Political Economy of M Industries

This book provides a critical political economic examination of the impact of increasingly concentrated global media industries. It addresses different media and communication industries from around the globe, including film, television, music, journalism, telecommunication, and information industries. The authors use case studies to examine how changing methods of production and distribution are impacting a variety of issues, including globalization, environmental devastation, and the shifting role of the State. This collection finds communication at a historical moment in which capitalist control of media and communication is the default status, and so, because of the increasing levels of concentration globally, allowing those in control to define the default ideological status. In turn, these concentrated media forces are deployed under the guise of entertainment but with a mind toward further concentration and control of the media apparatuses many times in convergence with others.

Randy Nichols is an Assistant Professor in the School of Interdisciplinary Arts and Sciences at the University of Washington Tacoma, U.S.A.

Gabriela Martinez is a Professor in the School of Journalism and Communication at the University of Oregon, U.S.A.

Routledge Studies in Media and Cultural Industries

Political Economy of Media Industries

Global Transformations and Challenges

Edited by
Randy Nichols and Gabriela Martinez

Routledge
Taylor & Francis Group

LONDON AND NEW YORK

First published 2020 by Routledge

2 Park Square, Milton Park, Abingdon, Oxon OX14 4RN
605 Third Avenue, New York, NY 10017

Routledge is an imprint of the Taylor & Francis Group, an informa business

First issued in paperback 2021

Publisher's Note

The publisher has gone to great lengths to ensure the quality of this reprint
but points out that some imperfections in the original copies may be apparent.

Library of Congress Cataloging-in-Publication Data
A catalog record for this title has been requested

ISBN: 978-1-138-60296-0 (hbk)
ISBN: 978-1-03-217674-1 (pbk)
DOI: 10.4324/9780429469336

Typeset in Sabon
by codeMantra

We dedicate this book to Janet Wasko for her continuing influence in the fields of media and communication, and her friendship, mentorship, leadership, and collegiality.

Onward!

Contents

Figures

Tables

Contributors

Jörg Becker (born September 17, 1946) is a Professor of Political Science at Marburg University in Germany. He was Guest Professor for Political Science and/or Communication Research at Universities in Roskilde in Denmark, Beirut in Lebanon, Hong Kong, and Innsbruck in Austria. His fields of interest include international and intercultural media politics, informatics and information technology, cultural studies, and peace research; numerous publications in more than ten languages. His most recent publication is *Medien im Krieg – Krieg in den Medien* (2016; *Media at War – War in the Media*).

Benjamin Birkinbine is an Assistant Professor of Media Studies in the Reynolds School of Journalism and Center for Advanced Media Studies at the University of Nevada, Reno. His research focuses on the political economy of communication with a specific focus on free and open-source software and the digital commons. He is the author of *Incorporating the Digital Commons* (University of Westminster Press, 2019), coeditor of *Global Media Giants* (Routledge, 2017), and his research has been published in the *International Journal of Communication*, *The Political Economy of Communication*, and the *Journal of Peer Production*.

Mary P. Erickson teaches media studies at Western Washington University. Her research focuses on regional and independent screen media, gender, distribution and marketing, and global media. She coedited *Independent Filmmaking Around the Globe* (University of Toronto Press, 2015) and *Cross-Border Cultural Production: Economic Runaway or Globalization?* (Cambria Press, 2008). She has also worked in independent films as a publicist, researcher, and distribution consultant.

Rodrigo Gómez is a Professor of Communication Policies and Industries at the Universidad Autónoma Metropolitana-Cuajimalpa and currently is the Chair of the Political Economy section of the International Association for Media and Communication Research (IAMCR). His research is grounded in the critical political economy of communication, examining ownership and public policies in cultural industries. He is coeditor (with Ben Birkinbine and Janet Wasko) of the series and book *Global Media Giants* (2017).

David Gracon is an Assistant Professor of Media Studies and Digital Production at Gonzaga University. His research/creative projects and teaching interests include cultural studies, film studies, media literacy, DIY cultural production, punk studies, political economy of media, documentary, and experimental production. His media works were screened at the Chicago Underground Film Festival, Seattle Underground Film Festival, New Art Film Festival (Champaign), the Mexican Centre for Music and Sonic Art, and many others. During the 2017/2018 academic year, David was an U.S. Fulbright Scholar teaching media literacy in Ivano-Frankivsk, Ukraine. He is a native of Buffalo, New York, and has been invested in post-punk, indie, experimental music scenes, zine communities, and college radio as well as activist-orientated experimental film, video, and documentary communities and collectives since the mid-1990s. David completed his PhD in Communication and Society at the University of Oregon and MA/BA at the University at Buffalo (SUNY) in the Department of Media Study and Sociology.

Wayne Hope is a Professor in the School of Communication Studies at the Auckland University of Technology, New Zealand. His specific areas of research include: New Zealand media history and public sphere analysis, the political economy of communication, sport-media relationships, and globalization and time. He is the author of *Time, Communication and Global Capitalism* (Palgrave, 2016 – described by a reviewer as "a virtuoso work of synthesis, provocative and pathbreaking. It needs to be read by anyone interested in the ways we live now, where we might be headed and how we might arrive at destinations not at the neoliberal route map"). His research has also been published in a range of journals, including *Media, Culture & Society*, the *International Journal of Communication*, and *Time & Society*. He is the founding coeditor of the online journal *Political Economy of Communication*. Within New Zealand, Wayne has appeared regularly as a media commentator on television and radio when not writing pieces against neoliberalism in *The Daily Blog*.

William M. Kunz is a Professor in the Division of Culture, Arts & Communication in the School of Interdisciplinary Arts & Sciences at the University of Washington Tacoma. He received his PhD in Communication and Society from the University of Oregon. He is the author of *Culture Conglomerates: Consolidation in the Motion Picture and Television Industries* as well as various articles and chapters focused on media ownership and regulation in the television industry. He has also worked in sports television at the network level for over 30 years, including ABC Sports, Turner Sports, and NBC Sports.

Randall Livingstone, Ph.D., is an Associate Professor in the School of Communication at Endicott College. He earned his PhD from the School of Journalism and Communication at the University of Oregon, where his dissertation work focused on the socio-technical nature of Wikipedia. At Endicott, he primarily teaches courses on social media, algorithmic culture, crowdsourcing, and research methods. Randall's research focuses on the role of automated robots ("bots") in social media, and his research has appeared in the *Journal of Communication Inquiry*, *M/C Journal*, *FLOW*, *Slate*, *First Monday*, *Social Science Computer Review*, and the *Newspaper Research Journal*.

Gabriela Martínez is a Professor in the School of Journalism and Communication at the University of Oregon. Martínez is a scholar who specializes in international communication and the political economy of communication. Her research addresses topics ranging from telecommunications to film industries to human rights and collective memories. While her primary geographical area of expertise is Latin America, she also looks at, weaves in, and analyzes historical, political, cultural, and economic connections highlighting the long-standing relationship of this region to others around the globe. She is the author of *Latin American Telecommunications: Telefónica's Conquest*. In addition, Gabriela Martínez is an international award-winning documentary filmmaker, who has produced and directed more than 14 ethnographic and sociopolitical documentaries. Her early documentary work includes *Ñakaj, Textiles in the Southern Andes, Mamacoca, and Qoyllur Rit'i: A Woman's Journey*, and her most recent work includes *Media, Women, and Rebellion in Oaxaca* and *Keep Your Eyes On Guatemala*.

Catherine McKercher is Professor Emeritus at Carleton University in Ottawa, Canada. She holds a BA in political science from Carleton, a Master of Journalism from Temple University, and a PhD in the Humanities from Concordia University. Before joining the faculty of the School of Journalism and Communication at Carleton University in 1987, she worked as a newspaper and wire service journalist in Ottawa, Toronto, and Kingston, Ontario, and in Washington, D.C. She is the author, coauthor or coeditor of a half dozen books, including *Shut Away: When Down Syndrome was a Life Sentence* (2019), *The Laboring of Communication* (2008), *Knowledge Workers in the Information Society* (2007), and *Newsworkers Unite: Labor, Convergence and North American Newspaper* (2002). In 2014, she and Vincent Mosco were named joint recipients of the AEJMC Professional Freedom and Responsibility Award.

Eileen R. Meehan is a Professor Emerita at Southern Illinois University, Carbdondale, and a political economist specializing in the culture industries and media arts. Her research examines the interplay of corporate structures, legal supports, and production processes in U.S.-based media industries. She is probably best known for her pioneering work on the television ratings industry, with particular attention to the operations and economics of the A. C. Nielsen Company (currently known as Nielsen Holdings) and her explication of transindustrial media conglomeration's impact on the creation, production, distribution, and recycling of specific media artifacts. The latter includes analyses of the *Star Trek* and *Batman* franchises. Among other publications, Meehan is the author of *Why TV Is Not Our Fault*, coeditor with Ellen Riordan of *Sex and Money: Feminism and Political Economy in Media Studies*, and coeditor with Janet Wasko of *A Companion to Television* (2nd edition).

Vincent Mosco (Ph.D, Harvard) is a Professor Emeritus of Sociology at Queen's University and Distinguished Professor of Communication, New Media Centre, Fudan University, Shanghai. At Queen's, he was Canada Research Chair in Communication and Society and Head of the Department of Sociology. His research interests include the political economy of communication, the social impacts of information technology, and the communication policy. Dr. Mosco is the author or editor of 26 books, including *The Digital Sublime* (2004) and *The Political Economy of Communication* (2009). His *To the Cloud: Big Data in a Turbulent World* was named a 2014 Outstanding Academic Title by Choice: Current Reviews for Academic Libraries. His latest books are *Becoming Digital: Toward a Post-Internet Society* (Emerald, 2017) and *The Smart City in a Digital World* (Emerald, 2019). In 2019 the International Communication Association named Dr. Mosco recipient of the C Edwin Baker Award, which recognizes outstanding scholarly contributions in the area of Media, Markets, and Democracy.

Graham Murdock is a Professor of Culture and Economy at the Department of Social Sciences at Loughborough University and Vice President of the International Association of Media and Communication Research. He has held the Bonnier Chair at the University of Stockholm and the Teaching Chair at the Free University of Brussels, has been a Visiting Professor at the Universities of Auckland, California at San Diego, Mexico City, Curtin Western Australia, and Bergen, and a Visiting Fellow at Fudan University in Shanghai. His work has been translated into 21 languages. His recent books include: as coeditor, *Money Talks: Media, Markets, Crisis* (2015), *New Media and Metropolitan Life: Connecting, Consuming, Creating* (2015) (in

Chinese), and *Carbon Capitalism and Communication: Confronting Climate Change* (2017).

Randy Nichols is an Assistant Professor in the Division of Culture, Arts & Communication in the School of Interdisciplinary Arts & Sciences at the University of Washington Tacoma. His work focuses on the critical political economy of video games. He has published two books: *The Video Game Business* (2014) and *Inside the Video Game Industry: Game Developers Talk About the Business of Play* (2016), as well as various articles and book chapters analyzing the interplay of the video games industry with other media industries and the implications of video games on cultural and creative industries policy.

Dan Schiller is a historian of communications and information in the context of the continuing development of capitalism. Successively a Professor at Temple University, UCLA, UCSD, and the University of Illinois, he is the sole –author of seven books, including *Digital Depression: Information Technology and Economic Crisis* (2014), and many research articles. He is presently moving toward completion of a book based on archival sources on the social history of U.S. telecommunications

H. Leslie Steeves is a Professor and Senior Associate Dean for Academic Affairs in the School of Journalism & Communication at the University of Oregon, U.S.A. Dr. Steeves' research addresses overlapping topics on media in and about sub-Saharan Africa, including gender, media, and development/social change; information and communication technologies (ICTs) for development; and entertainment and tourism representations of Africa. In 2017 she received the International Communication Association's Teresa Award for the Advancement of Feminist Scholarship. She coauthored with Srinivas Melkote *Communication for Development: Theory and Practice for Empowerment and Social Justice* (2015). She serves on a number of editorial boards and has published in leading journals in media studies, including *Journal of Communication, Communication Theory, Critical Studies in Media Communication, Communication, Culture & Critique, Media, Culture & Society, International Communication Gazette*, and *African Journalism Studies*. She has received two Fulbright Scholar grants for teaching and research in Kenya and Ghana; and she directs an annual study abroad program in Accra, Ghana, in collaboration with the University of Ghana.

Gerald Sussman is a Professor of Urban Studies and International Studies at Portland State University, where he teaches graduate courses in international development, political economy, political communication, and media studies. His latest book (as editor) is *The Propaganda*

Society: Promotional Culture and Politics in Global Context (Peter Lang, 2011). He is also the author of *Branding Democracy: U.S. Regime Change in Post-Soviet Eastern Europe* (Peter Lang, 2010), *Global Electioneering: Campaign Consulting, Communications, and Corporate Financing* (Rowman & Littlefield, 2005), and *Communication, Technology, and Politics in the Information Age* (Sage, 1997), and editor of two other books.

Téwodros W. Workneh is an Assistant Professor of Global Communication at the School of Communication Studies, Kent State University. Workneh's research agenda revolves around two areas of inquiry. His first research interest probes issues of regulation and policymaking in communication industries through the lens of critical political economy, especially as they pertain to freedom of speech in state-media relations in Ethiopia. His secondary research interest deals with postcolonial inquiries of African imagination in Western media. His most recent works investigate notions of hybridity, exoticism, and otherness in food-themed reality television programs.

Acknowledgments

We began this project several years back, and it is worth saying what a labor of love editing this book has been for us. Our work wouldn't have been possible if it wasn't for the help, support, and patience of many people involved. Thanks to Emma Rose, Alison Cardinal, Chris Demaske, Andrea Modarres, Ellen Bayer, Riki Thompson, and Ed Chamberlain at the University of Washington Tacoma, all of whom heard more than they probably cared to about the ins and outs of bringing this book together and always gave their support. Thanks to Leslie Steeves at the University of Oregon for her good disposition and encouragement. Special thanks to Micky Lee at Suffolk University for seeding the idea for the initial project. Erica Wetter at Routledge gave us invaluable feedback that allowed us to move the book on from its original idea to the form it is in today. Most importantly, there are no words that convey how thankful we are for the hard work and patience of our contributors, including those who for a variety of reasons couldn't continue on with the project.

Abbreviations

Chapter 4 – How Hollywood workers unite: Labor convergence and the creation of SAG-AFTRA

AFRA	The American Federation of Radio Artists
AFTRA	American Federation of Television and Radio Artists
AMPTP	Alliance of Motion Picture and Television Producers
CWA	The Communications Workers of America
IATSE	International Alliance of Theatrical Stage Employees
SAG	Screen Actors Guild

Chapter 5 – The Mexican Film Industry

COTSA	Operadora de Teatros y Cadena Oro
EFICINE	Inversión en la Producción y Distribución Cinematográfica Nacional (Fiscal Stimulus on Projects for Investment in National Film)
FIDECINE	Fondo de Inversión y Estímulos al Cine (Fund for Investment and Film Incentive)
FOPROCINE	Fondo para la Producción Cinematográfica de Calidad (Fund for Quality Cinema Production)
IMCINE	Instituto Mexicano de Cinematografía (Mexican Cinema Institute)
INEGI	Instituto Nacional de Estadística y Geografía
MFI	Mexican Film Industry
NAFTA	North American Free Trade Agreement
OTT	Over the Top
PAN	Partido de Acción Nacional (National Action Party)
PRI	Partido Revolucionario Institucional (Institutional Revolutionary Party)
PelMex	Películas Mexicanas (International Distribution Company)
PelNal	Películas Mexicanas (National Distribution Company)
USMCAN	United States-Mexico-Canada

Chapter 7 – Old Strategies in the New Paradigm: Web Series and Corporate Control

SVOD	Subscriber video-on-demand

Chapter 8 – State Monopoly of Telecommunications in Ethiopia: Revisiting Natural Monopoly in the Era of Deregulation

ADSL	Asymmetric Digital Subscriber Line
AfDB	The African Development Bank
ASC	(Ethiopian) Audit Services Corporation
BT	British Telecommunications
BTE	Board of Telecommunications of Ethiopia
ccTLD	Country Code Top-level Domain
CDMA	Code Division Multiple Access
ECOWAS	Economic Community of West African States
EDU	Ethiopian Democratic Union
EPLF	Eritrean People's Liberation Front
EPRDF	Ethiopian People's Revolutionary Democratic Front
EPRP	Ethiopian People's Revolutionary Party
ETA	Ethiopian Telecommunications Authority
ETC	Ethiopian Telecommunications Corporation
EU	European Union
EVDO	Enhanced Voice-Data Optimized
FDRE	Federal Democratic Republic of Ethiopia
GDP	Gross Domestic Product
GoE	Government of Ethiopia
GTP	Growth and Transformation Plan
IBRD	International Bank for Reconstruction & Development
IBTE	Imperial Board of Telecommunications of Ethiopia
IDA	International Development Association
IP	Internet Protocol
MCIT	(Ethiopian) Ministry of Communication and Information Technology
MDGs	Millennium Development Goals
MoFED	(Ethiopian) Ministry of Finance and Economic Development
MPLS	Multi Protocol Label Switching
NAFTA	North American Free Trade Agreement
NTT	Nippon Telegraph and Telephone
OECD	Organization for Economic Co-operation and Development
PASDEP	Plan for Accelerated and Sustained Development to End Poverty

PMAC	Provisional Military Administrative Council
PSRPs	Poverty Reduction Strategy Papers
PTO	Public Telecommunications Operator
PTT	Ministry of Posts, Telegraph and Telephone
SDPRPs	Sustainable Development and Poverty Reduction Program
TPLF	Tigrayan Peoples' Liberation Front
VSAT	Very Small Aperture Terminal
WTO	World Trade Organization

Chapter 9 – Through Being Cool: iTunes and the Political Economy of Music Retail

| DRM | Digital Rights Management |
| RIAA | Recording Industry Association of America |

Chapter 10 – In Practice and Theory? A Review of Scholarship on Wikipedia's Political Economy

| FLOSS | Free/Libre Open Source Software |
| WMF | Wikimedia Foundation |

Chapter 13 – Power Under Pressure: Digital Capitalism In Crisis

FDI	Foreign Direct Investment
ICT	Information and Communications Technology
IT	Information Technology
TNC	Transnational Corporations
WTO	World Trade Organization
VOIP	Voice-over Internet Protocol

1   Introduction

Randy Nichols and Gabriela Martinez

As is the case with many projects, this book began as something very different from the end result. When it was started, this book was born from a desire to acknowledge Dr. Janet Wasko and her contributions to our understanding of media and communication, particularly the critical political economy of communication. Wasko has, after all, been a major figure in the political economy of media in a variety of ways, both through her scholarship and through her important work with organizations like the International Association for Media and Communication Research and the Union for Democratic Communications. However, we realized that the best way to honor her and her work was not just to say thanks or to offer call-outs to her contributions, but rather to join her in the continued critical examination of media and communication. This is particularly true because over the course of the project, we have seen the rise and retrenchment of authoritarian regimes around the world, which have relied in no small part upon the media to fuel their rise. Mass media have also been front and center in escalating battles in the culture wars, playing a role both in combatting but also supporting virulent ethnocentrism and white supremacy as well as a deteriorating public trust in a range of social institutions. Perhaps the prime example of this (though certainly not the only one) is the role the media have played in the presidency of Donald Trump in the United States. At the same time, the surveillance state has extended itself via algorithms and capitalist enterprise. Finally, the mass media have been central to both the gradual awakening to the dire environmental consequences that come with overconsumption, even as it is part of the problem. Those are just a few of the threads the chapters of this book address. Ultimately, this book offers, through its collection of chapters by well-established and emerging scholars, a look at the broad landscape covered by the political economy of communication. In its three main sections – The Film Industry, Other Media Industries, and New and Enduring Challenges – it details a range of challenges and concerns posed by our modern communication landscape.

Such concerns are ideal for analysis through the critical political economic approach, which seeks to understand not just the nature of the various industries involved but also insists on seeing them in their relevant historical and social contexts. As such, political economy begins with the recognition that there are not merely economic concerns but political and moral concerns as well. This means that, in turn, political economy is inherently concerned with the ideological. Rather than focusing just on "wealth and the allocation of resources," as described by Smith (1993), critical political economy is more broadly concerned with, as Mosco (1996) describes it, "the study of power relations in society." This means that political economy seeks to understand and effect change in the struggle between capitalism and the social good (Golding & Murdock, 1991). As Wasko (2004) notes, these struggles may occur at a variety of levels, including the commodification and commercialization of media, the ways in which media have diversified, the ways media have integrated and synergized, how concentration has impacted communication, and the changing relationship between media and the State.

This means that the political economy of communication, unlike some other schools of thought that emphasize understanding media as a business such as media economics or the creative industries approach, is not only interested in understanding the production and distribution of media content, but also how we might resist the problems presented by the capitalist control of media and communication (Gandy, 1992; Garnham, 1990; Meehan, Mosco, & Wasko, 1994). That understanding, in turn, leads to praxis, by which we mean taking action based in the knowledge gained in order to advance the social good. Further, the political economy of communication gives itself a broader purview than, particularly, the creative industries approach and studies that emphasize digital and information technologies. Both of those examples emphasize particular areas while obscuring others, whether it is labor seen as "uncreative" within media production or the long history of non-digital technologies and media production (Wasko & Meehan, 2013). Rather, the political economy of communication sees these as part of a broader range of cultural industries that extend even beyond the media to all the avenues that are involved in the production, structuring, and dissemination of culture. These cultural industries are often interlocking and integrated even as they compete for our time, our dollars, and our understanding. Wasko offers us a fairly succinct articulation of these concerns, suggesting that concentrated media industries can be understood in terms of three key impacts: power, profit, and paucity (Wasko, 2003). Each of these impacts has become a crucial focus of examination for critical political economists because they represent key power relationships, both within particular industries, between industries, and between those industries and institutions and the broader public.

We would add that there are two other important features that are part and parcel of political economy of communication, though they are not always foregrounded. First, the political economy of communication grounds itself in empirical evidence. Often this evidence is drawn from the particular instances and institutions being studied, though it is used to demonstrate the many dangers posed. That means political economy uses the same evidence as other approaches, such as the creative industries approach; the difference is not in the evidence but is rather how that evidence is used. Political economic research on media should lead not just to an understanding of particular power relations but to a suggestion of how things might be improved for everyone impacted by what is being studied. Second, while there is often an emphasis on the importance of the political economy of information media (for example, journalism or search engines), understanding media focused on entertainment and leisure are also of vital importance. That emphasis on information media holds particularly true in the North American strand of political economy, which, as Mosco (1996) noted, can be traced back to the work of Herbert Schiller and Dallas Smythe and which often emphasizes their same concerns, particularly the continued consequences of the New World Information and Communication Order and the importance of the audience commodity. Consider for a moment the role entertainment media played not just in the election and presidency of Donald Trump to President of the United States but also of the range of hard-right conservative movements around the world. Entertainment media were not only instrumental in helping Trump rise to prominence in the public imagination, but the norms of entertainment media have also increasingly been deployed against those of informational media, particularly journalists, and have been seen to increasingly infiltrate the norms of informational media production, as well.

In this regard, Wasko's work serves as something of a bridge between the North American approach to critical political economy and the European articulation which, in addition to considering matters of the control of information, has maintained a focus on understanding the broader range of cultural life and practices (Mosco, 1996). Her work with H. Leslie Steeves (2002), for example, attempts to bridge the uneasy relationship North American political economy has sometimes had with feminist studies, while her work with the Global Disney Project not only drew attention to the impact of global media giant Disney but also bridged the work of political economy with that of audience studies (Wasko, Phillips, & Meehan, 2001). This global concern has long punctuated her approach, both through her years of work and leadership with the International Association for Media and Communication Research and in her own research as exemplified by *Global Media Giants*, a book that opens the space for discussion about media companies shaping the lives of people around the world through their global dominance (Birkinbine, Gómez, & Wasko, 2016).

This collection picks up many of those threads and attempts to extend them. We find ourselves at a historical moment in which capitalist control of media and communication is the default status, and so because increasing levels of concentration globally allow those in control to define the default ideological status. In turn, these concentrated media forces are deployed under the guise of entertainment but with a mind toward further concentration and control. In some cases, such concentrated media serves as an extension of the State, while in others it functions almost as an entirely separate entity, governed solely by the rules of the market or – more accurately since they are typically the most powerful entities in their markets – setting the rules that govern the transactions, the commodifications, and the very nature of how and whom that market serves. New methods of production and distribution are fundamentally altering the relationships between a variety of social institutions while building on long-term trends – globalization, environmental devastation, and a shifting role of the State among them.

Organization of the Book

With those concerns in mind, we have structured the book in a way that mirrors much of the trajectory of both Wasko's work and of the critical political economy of communication itself.

Part I examines the medium Wasko has focused on most explicitly: film. It begins by assessing her impact on the study of film and media and continues by examining key developments in labor, technology, and global impacts of the film industry.

Chapter 2: "The Hollywood Trilogy, The Disney Duo" by Eileen Mehan offers a succinct overview of Wasko's contributions to the study of media and the major implications her work suggests for other political economists.

Chapter 3: In "Movie Theaters and Money: Integration and Consolidation in Film Exhibition," Ben Birkinbine examines the changing status of film exhibition in the United States in light of major technological changes.

Chapter 4: In "How Hollywood Workers Unite: Labor Convergence and the Creation of SAG-AFTRA," Catherine McKercher and Vincent Mosco examine the 2012 merger of the Screen Actors Guild (SAG) and the American Federation of Television and Radio Artists (AFTRA), seeking to understand how advocates turned a defeated 2003 merger attempt into victory nine years later.

Chapter 5: "The Mexican Film Industry, 2000–2018: Resurgence or Assimilation?" by Rodrigo Gómez offers a probe at global impacts, providing a history of the role of the Mexican State and of Hollywood on the Mexican Film Industry.

Part II expands beyond film to consider a range of other industries, their impacts, and changing natures, providing key touchstones both for our understanding of new forms of production and distribution via digital technologies and changing State practices.

Chapter 6: "The New Holy Grail: Scripted Television Production and State, Provincial & National Incentives" by William Kunz offers a detailed examination on the impact of State production incentives as an extension of runaway television production, using examples drawn from television, cable, and internet services.

Chapter 7: "Old Strategies in the New Paradigm: Web Series and Corporate Control" by Mary Erickson details the impacts of serialized dramas produced for the web have both as a mechanism for competition with and control by television producers.

Chapter 8: "State Monopoly of Telecommunications in Ethiopia: Revisiting Natural Monopoly in the Era of Deregulation" by Tewodros Workneh and H. Leslie Steeves provide an in-depth history of Ethiopian telecommunication regulations while analyzing its changes and impact on a range of markets.

Chapter 9: "Through Being Cool: The Critical Political Economy of iTunes" by David Gracon uses the example of Apple's music products, particularly iTunes, to demonstrate the impact of market concentration, corporate power, and monopolistic policies' impact on the music industry.

Chapter 10: "In Practice and Theory? Scholarship on Wikipedia's Political Economy" by Randall Livingstone concludes the section providing an overview of how political economy has addressed one of the key developments of Web 2.0 and audience production, Wikipedia.

Part III closes the volume by providing longer histories for some of the most consequential challenges political economy must consider as well as offering some provocations both in their approach and conceptualization to the field at large.

Chapter 11: "Bribe and Journalism" by Jörg Becker begins the section by bringing together history, literary analysis, and political economy of modern journalism in Germany to detail the long history of distrust about the impact of capitalist ownership of journalism, as seen in the work of Gustav Freytag, Emile Zola, and Mario Vargas Llosa.

Chapter 12: "Labor in the Age of Digital (Re)Production" by Gerald Sussman revisits the history and implications of digital technologies and production on labor, examining the relationship between ideology and propaganda in the modern information-rich workplace.

Chapter 13: "Power Under Pressure: Digital Capitalism in Crisis" by Dan Schiller expands on the concerns about digital technologies to critique how the ideology and practices of digital capitalism poses significant problems for the economy.

Chapter 14: "Minutes to Midnight: Capitalist Communication and Climate Catastrophe" by Graham Murdock details the role that communication continues to play in the worsening environmental crisis in the West, but also across the world.

Chapter 15: "Time, Globality, and Commodity Fetishism" by Wayne Hope closes the book, tying many of these threads together with the political economy of memory and the question of consumption to offer a provocation to political economic researchers.

References

Birkinbine, B., Gómez, R., & Wasko, J. (Eds.). (2016). *Global Media Giants*. New York: Routledge.

Gandy Jr., O. H. (1992). The Political Economy Approach: A Critical Challenge. *Journal of Media Economics*, 5(Summer), 23–42.

Garnham, N. (1990). Contribution to a Political Economy of Mass Communication. In F. Inglis (Ed.), *Capitalism and Communication: Global Culture and the Economics of Information* (pp. 20–55). London: Sage.

Golding, P., & Murdock, G. (1991). Culture, Communication, and Political Economy. In J. Curran & M. Gurevitch (Eds.), *Mass Media and Society* (pp. 15–32). London: Edward Arnold.

Meehan, E. R., Mosco, V., & Wasko, J. (1994). Rethinking Political Economy: Change and Continuity. In M. R. Levy & M. Gurevitch (Eds.), *Defining Media Studies* (pp. 347–358). New York: Oxford University Press.

Mosco, V. (1996). *The Political Economy of Communication*. Thousand Oaks, CA: Sage Publications.

Smith, A. (1993). *An Inquiry into the Nature and Causes of the Wealth of Nations*. Indianapolis: Hackett Publishing Company.

Steeves, H. L., & Wasko, J. (2002). Feminist Theory and Political Economy: Toward a Friendly Alliance. In E. R. Meehan & E. Riordan (Eds.) *Sex & Money. Feminism and Political Economy in the Media* (pp. 16–29). Minneapolis: University of Minnesota Press.

Wasko, J. (2003). *How Hollywood Works*. Los Angeles, CA: Sage.

Wasko, J. (2004). The Political Economy of Communications. In J. Downing, E. Wartclla, & D. McQuail (Eds.), *Sage Handbook of Media Studies*. London: Sage.

Wasko, J., & Meehan, E. R. (2013). Critical Crossroads or Parallel Routes? Political Economy and New Approaches to Studying Media Industries and Cultural Products. *Cinema Journal*, 52(3), 150–157.

Wasko, J., Phillips, M., & Meehan, E. R. (Eds.). (2001). *Dazzled by Disney?: The Global Disney Audiences Project*. London: Burns & Oates.

Part I
The Film Industry

2   The Hollywood Trilogy, The Disney Duo

Eileen R. Meehan

Since receiving her doctoral degree in 1980, Janet Wasko has demonstrated an acute understanding of and fascination with Hollywood. In this essay, I argue that Wasko's unique focus on Hollywood has produced research that is remarkable for its scholarly depth and intellectual breadth. My discussion is rooted in a close rereading of four single-author books and one edited volume: *Movies and Money* (1982); *Hollywood in the Information Age* (1995); *How Hollywood Works* (2003); *Understanding Disney* (2001); and *Dazzled by Disney?: The Global Disney Audiences Project* (Wasko, Phillips, and Meehan, 2001). But, before moving to that task, I will provide some background on the academic context of Wasko's research – critical communications theory and radical political economy – as well as the dominant position in academic research on media industries, which celebrates the "genius of the system" (Schatz, 1996). Because my space is necessarily limited, my sketch of those contexts will be brief.

Critical and Celebratory Research: Hooray for Hollywood?

In 1980, Janet Wasko deposited her dissertation, "Relationships between the American Motion Picture Industry and Banking Institutions," in the University of Illinois Urbana-Champaign's library. She approached this topic from a critical perspective grounded in radical political economy and respectful of both materialist cultural and social research. Undeterred by Hollywood's glitz and glamour, Wasko traced the finances, technologies, persons, corporations, market structures, governmental protections, and political supports that combine to form and prop up the American "dream factory" (Powdermaker, 1951). In her case studies of Walt Disney, the Disney company, its oeuvre, fans, and critics, Wasko has taken an interdisciplinary approach that both traces the operations of Disney's dream factory and people's engagement with or against all things Disney. Overall, Wasko's goal has been to discover the facts, arrange them in an accessible and understandable fashion, and to contextualize them within a larger, critical framework so that their meaning and significance is clear.

That goal may seem prosaic – "ho-hum, all researchers do that." However, not all research has a commitment to critical thinking and clear, jargon-free writing. Critical thinking requires careful questioning of the "industry wisdom" and "common sense" that circulates through sources as varied as trade publications, elite newspapers, memoirs, public relations, popular books, popular criticism, governmental hearings, "infotainment" programs, advertising, and also some academic publications. Historically, within academic film studies, most research has described and celebrated the movies, the individuals on screen or behind the scenes, and the movie industry's unique status as "show business." That celebratory approach remains pervasive in film industry studies – indeed, in most media industry studies. It is particularly evident among practitioners of the newer forms of celebratory industry studies. Using "midlevel ethnography" (Havens et al., 2009), their research focuses on how individuals deal with their employment by media corporations, with an emphasis on individuals' agency, creativity, contestation, and resistance (Havens et al., 2009). Missing are immediate but abstract contexts like corporate structure, oligopolized markets, industrial integration, and trade policies regarding cultural production. Absent is any reference to the dynamics, systems, structurations, and relationships that combine to form the ultimate contexts for the Hollywood film industry: American capitalism and its role in a globalized, capitalist economy (Meehan and Wasko, 2013; Wasko and Meehan, 2013).[1]

But can scholars effectively contextualize the microscopic and mesoscopic within the macroscopic? To answer that question, we turn to *Movies and Money* (1982); *Hollywood in the Information Age* (1995); *How Hollywood Works* (2003); *Understanding Disney* (2001); and *Dazzled by Disney?: The Global Disney Audiences Project* (Wasko, Phillips, and Meehan, 2001).

Overview: Five Key Works

Wasko's titles are straightforward, identifying the separate focus of each volume. However, if we were to group them, then *Movies and Money*, *Hollywood in the Information Age*, *How Hollywood Works* may be seen as Wasko's Hollywood trilogy. Here Wasko digs deep into the historical and contemporary workings of the film industry from the 1890s to the early 2000s. Her accounts are detailed, data-driven, and analytic, working across the microscopic, mesoscopic, and macroscopic levels and building a complex representation of an industry-in-process across the decades and within changing circumstances. Wasko recognizes the roles played by individuals and social groups, by corporations and governmental organizations, by careful planning, and sheer luck in the ongoing articulation of "Hollywood." Taken together, the trilogy provides us with an unparalleled depth of critical inquiry into the political economy of Hollywood.

But as Wasko often reminds us, Hollywood's *raison d'être* may be profits, but for us – whether movie buffs, kids of all ages, or film critics – movies play many different roles. At the theater, films can be a communal experience, an excuse to socialize, or a means of escape. Watched in a home theater, movies become a more personal activity that may involve family or friends. On an ordinary television set, films can be the center of attention or merely background noise. On a personal computer, laptop, tablet, or cell phone, movies shrink to fit screens and sound systems that are designed for single users. In any of these situations, we may engage a film as a cultural artifact, artistic statement, hack job, cheap entertainment, amusing confection, time killer, reflection of the times, template for our next screenplay, work of a genius, or "the stuff that dreams are made of."[2]

To comprehend Hollywood in all of these terms, Wasko has blended political economy, cultural studies, and social research. That interdisciplinary breadth is manifested in the Disney Duo. In *Understanding Disney*, Wasko tackles all things Disney, including Walt Disney's public persona, classic and new animations, theme parks, and hidden Mickeys. She also examines peoples' reactions to "Disney" and how some people use Disney in constructing their identities and their social lives. In *Dazzled by Disney?*, Wasko led an international team of researchers to explore Disney's local presence and meaning as well as their students' experiences with and evaluations of Disney. The Disney Duo provides a notable synthesis of political economy, cultural studies, and social research. On one hand, it illuminates the complex and contested phenomena that are Disney. On the other, it reminds us as scholars that we need such interdisciplinary research if we are truly to comprehend the political, economic, cultural, and social phenomena called "the media."

To see how this all works, I turn next to a brief synopsis of each volume in the Hollywood Trilogy and then the Disney Duo.

How the Money Men Launched the Movies

Movies and Money traces the financial history of the American film industry from the 1890s to 1979. Wasko begins by showing how a rough-and-tumble aggregation of inventors, speculators, entrepreneurs, and an occasional banker created a movie business oriented to the production of inexpensive shorts that were sold to vaudeville houses as entertainment for working people. Using the case study of film pioneer D. W. Griffith, she shows how the industry's transition to longer films, large studios, middle-class audiences, and theatrical rental was achieved. Detailing Griffith's relationships with bankers, Wasko explains how the institutionalization of film financing initially supported Griffith, then limited the kinds of films that he could make, and finally ended his career. In the microcosm of Griffith's career, Wasko illuminates a radical shift in film economics and one film director's struggle to capitalize on and later cope with that on-going change. She examines the banking industry's roles in the introduction of sound, "golden age" of Hollywood studios, rise of independent production, and the acquisition of studios by conglomerates like Gulf + Western in the 1970s. In this, her analyses of individual case studies, industrial structure, and capitalist dynamics produces evidence of both change and continuity.

Throughout *Movies and Money*, Wasko deftly traces the relationships between directors, moguls, studios, individual investors, and banks, explicating the nuances, ambiguities, strains, conflicts, and shared interests between and among individual and corporate actors across the decades. She locates these actors and their relationships within their industrial context, that is, within impersonal markets for labor, finance, product, distribution, exhibition, technologies, and financing. Wasko recognizes the legal basis that undergirds those structures, that is, patents, copyrights, anti-trust regulation, export policies, etc.

Having integrated the microscopic and mesoscopic levels on which the film industry operates, Wasko situates them within the larger, macroscopic context of U.S. capitalism where movies are commodities and where success is defined as profits. Of course, Wasko recognizes the disparate and mixed motives of individual and organizational participants in the film industry and of film audiences as well as the artistic, ideological, and social significance of films, which themselves are sites for cultural negotiation, contestation, and appropriation. But, despite all of that, films as we know them exist as commodities, which places them in a series of institutional relationships that are organized in the context of rationalized production dependent on investment in order to feed operations in distribution and exhibition – initially within the confines of the film industry and subsequently across multiple media industries. With finance as the lynchpin of the film industry, financial institutions necessarily treat Hollywood as a "dream factory," where inputs and outputs are rationalized, where success is defined monetarily, and where profits have become relatively reliable. To realize the dream on a quarter-by-quarter basis requires tacit agreement on the process of filmmaking, on the selection of personnel to do the basic work of filmmaking, and on the uses of and goals for the end products themselves. In this way, Wasko reminds us that "the stuff that dreams are made of" lies behind the screen.

Hollywood's Myth-Buster

In *Hollywood and the Information Age*, Wasko takes on two myths that were widely circulated from the late 1970s through the 1990s: that, first, Hollywood has always been technophobic and, second, a techno-economic revolution was sweeping the nation, ushering in a new Information Age that broke radically with industrial capitalism and thus eliminated problems ranging from the exploitation of workers to war and environmental pollution. Nowadays, such claims seem preposterous. On one hand, Hollywood has embraced cable television, surround sound, 3-D movies, online ticket sales, HDTV, and streaming films as well as trailers to computers, smart phones, and tablets. On the other, new technologies introduced between the late 1970s and early 2000s have not ended industrialism, pollution, economic exploitation, or war. However, when Wasko published the book in 1994, the technophobe and Information Age claims had well-placed advocates within the film industry and film scholarship. Thus, Wasko swam against a rhetorical tide that had become common sense on the streets of Hollywood, in the towers of academe, and in the halls of government.

Wasko begins by analyzing the arguments mustered in favor of the Information Age, pointing out that the commercialization of new technologies is not the same as a radical restructuring of economic, political, social, or cultural relationships and institutions. For example, more people may have been employed by companies to produce information, but allocative control was still wielded by corporate boards of directors while operational control remained in the hands of executives. Companies may have relocated their industrial plants or outsourced some manufacturing, but such Information Age products as fiber optics and computers still had to be manufactured somewhere. Further, much of the content carried or accessed through those technologies was informational only in the most abstract sense. As a category of production, information easily described a data bank – but seemed odd and ill-fitting when applied to Madonna's music video "Like a Virgin" (1984) running in heavy rotation on Warner-Amex's MTV. In pointing this out, Wasko suggests that the Entertainment Age might be a more accurate moniker.

Wasko takes her entertainment seriously, recognizing that such commodities have cultural and ideological significance as well as a significant role to play in national and global economies. She shows how the Hollywood studios sought to become major players in the development of sound film, radio, and network television historically. She profiles the major companies involved in the Hollywood film industry, describes their adoption of new technologies as part of the production process, and then traces the majors' expansion "beyond the silver screen." Using the buzzwords of the day, she notes that Hollywood's role in the Wired Nation, Electronic Superhighway, and Home Video Revolution. In this way, she demonstrates how the film, television, and video industries are integrated in the Hollywood majors' operations. Along the way, she identifies key individuals and their attempts to advance or limit changes affecting the major Hollywood companies.

She also tackles Hollywood's return to vertical integration through theater ownership and its increasing dependence on revenues from product placements, tie-ins, licensing, merchandising, and video games. In this way, films take on a double role: commodities expected to earn profits and movie-length ads that showcase and sell other commodities. This new role necessarily reshapes the creative process and opens the way to direct and early participation by advertisers in preproduction, both with the major companies and with independent firms. Wasko is clear about the impact of economic practices on film culture and the potential to limit expression to stories, representations, ideas, and values that are brand friendly. This illuminates the structuration that makes the selection of brand-friendly elements into a decision that is sensible, creative, and professional.

In the 1990s, the companies that comprised Hollywood continued to strategize and maneuver, as indicated by her discussion of European cultural policies, the General Agreement on Tariffs and Trade, and presidential advocacy of Hollywood's interests. The Hollywood majors were transindustrial conglomerates that often operated as a cartel on the global stage and that relied heavily on support of the various nation-states that they called "home." While outcomes are never predetermined, these companies struggled to expand operations, enter new markets, amass more profit, push some firms aside, and make profitable alliances with others – all historical features of capitalism.

Wasko clearly understands the difference between capitalism as a system and the ongoing struggles among and across governments, industries, companies, trade organizations, reformist groups, and individual persons within particular times and places. Where *Movies and Money* traced the rise and establishment of the film industry, *Hollywood and the Information Age* examined how neoliberal deregulation fostered integration of industries through vertical and horizontal integration as well as the acquisition of operations across multiple media industries. Those developments served as the focus for the third installment of this trilogy.

Industrial Identity, Conglomeration, and Convergence

How Hollywood Works provides a detailed analysis of the Hollywood film industry's operations in an age of media convergence and transindustrial media conglomeration. Among celebratory scholars in the late 20th and early 21st centuries, "media convergence" became a popular catch phrase. Convergence was conceptualized as a battle between old and new media that would ultimately give consumers influence over media production (Jenkins, 2006). For some critical scholars, media companies' reorganization into transindustrial media conglomerates suggested that traditional separations between media like film, broadcast television, and cable or satellite television were collapsing (Meehan, 2011). In *How Hollywood Works*, Wasko demonstrates that media convergence has not yet eliminated the "distinct differences in the ways that specific media...are produced and distributed" (p. 1). She recognizes that the Hollywood majors are no longer studios with secondary operations that turn parts of soundtracks into records or license movies to television networks. The major studios have either rebuilt themselves as transindustrial media conglomerates or been absorbed into such conglomerates. Now, they own television networks and cable channels as well as film studios and distribution systems, among other things. As she pointed out in the previous book, Hollywood lobbied for the political economic policies and practices that allowed this transformation. Using that corporate structure, conglomerates like Time Warner or Disney coordinate internal operations across multiple media industries to secure every last penny of profit that can be wrung from any particular film or any other media product.

That general tendency in corporate structure, however, does not translate into a single template at the level of commodity production, distribution, and circulation for every media industry within such a conglomerate. For film, Wasko finds the classic divisions between production, distribution, and exhibition still very much in evidence. She breaks down each area, identifying its key phases, roles, markets, relationships, corporations, and organizations (including labor unions and guilds). She starts with production, noting the news/infotainment media's extensive coverage of stars, directors, film premieres, awards, etc. Her focus, however, is on the process by which an idea may move through the processes of copyright, acquisition, development, financing, preproduction, hiring, production, and postproduction – discussing each process and its key players in detail. Her discussion of labor unions and guilds as well as companies that service the Hollywood industry and issues like runaway production provide a much needed balance to the steady flow of infotainment coverage promoting stars and star-like studio executives.

She moves next to distribution, reminding us that "to understand how Hollywood works, one must ultimately confront distribution and thus ultimately encounter the Hollywood majors" (p. 60). With distribution, Wasko shows how Hollywood film has become integrated into media operations and retail markets outside the film industry. This is clear from her profiles of the six major conglomerates and the dearth of minor firms or independent distributors. Recognizing that the proverbial Big Six are major players across media industries, Wasko traces the dynamics between the Big Six's costs, ticket sales, and accounting practices combine to define when a film officially breaks even or profits. More importantly, Wasko notes, film distribution beyond the silver screen to every other media operation serves as the main force driving a transindustrial media conglomerate's operations across the entertainment-information sector.

Recognizing that Hollywood's product goes far beyond film, Wasko discusses exhibition and retail in the same chapter. She then examines how the majors push ever harder to expand the film industry through product placement, video games, and licensed merchandise as well as through corporate synergy, globalization of operations, and utilizing governmental assistance in furthering industry goals. She concludes by reminding us of why Hollywood's modus operandi matter and how we can use our new understanding to explode the myths of Hollywood's being a unique and competitive business that gives us what most of us want: mere entertainment lacking any ideological significance at all. Those myths are well and truly debunked in the last book in Wasko's Hollywood Trilogy.

The Disney Duo: Interdisciplinary Research on a Complex Phenomenon

In *Understanding Disney* and *Dazzled by Disney?*, Wasko immerses herself in "the Disney universe" in order to contemplate Disney Brothers, the Walt Disney Company, their histories, various corporate structures, forms of cultural production, imagination, social impact, fans, and detractors. To do that, Wasko balances theories and methods from social research, political economy, and cultural studies. While these books are best read in tandem, they can stand alone. We begin our discussion with *Understanding Disney: The Manufacture of Fantasy*.

From Personal Experience to Interdisciplinary Inquiry

In the preface to *Understanding Disney*, Wasko notes her personal connection to Disney. Not only is Disney necessarily a part of her research as a political economist of film, but also the company echoes across her life as a teacher, sports fan, former Disney employee, and Southern Californian for whom Disney and Disneyland were an integral part of growing up. Whether teaching her class on Disney, cheering along with Donald Duck at the University of Oregon sports events, or reminiscing about "working down on 'Uncle Walt's farm'" (viii), Wasko understands Disney's complexity in terms of lived experience. On one hand, "everybody knows" Disney through first-hand or mediated experience as a special company dedicated to fun, family, and fantasy. On the other, the Disney Company has worked hard to shape and control what "everybody knows" in order to advance its economic interests. Wasko's challenge is to balance this doubleness in order to affirm people's lived experiences (and the differences among those lived experiences) while also illuminating the impersonal structural and economic dynamics at work behind the fun and fantasy.

To do this, she begins by inviting us into the Disney universe, telling us some of the many stories that Walt Disney and his company have told about themselves and their initial struggles in the film industry. She also relates stories that are less well known, for example, Walt's claim before the House Committee on UnAmerican Activities that Communists caused his employees to strike for higher pay and better working conditions. Blending together Disney's official history and independent records and research, Wasko takes us from the Walt and Roy Disney's earliest ventures to Disney Company's days as a poverty row studio, its emergence as a specialty studio, and its transformation into a media empire.

This positions readers to understand Disney's films, etc., as media products that are consciously produced in routine ways. That routinization raises questions about types of representations, themes, and narratives that persist across Disney's multiple media products through the decades. While a film may be "mere entertainment" in terms of my lived experience, it is much more in its larger economic, cultural, and historical contexts.

Wasko also examines Disney's "worlds" – that is, its built environments designed, regulated, and staffed to reproduce a similar lived experience for park visitors, hotel guests, and home buyers in the Celebration housing development. This raises the issue of Disneyfication, that is, the importation and generalization of Disney's profit-driven aesthetics to settings that are not owned or licensed by Disney, for example, Times Square in New York City. The issue is particularly important in terms of publicly owned space in urban spaces or wilderness areas.

Having established the multiple contexts in which Disney offers lived experiences to its consumers, Wasko returns to an examination of people and their lived experiences. Noting that Disney conducts a significant amount of proprietary research, which is not circulated outside the company, she reviews the research literature and discusses her students of impressions of Disney as well as attempts by organized groups to celebrate, critique, or condemn Disney. From all this, she proposes a typology of aggregated responses to Disney, using brief case studies to make the types come to life: fanatic, fan, consumer, cynic, uninterested, resister, and antagonist.

Thus, we are reminded that Disney's success never was and still is not a foregone conclusion. While Disney fanatics and fans still grant it universal and sacred status, the response is but one of many. As Wasko notes, Disney consumers range from eager to admiring to reluctant. The rest of the spectrum varies in terms of activities with Disney antagonists perhaps the most notable. Whether operating from the religious right or the anti-consumerism/prolabor left, Disney antagonists are a force to be reckoned with, particularly given their use of the Internet to spread their message. Further, Disney's highly disparate holdings and involvements have fostered tensions and contradictions between the Disney image that Walt built and the transindustrial conglomerate whose profits depend on its chunk of the worldwide oligopoly in media, information, entertainment, and packaged experiences. Maintaining Disney's "Disney-ess" is not easy. But, as Wasko demonstrates, adequately tracing Disney and Disney-ess requires theories and methods drawn from history, political economy, cultural studies, and social research. That realization undergirded the global Disney audiences' project.

Touring Disney's World: 28 Researchers, 18 Countries, 1 Collection

As Wasko worked on *Understanding Disney*, she initiated a discussion with Mark Phillips and me about organizing a global study of Disney. Given her work with students, we were particularly interested in people's reports of their lived experiences of Disney as well as the availability and marketing of Disney products. From informal observations and discussions with colleagues, we knew that local, national, and regional differences existed – despite the fact that Mickey Mouse had enjoyed global recognition for decades. We decided to recruit colleagues who would query their students about their experiences and impressions of Disney, observe Disney's presence in their local and national markets, and provide an historical context for their country's relationship with Disney. Every researcher was given the same questionnaire, interview schedule, and market survey. Everyone was asked to use those tools to get an informational basis that could be blended with everyone else's results and analyzed by us. We also encouraged colleagues to pursue their research interests as well. Some researchers collected data for us; others also wrote national profiles based on their data and areas of expertise.

This was not a top-down enterprise in which powerful coinvestigators commanded the labor of academic "worker bees." We invited colleagues because we admired their research and because their scholarship was sensitive to interconnections between social research, cultural studies, and political economy. In their chapters, colleagues addressed Disney as a part of their lives and their respondents' lives as well as Disney's presence as a fixture on the national media scene and as a major force in global markets for media. In that way, they contextualized Disney in terms of its history within their respective countries and explored people's understandings of and exposure to Disney. Disney was ubiquitous in each country and its official messages, narrative patterns, and fantasies were "gotten" by respondents. Despite that, different patterns emerged in terms of respondents' personal relationship to Disney, their interpretation and evaluation of Disney representations, and their ownership of merchandise. These patterns recalled Wasko's typology mentioned above.

The national profiles were framed by three chapters. In the first, Wasko introduced the study and reviewed the research literature. In the second, Phillips presented the research and data, using quantitative and qualitative methods. The 18 national profiles were presented in alphabetical order from Australia to the United States. Following them was the final chapter presenting an overall discussion of the studies' findings as well as noting some themes pursued by individual authors that resonated across multiple chapters. Here I will briefly summarize two points from the overall discussion.

Among the key findings were the high degree of agreement among respondents regarding Disney's pervasiveness and its core values as well as its narrative formula, types of characters, and use of stereotypes. For most respondents, exposure to Disney products was a key feature of their lives from infancy through childhood and into their years in college. Family and social rituals kept them in contact with Disney regardless of whether they liked or disliked Disney. Looking toward the future, most could imagine themselves exposing their children to Disney. For the majority of respondents, regardless of country, Disney was one key to a good childhood and, after childhood, a part of life. While this mirrors Disney's marketing, it also suggests that immersion in Disney's symbolic universe teaches us what Disney ought to mean and that the lesson is learned even by those who see themselves as Disney cynics, resistors, or antagonists.

For many who liked Disney, the company was above criticism. But some of the "likes" separated Disney films, parks, etc. from Disney's marketing and synergistic strategies. While Disney products were beloved, its corporate strategies were too aggressive. The "dislikes" also decried Disney's strategies while regarding its products with suspicion. They tended to decode Disney's products in critical terms, for example, finding the same-gender stereotypes in classic and new Disney films despite the company's marketing claims that newer films depicted girls and women as independent. While "dislikes" recognized the traits deployed to mark female characters as independent, they deconstructed those characters revealing the gender stereotype that lurked below the feminist sheen. This deconstructive work suggested that readings "against the grain" (Hall, 1993) were themselves shaped by Disney's preferred reading of its films.

Even this highly truncated account suggests the interdisciplinary approach required by the Global Disney Audiences Project. As Wasko and I argued, the national profiles and overall discussion demonstrated that respondents were:

> ...engaging and negotiating Disney texts, but within the context of national cultures, ritualized use of media, expectations and predispositions learned from Disney about Disney texts, and the relative degree of critical consciousness achieved by individuals. This suggests that although some negotiation occurs, it takes place within the intersection of the political economy of the mediated text, the

national context within which that text plays economic as well as cultural roles, the cultural practices of a society and its social units (like families), and finally individual consciousness. This indicates that negotiation is quite diverse and often complex, requiring an interdisciplinary approach that integrates political economy, cultural studies, sociology, and anthropology. While each approach is crucial, no one approach is enough.

(Wasko and Meehan, 2001, p. 336)

On the Virtues of Breadth and Depth

In the Hollywood Trilogy, Wasko demonstrates the intrinsic value of depth: the ability to pursue research into a complex phenomenon – the Hollywood film industry – through its history and over the course of one's graduate study and an academic career spanning more than three decades. The result is an on-going account of agency, structuration, and structure that examines both change and continuity in a crucial nexus of cultural production. Films may well be "the stuff that dreams are made of" but, as Wasko shows, they are also an outcome of relations of production, technological and financial innovation, industrial concentration, and governmental supports at the local, national, and global levels. These economic and political dynamics set up the stage upon which artists, crews, executives, bankers, politicians, cinephiles, and movie viewers exercise their agency within the particular confines of their historical contexts. Wasko makes clear that outcomes are not predetermined and that individuals do exert agency. But she is keenly aware that some cultural, economic, political, social, and personal choices are systemically more easily made than others. To understand the movies, we must understand how agency, structuration, and structure combine to make the differences between the obvious choice, the difficult choice, and the unthinkable choice.

In the Disney Duo, Wasko demonstrates how depth can pave the way for breadth. Her keen understanding of how Hollywood worked historically and works contemporaneously provides the context for both *Understanding Disney* and *Dazzled by Disney?*. By narrowing her focus to a single company, Wasko is able to examine Disney as an economic entity, political collaborator, and sociocultural force that operates in local, national, and global contexts. Doing all of that requires an immersion in research from sociologists, anthropologists, cultural historians, and textual analysts as well as political economists. But it allows Wasko to examine the full range of Disney's activities from moneymaker to employer to storyteller. In that way, depth links to breadth, giving us a way to think about the non-Disney companies that also manufacture "the stuff that dreams are made of."

Notes

1 I realize that China, Cuba, Laos, North Korea, and Vietnam are still officially Communist countries. The degree to which their economies remain State-centralized varies as does their economic integration into globalization.
2 Sam Spade (Humphrey Bogart) utters these words in the closing scene of *The Maltese Falcon*. Sam Spade has explained the case to two police detectives and identified Brigid O'Shaughnessy as one of the criminals. As one detective takes her out of Spade's apartment, his friend, detective Tom Polhaus, picks up the statuette of the black falcon, notes that it is quite heavy, and asks Spade what it is. Touching the bird and looking in the direction that O'Shaughnessy exited, Spade answers "The stuff that dreams are made of."

References

Hall, S. (1993). Encoding, Decoding. In S. During (Ed.), *The Cultural Studies Reader* (pp. 90–103). London and New York: Routledge.

Havens, T., Lotz, A., & Tinic, S. (2009). Critical Media Industry Studies: A Research Approach. *Journal of Communication, Culture, and Critique*, 2(2), 234–253.

Jenkins, H. (2006). *Convergence Culture: When New and Old Media Collide*. New York: New York University Press.

Meehan, E. R. (2011). A Legacy of Neoliberalism: Patterns in Media Conglomeration. In J. Kapur & K. Wagner (Eds.), *Double Take: Neoliberalism and Global Cinema* (pp. 38–58). London and New York: Routledge.

Meehan, E. R., & Wasko, J. (2013). In Defense of a Political Economy of the Media. *Javnost-The Public*, 20(1), 5–19.

Powdermaker, H. (1951). *Hollywood, the Dream Factory: An Anthropologist Looks at the Movie Makers*. London: Secker & Warburg.

Schatz, T. (1996). *The Genius of the System: Hollywood Filmmaking in the Studio Era*. New York: Henry Holt and Company.

Wasko, J. (1982). *Movies and Money: Financing the American Film Industry*. Norwood, NJ: Ablex.

Wasko, J. (1995). *Hollywood in the Information Age: Beyond the Silver Screen*. Austin, TX: University of Texas Press.

Wasko, J. (2003). *How Hollywood Works*. London: Sage.

Wasko, J. (2001). *Understanding Disney: The Manufacture of Fantasy*. Malden, MA: Blackwell.

Wasko, J., & Meehan, E. R. (2001). Dazzled by Disney?: Ambiguity in Ubiquity. In J. Wasko, M. Phillips, & E. R. Meehan (Eds.), *Dazzled by Disney?: The Global Disney Audiences Project* (pp. 329–343). London: Leicester University Press.

Wasko, J. & Meehan, E. R. (2013). Critical Crossroads or Parallel Routes?: Political Economy and New Approaches to Studying Media Industries and Cultural Products. *Cinema Journal*, 53(3, Spring), 150–157 (P. McDonald (Ed.), *Focus Section*).

Wasko, J., Phillips, M., & Meehan, E. R. (2001). *Dazzled by Disney?: The Global Disney Audiences Project*. London: Leicester University Press.

3 Movie Theaters and Money

Integration and Consolidation in Film Exhibition

Ben Birkinbine

In the wake of the Paramount Decree, which forced vertically integrated film studios in the United States to divest their theater chains, film studios continued on a path of integration and consolidation in their production and distribution operations. Theater chains, it seemed, were left to fend for themselves while still being highly dependent on the studios for films to exhibit. Because the major studios continued to grow, and some were integrated into larger transnational media conglomerates, they have been the subject of important and critical inquiries. The theater chains, however, have received decidedly less attention. Drawing on the work of critical political economists of communication, this chapter explores the integration and consolidation of movie theater chains in the wake of a recent period of technological change. I focus specifically on the transition to digital projection technology, including three-dimensional (3-D) projection, as a way to highlight the ways in which the film exhibition industry in the United States has become increasingly consolidated.

Throughout this chapter, I focus on the ways in which technology and capital can play an important role in consolidating ownership within the film exhibition industry. However, my intent is not to privilege technology as an agent of change. Rather, I want to demonstrate how the introduction of a new technology within an industry can provide a critical juncture, whereby the industry becomes restructured according to distinct lines of power. Those firms that have access to the capital necessary for acquiring the technology may also be in a position to control access to that technology, especially when their competitors do not have access to capital for funding adoption of the technology. Therefore, new forms of dependency can arise within an industry when disadvantaged firms become reliant on competitors for access to the technology. This, in turn, leads to greater consolidation within the industry. In this sense, the technology itself is not the agent of change, but the relations of power and capital that underlie the technology are the primary agents of change. The key issues at stake for my analysis, then, are power, capital, and technology.

In what follows, I begin by framing the study within a critical political economy of communication and media perspective. In particular,

I focus on the reasons why such a perspective is a useful lens for understanding the transition to digital projection technology. Next, I provide some background information on how the transition to digital projection technology developed, including the key partnerships that enabled the transition to take place on a widespread scale. After this introductory information, I proceed by explaining exactly how the three largest exhibitors in the United States – Regal Cinemas, AMC Entertainment, and Cinemark – have colluded to control the transition to digital projection systems. Moreover, I explain how this collusion was made possible by these firms' unique access to the capital necessary for such control to take place. Finally, I discuss how the film exhibition industry in the United States has been restructured in the wake of the transition to digital projection systems, and the ways in which the film industry may be headed toward new ways of integrating production, distribution, and exhibition of film commodities.

Critical Political Economy of Communication and Media

The present study is informed by a critical political economic perspective. Critical political economists investigate the "social relations, particularly the power relations that mutually constitute the production, distribution, and consumption of media resources" (Mosco, 2009, p. 24). Such an approach is differentiated from neoclassical economics or, more simply, economics, in that political economists recognize that economic decisions are intimately entwined with politics. As Myrdal (1971) notes, political and economic decisions are both normative and teleological, implying that such decisions cannot be made without asserting how human activity *ought* to be organized in order to reach a certain end. Moreover, *critical* political economists explicitly expose contradictions within both political and economic spheres as a way to identify possibilities for working toward more just and democratic forms of human organization.

As applied within the field of communication studies, the critical political economy approach was pioneered by the work of Dallas Smythe (1960), Nicholas Garnham (1979), Peter Golding and Graham Murdock (1973), and others. These scholars and others working within this tradition have consistently sought to expose the unequal power relations underlying communications systems. Such unequal distributions of power can be seen in the ways that the majority of informational production, distribution, and access or exhibition are controlled by only a handful of large corporations. These large, often multinational and transindustrial conglomerates hold oligopolistic power within markets, which limits the possibility for alternative or counter-hegemonic forms of communication (Meehan, 2005).

In addition to critiques of large multinational conglomerates, critical political economists have supplied important industry-specific studies of how those industries are structured and how texts within a particular industry are produced, distributed, and consumed. Of particular value for the purpose of this study is the work done by those political economists who have studied the film industry and, more specifically, the film exhibition industry. While film exhibition has been relatively overlooked within the field of film studies, a small but growing corpus of scholarship is taking note of the importance that film exhibition has played throughout film history (Musser, 1991; Gomery, 1992; Waller, 1995; Acland, 2003). In addition, the work of Thomas Guback and Janet Wasko (1982, 1994, 2002, 2003) is notable for their treatment of film exhibition from a critical political economy perspective.

In a study of ownership and control, Guback (1986) analyzed some of the largest publicly held companies in the film exhibition industry to determine whether owners or managers controlled their respective corporations. He was working from the managerial control hypothesis proposed by Berle and Means (1933), which argued that large corporations are controlled by managers who do not own the company while the actual owners do not control the daily operations of the company. Guback concluded that the managerial control hypothesis could not be supported, as "major suppliers of equity and debt capital participate in, and share, the direction of business affairs" (Guback, 1986, p. 17). Here, Guback affirms that those who control capital flows for a particular organization have considerable influence over the decisions made within the organization. He continues by claiming that equity owners and lenders form a "community of interest" that share the common goal of achieving financial gains. This, in turn, suggests that "there still are identifiable sites where substantial ownership is concentrated in a few hands, and that this power to control often is shared with the financial community" (p. 17). With this observation, Guback extends his critique beyond the level of the firm to show that equity owners and lenders form a broader community for whom the power to control is of tantamount concern. Moreover, the power to control is limited to an increasingly concentrated community of interest that holds extensive ownership rights or equity claims throughout the economy, and the film exhibition industry is no different. Although Guback was writing within the context of the late 1980s, the content of his critique remains applicable today.

The same could be said about the work of Janet Wasko, who has consistently investigated the concentration of power and money within the film industry. In her first book, *Movies and Money*, Wasko (1982) investigated the links between financial institutions and the American film industry. In later projects, she specifically addressed concentration and consolidation within the film exhibition industry by focusing on the political economic context within which the theater chains were situated (see Wasko, 1994, 2003). Specifically, Wasko (2003) notes how, after the tremendous growth in multiplex cinemas during the 1990s, the film exhibition industry had become highly concentrated during the early 2000s. This was the result of overbuilding during the 1990s, which led to financial instability on behalf of the exhibitors. The solution to the instability was found in restructuring and consolidation, which left the exhibition industry dominated by fewer but larger cinema chains. This historical context helps to illuminate the present study, especially because the exhibition industry is still dominated by fewer and larger cinema chains. What has changed, however, is that the recent transition to digital projection technology has provided another critical juncture, whereby consolidation and control are reaching new levels.

Technology, in this case, is not the primary driver of this change. Thus, I am not espousing a form of technological determinism. Rather, I understand technology, writ large, as dialectically situated between democracy and capital. When put to use for democratic purposes, technology facilitates greater productivity through cooperation and participation with the goal of satisfying a pressing human need. Communication technologies, put to similar uses, can connect citizens from around the globe for purposes of organizing political action, facilitating dialogue, or enabling cultural exchanges. When controlled by capital, however, technology may be used to extract greater surplus value from commodities and labor by supplanting labor processes or eliminating spatial and temporal barriers that impede the rapid circulation of commodities (Braverman, 1974). Therefore, technology needs to be situated within the context that it is developed and how it is used. The technological changes discussed here occur within the industrial context of the U.S. film industry and have been carefully orchestrated by certain key corporations for the maximization of profit. In this sense, the power to control technology and ensure that it is used in particular ways is the primary determining factor at the heart of my analysis. By viewing technology in this way, a critical political economic approach is particularly valuable, especially when considering the effects of a new technology: rather than focusing on the technology per se, political economy draws attention to context within which the technology is developed as well as the corporations and their respective ownership structures to determine who holds an interest in the development of the technology. This type of perspective can illuminate who is truly benefiting from the so-called "revolutionary" changes in technology.

In sum, then, critical political economy provides a useful framework for investigating the transition to digital projection systems specifically because it draws our attention to the unequal power relations that shape the decisions made, by whom, and for whose benefit. In particular, the work of Thomas Guback and Janet Wasko provides a useful frame for the current study because of their work on the film exhibition industry. In what follows, I focus on a recent period of technological change and expose how the transition to digital projection systems has been con-trolled by the top three theater chains in the United States and Canada. Moreover, I will demonstrate how these three chains – Regal Entertain-ment, AMC Entertainment, and Cinemark – had access to the capital necessary to fund the transition, and as a result, the film exhibition industry has become increasingly consolidated in the wake of the dig-ital transition. I begin with a discussion of the transition to digital pro-jection systems and then I discuss how the three largest theater chains controlled the transition and solidified their position atop the film exhi-bition industry.

The Transition to Digital Projection

In 2002, six major film studios – Disney, Fox, Paramount, Sony Pictures Entertainment, NBC-Universal, and Warner Bros. Studios – formed a coalition known as Digital Cinema Initiatives (DCI), which was created to establish standards and specifications for digital cinema. The DCI specifications established standards for digital cinema systems in the following areas: digital cinema system frameworks, digital cinema dis-tribution, packaging, compression, transportation, exhibitor or theater specifications, projection standards, and security measures. The DCI specifications were meant to ease the transition to digital projection tech-nology by establishing standards to which the studios, distributors, and exhibitors could adhere. After the specifications were released, however, the transition still suffered from unresolved issues relating to adequate security measures and, perhaps most importantly, a lack of funding for the implementation of digital cinema systems (Culkin and Randle, 2003; McQuire, 2004). Exacerbating the urgency of these problems was the fact that the studios were planning the production of digital and 3-D content, and theaters needed digital projection systems to exhibit that content. However, neither the studios nor the exhibitors wanted to fully fund the installation of digital projectors.

The digital transition, it seemed, was at a standstill during the critical period between 2006 and 2009. Unresolved issues, especially a financ-ing agreement, combined with the then-developing financial crisis in the United States at the end of 2007 provided little evidence that the tran-sition would occur anytime soon. These specific and more general fi-nancial concerns were compounded by the fact that Twentieth Century Fox had announced the production of *Avatar* a year earlier, which was to be the first film produced entirely for 3-D exhibition. *Avatar* was set to be released during the summer of 2009, but the release was delayed until December to give theaters more time to install digital projectors (McClintock, 2007). During this critical period, the three largest exhib-itors in the United States and Canada combined forces to ensure that audiences would be able to enjoy *Avatar* in the manner it was meant to be viewed. To understand exactly how the three largest exhibitors accomplished this, I provide some contextual information on the film exhibition industry and background information on each of the companies involved before explaining the ways in which these companies worked together.

Theatrical Exhibition

The theatrical exhibition market in the United States and Canada is highly concentrated, with only a few extremely large theater chains owning the majority of the theaters and screens. Table 3.1 illustrates just how concentrated the industry has become. The top three theater chains – Regal Cinemas, AMC Entertainment, and Cinemark (collectively referred to as "the Big Three") – have consolidated their power at the top of the industry through acquisitions and mergers. The mergers and acquisitions have continued in the wake of the transition to digital projection technology, which became widespread in 2008. In 2010, AMC Entertainment acquired Kerasotes Theaters, which was listed as the sixth largest theater circuit in the United States and Canada at the time. In addition, Regal announced its acquisition of Hollywood Theaters during February 2013 (Regal Entertainment, 2013a). At the time of writing, Hollywood Theaters is listed as the eighth largest theater circuit. The upshot of the acquisition was the addition of 43 theaters with approximately 513 screens to Regal's already large circuit of theaters (Rozeman, 2013). Cinemark also agreed to acquire Rave Cinemas for $220 million in May 2013, and Rave Cinemas is listed as the ninth largest theater chain at the time of writing. Because this merger would further consolidate the film exhibition industry, the United States Department of Justice reached a settlement with Cinemark, whereby Cinemark will need to divest itself of theaters in Kentucky, New Jersey, and Texas in order to preserve competition in those markets (United States Department of Justice, 2013).

Because these two new acquisitions were reported during the preparation of this chapter, the exact numbers for the combined power of the Big Three are difficult to determine exactly. However, statistics from 2012 show that the United States and Canada had a total of 39,918 screens (Motion Picture Association of America, 2012). Collectively, and including the recent acquisitions by Regal and Cinemark, the Big Three now controls approximately 16,848 screens or 42% of all screens in the market. This gives the Big Three an incredibly strong market position. For some perspective on how dramatically the theatrical exhibition market has changed, Guback (1986) noted that the largest cinema chain in the United States during the mid-1980s was the General Cinema circuit,

Table 3.1 Top ten movie theater chains in the United States and Canada in 2012

Company	Screens	Sites
Regal Cinemas	6,880	540
AMC Entertainment	4,988	346
Cinemark USA[1]	3,916	298
Carmike Cinemas	2,502	249
Cineplex Entertainment Ltd. Partnership[a]	1,455	136
National Amusements[b]	920	67
Marcus Theaters Corporation	694	56
Hollywood Theaters[a]	546	49
Rave Cinemas[a]	518	35
Harkins Theaters[b]	429	30

Note: Unless otherwise noted, all data was compiled from 10-K annual reports filed with the SEC for 2012.

References: AMC Entertainment (2013), Carmike Cinemas (2013), Cinemark Holdings (2013), Cineplex Entertainment (2013), Hollywood Theatre (2013), Marcus Corporation (2012), Rave Motion Pictures (2013), and Regal Entertainment (2013b).

a From company Web site.
b From National Association of Theater Owners (NATO).

which owned more than 1,100 screens. At the other end of the spectrum was the Marcus Corporation, which owned only 98 screens. In spite of its relatively small size, Guback argued that the Marcus Corporation held considerable market power since it was geographically limited to the state of Wisconsin. In the wake of the digital transition, however, these smaller regional chains are disappearing or becoming integrated into the largest chains. More specifically, these chains are being acquired by the three largest exhibitors, which only consolidates their position atop the film exhibition industry. In what follows, I discuss each of the Big Three individually.

Regal Entertainment Group

Regal Entertainment Group is the parent company of Regal Cinemas, which owns the largest theater chain in the United States.[2] Regal's holdings include the wholly owned subsidiaries Edwards Theaters, Regal CineMedia, and the United Artists Theater Company as well as the recently acquired Great Escape Theaters and Hollywood Theaters, which were acquired in 2012 and 2013, respectively. The company's theaters are located solely in the United States, where the company has a presence in 39 states as well as the District of Columbia. The highest concentration of its theaters is in the state of California, where the company owns 97 theaters. Furthermore, Regal's theaters are located in 43 of the top

50 markets in the United States, which gives the company a significant presence in major urban areas.

In 2012, the company earned approximately \$2.8 billion for the 2012 fiscal year. Of those revenues, approximately 68.2% came from admissions sales, while 26.5% came from concessions sales and the remaining 5.3% came from "other operating revenues," which include its joint ventures with the other Big Three exhibitors. Although 5.3% may be a small part of the company's total revenues, the "other operating revenues" category has grown as a percentage of total revenues since 2009. Depending on how many other operations are reported under this category, this may suggest that the joint ventures are becoming a more important part of Regal's overall operations.

AMC Entertainment

AMC Entertainment owns the second largest theater chain in the United States. AMC Entertainment currently owns theaters in 33 states as well as the District of Columbia in the United States. Similarly to Regal, AMC's theaters are primarily located in major urban markets throughout the United States. Outside the United States, AMC owns theaters in the United Kingdom and Canada as well as a partial interest in two theaters located in Hong Kong. In 2012, AMC reported approximately \$2.018 billion in revenue, but that revenue was split into separate reporting segments due to a recent restructuring of the company. Indeed, the most interesting aspect of AMC's operations is the massive corporate restructuring that has taken place during the past decade. A brief overview of this history will help to understand why and how the Big Three had access to capital during the financial crisis as a way to fund the installation of digital projection systems.

From 2004 until 2012, AMC Entertainment was owned by Marquee Holdings Inc., which was ultimately owned by J.P. Morgan Partners L.C. and other funds affiliated with J.P. Morgan Partners and Apollo Investment Fund V, L.P. Marquee Holdings Inc. conducts no business operations of its own, but serves strictly as a holding company for AMC Entertainment. After Marquee Holdings became the parent company for AMC Entertainment, AMC underwent significant transformations to its operations beginning in March 2005. These changes included the divestiture of its theaters located in foreign markets, such as Japan, Hong Kong, Spain, Portugal, Argentina, Brazil, Chile, and Mexico. In addition, Marquee Holdings acquired LCE Holdings Inc., which served as the parent company for the Loews Cineplex Entertainment Corporation. Interestingly, LCE Holdings was formed by investment funds associated with Bain Capital Partners, Spectrum Equity Investors, and The Carlyle Group, all of which are major private equity firms. These ties to major sources of capital would be one of the primary ways the Big Three were able to finance the installation of digital projectors and facilitate the broader transition to digital projection within the exhibition industry. Moreover, the ties with private equity and one of the largest banks in the United States were particularly important during the critical period of the digital transition from 2006 to 2009.

In 2011, Marquee Holdings merged into AMC Entertainment. AMC Entertainment became a wholly owned direct subsidiary of AMC Entertainment Holdings, Inc., which took over as the parent company of AMC. In 2012, however, AMC announced a merger between its parent company and Wanda Film Exhibition Co. Ltd., which is a wholly owned indirect subsidiary of the Dalian Wanda Group. Dalian is a Chinese private conglomerate with holdings in real estate, tourism, hotels, and entertainment. Figure 3.1 illustrates the new corporate structure for AMC, which represents the changes that took place after the merger with the Dalian Wanda Group. While the merger has effectively separated AMC from its ties to major private equity firms, AMC and the rest of the Big Three benefited from these connections during the critical period of the transition.

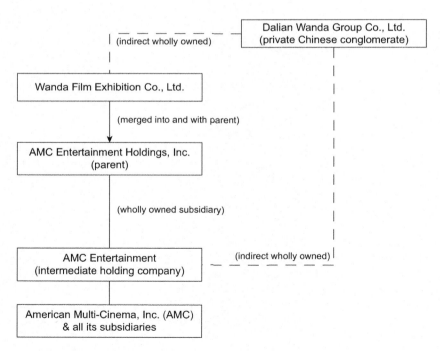

Figure 3.1 New ownership structure for AMC.

Cinemark Holdings, Inc.

Cinemark is the last of the Big Three theater chains involved in controlling the transition to digital projection technology. The Cinemark chain is owned by Cinemark Holdings, Inc., which also owns the Century Theaters chain and recently acquired Rave Cinemas. Cinemark is unique among the Big Three for its geographic scope; the company owns theaters both domestically and internationally. Within the United States, Cinemark owns theaters in 39 states, and its largest presence is in the state of Texas where it owns 80 theaters that account for 1,051 screens. While both Regal and AMC tend to be concentrated within major urban markets, Cinemark's theaters are primarily located in mid-sized markets and suburban areas. Outside the United States, Cinemark owns 167 theaters that are located throughout Latin America, including Brazil, Mexico, Argentina, Colombia, Chile, Peru, Ecuador, Honduras, El Salvador, Nicaragua, Costa Rica, Panama, and Guatemala. In Brazil and Argentina, Cinemark is currently the largest exhibitor, and the company often faces little or no direct competition throughout Latin America.

Although Cinemark is listed as the third largest of the Big Three in the figures reported in Table 3.1, these figures do not include Cinemark's international holdings. When those theaters are included, the exhibitor owns 465 theaters with 5,240 screens, which would position Cinemark as the largest theater chain in terms of total theaters and second in terms of total screens. Indeed, Cinemark reported approximately $2.5 billion in revenues for 2012, which would also position it second among the Big Three in terms of revenue. While these numbers certainly indicate the size and scope of the individual companies, the Big Three combined forces to control the transition to digital projection. In what follows, I describe exactly how they managed to do so by focusing on their unique access to capital and their joint ventures.

The Big Three Unite

The Big Three combined forces during the critical period between 2006 and 2009 to control the transition to digital projection. While installation of digital projectors languished during this period, the Big Three initiated the push for widespread installation of the projectors. To do so, they relied on AMC and Marquee Holding's connections to J.P. Morgan and large private equity firms. In 2009, J.P. Morgan and other private equity firms pledged $525 million to the Big Three (DiOrio, 2009)[3]. This enabled the Big Three to facilitate the installation of digital projection systems by offering financing and installation to their competitors through one of their joint ventures, Digital Cinema Implementation Partners (DCIP). The Big Three also offered distribution and advertising services to their competitors through its second joint venture, National

CineMedia (NCM) and its subsidiary Fathom Events. Beyond these initial joint ventures, the Big Three have continued to negotiate joint ventures and other partnerships. The most recent examples of this type of cooperation are the Digital Cinema Distribution Coalition (DCDC) and Open Road Films – each of which will expand the Big Three further into distribution operations. In what follows, I discuss each of these joint ventures in more detail.

Digital Cinema Implementation Partners – Financing and Installation

Most of the Big Three's business operations related to digital cinema take place through DCIP. DCIP began in 2007 as an independent corporation that secures funding and negotiates agreements with major film studios for the implementation of digital cinema systems. Each of the Big Three maintains an equal voting interest in the company, but their economic interests in the venture differ. Regal maintains the largest economic interest in DCIP with 46.7% while AMC and Cinemark hold 29% and 24.3%, respectively. In 2010, DCIP secured a total of $660 million to aid in the transition to digital projection systems, with $445 million of that sum coming from major financial institutions, including J.P. Morgan, Morgan Stanley, Bank of America Merrill Lynch, GE Capital, Sumitomo Mitsui Banking Corporation, Barclays Bank, Credit Suisse, Deutsche Bank, and Citi (Digital Cinema Implementation Partners, 2010). The inclusion of J.P. Morgan in this group is notable for its ties to the Big Three through AMC, while GE Capital maintained indirect ties to the film industry at that time through its partial ownership of NBC-Universal. In February 2013, however, Comcast agreed to purchase General Electric's remaining 49% common equity interest in NBC-Universal (Comcast, 2013).

DCIP was created by the Big Three to finance, procure, and deploy digital cinema projection systems. One way DCIP deploys digital cinema equipment to other exhibitors is by negotiating leasing agreements with its competitors. Since smaller independent or regional theater chains do not have access to the types of funding provided to the Big Three via DCIP, those exhibitors may rent digital cinema equipment from DCIP if they are unable to secure independent funding for the transition. DCIP also collects virtual print fees from the studios through its subsidiary, Kasima. The studios and distributors agreed to pay virtual print fees to the exhibitors in order to offset the savings that the studios would enjoy for not having to ship rolls of film to exhibitors. While DCIP is primarily focused on the financing and deployment of hardware for digital cinema projection, the second joint venture of the Big Three provides a means to exploit distribution and content-related business operations.

National CineMedia – Distribution, Advertising

The second joint venture is known as NCM, which serves as an in-theater advertising network and distributor of non-feature film content. NCM is slightly different from DCIP in its ownership structure. The Big Three hold differential ownership stakes in NCM: Regal owns 25%, AMC owns 18.5%, and Cinemark owns 15%, which accounts for 58.5% of the total ownership. The remaining 41.5% is owned by National Cine-Media Inc., which serves as a holding company for the operating company National CineMedia LLC. Through the operating company, NCM develops, produces, sells, and distributes content that is exhibited via its on-screen pre-feature program called *FirstLook*. The advertising programs featured in *FirstLook* primarily come from national advertisers, but the NCM network allows local vendors to purchase advertising spots within the program cycle. In addition, NCM produces advertising and promotional materials for display in theater lobbies throughout its network. NCM has also expanded into mobile application development with its *Movie Night Out* and *MovieSync* applications, which deliver advertising and promotional materials to consumers via mobile devices. For the 2012 fiscal year, advertising revenues accounted for 91.2% of the company's total revenue.

NCM also markets and distributes live or prerecorded content to its network of theaters through its Fathom Events subsidiary. The programming offered by Fathom Events is typically live music, opera, theatrical performances, or sporting events. These events are streamed directly to theaters, thereby extending the reach of a live performance that would otherwise be bound to a specific place. In this sense, Fathom Events functions similarly to pay-per-view or on-demand television, although it takes place within a theatrical setting, thereby giving viewers access to a large screen and surround sound. In 2010, Fathom Events began streaming of 3-D programming as well. Because the digital projectors enable an entire network of theaters to view the same content at the same time, live performances or other presentations may be supplemented with interviews, lectures, discussions, or other materials that would generally be included on the DVD or Blu-Ray release. This supplemental material can also be combined with the feature presentation, thereby allowing for commentary on a particular film. For example, *Rifftrax* Live features former cast members of the cult comedy show *Mystery Science Theater 3000*, providing satirical comments alongside the broadcast of a film. In addition to providing content to its network of theaters, the digital projection systems also allow for theaters to be repurposed for other types of events like corporate meetings, training seminars, or religious services. For an exhibitor to gain access to the advertising, programming, and functionality provided by NCM and Fathom, exhibitors must enter into an agreement with NCM that grants NCM exclusive rights to sell advertising as well as meeting and communication services in those theaters.

These two joint ventures and their subsidiaries represent the ways in which the Big Three worked together to control the transition to digital projections systems, particularly during the critical period between 2006 and 2009. Figure 3.2 provides an illustration of how these joint ventures fit into the combined structures of the Big Three, including the economic interests that each of the Big Three holds in the joint ventures. Figure 3.2 also illustrates how the Big Three had access to capital through AMC's ties to J.P. Morgan and major private equity firms. The joint ventures contained within the illustration were established during the critical period and gained prominence when the more widespread transition to digital projection systems was underway. As certain exhibitors relied on agreements with the Big Three to gain access to the programming and other services available through digital projection systems, the Big Three became more firmly entrenched atop the film exhibition industry. Since this initial period, however, the Big Three have continued to expand their business operations through additional joint ventures and partnerships.

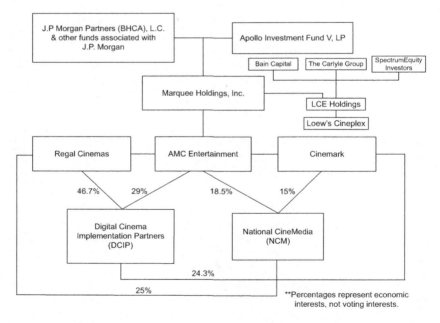

Figure 3.2 Ownership and corporate interlocks in digital film exhibition.

Digital Cinema Distribution Coalition and Open Road Films – Distribution

In 2012, the Big Three worked in connection with Universal and Warner Brothers to establish the DCDC, which will distribute films via satellite. Since the formation of DCDC, three other studios – Disney, Paramount, and Lionsgate – have agreed to join the coalition, while Sony and Fox are still in negotiations with the group (Stewart, 2013). The coalition has been formed with the goal of eliminating the need for distributing material prints or discs of films to exhibitors. DCDC is significant because it expands the distribution operations of the Big Three, which started with their involvement in NCM and Fathom Events. DCDC is also significant for the combined business operations of the studios and exhibitors, which have been officially separated since the Paramount Decree in 1948.

In addition to DCDC, in which all of the Big Three are involved, Regal and AMC jointly own Open Road Films. This company distributes films as well, but focuses on the "unique opportunity to fill a gap in the marketplace created by the major studios' big-budget franchise film strategy by marketing smaller budget films in a cost-effective manner" (Regal Entertainment Group, 2013b, 6). In other words, Open Road Films is focused on niche programming rather than a more large-scale, general interest audience. For example, during the summer of 2013, Open Road Films distributed *Machete Kills*, an ultraviolent action film, and *Jobs*, which is a biopic about Apple cofounder Steve Jobs.

These two additional joint ventures represent the ways in which the Big Three continue to expand their business operations after positioning themselves to control the transition to digital projection systems. By controlling the digital transition during a period of financial difficulty, the Big Three established distinct lines of dependency within the film exhibition industry. The fact that the Big Three continue to acquire smaller regional and independent cinema chains demonstrates the consequences of such concentrated power within the industry.

Toward a New Integration

In this chapter, I have demonstrated how the Big Three exhibitors – Regal Cinemas, AMC Entertainment, and Cinemark – colluded to solidify their position atop the film exhibition industry in the United States and Canada. The Big Three created DCIP to secure the funding and hardware necessary to equip their theaters with digital cinema projectors. After doing so, they sold installation services to their competitors through DCIP. Then, the Big Three created NCM to serve as an in-theater advertising network as well as a distributor of non-feature film content. Fathom Events, a subsidiary of NCM, markets and distributes content to those exhibitors that subscribe to the service. By subscribing to the services offered by NCM and Fathom Events, competitors grant exclusive rights to NCM to sell advertising as well as meeting and communication services within their theaters.

The Big Three were able to undertake these two joint ventures for two primary reasons. First, some of the Big Three's competitors were unable to fund their own transition to digital projection systems because of the large up-front costs, especially as the transition was taking place during the onset of the financial crisis during 2007–2008. Second, the Big Three were uniquely positioned in their access to capital with AMC having ties to J.P. Morgan and other private equity firms. By having access to the necessary capital, the Big Three became early adopters of the technology and expanded their business operations through joint ventures and partnerships that allowed them to provide goods and services related to digital projection technologies to other exhibitors. These joint ventures also included business operations that exhibitors have not conducted since they were integrated with the Hollywood studios prior to the Paramount Decree in 1948 such as production, distribution, and financing.

While the Big Three are still in the process of acquiring more theaters and expanding their business operations, certain trends are emerging that could have a significant impact on the broader film industry. The recent partnership between the film studios and the Big Three in the DCDC seems to indicate that the film industry is again headed toward greater integration. The studios are working directly with exhibitors to streamline the distribution of films via satellite. In this sense, a highly consolidated exhibition industry would make it easier for the studios to negotiate distribution deals with exhibitors. The Big Three are currently the only exhibitors involved in the DCDC, and their close ties with the studios through this partnership will only increase their competitive advantage in the exhibition industry.

However, the close partnership that the Big Three have with the studios through DCDC will most likely have consequences beyond a mere competitive advantage. DCDC could ultimately lead to a tiered distribution and exhibition system. In this scenario, smaller, independent, and regionally based theater chains may be forced into a situation similar to the block booking techniques that occurred at the height of the vertically integrated film studios of the 1920s and 1930s. During that time, studios packaged film distribution into blocks, whereby a single A-list film was combined with other B-list films in order to make production and distribution more cost-effective. To get access to the A-list material, theaters were forced to rent the B-list movies. In the present case, the Big Three may end up controlling access to premium content, whereas theaters not affiliated with the Big Three through subscriptions or other agreements may not receive favorable distribution deals. The difference with the present scenario is that access to the material relies also on technology necessary for viewing the content rather than a rent agreement with distributors. However, the technology for exhibiting such content may be rented to the "lower tier" of movie theaters via DCIP. After the technology has been acquired, the Big Three may also require that the lower tier of theaters agree to exhibit some of the content distributed by NCM or Fathom Events. This, in effect, would be similar to the block booking techniques used by the vertically integrated film studios. While the Big Three are not technically integrated with the studios, DCDC represents one way in which the Big Three are working closely with the studios to streamline satellite distribution of films. The compelling question for regulators and independent exhibitors is whether this level of cooperation will become sufficiently similar to the block booking techniques used by the vertically integrated studios. During the 1930s, independent exhibitors lobbied for antitrust regulation against the studios, which culminated in the Paramount Decree and forced the studios to divest their theater operations.

Furthermore, Dalian Wanda Group's acquisition of AMC will likely have consequences both within the domestic market as well as internationally. The acquisition now makes Dalian Wanda the owner of the largest chain of theaters in the world, and the company may have plans to acquire additional theater chains in the United States as well as in Europe (Mider, 2013). At the time of writing, Wanda's acquisition already marked the largest takeover of a U.S. company by a Chinese company, and China now represents the third largest market for Hollywood films after the United States and Japan. While this chapter specifically focused on the connections between movie theaters and money within the United States and Canada, additional research will be needed to investigate whether a similar trend is occurring around the world. Certainly, Wanda's recent acquisition seems to suggest that we may be headed toward a more fully integrated global film industry. In part, this integration will rely on the control of digital technologies.

Indeed, the Motion Picture Association of America (MPAA) has long bemoaned the effect that piracy is having on the economic performance of the film industry. The organization frequently produces industry reports and educational materials that are intended to demonstrate how piracy is adversely affecting its constituents. In response, Hollywood has attempted to combat piracy by manipulating release schedules for its films. For example, a single film may be released simultaneously around the world on the same date to prevent unauthorized copies of the film from showing up in black markets. These measures have been largely ineffective, even by the MPAA's own accounting measures. The transition to digital projection systems would enable films to be exhibited without a material copy of the film. Originally, digital prints were distributed in one of three ways: by satellite, by fiber-optic cables, or by hard drive. Satellite and fiber-optic delivery do not require material versions of the film to be sent, which might explain why the Big Three and the studios have been working closely to streamline the satellite distribution process.

While these methods are aimed at eradicating piracy, the extent to which such measures can be effective is yet to be seen. What is clear, however, is that the studios and the MPAA are working to more effectively control the technologies used for the storage, transmission, reception, and exhibition of theatrical film.

While these are only possible scenarios, the transition to digital projection systems appears to be having dramatic effects on the overall structure of the film exhibition industry. Popular rhetoric and corporate publicity campaigns tend to emphasize the unique aesthetic novelties provided by these technologies. What I have tried to do throughout this chapter is demonstrate how the Big Three's control of these technologies is being used to restructure the industry. Behind the technological transition was a broader community of financial interests with an economic stake in the transition. In the wake of the digital transition, the Big Three have continued to pursue joint ventures and strategic partnerships that will more fully consolidate and integrate the film exhibition industry. As an increasing array of options for viewing filmed entertainment become available to consumers, the consolidation and integration within theatrical exhibition may be overlooked by regulators. For this reason, the digital transition provides an important and germane moment for political economic analysis. Rather than focusing on the technology and its attendant aesthetic novelties, we ought to consider the connections between movie theaters and money.

Notes

1 These figures only include Cinemark's theaters in the United States and Canada. Cinemark also owns 167 theaters in 13 Latin American countries. When those theaters are included, the exhibitor owns 465 theaters with 5,240 screens.
2 Unless otherwise noted, the information about the Big Three exhibitors has been taken from the most recent 10-K filings for each of the companies.
3 JP Morgan contributed $325 million to this sum, while the additional $200 million was equity-based contributions from private equity firms and the circuits themselves. While we do not know exactly which private equity firms contributed to this amount, AMC's connections to the private equity firms Bain Capital, the Carlyle Group, and Spectrum Equity Investors suggests that at least a portion of the equity-based contributions may have come from these sources.

References

Acland, C. R. (2003). *Screen traffic: Movies, multiplexes, and global culture.* Durham, NC: Duke University Press.

AMC Entertainment, Inc. (2013, March 13). Form 10-K. Annual Report. Last accessed March 28, 2013, from http://www.investor.amctheatres.com/sec.cfm?CIK=722077

Berle, A. F. & Means, G.C. (1933). *The Modern Corporation and Private Property*. New York: The Macmillan Company.

Braverman, H. (1974). *Labor and monopoly capital: The degradation of work in the twentieth century*. New York: Monthly Review Press.

Carmike Cinemas, Inc. (2013, March 14). Form 10-K. Annual Report. Last accessed March 28, 2013, from http://www.carmikeinvestors.com/SECFilings/Annual

Cinemark Holdings, Inc. (2013, February 28). Form 10-K. Annual Report. Last accessed March 27, 2013, from http://phx.corporate-ir.net/phoenix.zhtml?c=192773&p=irol-sec

Cineplex Entertainment, LP. (2013). Company Web site. Last accessed March 28, 2013, from http://www.cineplex.com/

Comcast Corporation. (2013). Form 10-K. Annual Report. Last accessed July 28, 2013, from http://files.shareholder.com/downloads/CMCSA/2608951310x0xS1193125-13-67658/1166691/filing.pdf

Culkin, N. & Randle, K. (2003). Digital cinema: Opportunities and challenges. *Convergence*, 9(4), pp. 79–98.

Digital Cinema Implementation Partners. (2010, March 10). Digital cinema implementation partners announces completion of $660 million financing for digital cinema upgrade [Press Release]. Last accessed July 28, 2013, from http://www.dcipllc.com/press/DCIP_closing_release_final_March_10.pdf

DiOrio, C. (2009, September 11). D-cinema gets $525 mil boost [Electronic version]. *Film Journal International*. Last accessed July 28, 2013, from http://www.filmjournal.com/filmjournal/content_display/news-and-features/news/digital-cinema/e3i769003baee0c3e51613eeeef2a1e0aa4

Gomery, D. (1992). *Shared pleasures: A history of movie presentation in the United States*. Madison, WI: The University of Wisconsin Press.

Guback, T. (1986). Ownership and control in the motion picture industry. *Journal of Film and Video*, 38(1), pp. 7–20.

Hollywood Theaters, Inc. (2013). Company Web site. Last accessed March 28, 2013, from http://www.gohollywood.com/about-us/

Marcus Corporation. (2012, August 14). Form 10-K. Annual Report. Last accessed March 28, 2013, from http://phx.corporate-ir.net/phoenix.zhtml?c=99966&p=irol-sec

McClintock, P. (2007, December 11). Fox shifts 'Avatar,' 'Museum.' *Variety*. Last accessed July 25 from http://variety.com/2007/film/news/fox-shifts-avatar-museum-1117977544/

McQuire, S. (2004). Slow train coming?: The transition to digital distribution and exhibition in cinema. *Media International Australia*, 110 (February), pp. 105–119.

Meehan, E. R. (2005). *Why TV Is Not Our Fault*. Lanham, MD: Rowman and Littlefield.

Mider, Z. R. (2013). China's Wanda to buy AMC cinema chain for $2.6 billion. Bloomberg. Last accessed July 30, 2013, from http://www.bloomberg.com/news/2012-05-21/china-s-wanda-group-to-buy-amc-cinema-chain-for-2-6-billion.html

Mosco, V. (2009). *The political economy of communication* (2nd ed.). London: Sage.

Motion Picture Association of America. (2012). *Theatrical market statistics 2012.* Last accessed July 25, 2013, from http://www.mpaa.org/Resources/3037b7a4-58a2-4109-8012-58fca3abdf1b.pdf

Musser, C. (1991). *Before the nickelodeon: Edwin S. Porter and the Edison Manufacturing Company.* Berkeley, CA: University of California Press.

Myrdal, G. (1971). *The political element in the development of economic theory.* London: Routledge.

Rave Motion Pictures. (2013). Company Web site. Last accessed March 28, 2013, from http://www.ravemotionpictures.com/aboutus.aspx

Regal Entertainment Group, Inc. (2013a, April 1). Regal Entertainment Group completes the acquisition of Hollywood Theaters. Press Release. Last accessed April 2, 2013, from http://investor.regmovies.com/

Regal Entertainment Group, Inc. (2013b, February 25). Form 10-K. Annual Report. Last accessed March 27, 2013, from http://investor.regmovies.com/phoenix.zhtml?c=222211&p=irol-sec

Rozeman, M. (2013, April 2). Regal Entertainment Group acquires Hollywood Theaters for $191 million. *Paste Magazine.* Last accessed July 25, 2013, from http://www.pastemagazine.com/articles/2013/04/regal-entertainment-group-acquires-hollywood-theat.html

Stewart, A. (March 7, 2013). Studios, exhibitors partner for digital delivery service that will eliminate physical discs. *Variety.* Last accessed July 28, 2013, from http://variety.com/2013/digital/news/coming-soon-to-theaters-movies-via-satellite-1200005115/

United States Department of Justice. (2013, May 20). Justice Department reaches settlement with Cinemark Holdings Inc. and Rave Holdings LLC movie theaters. *Press Release.* Last accessed July 25, 2013, from http://www.justice.gov/opa/pr/2013/May/13-at-582.html

Waller, G. A. (1995). *Main street amusements: Movies and commercial entertainment in a southern city, 1896–1930.* Washington, DC: Smithsonian Institution Press.

Wasko, J. (2003). *How Hollywood works.* Thousand Oaks, CA: Sage Publications.

Wasko, J. (2002). The future of film distribution and exhibition. In D. Harries (ed.), *The new media book.* London: British Film Institute Publishing.

Wasko, J. (1994). *Hollywood in the information age: Beyond the silver screen.* Austin, TX: University of Texas Press.

Wasko, J. (1982). *Movies and money: Financing the American film industry.* Norwood, NJ: Ablex Publishing Corporation.

4 How Hollywood Workers Unite

Labor Convergence and the Creation of SAG-AFTRA

Catherine McKercher and Vincent Mosco

In 2012, the Screen Actors Guild (SAG) and the American Federation of Television and Radio Artists (AFTRA) pulled off a historic merger. By overwhelming majorities, the members of both unions voted to create SAG-AFTRA, "the newest, strongest union for talent in media and entertainment," according to President Ken Howard (2013). To most members of the two unions, to the labor movement, and to those who study communication labor, the idea of a SAG-AFTRA merger has been a no-brainer for decades. If ever a compelling argument could be made for two unions to unite, it was the case with SAG and AFTRA. They represented workers in the same industry, doing the same work, often under identical contracts. For more than 30 years, the unions had bargained jointly on their major national contracts with the advertising and entertainment industries. While AFTRA covered a broader range of workers – sound recording artists, radio and television journalists, performers in soap operas, talk shows, reality shows, and game shows – the core constituency of both unions was actors. In fact, roughly 44,000 film, television, and commercial actors belonged to both unions, which meant that 40% of SAG's 120,000 members were AFTRA members too and 60% of AFTRA's 70,000 members also belonged to SAG. Yet, all previous efforts at merger – in the 1980s, 1990s, and early 2000s – had collapsed when SAG chose to go alone (McKercher and Mosco, 2007; McKercher, 2008).

This chapter focuses on the 2012 merger effort, seeking to understand how merger advocates turned the defeat of 2003 into victory nine years later. What happened in those years to convince a significant proportion of SAG voters to change their mind on merger? More significantly, what does this mean for members of the new union, and for members of other unions contemplating similar mergers? It concludes that SAG and AFTRA have put themselves in a better position to represent the needs of their members and to serve as a model for other unions seeking a way to thrive, not just survive, in the transformation to digital communication.

Labor, Convergence, and Technology

These are tough times for trade unions across the United States, not just in Hollywood. Union density – the proportion of workers who belong to a trade union – hit a new low of 11.3% in 2012, the year SAG and AFTRA merged, and has declined since then to 10.7% in 2017. In the public sector, the union membership rate was 34.4% in 2017, but in the private sector it was just 6.5% (Bureau of Labor Statistics 2013, 2018). A number of factors account for this. So-called "right to work" laws – which have nothing to do with guaranteed jobs and everything to do with undermining trade unions by allowing workers in a unionized workplace to decide whether they wish to pay union dues – continue to spread, at last count, to 28 states. In addition, a number of states have sought to strip collective bargaining rights from public sector workers. Meanwhile, the balance of power between trade unionists and the companies that employ them continues to shift in favor of business. The six biggest film producers in Hollywood, commonly known as the majors, include some of the world's largest communication and media companies: Sony, Time Warner, the Walt Disney Company, Comcast, Twenty-First Century Fox (a spinoff of News Corp.), and Viacom. Filmmakers, like other manufacturers, continue to export work to lower-wage, often nonunion, locales. A number of jurisdictions, both inside the United States and abroad, offer generous incentives to lure film production and the local spending it generates. Finally, it is almost impossible to overstate the impact digital technology is having on communication and information workers of all sorts, including creative workers in Hollywood. The boundaries between previously separate forms of work – acting for film cameras or for TV cameras, for example, or voicing characters for radio or for video games – have blurred as communication work goes digital. While the film industry has diversified and expanded both horizontally and vertically, Wasko quite rightly notes that entertainment unions in Hollywood have traditionally been organized along craft lines. This has, she concluded, "tended to inhibit labor unity within the industry" (2003, p. 43).

In recent years, a number of trade unions have begun to explore new ways to stop the erosion of – and perhaps increase – labor power. This is especially the case in the communication sector, which provides the equipment that makes globalization possible, and produces and distributes the ideas and images that make it work. One approach is to pursue trade union mergers, designed strategically to restructure unions along much the same lines as the corporations that employ their members. The Communications Workers of America (CWA) has brought together workers in what were once independent industries – newspapers, telecommunications, sound recording, broadcasting – but now are part of cross-media conglomerates. As a CWA official quoted by Wasko put it:

> (W)ith all the concentration of corporate power, it's become an advantage for unions to band together and join their resources and strength. It certainly helps when unions have to take on these multinational corporate structures, as especially evidenced in the communications and broadcasting fields.
>
> (2003, p. 49)

In Canada, the Communications, Energy and Paperworkers Union, itself a converged union much like the CWA, took labor convergence one step further in 2013 when it merged with the Canadian Auto Workers Union. With more than 300,000 members, the new union, known as Unifor, is the largest private sector union in Canada (CBC News, 2013).

Mergers are not the only form of labor convergence. Another approach is to take joint action to address a specific problem or issue. The best example in Hollywood is the fight against runaway film and video production. This began in 1999 when SAG and the Directors Guild of America commissioned a study that defined the issue simply and clearly – runaways are TV productions or films intended for a U.S. audience but filmed in another country to cut production costs – and set the terms on which it would be debated (Vlessing, 2004). Over the next few years, a coalition of labor and industry groups, spearheaded by the Directors Guild, lobbied Congress successfully for changes in the tax law aimed at keeping production in the United States. At its peak the Runaway Production Alliance was composed of 19 organizations with a stake in the issue, including the major labor unions in Hollywood: SAG, AFTRA, the Teamsters, the International Alliance of Theatrical Stage Employees (IATSE), and the Writers Guild.

Joint collective bargaining is another way of expressing labor unity, and it has a long history in Hollywood. In 1981, in a move intended to be the first step toward a full merger, SAG and AFTRA agreed to bargain jointly on their major contracts. The hoped-for merger didn't follow, but the commitment to joint bargaining endured, with one major exception which we describe below, for more than 30 years.

Whatever form it takes, labor convergence recognizes that it is not just the boundaries between employers that have become blurred; the rise of digital technology has blurred the boundaries between what were once distinct forms of work. Workers in the converging communications industries are increasingly involved in knowledge labor that requires similar sets of skills and training. Although specific differences among jobs exist, these are eroding as knowledge workers go through similar processes of deskilling and reskilling, and often deskilling again, and face similar challenges such as outsourcing their work (Huws, 2003; Mosco,

2005). There is considerable research on the value of merger or convergence among trade unions, including in the communication and information industries (Batstone, 1984; Katz, 1997; Stone, 2004; Mosco & McKercher, 2006). Labor convergence, therefore, may be an appropriate response to technological and corporate convergence (Bahr, 1998; McKercher, 2002; Swift, 2003; Mosco & McKercher, 2008). However, trade union mergers do not arise from simply technocratic cost-benefit analyses (Chaison, 1986). Nor is there a natural path to unity among knowledge and cultural workers, as some have predicted (Terranova, 2004). Rather, trade unions are social, cultural, and political institutions, with distinctive histories, norms, and power structures. A merger may mean that factions or individuals have to give up power and say goodbye to treasured traditions. The fact that potential merger partners often have a shared history of competition and conflict as well as cooperation complicates matters for trade unions.

Cultural and political conflicts derailed all prior attempts at a merger between Hollywood's two actors unions most spectacularly in 2003. After describing the series of failed attempts to merge, the chapter looks at what happened to SAG and AFTRA after the failure of 2003, and explores why and how they managed to accomplish the successful merger of 2012. The chapter concludes by assessing how well the new union, SAG-AFTRA, has managed the transition from two separate unions with their own cultures and histories to a converged union, and what lessons can be drawn from the new structure.

No, No, No to Merger

By the time they merged, SAG and AFTRA's core jurisdictions were virtually indistinguishable from one another. Originally, though, they represented distinct groups of workers employed by distinctly different industries, working on opposite ends of the country, in New York and Los Angeles. They also had their own administrative structures, approaches to organizing, craft traditions, and political cultures.

SAG was founded in Los Angeles in 1933. For legal reasons relating to the state of labor law at the time, it was set up as a corporation (Prindle, 1988: p. 22). This meant that it was a centralized organization, run by directors elected by the full membership. From its earliest days, SAG had progressive and conservative elements – the fact it chose to call itself a "guild" rather than a "union" reflects this – and the struggle between the two has been a "constant but muted" undercurrent in SAG politics (Prindle, 1988: p. 8). This was not the only fault line in the union, however. There have been tensions between the Hollywood, New York, and regional divisions, between people who made their living as actors and people who saw acting as a sideline (and a SAG membership as a status symbol), between those who saw AFTRA's more diverse membership as a strength and those who saw it as a weakness, between factions that believed in confrontation and factions that pursued labor peace as the prime objective, and between groups that saw themselves as part of the labor movement and groups that saw actors as creative artists whose concerns were far removed from those of working-class Americans. One of SAG's most distinctive features was its *de facto* party system and lively political culture, characterized by shifting alliances contesting over whatever issue was most pressing at the time.

The American Federation of Radio Artists (AFRA), the precursor of AFTRA, was nothing like that. It was founded in 1937 in New York, home of the U.S. radio business. AFRA's constitution vested power in the locals, which elected their own boards and chose representatives to the national board. It was much more like a traditional North American trade union than was SAG. Performance was the common denominator of both SAG and AFRA, but in the early days their jurisdictions were clearly and sharply delineated. Performing live on radio was AFRA work and most AFRA members worked in New York, the home of the radio business; acting before film cameras for later projection on a screen was SAG work and most SAG members worked in Hollywood, the home of the film business. Actors who did both had to join both unions, and many did.

As television appeared in North American homes after the Second World War, the neat division began to break down. Both AFRA and SAG claimed jurisdiction over the new mass medium. After a lengthy struggle, SAG won the right to represent actors in filmed television programs. AFTRA – the "T" added to the name stands for television – was given jurisdiction over live television. Over the next three decades, this division also began to break down. Meanwhile, the television business migrated west, from AFTRA's base to SAG's, and AFTRA work migrated along with it. The development of videotape, which allowed for productions that were neither live nor on film, created new jurisdictional confusion. Television's ability to reuse material – by televising theatrical films or reruns of TV programs – launched the unions on long and costly fights over residuals, which are basically royalties for repeat airing. Writes Prindle:

> Periodically, the notion of eliminating the tangle of jurisdiction by merging all screen actors into one union would gain favor. SAG and AFTRA would consult about it and hire a professional researcher to do a study, there would be a good deal of argument back and forth, and after a while the impulse would peter out.

(p. 77)

Distinct craft traditions and decades-old conflicts would win the day over the ostensibly sensible idea of joining forces in merger.

In 1981 these discussions resulted in a significant step toward uniting: an agreement to jointly negotiate and ratify all major film and television contracts. For both SAG and AFTRA, cooperation at the bargaining table was simultaneously an act of self-promotion (a way to get better deals with the employers) and an act of self-preservation (a way for the unions to prevent employers from playing one union off against the other). It was also meant to be the first step toward a bigger goal. The agreement to bargain jointly was known as Phase One of Merger. Phase Two, the adoption of a new joint governing structure, did not materialize, however. Nor, of course, did Phase Three, the uniting of the pension and health plans.

In that failed merger attempt, as in the 1998 and 2003 failures, the stumbling block was the internal debate at SAG over whether actors would be best served by a narrowly focused craft union or by a union with a broader vision.

In the 1980s effort, a pro-merger faction won control, first of AFTRA's Los Angeles local and then of the SAG board. But SAG also had a new president, the outspoken and left-leaning Ed Asner, who angered conservatives in the union. Almost immediately, a conservative coalition coalesced in opposition to Asner's radicalism in particular and to the direction SAG was heading in general. The SAG-AFTRA merger effort was knocked off the agenda by a vicious fight over what was supposed to be a precursor merger between SAG and the Screen Extras Guild. That deal was rejected by the SAG membership twice, the second time more decisively than the first. The next serious merger attempt came in the late 1990s, when a moderate and pro-merger faction rose to power at SAG. The Guild and AFTRA negotiated an agreement for a new body to be called SAG/AFTRA that would unite everything but the health and pension plans. The goal was to end jurisdictional disputes between the two unions, including a looming battle with the media conglomerates over revenues from high-definition television. Proponents argued that it would also streamline operations and give the union more power at the bargaining table. This time, the opposition came from a right-leaning bloc at SAG that dismissed the prospect of a jurisdictional dispute as a scare tactic. The group also questioned the decision on health and pension plans. In the end, it convinced members to choose the "purity" of an actors' union over one that included broadcasters and musicians too (Cooper, 2001). According to their respective constitutions, the merger required 60% approval from both unions to pass. AFTRA members endorsed it, decisively if somewhat narrowly, with 67.6% approval. SAG turned it down flat, with just 46.5% of members voting yes. Soon after, SAG's pro-merger president, Richard Masur, was replaced by the conservative-leaning William Daniels, who promised to get tough with the employers. His combative two-year term included the bitter six-month SAG/AFTRA commercials strike in 2000. A political moderate who supported merger with AFTRA, Melissa Gilbert, replaced Daniels in 2001 and negotiations with AFTRA were on again. In 2003 the unions reached a new agreement, this time for an affiliation to be called the Alliance of International Media Artists, with three autonomous and self-governing subunits covering actors, broadcasters, and musicians. The structure was intended to avoid one of the hurdles that tripped up the previous merger attempt: SAG members didn't want to lose their identity or their traditions, and the creation of an autonomous subunit would recognize that. As with the previous merger vote, the ratification campaign was heated. The antimerger faction argued that SAG would lose direct fiscal control over its budget and that the actors union would be reduced to a "glorified committee" of a larger union (Kiefer, 2003). Former SAG President Daniels attacked AFTRA directly in an interview with the *New York Times*: "AFTRA is a crummy little union, and they're undercutting our contracts, so we should join them? To us it's a very, very bad deal" (Lyman, 2003). The opponents also made much of some unavoidable uncertainty about the future of the SAG and AFTRA pension and health plans. In a 2006 interview with the authors of this chapter, Matt Kimbrough, then AFTRA's National Recording Secretary and a SAG member, explained that because the plans were created and governed separately from the unions, "you couldn't even begin the process of merging the plans until you actually merged the unions." But this meant that merger proponents had no clear answers about what the merger would mean for actors' pensions. Opponents also appealed, as they had in 1999, to craft solidarity – the notion that actors are artists and shouldn't be comingled in a union with broadcast journalists or musicians. Ron Morgan, then president of AFTRA's Los Angeles local and a SAG member, said this argument "resonated stronger than anything else" (interview with authors, 2006). In the end, AFTRA members approved it easily, with 75.8% in favor. At SAG it netted 57.8% approval, just short of the 60% margin required. In July 2005 Gilbert announced she would not seek a third term as SAG president. She was replaced by Alan Rosenberg. Though liberal-leaning rather than conservative, Rosenberg – like Daniels – opposed merging with AFTRA and promised to get tough with the employers. Also like Daniels, his time at the helm of SAG would be marked by controversy.

Building Unity Out of Division

While SAG and AFTRA debated the merits of labor convergence, the businesses that employed their members were consolidating and going digital. *AFTRA Magazine* noted that the number of major employers of performers and broadcasters had declined from 26 in 1985 to 6 in 2003

("AFTRA consolidation plan," 2003). Eight studios controlled 88% of all domestic theatrical production and distribution. Five record companies controlled 84% of the recording industry. Two cable system owners, AT&T and Time Warner, accounted for 40% of all cable households. Two companies owned more than 1,400 radio stations (Winter, 2003: p. 4). "While AFTRA and SAG have been *thinking* about consolidating, our employers have actually done it. The industry *already* has consolidated" (p. 4, emphasis in original). The magazine also pointed out that digitization, which would replace both film and tape, presented a growing threat. "The emergence of digital production has rapidly escalated the jurisdictional conflict. This serves to: 1. Drive down terms and conditions for performers. 2. Divert resources from critical union initiatives" (p. 5). The magazine pointed out that one of the "common perceptions" in the 1999 merger attempt was that there was "no imminent or compelling need to take action" (p. 5). That was no longer the case, it argued. Over the years following the failed 2003 merger, the consequences of industry changes and the failure to unite would become more apparent.

In 2007 and 2008, the collective agreements between the major creative Hollywood unions and the Alliance of Motion Picture and Television Producers (AMPTP) came up for renewal. Compensation for new media use was one of the key issues for most of the unions, but especially for those representing writers and actors. The Writers Guild of America went on strike in November 2007 after talks broke down over new media royalties. Two months into the 14-week strike, the Directors Guild of America reached a collective agreement with the producers association. SAG's Rosenberg, who strongly supported the writers, criticized the new media provisions in the directors' deal as inadequate. The writers settled a few weeks later, clearing the way for SAG and AFTRA, bargaining jointly as they had so many times before, to reach their own deal.

That didn't happen. AFTRA announced in March 2008 that it would go it alone. The immediate cause of the rift was an accusation that SAG tried to poach AFTRA work on a soap opera. However, comments reported in *Inside TV* from the presidents of both unions show deeper tensions, tensions that had been building ever since Rosenberg's election as SAG chief. Here's what Roberta Reardon of AFTRA had to say:

> Actually, the *Bold and the Beautiful* event had significant impact, but really, it was the culmination of what we saw as a year-long campaign from the Screen Actors Guild Hollywood leadership to defame AFTRA. ... [I]t's clear that for a year they were trying to get out of Phase One. So now, all of a sudden we're the bad guys for saying, 'You lied to us, we're leaving.' It's been very disingenuous to say the least.

Rosenberg told a different story, and in intemperate and accusatory terms:

> I really thought [AFTRA] would [at] the last minute find some flimsy excuse – which this *Bold and the Beautiful* thing is – to end this relationship. ... And if it hadn't happened now it would have happened a week or two into negotiations, I'm convinced. Their goal all along has been to be separated from us so they can compete with us. It was despicable.
>
> (Juarez, 2008)

AFTRA reached a deal with the AMPTP in May. SAG, unhappy with the provisions in that deal and concerned that AMPTP would demand the same from SAG, reacted in a stunning and unprecedented way. It launched a vigorous public campaign to convince the 44,000 dual members – actors who belonged to both SAG and AFTRA – to turn down the AFTRA deal. This tactic was distinctly unusual; typically trade unions avoid interfering in each other's operations. It also proved unsuccessful. AFTRA ratified the deal with a 62% margin ("Timeline ...," 2009). Given that 60% of AFTRA members were also SAG members, the result suggests a significant repudiation of the SAG tactic by dual members. By this point, SAG was the only union that had still not reached a deal. This raised questions among its own members about whether SAG leaders were fooling themselves by thinking that their union could do better than the others. The pattern had already been set, despite SAG's desire to alter it.

SAG's negotiations with the AMPTP went nowhere. By the end of June 2008, when the existing collective agreement expired, the two sides were at an impasse. Meanwhile, member discontent with Rosenberg's hardline stance was growing in the union. This was reflected in the results of the SAG board election that fall, which shifted the balance of power from Rosenberg's faction, known as Membership First, to a more moderate group, known as Unite for Strength. A federal mediation effort failed in November. Almost immediately, Rosenberg announced plans to hold a strike vote. The membership erupted. The New York region's board voted against holding a strike vote. More than 130 high-profile Hollywood actors released statements calling on the union to drop the idea. Citing the deepening recession and the fact the other unions had signed contracts, the actors argued that this was not the time to take a hard line. Instead, they urged SAG to unite with the other unions and negotiate from a stronger position the next time the contracts come up (Callan & White, 2008). The strike vote, which needed 75% approval to authorize a walkout, was set for January 2. Just before Christmas, SAG Executive Director Doug Allen, head of the bargaining committee and a Rosenberg loyalist, emailed members to say he and

Rosenberg had agreed to postpone the strike vote until after a national board meeting in January (Verrier, 2008). By that meeting, the moderates on the board were in open revolt. Rosenberg led a 29-hour filibuster to stave off an effort to fire Allen and replace the negotiating committee. A couple of weeks later, the board succeeded on both actions. It took several months – in part because of a lawsuit Rosenberg and some other Membership First board members filed against their own union to reinstate Allen and impede the negotiations – but eventually SAG and the AMPTP reached an agreement. While the union prepared for ratification, SAG's Hollywood board, still controlled by the hardline Membership First faction, took a final shot at AFTRA, passing a resolution to establish a task force "to explore the acquisition of actors of AFTRA" (Handel, 2009). This would violate the agreement between the two unions that prohibits disparagement and raiding. The resolution went nowhere. Rosenberg's presidency ended later in 2009 and Ken Howard, a moderate and leader of a pro-merger Unite for Strength faction, became the leader of the union.

The 2007–2008 negotiation cycle had significant – and almost immediate – consequences for members of both SAG and AFTRA. In a 2012 analysis, Jonathan Handel, an entertainment lawyer who closely tracks labor in Hollywood, found that SAG's share of prime-time television took "a stomach-churning plunge more typical of a double-black-diamond ski run than a business graph." It fell from 93% in 2008 – the year AFTRA had a deal with the producers and SAG did not – to 50% just three years later. AFTRA's share, which stood at less than 10% in 2008, had risen to 45% and was expected to pass 55% in 2012. Handel said SAG's drop in market share was especially sharp in prime-time pilots. Overall, the total number of pilots fell during the year of the writers' strike and had not fully recovered. Producers, still feeling the effects of that stoppage and concerned about what was going on at SAG, chose to sign with AFTRA. After the leadership change at SAG, the producers began to return to SAG. Even so, though, SAG's share of pilots in 2012 was just 20%. Given that SAG was the larger union and had historically been the stronger of the two, the reversal was worrisome. Handel noted that the drop in SAG's market share was of "grave concern" to the union's health and pension plan because employer contributions are related to the amount of earnings covered (Handel, 2012a).

While this shift was taking place, relations between SAG and AFTRA were beginning to thaw. The pro-merger faction expanded its control of the SAG board in 2010 and the two unions agreed to return to their traditional pattern of joint bargaining. They reached an agreement with AMPTP for a new three-year contract in November 2010, almost eight months ahead of the expiry date. As Handel put it, "That early deal left the unions free to spend 2011 focused on merger" (2011). They struck a joint committee, known as the Group for One Union or G1, and several subcommittees to handle specific issues. SAG President Ken Howard and AFTRA President Roberta Reardon went on a national "listening tour" to hear what the members had to say. Things proceeded swiftly, and by the end of January 2012, the two sides had reached a merger agreement. As always, the campaign was lively, featuring antimerger protests outside the building housing the SAG and AFTRA offices and an unsuccessful lawsuit filed by a number of prominent SAG political figures – including former presidents Rosenberg and Ed Asner – aimed at derailing the ratification (Handel, 2012c). Ballots went out in February. As in the past, AFTRA members supported the merger, this time by 86%. But this time, 81.9% of SAG voters said yes. It was a stunning turnaround.

How can we account for this change? A number of factors come into play. Among the most significant is the growing recognition in the U.S. labor movement that trade unions need to adapt and grow if they are to survive. In cases like SAG and AFTRA, where digital technology and corporate convergence have blurred and even erased traditional jurisdictional lines, labor convergence becomes not just increasingly possible but desirable. Sue Schurman, a Rutgers University dean who was brought in to facilitate the merger, summed up the situation:

> There was once a difference between the big screen of movies and the small screen of television – now there are screens everywhere showing digital content. Ownership in the entertainment industry is highly concentrated. A small number of conglomerates own virtually all the networks and other content creation and distribution channels. These companies have learned to make more money with fewer performers thanks to technology. There are growing numbers of skilled non-union performers, not to mention the popularity of reality shows. When the basic conditions of an industry change, workers and their organizations have to adapt.
>
> (Hopkins-Jenkins, 2012)

Support at SAG for merger had been growing, if more slowly than at AFTRA, for a number of years, from under 50% in the 1990s to just under 60% in the early 2000s to over 80% in 2012. The step away from joint bargaining in 2008 offered a sharp reminder about the practical values of labor solidarity and the negative consequences that can happen when unions fight each other. Instead of cooperating with each other the unions wound up competing – a situation that tends to benefit employers rather than workers. As AFTRA's Kimbrough puts it, "The only way a union competes with another union for a job is to offer the producers a better deal. That's a hard truth and it's not good for the members" (interview with authors, 2006). Schurman makes a similar point: "SAG and AFTRA have both been weakened already by the changes in their industry, and by fighting with each other instead of cooperating to bring workers in the new media parts of the industry into their unions" (Hopkins-Jenkins, 2012).

Certainly, SAG's internal politics played a critical a role. The union's unusual party system was remarkably successful at engaging members in the governance of the union. However, the numerous fault lines that run through SAG tended to show up in sharp swings in the composition and direction of the board. In the years leading up to the 2012 vote, control of the board swung between narrow, craft-oriented factions (Artists Working for an Actor's Guild, Membership First, Save SAG) and factions that sought stronger ties with a broader range of creative workers (Caucus of Artists for Merger, Restore Respect, Unite for Strength). Rosenberg, in advocating a get-tough approach with the studios despite the fact that the other unions had settled and despite the perilous state of the national economy, ended up alienating many of the very people his Membership First faction sought to represent. By the time the merger agreement was back on the table, his faction had more or less drawn down its political currency. As Handel put it:

> Credit not only the advocates, but also Membership First. Under their watch – and despite their intentions – the events of 2007–2008 weakened SAG, strengthened AFTRA, accentuated the split earnings problem, allowed the studios to play one union off against the other, and led SAG members to reject intra- and inter-union battles and seek merger instead.
>
> (2011)

From Merger to Convergence

Negotiating a merger is one thing; making it work is quite another. SAG-AFTRA has faced both challenges and opportunities. In an effort to rationalize its structure, the merged union almost immediately reduced the number of seats on its board, bought out 80 paid staff members, consolidated 33 locals into 25, and closed a number of regional offices. Inevitably, this prompted some angry reaction. The new union also inherited a simmering misappropriation scandal about SAG's benefits plans, resulting in a Labor Department investigation that wrapped up in 2016 (Robb, 2017a), and a lawsuit filed by Ed Asner and 15 others over how the union handled foreign residuals (McNary, 2013). Positive developments included signing a first-ever contract with record labels covering music video dancers (McNary, 2012), a successful campaign to organize Southern California public radio workers (Verrier, 2013a), and a polished and well-received SAG awards show. It also began what would turn out to be four years of work to merge the health plans. That happened in 2016 (McNary, 2016).

The biggest challenge – and the biggest success – in the union's first year was negotiating a new commercials contract, one of the largest contracts covering members of both SAG and AFTRA. Although the unions had a long record of bargaining jointly, the new structure meant that they had to bargain as a single unit, putting together a team that would represent everyone. Reardon, who was copresident with SAG's Ken Howard until 2013, chaired the bargaining team; David White, formerly chief counsel for SAG and national executive director of the merged union, was the chief negotiator. Part of the promise of a merger was that a merged union would have more clout at the bargaining table. This meant the negotiators were under pressure to sign a deal demonstrating that SAG-AFTRA was greater than the sum of its parts. The deal seemed to have done the trick, and the proof was in the ratification vote. It passed by an astounding 96% – a strong endorsement not just of the contract but of the new union as well (Verrier, 2013b).

The result boded well for the next round with the television and film producers in 2014. The contract negotiated that year unified the separate SAG and AFTRA agreements and included a first-ever, industry-wide agreement on basic cable production. The ratification vote was marginally lower this time, but still impressive at 92.12% in favor (Handel, 2014).

The 2017 contract was considerably more hard-fought, however. In fact, the question of whether to ratify it at all became an issue in the SAG-AFTRA presidential election that year. Two of the five candidates – Esai Morales, head of the Membership First faction, and Peter Antico, a stuntman, pushed for a "no" vote. Gabrielle Carteris, who became president following the death of Ken Howard and chaired the negotiating committee, won reelection and the contract was approved by 76% of members (McNary, 2017a). However, the bitterness of the 2017 union presidential election campaign and the fact that Membership First won 7 of the 15 seats on the SAG-AFTRA board in elections that year suggest the union still has work to do to create a unified political culture (Robb, 2017b).

Without doubt, SAG-AFTRA faces difficulties from sources outside its own internal workings. The increasingly anti-union climate in the United States, the growing power of conglomerates, the push toward nonunion labor, and the continuing expansion of digital technology all pose challenges. Many of these were at play in what would turn out to be SAG-AFTRA's longest strike ever, which began against the video game industry in October 2016 and lasted until September 2017. A key issue in the 19 months of negotiations leading up to the strike was the union's push for residuals. SAG-AFTRA argued that the gaming industry had grown into one of the largest segments of the entertainment business, and it should pay voice actors the same kind of residuals as the film and television industries. It also wanted improvements in working conditions – voicing video games may require a lot of screaming, which can cause physical harm – and more transparency in hiring practices. During the strike, the companies repeatedly blasted the union leadership for not allowing members to vote on what it called its final offer, which would have provided an immediate 9% pay hike (McNary, 2017b). It also refused to budge on the residuals question. In the end, the three-year contract included a sliding scale bonus system instead of residuals and improvements on the other key issues. The contract gained 90% approval in the ratification vote (McNary, 2017c). But a lengthy strike, even if it concludes successfully, takes a toll.

After the 2012 merger, Handel identified three big challenges for the merged union: mobilizing members, picking up the pace on merging the pension and health plans, and capitalizing on the leverage unity can bring to contract negotiations (Handel, 2012b). Schurman, who as merger facilitator addressed the cultural clashes that defined relations between the former SAG and the former AFTRA, says melding two cultures into one may well in the long run, be the most important outcome of the merger. "If the new SAG-AFTRA does its job well, I suspect some of the other unions will want to merge as well – if for no other reason than to concentrate their pension and health contributions," she says (Hopkins-Jenkins, 2012).

Actors Equity Association – which represents 45,000 theatrical actors and stage managers, many of whom also belong to SAG-AFTRA – endorsed the SAG-AFTRA merger in 2012. Equity and SAG-AFTRA continue to cooperate with other performers unions through a long-standing federation known as the Associated Actors and Artistes of America. The writers and directors guilds also share some members with SAG-AFTRA. Given the challenges of bringing together SAG and AFTRA, it is difficult to imagine a converged union of all creative workers in Hollywood, at least not in the short term. With SAG-AFTRA's house in order, however, interunion cooperation is likely to increase and become more effective.

And as a united force, the union will be in a stronger position to represent, protect, and promote the needs of its members. Like the CWA and other unions that pursue a labor convergence agenda, it may also serve as a model, offering a lesson in how to adapt democratically, how to grow financially, and how to promote workers individually and collectively.

References

"AFTRA consolidation plan." *AFTRA Magazine*, Winter 2003, pp. 3–5.

Bahr, M. 1998. *From the telegraph to the Internet*. Washington, DC: National Press Books.

Batstone, E. 1984. *Working order: Workplace industrial relations over two decades*. Oxford: Basic Blackwell.

Bureau of Labor Statistics. 2013. "Union members – 2012." News release USDL-13-0105. Jan. 23.

———. 2018. "Union members – 2017." News release USDL-18-0080. Jan. 19.

Callan, J. & White, M. 2008. "Baldwin, Hanks urge actors to drop strike vote as rift deepens." *Bloomberg*. Dec. 16.

CBC News. 2013. "CAW, CEP unions now known together as Unifor." *cbc.ca*. May 31.

Chaison, G. 1986. *When unions merge*. Lexington, MA: Lexington Books.

Cooper, M. 2001. "Residual Anger." *The Nation*. April 2.

Handel, J. 2009. "SAG's strange voyage." *Huffington Post*. May 19.

———. 2011. "The SAG-AFTRA merger attempt: Why is it happening now?" *The Hollywood Reporter*. July 12.

———. 2012a. "SAG's primetime market share set to fall below 50% this fall." *The Hollywood Reporter*. March 25.

———. 2012b. "SAG-AFTRA: 3 big challenges for the merged union." *The Hollywood Reporter*. April 3.

———. 2012c. "SAG-AFTRA merger lawsuit to be dropped." *The Hollywood Reporter*. May 16.

———. 2014. "SAG-AFTRA ratifies 2014 TV and theatrical contracts." *The Hollywood Reporter*. Aug. 22.

Hopkins-Jenkins, A. E. 2012. "One union, two cultures." Q&A with Sue Schurman. Rutgers University. April 3.

Howard, K. 2013. Comments made introducing the 2012 Screen Actors Guild awards.

Huws, U. 2003. *The making of a cybertariat: Virtual work in real world*. New York: Monthly Review.

Juarez, V. 2008. "The SAG/AFTRA divorce: What went wrong, and what's next?" *Inside TV*. April 4.

Katz, H. C. 1997. "Introduction and comparative overview." In H. C. Katz (Ed.) *Telecommunications: Restructuring work and employment relations worldwide*. Ithaca: Cornell University Press, pp. 2–28.

Kiefer, P. 2003. "SAG-AFTRA merger proposal shot down." *The Hollywood Reporter*. July 2.

Lyman, R. 2003. "It's Take 2 For Merger Of Actors' Unions." *The New York Times*. June 18.

McKercher, C. 2002. *Newsworkers Unite: Labor, convergence and North American newspapers*. Lanham, MD: Rowman and Littlefield.

———. 2008. "Hollywood unions and the fight for work." In Janet Wasko and Mary Erickson (Eds.) *Cross-border cultural production: Economic runaway or globalization?* Youngstown, NY: Cambria Press, pp. 117–137.

McKercher, C. & Mosco, V. 2007. "Divided they stand: Hollywood unions in the information age." *Work Organisation, Labour and Globalisation*. Vol. 1, No.1, pp. 130–143.

McNary, D. 2012. "SAG-AFTRA, labels ink dancer deal." *Variety*. June 1.

———. 2013. "Ed Asner, 15 others sue SAG-AFTRA over unpaid funds." *Chicago Tribune*. May 24.

———. 2016. "SAG, AFTRA health care plans merge." *Variety*. June 8.

———. 2017a. "SAG-AFTRA members ratify new film-TV contract." *Variety*. Aug. 7.

———. 2017b. "SAG-AFTRA video game strike ends after a year." *Variety*. Sept. 25.

————. 2017c. "SAG-AFTRA members ratify three-year video game contract." *Variety*. Nov. 7.

Mosco, V. 2005. "Here today, outsourced tomorrow: Knowledge workers in the global economy." *Javnost/The Public*. Vol. 12, No. 2, pp. 39–56.

Mosco, V. & McKercher, C. 2006. "Convergence bites back." *Canadian Journal of Communication*. Vol. 31, No. 3, pp. 733–752.

————. 2008. *The laboring of communication: Will knowledge workers of the world unite?* Lanham, MD: Lexington.

Prindle, D. F. 1988. *The politics of glamour: Ideology and democracy in the Screen Actors Guild*. Madison: University of Wisconsin Press.

Robb, D. 2017a. "Department of Labor finds $750,000 misappropriation from SAG pension and health plans." *Deadline Hollywood*. Jan. 20.

————. 2017b. "Gabrielle Carteris re-elected as SAG-AFTRA president." *Deadline Hollywood*. Aug. 24.

Stone, K. 2004. *From widgets to digits: Employment regulation for the changing workplace*. Cambridge: Cambridge University Press.

Swift, J. 2003. *Walking the union walk*. Ottawa: Communication Energy and Paperworkers Union of Canada.

Terranova, T. 2004. *Network culture: Politics for the information age*. London: Pluto.

"Timeline: SAG's contract dispute." 2009. *Variety*. June 10.

Verrier, R. 2008. "SAG delays strike vote." *Los Angeles Times*. Dec. 23.

————. 2013a. "KPCC employees join SAG-AFTRA union." *Los Angeles Times*. Jan. 18.

————. 2013b. SAG-AFTRA gives big thumbs up to new commercials contracts." *Los Angeles Times*. May 31.

Vlessing, E. 2004. "Canada launches attack in runaway prod'n war." *The Hollywood Reporter*. Oct. 14.

Wasko, J. 2003. *How Hollywood works*. London: Sage.

5 The Mexican Film Industry 2000–2018

Resurgence or Assimilation?

Rodrigo Gómez

This chapter understands the Mexican film industry (MFI) as part of the cultural industries, which means that these industries have the "ability to make and circulate products that influence our knowledge, understanding and experience; a role as system for the management of creativity and knowledge; and its effects as agent of economic, social and cultural change"(Hesmondhalgh, 2013, p. 4). Thus, the products of cultural industries must be understood in relation to their economic and cultural dynamic duality and as distinctly different from other industrial products and commodities (Guback, 1989). They are, at the same time, commodities that have the main purpose to make profits as well as symbolic texts that have a pivotal role in how our societies create sense. Cultural products shape our imaginaries, ideologies, and identities (Murdock, 1988; Sánchez-Ruiz and Gómez, 2009). In addition, one of the main differences from any other commodity is that these cultural products/symbolic texts (songs, narratives, performances, movies, news, TV series and formats, video games, documentaries) have as their primary aim to communicate to an audience to make profits (Hesmondhalgh, 2013, p. 4).

This chapter uses a political economy of film approach, as Wasko established: "The political economy of film analyzes motion pictures as commodities produced and distributed within a capitalist industrial structure...." Thus, "the approach is most definitely interested in questions pertaining to market structure and performance, but...would challenge the myths of competition, independence, globalization, etc., and view the film industry as part of the larger communication – *and cultural* – and media industry and society as a whole" (2003, pp. 9–10).

Another aspect needed to understand the complexity of the cultural industries from a political economy of communication perspective is that these industries are interconnected, particularly the audiovisual industries, because as Garnham has noted, these industries compete with each other for the same resources: "1) for a limited pool of disposable consumer income; 2) for a limited pool of advertising revenue; 3) for a limited amount of consumption time; 4) for skilled labor" (1990, p. 158).

In addition, in my view, we have to add that these industries and their products are in both continuous interactions and transformation; sometimes that transformation is stable and at other times it is more unsettled. Thus, to understand any film industry, local or global, it has to be analyzed from a multidimensional perspective and in a dynamic relation with the interlocks with other cultural industries throughout time (Hesmondhalgh, 2013).

Historically the film industry is a prime example of these complex dynamics, interlocks, and changes throughout time. In fact, the film industry, as one of the first cultural industries, has experienced those transformations since its beginnings. For example, in the early days of the 20th century, film was the central cultural industry and competed just with the press, primarily newspapers. When the radio industry emerged as a challenger, it did so with an alternative business model as well as different practices of cultural consumption. Not long after the radio's emergence, the TV industry brought another important change, displacing film as the nucleus of the cultural industries core. Television impacted other cultural industries at a variety of levels, from their formats and genre to cultural labor, particularly symbol creators, among others. Thus, in a very short time, the film industry had to change, in order to compete and adapt to the interactions and transformations with the different additions of new cultural industries.

Golding and Murdock (2000) and Meehan, Mosco, and Wasko (1993) have established that structural historical analysis is central to provide insight into social change. As well to understand and analyze relations of power through the study of ownership and control of the cultural industries, with the aim "through identification of contradictions, political economy analysis provides strategies for intervention, resistance and change" (Wasko, 2003, p. 9).

In that regard, the political economy of film has been interested in studying Hollywood's domination and hegemony of the international markets and the role of the national State to defend their film industries for cultural and economic reasons (Guback, 1989). Thus, the political economy of communication, as Golding and Murdock (2000, p. 72) established, "…is centrally concerned with the balance between capitalism enterprise and public intervention" at local and international levels.

State Intervention and the Historic Mexican Film Industry

The MFI underwent different processes in its development to generate its current consolidation. Some could be explained in relation to national political and economic dynamics and circumstances. But at the same time, its development can't be explained without the international historic context and the proximity to the United States of America.

This section presents a snapshot of the MFI structure from its beginning until the end of the 1980s through a historical analysis.

It is important to recall that the MFI from 1939 to 1992 was a key industry for the Mexican government. The importance of film was clearly established through the state's role as an active protector, funder, producer, distributor, and exhibitor (García-Riera, 1971; Getino, 1998; Saavedra and Ávalos, 2012). However this role of the Mexican State, through the different Partido Revolucianario Institucional (PRI)[1] administrations, was primarily a response in the moment to national and international political, economical, and sociocultural situations rather than a master plan or long-run State public policy planning (Peredo, 2012). In fact, this reactive performance of the various Mexican governments was a constant of the dynamics and logics of the clientelist, centralist, authoritarian, and presidentialist Mexican political system of the second half of the 20th century (Gómez, 2007).

The central role of the State in the MFI had six key components during this period. First, it offered support for the National Cinematographic Bank, the public institution which financed the production branch for filming and technological equipment as well as the national distribution and exhibition branches. This institution operated with different names from 1942 to 1979 and was a keystone. Second, it issued the Federal Cinematographic Industry Law (1949/1952–1992). This law mandates promotion of and support for the film industry. Furthermore, one of the most important articles within this law addresses the screen quota system for the protection of Mexican productions. Since 1950, the screen quota was set at 50% devoted to the showing of Mexican films; another important issue of this law was that it prohibited the horizontal commercial ownership in the industry. Third, the price of the movie ticket was controlled by the government. The year 1947 is when the State first intervened and later governments included film as part of the *canasta básica familiar* or basic basket of goods[2] (from 1970 to 1991). Fourth was the ownership of Pelmex (1945) and partial ownership of PelNal (1947), the most important distribution companies. Pelmex exported Mexican productions throughout the Ibero-American countries and PelNal distributed domestically within Mexico. Fifth was the takeover of Operadora de Teatros y Cadena Oro – better known as COTSA – two of the most important national exhibition chains acquired in 1961. It later invested in Estudios Churubusco-Azteca, the most emblematic Mexican studios acquired in 1969. Finally, it invested in Estudios América, acquired in 1975 (García-Riera, 1985; Paranaguá, 1995). It is important to point out that all film assets of the MFI were located in Mexico City, clearly reflecting the centralism of all cultural industries in Mexico (Sánchez Ruiz, 2005).

The above shows as an example how the Mexican administrations took part in different initiatives and policies to maintain and protect the MFI during the second half of the 20th century. Certainly, there were economic, political, and sociocultural reasons to protect this industry. We have to remember that before the expansion of television, cinema was Mexico's national entertainment, and it was the place where the public accessed national and international news in audiovisual form (Monsiváis, 2000). Other aspect that has to be highlighted in relation to the Mexican society of those years is the level of literacy; for example, in 1950, 42.6% of the Mexican population was illiterate. Thus, for the PRI regime, the film industry and its national products were key to control political information and cultural consumption through this mass medium (Sánchez Ruiz, 2005).

In political terms, the film industry was controlled by the government, meaning that Mexican movies did not criticize the regime or raise for public discussion political issues that may inconvenience the government (Sánchez Ruiz, 2005). In fact, the government had a special office in the *Secretaria de Gobernación* (Interior Ministry) where film producers obtained permission for financing their films, distribution, and screening. That office began its operations in 1949 with the name of *Dirección General de Cinematografía* (General Direction of Film). To illustrate the role of that office and political censorship, I would like to point out the movie *La Sombra del Caudillo* (1960), which was not allowed for release until the fall of 1990, 30 years after its production.

In terms of the economic dimension, the Mexican State's economic policies and their implementation presented a mixed economy "where the State protected the capitalist system, dictated the rules for development and take part as any other big private entrepreneur" (Smith, 2001, p. 332). The film industry was a reflection of this because the state participated in all the activities of the productive chain of the film industry (Sánchez Ruiz, 2005). Another aspect that must be emphasized and which helps explain the long-running active role of the State's control of the film industry: it is an economic structural fact that the industry gave financial fuel to the different Mexican administrations. From the 1940s to the 1970s, the Mexican gross domestic product (GDP) grew on average around 6%. No Latin American country grew at that pace during those years (Meyer, 1992). This situation in combination with the proximity to the United States gave an important competitive structural advantage, allowing the MFI to become the most important film industry in the Ibero-American geo-cultural zone (Getino, 1998). From 1926 to 1989, the MFI produced 4,609 movies (Gómez, 2005).

However, despite government support, the history of Mexican film productions was still cyclical, with ups and downs, as Figure 5.1 illustrates. Historically, during the 20th century the most productive year was 1958 with 136 movies, and from 1945 to 1970 the production of films was consistently around 80 films per year. But the most important occurrence of those years, particularly during the "golden age of

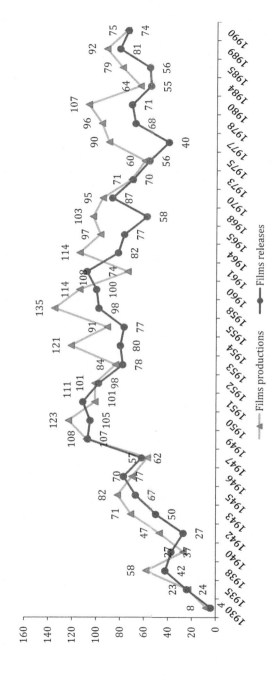

Figure 5.1 Selected years of historic film production and release performance from 1930 to 1990.

Source: Elaborated by the author with information from: Imcine 2011: 134–135.

Mexican cinema," was the consolidation of the MFI, especially in the following aspects:

- The movies reflected, in general, different social issues of Mexican society, and above all showed some aspects of Mexican popular culture through original cinema genres as *melodrama, rancheras, lucha-libre*, and *comedy*;
- The average productions were technically and creatively produced and directed with international standards and were recognized in international circuits;
- The actors and actresses became national figures and generated a Mexican Star System;
- The movies were distributed efficiently at national level as well as throughout Latin America, Spain, and U.S. Hispanic markets. In other words, Mexican players controlled the distribution in Mexico;
- The Mexican and Latin American public/audiences were heavy viewers of these films, and it was included as a central part of their everyday cultural diet, providing some cultural counterbalance to Hollywood productions (Gómez, 2007).

In addition, the film labor unions played an important role during the second half of the 20th century. The unions were active agents in the development, formation, and consolidation of the industry. However, they weren't exempt from internal conflicts, clientelist practices, or harsh negotiations with the government and the private companies (García Riera, 1985).

It is important to underline that the relationship with Hollywood film production was complicated from the beginning of the industry, particularly between the 1940s and the 1960s. In fact, the Mexican government had to intervene many times as protector and defender of the Industry to maintain the ownership of many assets in Mexico.[3] One action that illustrates that protection was the decreet to limit the foreign ownership at 49% in 1944 (Peredo, 2012).

In the 1960s the industry entered a period of production spoilage, because the star system remained unchanged without new fresh actors and same directors while at the same time the film industry experienced big competition from TV in terms of cultural consumption. As a result, the industry started to adapt to that new cultural mass media landscape and new market dynamics of those years. As Figures 5.1 and 5.2 show, during that decade, the result of those changes was a decrease in the number of films produced and in the number of theaters themselves (De la Vega, 2012).

During the second half of the 1970s, Mexican film production experienced an important wave of creativity and innovation in both formats and in ways to interpret the cinema as an art (García-Riera, 1985, p. 285).

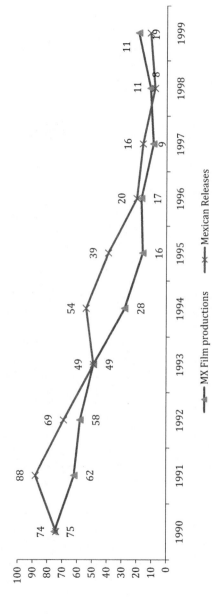

Figure 5.2 Mexican production and releases from 1990 to 1999.
Source: Imcine 2011: 134–135.

Table 5.1 Number of cinemas in Mexico from 1938 to 1990 (selected years)

Year	Number of cinemas	Attendance (in millions)
1938	830	66
1942	1,125	No data
1946	1,140	No data
1953	2,459	162
1968	1,836	358
1970	1,769	253
1975	2,632	254
1980	2,831	264
1985	2,246	450
1990	1,896	54.8

Source: Gómez, 2007: 258.

As Table 5.1 shows, these advances coincided with positive momentum as the number of cinema screens increased significantly. In fact, this period of the MFI was characterized by the consolidation of the State's intervention into all parts of the industry and as the most important investor (Sánchez Ruiz, 2012).

However, it is important to remember that the figures related to the number of cinema screens have to be linked not just to Mexican productions. In fact, since the beginning of Mexican movie theaters, Hollywood movies have been an important part of the Mexican cinema consumption diet (Ugalde, 1998, p. 55). This was particularly true of the middle and upper classes.[4] Hence, the increase of the screens is related with two main developments: the momentum and quality of the Mexican and U.S. movies as well as their balanced distribution, and the economic performance of the country impacting the whole film industry, particularly through the disposable income power of the public. Another aspect that has to be noticed: toward the end of the 1970s and the beginning of the 1980s, the Mexican commercial TV company Televisa[5] dabbled in cinema production, particularly through its subsidiary *Televicine*. From 1978 to 1982, it was the most productive private film company (Gómez, 2007).

This continued into the 1980s and experienced other important cultural, technological, and market dynamic mutations in relation to the cultural industries. The invention of the VCR and distribution of movies through video rentals as well as satellite television provoked a clear transformation in cultural consumption in general and that of movies in particular (Rosas, 2017). Also in this period, Mexico experienced an economic crisis combined with increased migration from the rural areas to the cities, particularly to Mexico City, Guadalajara, and Monterrey (De la Vega, 2012). But there was another route for the migration processes, which focused on crossing the U.S. border. During the decade of the 1980s, Mexican immigration to the United States without proper documentation experienced higher levels. According to the Consejo Nacional de Población (CONAPO),[6] it was estimated that 2.6 million crossed the border (CONAPO, 2001).

In 1983 the Mexican government created the Instituto Mexicano de Cinematografía (IMCINE).[7] Since then, IMCINE has been the key public player to support and promote the Mexican film productions through a range of funds and public policies. These interventions always included the accompaniment and participation of the cinematographic community – organizations, unions, federations, etc. (Carmona and Sánchez, 2012).

As other researchers have pointed out, during the 1980s the MFI experienced the erosion of their Statist model, and the De la Madrid (1982–1988) and Salinas (1988–1994) administrations started the turn of the economic model toward neoliberal policies (Davalos, 95; Sánchez Ruiz, 2001). This situation was reflected mainly in the bad quality of the films but also in a lack of directors and of new cinema actresses and actors (Gómez, 2007). Because of that scenario, the middle and upper classes abandoned Mexican movies (Rosas, 2017). Thus, the industry experienced a clear deterioration. Furthermore, the technological and cultural changes combined with the economic crisis of that decade[8] (better known as the economic "Lost decade") produced further losses in the Mexican film production and in the number of movie theaters. Under those circumstances, the exhibition companies started a new model of business, as in the United States, begging to build the multiplex multi-cinemas (Rosas, 2017). During this period, two genres had blockbusters in the popular cinemas of COTSA: the *Cabrito-western* and *sexi-comedy*; the former focusing on stories of the northern border and immigration and the latter emphasizing stories about Mexico City and other urban areas. Most of those productions were funded by private investors but screened in state-owned exhibition chain. That kind of Mexican movies was common during the 1980s so-called "lost decade" (Gómez, 2007). Under that context of attrition the MFI continued to change into the 1990s.

This brief historical structural analysis of the MFI established how the processes, dynamics, trajectories, policies, and agents developed the industry before the North American Free Trade Agreement (NAFTA). In fact, even its cyclical performance and strong intervention of the Mexican State, both economically and politically, were successful, particularly as both an important economic driver industry as well as a dynamic and central cultural vector for Mexican society. As De la Garza said: "…for most part of the twentieth century Mexican cinema was truly national in that it helped to forge and disseminate a common cultural background that cut across class, gender and ethnic cleavages, both in terms of narrative content and outreach and engagement. It also served to shape and develop a cultural industry that had national scope" (2016, p. 760). At the same time, it must be noted that Hollywood movies before the 1990s maintained an interesting balance, competing with Mexican production releases and attendance. This was true even when Hollywood represent just 30% of the releases (Ugalde, 1998; Sánchez Ruiz, 2012).

Free Market Logic and Consolidation Reshape the Mexican Film Industry

The decade of the 1990s has been characterized as the worst period of the MFI (Sánchez Ruiz, 2001; Hinojosa, 2014; McLaird, 2013). As seen in Figure 5.2, Mexican film production hit bottom in 1997 with only nine films. Not surprisingly, exhibitors experienced a catastrophic time in the next year with just eight new Mexican releases. Since then, it has been difficult for the industry to launch films that attract audiences and, consequently, to have an important box office share in the film market. In fact, regaining and maintaining a constant Mexican audience has been one of the main problems.

The need to respond to these structural conditions shaped the Film Law of 1992, and it can also be linked to the liberalization context of NAFTA. Since 1988, particularly under the Salinas administration, there were many economic structural changes, especially the liberalization of many strategic sectors as well as the privatization of state-owned companies. At the same time, many public policies reforms were established to accomplish those changes (Gómez, 2007). In the case of the cultural industries, and particularly the MFI, its former law from 1949 was repealed and replaced with a new one in 1992. In brief, the logic of that new law was to align the MFI to free market imperatives. With that in mind, the most significant change, among others, was the abolishment of the 50% screen quota in favor of Mexican film productions. Further, in 1993, the Salinas administration privatized the national state-owned cinema chain COTSA. It should be recalled that this chain had controlled ticket prices, keeping them at lower cost and focused primarily on the low income and poor classes across the nation. The company that purchased COTSA was TV Azteca, which closed down the entire operation two years later (Sánchez Ruiz, 2001).

Also in 1992, the Foreign Investment Law was modified to allow more foreign capital participation, giving national treatment to offshore companies involved in film production, distribution, or exhibition. In addition, the *Secretaria de Hacienda* (Secretary of the Treasury) gave tax incentives to exhibitors and film production foreign investors. Surprisingly, such incentives were not considered for national producers (Muñoz and Gómez, 2011).

As is well known NAFTA came into force in 1994 when the Mexican government rejected the possibility of introducing the cultural exception clause, affecting the cultural sector and particularly the cultural industries. The government took the position that Mexican culture and identities were sufficiently solid to withstand any foreign cultural influence. In addition, the government argued that having a different language would serve as a natural barrier against foreign cultural product consumption (Gómez, 2007). The implication of this position was clear: the Mexican government canceled the right to implement cultural public policies as strong screen quotas or other protection initiatives under the argument that those policies have an important impact as market distortions (Lozano, 2016).

In the case of culture, George Yúdice established that NAFTA defined "culture" as a matter of *property* through the inclusion of copyrights, patents, registered trademarks, phylogenetic rights, industrial designs, trade secrets, integrated circuits, geographical indicators, codified satellite signals, audiovisual production, and others (2002, p. 266). This is important because since then, this is the frame and logic that shapes the cultural sector in Mexico. In fact, agreeing with D.Y. Jin that suggests that NAFTA was the first experiment by the United States to implement and establish a strategy to shift global political culture by making it significantly more difficult for future national governments to develop national institutions and culture. Instead, it crafted a policy that favors transnational film corporations and the Motion Picture Association of America (MPAA) (2011, p. 665).

Another factor needed under the film industry's dynamic interaction with the rest of the cultural industries was the expansion of pay-TV across Mexico. The consumption of pay-TV in the 1990s increased exponentially; in 1990 there were 545,000 pay-TV subscribers, and by 1999, there were 2.8 million subscribers (Gómez and Sosa, 2010, p. 121). In fact, the pay-TV programming consumed in Mexico reinforces U.S. cultural products and consolidates their centrality in the Mexican cultural audiovisual consumption offer because the majority of the pay-TV channels are U.S. cable networks (Sánchez Ruiz, 2001).

According to Sánchez Ruiz, during the 1990s "the Mexican film industry went through a process of contraction, concentration, and transnationalization" (2001, p. 98). I have argued in previous research that there is an additional process: the elitization of its public (Gómez, 2005). In fact, those public policies and the structural economic changes as well as the continuous transformation of the cultural industries reshaped the MFI. The winners of those changes were clearly identified. First the Hollywood majors – Disney, Paramount, Universal, Columbia Pictures, Sony, Twentieth Century Fox, and Warner Bros. – finally started to control the distribution of the Mexican cinemas. Since the 1990s, the majors controlled approximately 80% of the market share revenues (Gómez, 2005). Second, but in close relation, the exhibition chains began an important growth period, privileging Hollywood films. In other words, after the Mexican production almost vanished, the terrain was wide open to fill that void with the Hollywood steamroller and set their conditions, since then, as "home field advantage."

In response to these circumstances, the Mexican cinema community (unions, directors, actors, writers, etc.) reacted by organizing themselves toward recovering some ground. They continue to defend their labor and reinforce the idea of the value in supporting Mexican film productions in cultural and economic terms. They have created an important lobby in Congress and the results have been interesting. In 1998, film professionals gained some reforms to the 1992 Film Law to help film production. For example, a 10% screen quota devoted to Mexican productions was reinstated. They have also continued to push to get some public funds to be administered by IMCINE. By the year 2000, there were two funds for domestic film production: the Fund for Quality Cinema Production or Foprocine and the Fund for Investment and Incentive to Film or Fidecine. The former was targeted to support art or less commercial films and the latter to commercial film productions (Lay, 2011).

Because of those changes, during the 1980s and 1990s, the union system experienced a significant crisis as well. The labor environment shifted from labor stability to "flexible production." As Muñoz and Gómez noted:

> At an internal level, the unions have had to accept the negative repercussions of historic corruption practices like clientelism and fraud, as well as corporatist attitudes that generate rigidity, distrust, stagnation of expertise, and decreasing rates of formal union membership. At an external level, unions have had to face the disappearance of a corporatist welfare state in favor of a neoliberal-oriented re-regulation that resulted in the dismantling both the sources of work and also the social benefits achieved by unions in the past.
>
> (2011, p. 863)

Paradoxically, as De la Garza (2016) noted, under that context of crises "The three amigos" made their debuts: Alfonso Cuaron's *Sólo con tu pareja* (1991), Guillermo del Toro's *Cronos* (1993), and Alejandro González Iñarritu's *Amores Perros* (2000). It is important to note that the professional as well as creative trajectories of these directors were different and their successful careers are the result of their own merits as well as their crews and not as a result of the MFI infrastructure. It should also be noted that at the same time three women filmmakers made their debut or consolidation: Maria Novaro's *Danzon* (1991), Busi Cortés's *Serpientes y Escaleras* (1991), and Maryse Sistach's *Anoche soñé contigo* (1992) (MacLaird, 2013). These women were pioneers in a field dominated by men.

The Recovery of Mexican Film Production and Distribution?

The 21st century presented a lot of challenges, trends, and doubts for the MFI. First, after the worst decade ever, there were numerous questions about how the MFI would recover: what kind of strategies and actions needed to be implemented, especially in production and distribution? What will be the role of IMCINE? How Mexican films will recover the audience's preference? Second, what would the result be of the digitization and convergence process which created accelerated transformations throughout all cultural industries, including the MFI, forcing a response to the consolidation of global capitalism. As Bárcenas (2015) noted, these changes presented trends and a window of opportunities, including how to take advantage of distribution through new platforms thanks to digitization; the possibility of launching digital channels on broadcast TV; and how to use Over the Top media services (OTT) including Netflix, Amazon Prime, Claro, etc. But the main challenge remained in relation to theatrical distribution: how to advance past the 10% line of market share and ticket attendance at the national level? Each presented a difficult challenge because those variables are all linked together.

In political terms, the year 2000 is an important moment for Mexico's political system, because after 71 years the ruling party (PRI) lost the presidency, and a time of political alternation and some acceleration of the Mexican democratic transition began. However, in spite of this political and democratic reframing, the support and impulse of economic policies under the logic of free market and neoliberal imperatives of global capitalism continued with support by the two Partido de Acción Nacional (PAN; Action National Party) administrations with Vicente Fox (2001–2006) and Felipe Calderon (2007–2012) as well as Peña Nieto's PRI administration (2013–2018).

Public Policies and Programs

From the 2000s onward, the main public policies or initiatives related to boosting film production and distribution were, first, the implementation of the Fiscal Stimulus on Projects for Investment in National Film, known as Eficine 226 and 189. This initiative, established in 2006, opened a significative option to private investors. Second was the Stimulus for the Promotion of Mexican Cinema or Eprocine established in 2012. This program sought to promote film projects as well as their commercial distribution.

It is important to track the total spending of IMCINE through its different funds – Fidecine, Foprocine, and Eficine – because these funds have been the fuel to increase Mexican film productions. According to IMCINE reports from 2000 to 2018, it has distributed around 8,200 million pesos (Alvárez, 2018; IMCINE, 2016, 2018). Although the conversion to U.S. dollars is difficult due the instability of the peso, estimates suggest that amount represented around $500 million. This total has increased significantly since 2006 when Efecine started.

Previous research has demonstrated that MFI has not benefited from its proximity to Hollywood; instead, there is a one-way flow of labor mobility, as Mexican filmmakers move north to find better work opportunities. Social and economic instability and strong competition from English-speaking host countries like Australia, the United Kingdom, New Zealand, and Canada have made Mexico a less attractive location option for U.S. film producers (Muñoz and Gómez, 2011).

Last, it has to be mentioned that Mexico and the United States renegotiated NAFTA in 2018. This new agreement will be the United States-Mexico-Canada Agreement (USMCAN). In those negotiations the Mexican government did not require the inclusion of the cultural exemption clause for Mexico's cultural industries (Observacom, 2018), despite the fact that the cultural and particularly the film industry community had been asking for it since negotiations failed to exclude the audiovisual industries from the treaty, following the Canadian position to keep the clause in the new agreement (Rodríguez, 2017).

Economic Performance

The economic performance of the MFI[9] during the first 17 years of the new century has been positive. In fact, the MFI has been growing constantly since then. Accordingly, to IMCINE, the average annual total economic increase of the MFI between 2008 and 2016 was 6.5%, exceeding 4.5% of the national GDP. The gross value added of film increased 13.7% in 2016 with respect to 2015. Thus, the economic performance of MFI has been more dynamic than the Mexican economy overall (IMCINE, 2018, pp. 29–36). In addition, during 2016 the MFI in relation to the audiovisual media sector GDP represents just 8%. But it is important to note that this economic sector is constantly growing, because of the dynamism of internet platforms and their interlocks with all cultural industries. For example, the growth of the audiovisual media sector in real terms rose to 17.6% in 2016 (IMCINE, 2018). However, before overrating these figures, we should break and analyze the MFI performance separately by their branches: production, distribution, and exhibition.

Production

Production is the core and heart of any film industry. This branch is where the creative process and labor take place; it is closely related to the cultural specificities of society. Since the second half of 2006 and onwards, filmic production has experienced some signs of recovery. In fact as Figure 5.3 shows, from 2013 to 2017, it surpassed the historical landmark of 135 films produced in 1958. Nevertheless, it is important

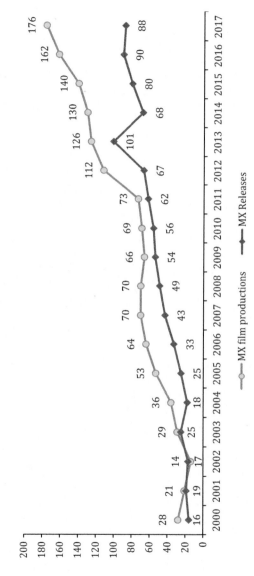

Figure 5.3 Mexican Film productions and releases from 2000 to 2017.
Source: Imcine, 2011–2018.

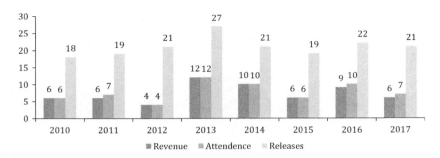

Figure 5.4 Performance of Mexican films in revenues, attendance, and releases by % from 2010 to 2017.
Source: Imcine, 2018: 81.

to analyze the extent and how the recovery occurred because Mexican films still hover around 10% of attendance and market share of the total tickets sales in Mexico as shown in Figure 5.4. Mexican releases remain in clear disadvantage compared to Hollywood films, particularly with their distribution in the number of copies and by extension their national reach and the costs of marketing (IMCINE, 2011, 2016, 2018). In terms of cost, the average for Mexican film productions from 2002 to 2017 has been around one million dollars (IMCINE, 2018, p. 55).

As discussed, the public funds administered by IMCINE have been the main funding source to get those numbers, as seen in Figure 5.5. Thus, the State and public funding still are the central resource to recover the Mexican film production, though still in the context of free market and competition. Fidecine, Foprocine, and Eficine have been the main tools to stimulate the film production branch (Lozano, Barragan & Guerra, 2017). In addition, since 2013, private investors have been increasing their participation and represent 45% of the total films produced in 2017. Furthermore, international coproductions have also been a factor in those productions, meaning that many of the productions funded by the State and private investors include other external investments. For example, from 2007 to 2017, there were 285 coproductions made with 41 countries. The countries leading in coproductions were the United States, Spain, Colombia, and Argentina (IMCINE, 2018, p. 53).

These last figures could suggest that the production branch is finally healthy and recovered. But this performance could also be a mirage if the positive increase is not reflected in the releases, number of copies distributed for national reach, attendance, and revenues. In other words, this positive production momentum has to be articulated closely with the other two branches – distribution and exhibition – and the whole circulation process of the MFI. This is the core issue: how to articulate

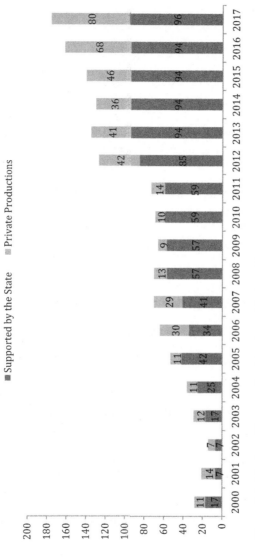

Figure 5.5 Mexican films productions from 2000 to 2017.
Source: Imcine, 2018: 49.

the Mexican production with the other two branches to accomplish an effective circulation? Even though the production has been increasing steadily and hitting historic figures, the attendance to Mexican films is not growing accordingly (Figures 5.3 and 5.4). Thus, it is time to firm up the circulation of those films across all the audiovisual platforms (Bárcenas, 2015). This must be accomplished without neglecting the centrality of movie theaters and continuing with audience creation and development (De la Garza, 2016, p. 765).

Other types of industrial indicators in relation with the production that have to be analyzed to evaluate these positive figures are the number of companies that are involved in producing those films. Accordingly with the last Instituto Nacional de Estadística y Geografía (INEGI)[10] report in 2015, there were 67 economic units registered related to film production. If we look back 20 years at that same indicator, we see that in 1995 there were 170 units reported. The sector hit bottom in 2005 with 41 units (Álvárez, 2018). In other words, the 2015 industrial indicator reflects a discreet increase and recovery.

Furthermore, previous research shows that the production remains centralized in Mexico City (Sánchez Ruiz, 2012; Muñoz and Gómez, 2011). The nature of those companies:

> …is dominated by temporary work because production projects last from approximately three to five months. Permanent employment is downsized and typically reserved for producers and administrative personnel. The temporary use of independent contractors, which makes labor relations flexible, allows the production companies to save on fixed costs and adapt for intermitent production by not having a payroll with permanent employees and social benefits.
>
> (Muñoz and Gómez, 2011, p. 861)

Thus, the film district in Mexico City is characterized by flexible production in its industrial organization and is motivated by the undercapitalization of the production branch and the "one project" model (Muñoz and Gómez, 2011). It is under this scheme that it could be explained how IMCINE has registered 325 film producers from 2002 to 2013, but they do not operate or qualify as an economic unit. However, it also identified around 20 film producers that had been active from 2000 to 2017 – Argos cine, Altavista Films, Canana Films, Astillero Producciones, Producciones Tragaluz, Alebrije, Bandido Films, Malayerba producciones, Interior Trece, Arte Mecánica, Lagartija Negra, Jaqueca Films, El Chilito Enmascarado, Tequila Gang, Ánima Estudios, Lemon films, Axolote cine, Huevocartoon productions, and Cinépolis producciones.

In addition, since the arrival of the OTT services – Netflix, Amazon Prime, Clarovideo, Blim, Cinepolis Klic, among others – and the competition with pay TV channels – HBO, TNT, Sony, Fox, etc. – some of those audiovisual film companies have been increasing their coproduction with those global players to attract Mexican, Latino, and Latin American audiences (Sánchez Prado, 2014; Gómez, 2016).

Examining the participation of women in the production process appears to show that there is a significant increase in participation in the creative film labor process as symbol creators. For example, during 2017, women worked as directors, scriptwriters, or producer on 52% of the productions. The number of women working as directors in that year was very promising with 42 movies (IMCINE, 2018, p. 57). This is important, because to some extent gender equity and women's participation seems to be working in a field dominated by men, and at the same time, their stories reflect women's points of view and preoccupations of our contradictory, patriarchal, and violent society.

Distribution

According to the IMCINE annual yearbook in 2017, the U.S. films accounted for 88% of the attendance in Mexico's cinemas (IMCINE, 2018). That figure has hovered at 85% since the 2000s onwards (Sánchez Ruiz, 2012; Canacine, 2014). In addition, Hollywood distribution majors maintained between 70% and 75% market share of revenues and attendance (Canacine, 2016; Huerta-Wong and Gómez, 2016). The actual Hollywood major companies are Disney Int, Fox Int, Sony/Columbia Pictures, Warner Bros, Universal, and Paramount. These companies get better results year by year in ticket sales (see Table 5.2). These figures show that beyond their economic performance, U.S. cultural products have been dominant in Mexican cinemas since at least the last decade of the 20th century and into the first two of the 21st century (Ugalde, 1998; Sánchez Ruiz, 2012; IMCINE, 2018). Hollywood dominance could be seen across all audiovisual industries. As such, Hollywood has dominated the Mexican box office and Pay-TV as well as OTT platforms for more than 20 years. In other words, Hollywood has the advantage

Table 5.2 Distribution companies that had record attendance from 2011 to 2017 in Mexican cinemas

Year	Distribution company	Record of attendance (in millions of pesos)
2011	Paramount	2,042
2013	Walt Disney	2,032
2014	Twentieth Century Fox	2,801
2015	Universal	3,064
2016	Walt Disney	3,205
2017	Walt Disney	3,316

Source: Canacine (2014, 2015, 2016, 2017, 2018).

to foster the development of audiences through and for the various audiovisual platforms.

Mexican distribution companies have had to incorporate U.S. films into their catalogs. For example, Videocine-Televisa company has had a number of different distribution agreements with U.S. studios in the past, and currently distributes the Lionsgate Film productions. Corazón, Cinepolis, and Gussi have been distributing some U.S. independent movies and other foreign films. However, it is important to indicate that their main film distribution is Mexican movies. Another distribution company that entered the Mexican distribution market since 2010 onwards is Diamont Films owned by Telefilms group from Argentina. This is important to note because clearly the majors are the main players in this branch, but there are some other distribution companies competing for around 20–25% of the market that is not in the hands of the global media giants (Birkinbine, Gómez & Wasko, 2017). In that vein, after the merger of Twentieth Century Fox with Disney in 2018, the global film distribution market will be even more concentrated. The impact will be global, and Mexico won't be an exception.

It must also be noted that the OTT services have begun to distribute movies, albeit not for theatrical release; for example, Netflix and Amazon Prime are the main players breaking in with this kind of disruptive practices. No doubt, there will be more adjustments and transformations across the circuits and consumers of the cultural industries in the coming years, guided by these new actors and competition with the Hollywood majors.

In particular the distribution of Mexican films have begun to see some efforts to increase their circulation with some IMCINE funds as well as the launch of digital platforms online (VOD) that offer Mexican productions. Examples include FilminLatino.mx and Plataforma Digital del Cine Mexicano. However, the process to build audiences is difficult due to competition with the power and scale of the Hollywood majors. At the same time, Netflix has been an up and coming player promoting Mexican cinema. In 2012, as an OTT, it had more Mexican movies in its catalog – 276 (IMCINE, 2013, p. 166).

As Janet Wasko has pointed out, the major distributors are the agents that dominate the film business (2003, p. 59). In the same vein, Nicholas Garnham noted: "It is cultural distribution, not cultural production, that is the key locus of power and profit. It is access to distribution which is the key to cultural plurality. The cultural process is as much, if not more, about creating audiences or publics as it is about producing cultural artefacts and performances" (1990, p. 162). This is important to remember because this key process in the MFI, as seen in the data analyzed here, was dominated by the Hollywood majors after the liberalization and privatization processes were implemented, starting in the 1980s. In other words, after the 1990s crisis of the MFI, the checkmate to the MFI was not the total scarcity of the Mexican films, but the control of film distribution and circulation.

Exhibition

This sector is the most concentrated of the MFI. It has experienced high levels of concentration since the merger of Cinemex to Multimedios Cinemas (Huerta-Wong and Gómez, 2016). According to Canacine figures, Cinépolis (50.3%) and Cinemex (42%) control 92.3% or 6,633 commercial screens (Canacine, 2016). The rest of the 7.7% is distributed by Henry, Cinemagic, and Citicinemas, among others (Canacine, 2016). Further, those screens are concentrated in urban areas, with Mexico City (26%), Monterrey (8%), and Guadalajara (6%) being the main markets (IMCINE, 2018, p. 105). In terms of market share, Cinepolis has 67.5% and Cinemex 29.1%. Thus, Cinepolis and Cinemex are the big winners of the retail companies. In the case of the former, it is ranked as the fourth largest exhibition group in the world in terms of screen count, with 5,334 in 240 cities distributed in 15 countries: Mexico, United States, Guatemala, Honduras, El Salvador, Costa Rica, Colombia, Panamá, Perú, Chile, Brazil, Argentina, Spain, and India. And it is second in the world by number of attendance (Cinepolis, 2018).

In addition, Mexican screens and cinemas have continued to grow. For example, from 2016 to 2017, there were 408 more screens. But that growth is concentrated in urban areas and in some states with positive economic growth. In that regard, it has to be pointed out that the national indicators have to be read carefully. For example, the State of Mexico and Baja California Sur reported decreases in their screens while Tabasco, Chiapas, Oaxaca, Durango, Campeche, Nayarit, and Zacatecas reported no new screens; in contrast, just in the metropolitan area of Mexico City, 252 new screens opened in the same period.

From 2000 onward, the economic performance of this branch has been remarkable. The number of tickets sales has increased, making Mexico the fourth globally in terms of ticket sales. Admissions doubled from 157 million in 2005 to 348 million in 2017. Furthermore, Mexico ranks number ten in the global market in terms of earnings in U.S. dollars, with $869 million dollars in box office revenues (Canacine, 2017).

The retail exhibition market also earns revenues from the advertising market. According to Merca 2.0, from 2005 onwards, media advertising total investment in the sector has been constant at around 1.2–1.5%. In 2017, this figure was approximately 1,200 million pesos or $60 million (Merca 2.0, 2018, p. 51). These figures have been growing constantly, year by year, in Mexican pesos, but after converting to U.S. dollars, it appears to reflect some stagnation because of the volatility of the Mexican peso in relation to the U.S. dollar. That same situation explains why in Mexico the ticket price of approximately $2.50 on average appears to be one of the lowest when compared with other international markets. However, when put in context of the purchasing power of the majority of the Mexican population, the cinema ticket is expensive. As such, it must be remembered that going to the movies in Mexico remains expensive, thus directed to the middle and higher classes (Gómez, 2005).

Cinepolis and Cinemex are a clear example on how the economic policies have promoted concentration and permitted the establishment of noncompetitive market structures as oligopolies. Under these circumstances, Cinepolis has taken advantage of that position and began its internationalization after its consolidation in Mexico.

Conclusions

The MFI has clearly showed some signs of recovery across the three sectors. However, it has to be underlined that this general performance has been shaped under the conditions, logic, and dynamics of the Hollywood majors and free market imperatives. Thus, this new era of the MFI should be characterized as its assimilation by the U.S. film industry as a significant market.

In the case of Mexican film productions, even though the output has broken historic figures, those numbers are not reflected in their circulation, attendance, and market share, which is still less than 10%. However, as Sánchez Prado suggested, after the first decade of the 21st century, the Mexican cinema "[has experienced] growing connections with international film markets and cultural flows" (2014, p. 157). But as this chapter shows, following De la Garza (2016), this experience has been more as film niche genre than a film industry as it was during the past century. This is important, then, to not overreact about the Mexican film productions performance and their circulation at domestic level and in some international market because, in actuality, it is still in the margins globally and nationally, and production remains centralized in Mexico City.

Further, the "one project" model serves as a constraint on the working conditions of the range of cultural workers involved with the industry and struggling with its industrial organization (Muñoz and Gómez, 2011; Bárcenas, 2015). As such, the production sector has not been able to consolidate, though its industrial performance suggests some recovery. This might allow for its reconfiguration in spite of the convergence and competition between the different platforms of the national and global cultural industries.

Finally, it is clear that IMCINE funds have been crucial to the industry, and the organization has been the key actor working to recover the MFI. Nevertheless, the MFI is limited by the competitive advantages that the Hollywood majors and the Mexican exhibition duopoly have, both of which have stymied the possibility of implementing strong screen quotas that, among other protection policies, could retake or at least rebalance the control of circulation.

Notes

1 Partido Revolucionario Institucional [PRI] – or The Revolutionary Institutional Party – ruled Mexico from 1930 to 2000.
2 During those years the ticket price was included in the basket of goods, which refers to a fixed set of consumer products and services set and protected by the Mexican goverment, guaranteeing access through low prices for the general public.
3 Peredo (2012) describes and analyzes different episodes of this circumstances during the 1950s.
4 Why particularly with those social classes? Because throughout the 20th century, starting with the Lázaro Cárdenas administration, dubbing foreign movies was not allowed. Thus, in Mexico, all foreign movies were subtitled, and as a result, the target audience were the literate or educated classes. This policy's rationale was to maintain the lower classes who were illiterate or functional illiterates as a secure market for Mexican productions. Rosas said that this policy "gave the possibility that the spectators -mainly middle classes and literate- knowed the original voices and dialogues, as well as the different accents" (2017: p. 177). This is important to note because in countries like France, Italy, and Spain they would rather have dubbing.
5 From 1973 to 1993, Televisa experienced its golden years because it was the only commercial TV company that operated as monopoly at national level with three national networks in the Mexican TV System and market. One of those networks, Channel 5, was the window to the American way of life through the consumption of U.S. cultural products: cartoons, series, movies, and U.S. professional sports (Gómez, 2017). Monsivais named that channel as the first U.S. TV channel outside the United States (Monsiváis, 2000). This is important to underline, because the Mexican urban middle classes, particularly in Monterrey, Guadalajara, and Mexico City, grew with the centrality of those cultural products (Gómez, 2017). This role of Channel 5 was central to build audiences with an important cultural consumption of U.S. audiovisual products (Monsiváis, 1992) and for sure reinforced the consumption of U.S. films.
6 The Mexican National Council of Population.
7 The Mexican Cinematography Institute.
8 In Latin America the economic crisis of the 1980s is known as the lost decade. Just to give an example, in Mexico the economic inflation in 1982, 1986, and 1987 was 98%, 105%, and 152%, respectively (Smith, 2001, p. 372).
9 Accordingly to INEGI, they consider the film industry economic activities as: production, postproduction, distribution, and exhibition of film and other audiovisual media. This value chain as a whole is generically known as the "film industry."
10 National Institute of Statistics and Geography.

References

Alvárez, C. (2018). *Las políticas públicas como mediaciones histórico-estructurales que impulsaron la expansión del cine estadounidense en México: el Tratado de Libre Comercio de América del Norte y sus repercusiones para la industria audiovisual mexicana.* (BA dissertation, Universidad de Guadalajara, Mexico).

Bárcenas, C. (2015). *Productoras cinematográficas en México ante la convergencia digital*. (Doctoral dissertation, Universidad Nacional Autónoma de México, Mexico).

Birkinbine, B., Gómez, R., & Wasko, J. (Eds.). (2017). *Global media giants*. New York: Routledge.

Canacine. (2018). *Resultados definitivos 2017*. México: Canacine. http://canacine. org.mx/wp-content/uploads/2018/02/Resultados-definitivos-2017-1.pdf

Canacine. (2017). *Resultados definitivos 2016*. México: Canacine. http://canacine. org.mx/wp-content/uploads/2014/04/Resultados-Definitivos-2016-1.pdf

Canacine. (2016). *Resultados definitivos 2015*. México: Canacine. http://canacine. org.mx/wp-content/uploads/2014/04/Resultados-Definitivos-2015-ATI-1-1.pdf

Canacine. (2015). *Resultados definitivos 2014*. México: Canacine. http://canacine. org.mx/docs/resultados-definitivos-2014.pdf

Canacine. (2014). *Resultados definitivos 2013*. México: Canacine. http://canacine. org.mx/docs/Presentacion_PRENSA.pdf

Carmona, C., & Sánchez, C. (2012). El fortalecimiento de la producción desde Imcine a través de la comunidad cinematográfica. In Carmona, C. and Sánchez, C. (Eds.) *El estado y la imagen en movimiento. Reflexiones sobre las políticas públicas y el cine mexicano*. México: Imcine, 313–338.

Cinepolis. (2018). Datos de la compañía. Diciembre 2018. https://intranet. cinepolis.com/SitePages/Fact%20Sheet.aspx

CONAPO. (2001). Migrantes mexicanos en Estados Unidos. In Boletín CONAPO, 5 (15). México.

De la Garza, A. (2016). Film policy under globalization: the case of Mexico. *International Journal of Cultural Policy*, 22(5), 758–769.

De la Vega, E. (2012). Del neopopulismo a los prolegómenos del neoliberalismo: La política cinematográfica y el "nuevo cine mexicano" durante el periodo 1971–1982. In Carmona, C. and Sánchez, C. (Eds.) *El estado y la imagen en movimiento. Reflexiones sobre las políticas públicas y el cine mexicano*. México: Imcine, 227–270.

García-Riera, E. (1985). *Historia del cine Mexicano*. SEP: México.

García-Riera, E. (1971). *Historia documental del cine Mexicano*, Tomo III. México: Era.

Garnham, N. (1990). *Capitalism and communication: Global culture and the economics of information*. London: Sage.

Getino, O. (1998). *Cine y televisión en América Latina. Producción y mercado*. Ciccus: Buenos Aires.

Gómez, R. (2017). Televisa. In Birkinbine, B., Gomez, R., and Wasko, J. (Eds), *Global Media Giants*. New York: Routledge.

Gómez, R. (2016). Latino Television in the United States and Latin America: Addressing networks, dynamics, and alliances. *International Journal of Communication*, 10, 20.

Gómez, R. (2007). *El impacto del Tratado de Libre Comercio de América del Norte (TLCAN) en la industria audiovisual mexicana (1994–2002)* (Doctoral dissertation, Universitat Autònoma de Barcelona).

Gómez, R. (2005). La industria cinematográfica mexicana 1992–2003: estructura, desarrollo, políticas y tendencias. *Estudios sobre las culturas contemporáneas*, 11(22), 249–273.

Gómez, R., & Sosa, G. (2010). La concentración en el mercado de la televisión restringida en México. *Comunicación y sociedad, 14*, 109–142.

Golding, P., & Murdock, G. (1991). Culture, political economy and communications. In Gurevitch, M. and Curran, J. (Eds.) *Mass media and society.* London: Edward Arnold.

Guback, T. (1989). Should a nation have its own film industry? *Directions, 3*(1), 489–492.

Hesmondhalgh, D. (2013). *The cultural industries.* Third edition. London: Sage.

Hinojosa, L. (2014). Economía política del cine mexicano: dos décadas de transformaciones. *Revista de la Asociación Española de Investigación de la Comunicación, 1*(2), 94–102.

Huerta-Wong, E., & Gómez, R. (2016) Media ownership and concentration in Mexico. In Noam, E. and the IMCC (Eds.) *Who owns the world media?* New York: Oxford University Press.

IMCINE. (2018). *Anuario estadístico del cine mexicano 2017.* México: Imcine.

IMCINE. (2016). *Anuario estadístico del cine mexicano 2015.* México: Imcine.

IMCINE. (2013). *Anuario estadístico del cine mexicano 2012.* México: Imcine.

IMCINE. (2011). *Anuario estadístico del cine mexicano 2010.* México: Imcine.

Jin, D. Y. (2011). A critical analysis of US cultural policy in the global film market: Nation-states and FTAs. *International Communication Gazette, 73*(8), 651–669.

Lay, T. (2011). Sociedad civil y participación legislativa: el proceso de discusión de la Ley Federal de Cinematografía como primer ejercicio. *Revista legislativa de estudios sociales y de opinión pública, 4*(7), 215–230.

Lozano, D., Barragán, J. N., & Guerra, S. (2017). El cine: el negocio de la cultura. *Innovaciones de Negocios, 6*(12), 207–224.

Lozano, J. C. (2016). Transnational forces, technological developments, and the role of the state in the Mexican audiovisual sector. In Graham, M. and Raussert, W. (eds.) *Mobile and entangled America(s).* New York: Routledge.

MacLaird, M. (2013). *Aesthetics and politics in the Mexican Film Industry.* New York: Springer.

Meehan, E. R., Mosco, V., & Wasko, J. (1993). Rethinking political economy: Change and continuity. *Journal of Communication, 43*(4), 105–116.

Meyer, L. (1992). *La segunda muerte de la revolución Mexicana.* México: Cal y Arena.

Merca 2.0. (2018). *Estudio anual de inversión en medios durante 2018.* Media Book. México: Merca 2.0.

Monsiváis, C. (2000). *Aires de familia.* Barcelona: Anagrama.

Monsiváis, C. (1992). De la cultura mexicana en vísperas del Tratado de Libre Comercio. In Guevara, G. and García Canclini, N. (Eds.), *La educación y la cultura ante el tratado de libre comercio.* México: Nueva Imagen.

Muñoz, A., & Gómez, R. (2011). Analysis of the film production district in Mexico City, 2006–2008. *International Journal of Communication, 5*, 31.

Murdock, G. (1988). Large corporations and the control of the communication industries. In Gurevitch, M., Bennett, T., Curran, J., and Woollacott, J. (Eds.), *Culture, society and the media.* Third edition. London: Routledge.

Observacom. (2018). TLCAN: México y EEUU alcanzan acuerdo preliminar. http://www.observacom.org/tlcan-mexico-y-eeuu-alcanzan-acuerdo-preliminarelimina-obligaciones-sobre-productos-digitales-y-establece-reglas-para-remocion-de-contenidos-por-propiedad-intelectual/

Paranaguá, P. A. (Ed.) (1995). *Mexican cinema*. London: British Film Institute-Imcine.

Peredo, F. (2012). Las intervenciones gubernamentales como estrategia de crecimiento y supervivencia durante la segunda guerra mundial y la posguerra (1940–1952). In Carmona, C. y Sánchez, C. (Eds.), *El estado y la imagen en movimiento. Reflexiones sobre las políticas públicas y el cine mexicano.* México: Imcine.

Rodríguez, A. (2017, de Agosto 31). En el TLCAN lo audiovisual debe cambiar, señala el director de Imcine. *Jornada.* http://www.jornada.com.mx/2017/08/31/espectaculos/a10n1esp

Rosas, A. (2017). *Ir al cine. Antropología de los públicos, la ciudad y las pantallas.* México: Gedisa-UAM.

Saavedra, I. y Ávalos, G. (2012). La reconfiguración de la industria cinematográfica mexicana. In Carmona, C. y Sánchez, C. (Eds.), *El estado y la imagen en movimiento. Reflexiones sobre las políticas públicas y el cine mexicano.* México: Imcine.

Sánchez Prado, I. (2014). *Screening neoliberalism: Transforming Mexican Cinema, 1988–2012.* Nashville: Vanderbilt University Press.

Sánchez Ruiz, E. (2012). El Tratado de Libre Comercio y la casi desaparición del cine Mexicano, in Carmona, C. y Sánchez, C. (Eds.) *El estado y la imagen en movimiento. Reflexiones sobre las políticas públicas y el cine mexicano.* México: Imcine.

Sánchez Ruiz, E. (2005). Los medios de comunicación masiva en México, 1968–2000. In Meyer, L. y Bizberg, I. (Eds.), *Una historia contemporánea de México: los actores.* México: Océano.

Sánchez Ruiz, E. (2001). Globalization, cultural industries, and free trade: The Mexican audiovisual sector in the NAFTA age. In Mosco, V. and Schiller, D. (Eds.), *Continental Order?* Lanham: Rowman & Littlefield.

Sánchez-Ruiz, E., & Gómez, R. (2009). La economía política de la comunicación y la cultura. Un abordaje indispensable para el estudio de las industrias y las políticas culturales de comunicación. In Vega, A. (Ed.), *La comunicación en México. Una agenda de investigación.*México: UNAM-AMIC, 53–68.

Smith, P. (2001). El imperio del PRI. In Timothy, A., Bazant, J., Katz, F., Womack, J., Meyer, J., Knight, A. y Smith, P. (Eds.), *Historia de México.* Barcelona: Cambridge University Press-Crítica.

Ugalde, V. (1998). Panorama del cine mexicano: cifras y propuestas. *Estudios cinematográficos, 14,* 45–59.

Wasko, J. (2003). *How Hollywood Works.* London: Sage.

Yúdice, G. (2002). *El recurso de la cultura.* Barcelona: Gedisa.

Part II
Other Media Industries

6 The New Holy Grail

Scripted Television Production and State, Provincial & National Incentives

William M. Kunz

The second season of *Marco Polo* was a testament to the new age of television when it premiered worldwide on Netflix on July 1, 2016. *Marco Polo* was one of the most expensive television productions of all time, with the Internet streaming service spending a reported $180 million for the production of 20 episodes over two seasons. The second season was available to over 83 million Netflix streaming subscribers worldwide, including over 36 million outside the United States, and featured locations around the world, with primary filming in Malaysia, Hungary, and Slovakia. The drama focused on the story of Marco Polo in Kublai Khan's court in 13th century China, but the end credits told a different tale. Following the names of all the personnel involved in *Marco Polo* were the titles of other important contributors: National Film Development Corporation Malaysia; Hungarian National Film Fund; and Slovakia Audiovisual Fund. Each of those nations had provided production incentives for Netflix and The Weinstein Group for filming on their soil. That was not the total story, however, as the end credits also acknowledged incentives from the Canadian and Ontario governments for special effects in Toronto and from the state of New York for postproduction in New York City. While the show averaged $9 million per episode to produce, much of that came back to Netflix in the form of rebates and other incentives.

The production of *Marco Polo* presents a fascinating snapshot into the current state of television program development and production. The major motion picture studios and television networks have long sought ways to reduce costs and concerns about so-called "runaway" productions that have been around since broadcast television was in its infancy. These have only intensified as technological changes have transformed the production process. *Marco Polo* challenges a basic tenet of the "runaway" debate, which focused on films and television programs that were "conceptually developed in the United States" and "intended for initial release/exhibition in the U.S., but filmed partly or entirely outside the U.S." (Jones, 2002). While the definition of a "runaway" production might still work with a scripted series such as *Once Upon A Time*, which was produced in Vancouver, British Columbia, to be first aired on the ABC Television

Network, such definition shows that flaws are quite clear with a drama series such as *Marco Polo*, given the fact that Netflix had more "international streaming" memberships in mid-2017 – 52.031 million – than "domestic streaming" memberships – 51.921 million (Netflix, 2017a). That change in the television marketplace points to the need for a broader, more sophisticated understanding of the flow of television series and program production, one Janet Wasko and others advanced in a 2006 conference and edited book of the same title: *Cross-Border Cultural Production: Economic Runaway or Globalization?*. That collection reframed the discussion to understand the "expansion of production away from traditional centers" that created the "increasingly contentious and complex issue of cross-border cultural production." (Wasko and Erickson, 2008). It is important to note, however, the one argument in that Ben Goldsmith and Tom O'Regan make in this collection is that these new productions sites are "increasingly interconnected and simultaneously integrated, informally and formally, into Hollywood's globalizing production system" (Goldsmith and O'Regan, 2008). In other words, it is the U.S.-based production companies and transnational media conglomerates that benefit most from this expansion.

This chapter explores some of the questions advanced in *Cross-Border Cultural Production* a decade down the road. The focus is on the use of incentives in the production of scripted series that populate three distribution platforms: the five main U.S. broadcast networks, prominent U.S. basic cable networks, and premium cable and streaming services. The analysis covers the first seven seasons of the 2010s, a period that followed the expansion of production incentives in the United States and around the world, which, in turn, led to a focus on such incentives in the preproduction process. This also corresponds to a period of significant growth in the production of scripted series, from 216 in 2010 to 487 in 2017 by one estimate, creating what FX Networks head John Landgraf calls a time of "peak TV" (Otterson, 2018). The basic questions that frame this analysis is how has the use of such incentives increased or decreased over the given time period and how does the use of incentives differ across different distribution platforms.

Theoretical and Historical Framework

The questions that are central to this analysis are the same that are at the foundation of the critical political economy of the media. Dallas Smythe outlined two basic questions in his seminal work that are fundamental to this topic: "(1) Who gets what scarce goods and services, when, where and how?... (2) Who takes what actions in order to provide what scarce goods and services, when, how and where?" (Smythe, 1960). The fact that state, provincial, and national governments allocate funds to transnational media conglomerates that could be used for social services in their respective communities ensures that these questions remain prominent. Peter Golding and Graham Murdock defined political economy as the "balance between capitalist enterprise and public intervention" that can be framed around four historical processes: "growth of media; extension of corporate reach; commodification; and the changing role of the state and government intervention" (Golding and Murcock, 2000). Once again, there is little question that the role of the state and the degree of government intervention has changed to a dramatic degree over the last decade, most evident in the State of California, which now allocates $330 million per year for film and television production.

The California tax credit program was launched in 2009 and was enriched in 2015 to stem the tide of productions moving outside of Hollywood, an exodus that gave rise to the debates around "runaway" productions. And while the notion of a "runaway" is far too simple to describe what are now interconnected and integrated parts of what is now "Hollywood's globalizing production system," the literature provides an important foundation for this analysis. In a report to the Select Committee on the Future of California's Film Industry in 2002, Martha Jones defined it as follows:

> Runaway production refers to films that were conceptually developed in the United States, but filmed somewhere else. If the conversation is at the federal level, runaway production goes to other countries. If at the state level, production that goes to other states is runaway.
>
> (Jones, 2002, p. 2)

The term is also used for "products developed in the U.S. and intended for initial release/exhibition in the U.S., but films partly or entirely outside the U.S." (Jones, 2002, p. 35). An important distinction can also be made between what some have called artistic runaways, those shot outside where they were developed for the service of story, and economic runaways, those shot outside where they were developed for economic advantage. Adrian McDonald makes a distinction between "natural economic runaways" and "artificial economic runaways." A "natural economic runaway" was defined as films shot "abroad to take advantage of natural economic occurring phenomenon – cheap labor – that lower production costs," while an artificial economic runaway was defined as films shot "abroad because of artificial, or legislatively created, incentives designed to lure productions" (McDonald, 2007, p. 900).

The Rise of Production Incentives

The state of Louisiana is often credited with the establishment of the first state-based incentive program in the United States. The Motion

Picture Investor Tax Credit, enacted in 1992, allowed residents to claim an income tax credit for losses incurred in the production of motion pictures with substantial Louisiana content, which made it more of an insurance plan and a clear departure from the programs that are now prominent. The move to direct subsidies can be traced to the mid-1990s when the Canadian government implemented the refundable Canadian Film or Video Production Tax Credit in 1995. That credit was designed to "encourage the creation of Canadian film and television programming" and was only available to Canadian-owned corporations whose main business was Canadian film or video production. In 1997, however, the Canadian government introduced the Film or Video Production Service Tax Credit, an 11% credit for qualifying labor expenses that could be claimed by either Canadian or foreign corporations. The Ontario and British Columbia governments introduced matching 11% tax credit schemes in 1997 and 1998, respectively. The first U.S.-based programs that could approach the combined federal/provincial credits available in Canada came in 2002 when New Mexico introduced its Film Production Tax Rebate Program, which started as a 15% credit for qualified production expenditures but increased to 25% by 2006, and Louisiana created its Motion Picture Investor Tax Credit Program, which allowed for a 15% credit on productions over $1 million with an additional 20% credit for Louisiana payroll.

There were a mere handful of states with production incentives in 2002 after the program in New Mexico was created and the program in Louisiana expanded. That changed in subsequent years when a number of prominent U.S. states launched programs, including Florida, Illinois, and Pennsylvania in 2004 and Georgia, New Jersey, and New York in 2005. At the start of 2009, there were 44 states with a program in operation or one slated to launch that year. The global financial crisis that followed had a staggering impact on state and local governments, with a dramatic decline in tax revenue generated and a rise in need for public goods and services. The total number of states offering incentives at the end of 2017 was down to 34. Among the states dropping their programs between the start of 2009 and the end of 2017 were Florida, Michigan, New Jersey, and North Carolina, with the lattermost replacing an uncapped tax credit scheme with a grant program with a cap of $31 million in the 2018–2019 fiscal year.

These production incentives take on different forms and represent different levels of funding. Some incentives take the form of production grants, a percentage of total costs that is allocated before production begins. Far more common are tax credits that are based on a percentage of labor costs and other qualified expenditures. These credits, however, vary a great deal; with some being transferable while others are nontransferable and still others are refundable if the tax liability is not reached. There is also great variance in terms of what can be included under such programs. Some of these programs require a minimum spend per episode, $1 million in the case of California, and some require a percentage of total costs to be spent within the state or province. There are also clear differences in the resources allocated for such programs, which is most evident as one travels north along the Pacific Ocean. As noted earlier, California raised the cap on its program to $330 million per year in 2015, which dwarfed the $14 million per year allocated in Oregon in 2017. Washington Filmworks offered a 35% for episodic series with at least six episodes, but that program had an annual cap of just $3.5 million.

The effectiveness of these production incentives is much debated. Studies sponsored by the Motion Picture Association of America (MPAA) often herald the return on investment from such programs, while those from public policy analysts reach a very different conclusion. This contradiction was most evident in New Mexico a decade ago. In August 2008, the Arrowhead Center at the New Mexico State University completed a study for the Legislative Finance Committee of the State of New Mexico and concluded that for every dollar in rebates, the state only received 14.44 cents in return (Popp and Peach, 2008). In January 2009, Ernst & Young completed a study for the New Mexico State Film Office and concluded that for every dollar extended in state tax credits, state and local governments received $1.50 in tax collections (Ernst and Young, 2009). Such discrepancies are related to various factors, including in this case the inclusion or exclusion of local revenue, but the biggest challenge relates to the use of various multipliers to predict how spending in one sector relates to spending in other sectors (Weiner, 2009). This issue is significant with production incentives since the workforce is often transient, with above-the-line personnel, in particular, oftentimes living outside the state where production takes place and, in turn, spending their incentive-supported salaries elsewhere.

The position of the MPAA is most evident in another analysis it commissioned from Ernst & Young that was released in 2012 (Weiner, 2009). In its conclusion, this analysis acknowledged that some would assert that the "credits must generate tax revenue equal to the cost of the program on an annual basis," but argued that one must focus on more long-term goals, concluding that production incentives that are not offset by additional state and local taxes that result from increased economic activity "may still provide relatively high benefit-cost ratios compared to other economic development programs" (Weiner, 2009, p. 18). There is a growing body of analysis that challenges such an argument. Various public policy think tanks have critiqued such incentive programs over the last decade, concluding that such programs are not a good use of public resources.[1] There is also an academic scholarship that challenges the merits of such programs in various locations, with a recurring question being whether such programs build a sustainable model.[2] The study that probably garnered the most headlines and elicited the strongest reaction was authored by Michael Thom from the School of Public Policy at USC. Thom concluded such incentive programs has "little to no sustained impact on employment or wage growth and the none of the incentives affected motion picture industry GSP [gross state product] or concentration" (Thom, 2016). The MPAA response to the study from Senior Vice President of Government Affairs Vans Stevenson attached not only Thom but also USC:

> It is troubling and without excuse that such a false claim and misleading study, without statistical or intellectual foundation, would be recklessly promoted by an otherwise respected educational institution such as USC. It severely tarnishes the reputation of the university as well as the academic credentials of the author, USC assistant professor Michael Thom. This is academic malpractice. Designed to make a provocative statement rather than offer sound policy analysis.
>
> (Motion Picture Association of America, 2016)

The success or failure of production incentives to create sustained growth in jobs and wages as well as infrastructure investment is beyond the scope of this analysis, but the reaction of the main lobbyist for the major film and television conglomerates illustrates the stakes in this battle.

Methodology

This analysis measures the number of programs eligible for state, provincial, or national production incentives over seven-year periods. For the broadcast networks, the sample includes the five major U.S. networks – ABC, CBS, CW, FOX, and NBC – and covers the 2010–2011 through 2016–2017 season. For the basic cable services, the sample includes the four that are most prominent in the production of hour-long scripted series, AMC, FX, TNT, and USA. Since the cable services do not adhere to the traditional broadcast season and often schedule against that calendar with series debuts in the summer months, the sample includes seven years, 2011 through 2017. The final group includes three premium cable services that also have prominent streaming profiles, HBO, Showtime, and STARZ, as well as three streaming services, Amazon, Hulu, and Netflix. While there are imbalances within the final group, with Netflix allocating far more resources to original productions than Amazon or Hulu, there is little question that this is an important part of the discussion.

The compilation of a comprehensive list of production incentives across these platforms is riddled with challenges. The most prominent is that there is great variance in how state, provincial, and national programs disclose the recipients of credits and grants, with the four most prominent production centers in North America providing examples. The expanded California tax credit program announces the projects selected to receive tax credits and the amount reserved for that project, but such disclosure is rare. In 2013, the New York state legislature called for increased transparency in its program and Empire State Development does eventually release the credit issued to a given project, although there is a significant lag time before such detail is released.[3] The initial applications for tax credits, moreover, are reported through anonymous identification numbers, with no disclosure of the project or parent corporation. British Columbia and Ontario, home to the production hubs in Vancouver and Toronto, respectively, report the amount allocated for such incentives in aggregate and do not release any project-specific financial information. Provincial agencies in British Columbia and Ontario do compile lists of projects produced in the province, so there is some information but not the desired depth.

A second related challenge is that many state, provincial, and national programs do not require screen credit for projects receiving production incentives. The High-End Television Tax Relief program in the United Kingdom, for example, does not require on-screen acknowledgment from productions taking advantage of the tax credit. The same is true for the provincial programs in British Columbia and Ontario. Conversely, California and New York both require screen credit. The State of Georgia is the most unusual in this regard, offering a 20% transferable tax credit on qualified expenditures, including both resident and nonresident labor, and a 10% bonus with the inclusion of a Georgia promotional logo in the end credits. There is a further complication with tracking television programs shot in Georgia. Full-length feature films that receive the 20% tax credit must acknowledge Georgia in the end credits with the following statement: "This project was completed with assistance from the Georgia Film Office, a division of the Georgia Department of Economic Development." That requirement does not extend to television programs, so there is no acknowledgment of those not taking the 10% bonus.

Netflix and other streaming services, and to a lesser degree premium cable, provide other challenges. First, as noted earlier, Netflix now has more streaming subscribers outside the United States than inside and produces original programming in numerous languages. For the purposes of this analysis, only primarily English language programming was included in the data set. Second, Netflix and other streaming services acquire programming from distributors around the world and sometimes, programs that were developed outside of its reach, include "A Netflix original series" label. For the purposes of this analysis, programs acquired after production was completed are not included, except for subsequent years in which Netflix or others continue production of a program dropped by its original distributor.

This analysis focuses on a subset of incentive eligible programs. For this analysis, series and miniseries at least 40 minutes per episode were included in the data set. This is the same requirement as for the current California state program, one that was refined from "a running time of no less than sixty (60) minutes (inclusive of commercial advertisements and interstitial programming)" in the first iteration of the program. The change reflects the rise of commercial free programs on premium cable and streaming services. End credits for all programs were screened to determine eligibility for incentives, with the Internet Movie Database (IMDB) and other sources used to determine the production site for programs with no disclosed location. Shows included in the broader analysis were based on network schedules and lists of original programs, cross-referenced with the IMDB.

Scripted Program Production in the 2010s

The headline in *Variety* following the announcement of the Primetime Emmy Award nominations for the 2016–2017 season provided a window into drama production in the mid-2010s. In the words of the Hollywood trade publication, the NBC drama *This Is Us* was so good that it put the broadcast networks "Back into the Drama Race" (Turchiano, 2017). There was a time when the battle for Emmy glory for outstanding drama was reserved for the broadcast networks, but that began to change with the rise HBO and the nomination of *The Sopranos* after its inaugural season in 1998–1999. HBO claimed its first Emmy for outstanding drama in 2004, thanks once again to *The Sopranos*, and provided bookend wins in a ten-year span from 2007 (*The Sopranos*) through 2016 (*Game of Thrones*) when the broadcast networks were winless. And while *Variety* believed that *This Is Us* was a strong contender in 2016, the other nominees provided clear evidence of how drama production had changed, with three nominations for Netflix (*The Crown, House of Card,* and *Stranger Things*) and one each for AMC (*Better Call Saul*), HBO (*Westworld*), and Hulu (*The Handmaid's Tale*). That slate of nominees, including broadcast networks, basic and premium cable outlets, and streaming media services, also supports the need to conduct research across these platforms to understand issues related to television production and distribution.

Broadcast Networks

There was a time when the bulk of the dramas on the primetime schedules of the major broadcast networks called Hollywood home. That was evident on the debut schedules for ABC, CBS, and NBC in the fall of 1986. While there were some shows shot on location in exotic locales, such as *Magnum P.I.* in Hawaii and *Miami Vice* in Florida, primary filming for the vast majority was conducted on sound stages and studio back lots in the Los Angeles basin. Even shows set elsewhere, like *Cagney & Lacey* (New York), *Dallas*, and *Dynasty* (Denver), were often shot in Southern California with additional exterior scenes shot on location. What is most interesting about the 1986–1987 season is that just one drama on the fall schedules of the three major networks was shot in New York, *The Equalizer* on CBS. FOX debuted its first primetime slate in April 1987 and the maiden drama on the new network was *21 Jump Street*. While that show is best remembered for starring a 23-year-old Johnny Depp, it was shot in Vancouver and is often credited for being one of the shows that put that city on the map. Show creator Stephen J. Cannell was so enamored with Vancouver that, in fact, he soon after teamed with Paul Bronfman to build North Shore Studios, at the time the largest studio space in Canada. The rise of New York and Vancouver and the transformation of primetime drama production are most evident when one moves forward 30 years.

The analysis of the primetime schedules of the major broadcast networks in the United States over a seven-season period, from 2010–2011 through 2016–2017, provides a clear picture of the changes in program production and the raising reliance on production incentives over three decades. Those totals are detailed in Table 6.1. The percentage of scripted programs produced in a state, province, or country with available production credits is the most dramatic change, from just under 50% in 2010–2011 with 59 hour-long dramas on the five networks to just over 80% with 81 hour-long dramas. Most of that change, moreover, is attributable to incentives in the United States, as the percentage of programs produced receiving credits in one of the 50 states increased from 27.1% in 2010–2011 to 50.6% in 2016–2017. The percentage of programs eligible for incentives in a Canadian province increased as well, from 20.3% in 2010–2011 to 27.2% in 2016–2017, but there is no clear trend line, with three year-over-year decreases and three year-over-year increases in the sample period. NBC was the most aggressive in 2016–2017, producing all 16 dramas in locations with incentive programs, including one that qualified for tax credits in California (*This Is Us*).

There are other patterns in the results of this analysis. In 2010–2011, there were only four broadcast dramas produced in New York, but those numbers increased after the New York State Legislature extended and expanded the film and television tax credit program in August 2010, allocating $420 million per year. While that was too late to impact on the 2010–2011 broadcast season, the increase in New York-based productions in subsequent years was clear: 11 hour-long dramas in 2011–2012, 14 in 2012–2013 and 2013–2014, 15 in 2014–2015, 16 in 2015–2016, and 13 in 2016–2017. CBS and NBC, in particular, took advantage of the largesse in New York, with those two networks accounting for 11 of the 15 broadcast dramas in 2014–2015 and 13 of 16 in 2015–2016. At the other end of the continent, CW accounted for 10 of the 16 broadcast dramas produced in Vancouver in 2016–2017.

Table 6.1 Original scripted series and miniseries, at least 40 minutes per episode, on selected U.S. broadcast networks – ABC, CBS CW, FOX, and NBC – with and without production incentives, 2010–2011 through 2016–2017

	2010–2011	2011–2012	2012–2013	2013–2014	2014–2015[4]	2015–2016[5]	2016–2017[6]
Total Dramas	59	57	60	69	74	76	81
State-Level Incentives in the United States	16	20	25	33	35	36	41
National- or Provincial-Level Incentives in Canada	12	10	14	14	15	19	22
Incentives in Other Countries	1	2	2	3	1	3	4
Total with Production Incentives	27 (48.2%)	32 (56.1%)	41 (68.3%)	50 (72.5%)	50 (67.6%)	54 (74.4%)	65 (80.2%)
Total without Production Incentives	31 (52.5%)	25 (43.9%)	19 (31.7%)	19 (27.5%)	24 (32.4%)	21 (27.6%)	16 (19.8%)

There was also a significant increase in incentive-supported production in California over the sample period. When the state introduced its film and television tax credit program in 2009, only broadcast network programs that relocated from a location outside of California were eligible. In 2011–2012, *Body of Proof* on ABC moved to California from Rhode Island, where it received a tax credit in its debut season, but that was the only broadcast drama to receive incentives in California from 2010–2011 through 2014–2015. As noted earlier, in 2015, the state approved an increase in funding for the program and expanded eligibility to include one-hour television series on all distribution outlets as well as television pilots. The impact of that change was evident in 2016–2017, when nine broadcast network dramas received tax credits under the California program, an increase from four in 2015–2016. It is important to note that three of the dramas produced in California with tax credits, *American Crime* and *Secrets and Lies* on ABC and *Scream Queens* on Fox, relocated after shooting earlier seasons in other states, Texas, North Carolina, and Louisiana, respectively.

The number of broadcast dramas produced in states other than California and New York is another trend, with an increase from an average of 10.0 per season from 2010–2011 through 2012–2013 to an average of 18.5 per season from 2013–2014 through 2016–2017. Two states that stood out in that area were Illinois and Georgia. In 2016–2017, there were seven dramas shot in Chicago under the Illinois state incentive program, the Dick Wolf produced quartet on NBC, *Chicago Fire*, *Chicago PD*, *Chicago Med*, and *Chicago Justice*, and three FOX dramas, *Empire*, *APB*, and *The Exorcist*. FOX was also the most prominent in Georgia with three dramas shot in that state, *24: Legacy*, *Sleepy Hollow*, and *Star*, with CW (*The Originals* and *The Vampire Diaries*) and CBS (*MacGyver*) bringing its total to six broadcast dramas in 2016–2017.

The value of production incentives to the media conglomerates that chase them are often hard to determine. As discussed earlier, most states and provinces do not report the allocation of credits and rebates on a case-by-case basis, claiming that it is proprietary information. California and New York now provide some specific information on their programs but at different points in the process. As noted earlier, the Empire State Development Corporation now reports the final allocation of funds, albeit multiple years after completion of a given season in the case of television, after identifying new projects that receive approval of an initial application by number without attribution to a project, studio, or corporate parent. California, however, reports the amount allocated for a given project when it qualifies for the tax credits.

The tax credits allocated for CBS dramas show the value of such programs to the studios and their corporate parents. In 2013–2014, CBS broadcast a total of 16 dramas over the course of the season, with 9 shows eligible for tax credits. The tax credits allocated for the six shows produced in New York are detailed in Table 6.2. The New York

Table 6.2 New York state tax credits issued for original scripted series or miniseries on CBS, 2013–2014

Production Title	Season(s)	Episodes	Production company	Qualified costs	New York state spend	Tax credits issued
Blue Bloods	4	22	CBS Studios Inc.	65,862,252	$91,456,252	$19,758,722
Elementary	2	24	CBS Studios Inc.	$62,486,380	$77,648,744	$18,754,914
The Good Wife	5	22	CBS Studios Inc.	$51,800,752	$73,091,630	$15,540,226
Hostages	1	15	Warner Bros. Entertainment Inc.	$34,954,201	$44,664,827	$10,486,260
Person of Interest	3	23	Warner Bros. Entertainment Inc.	$66,828,512	$81,847,585	$20,048,554
Unforgettable	2 & 3[7]	19	Sony Pictures Television & CBS Studios Inc.	$47,435,940	$60,119,956	$14,230,782
						$98,819,458

le 6.3 Original scripted series and miniseries on broadcast network in 2016–2017 receiving California tax credit

duction Title	Network	Season	Episodes	Production company	Qualified expenditures	Reservation of Credits
erican Crime	ABC	3	8	ABC Studios	$20,895,000	$5,223,000
le Black	CBS	2	16	ABC Studios	$36,876,000	$7,411,000
zy x-Girlfriend	CW	2	13	CBS Studios & Warner Bros.	$29,518,000	$5,873,000
h	FOX	1	10	Twentieth Century Fox	$34,543,000	$7,234,000
e Genius	CBS	1	13	ABC Studios & CBS Studios	$39,225,000	7,977,000
ewood	FOX	2	22	Twentieth Century Fox	$55,977,000	$11,387,000
am Queens	FOX	2	10	Twentieth Century Fox	$49,729,000	$9,200,000
rets & Lies	ABC	2	10	ABC Studios	$22,938,000	$5,734,000
s is Us	NBC	1	18	Twentieth Century Fox	$51,427,000	$10,332,999
						$70,371,000

State credits allocated to shows varied from just over $10 million for a 15-episode run of *Hostages* to over $20 million for a 23-episode run of *Person of Interest*. The total tax credits issued to CBS, Warner Bros., and Sony for those six shows surpassed $98 million, an average of $16.5 million per drama. That, moreover, does not include credits or rebates for CBS productions in Hawaii (*Hawaii Five-0*), North Carolina (*Under the Dome*), and South Carolina (*Reckless*) in 2013–2014.

The collection of broadcast network programs on the 2016–2017 schedules that received tax credits for productions in California provide additional insights into the value of such incentives. Those nine programs are listed in Table 6.3. At $7,819,000 per drama, the average tax credits reserved for the nine dramas approved under the California program in 2016–2017 is somewhat lower than the New York average from 2013 to 2014. Four of those programs were designated as a new television series eligible for a 20% tax credit, while the three others were relocating television series eligible for a 25% tax credit: *American Crime* and *Secrets & Lies* on ABC and *This Is Us* on NBC. What is interesting about this trio is that all were originally produced in states with incentive programs that were altered in some form or fashion in 2015 – Louisiana, North Carolina, and Texas, respectively.

Basic Cable Networks

The arrival of basic cable networks in the production of scripted dramatic series was clear at the 60th Primetime Emmy Awards on September 21,

2008. On that night, AMC's first-year drama, *Mad Men,* became the first-ever basic cable show to win the Emmy for Outstanding Drama Series. That year, basic cable also claimed the awards for outstanding lead actor and actress for a drama, Bryan Cranston for AMC's *Breaking Bad* and Glenn Close for FX's *Damages.* Over a ten-year period, from 2007–2008 through 2016–2017, basic cable claimed six of ten best drama awards, four for *Mad Men* and two for *Breaking Bad.* Some of the finest character portrayals were found on basic cable, as Cranston claimed a record equaling four Emmy's for his portrayal of Walter White, and shows on AMC, FX, TNT, and USA won at least one lead actor or actress Emmy over that same period. In total, those four basic cable services collected a total of nine lead and seven supporting drama awards in the lead and supporting actor or actress categories over that ten-year period.

The expansion of basic cable services into the production of original dramas was fueled in large part by state and provincial production incentives. The analysis of scripted series on the four selected basic cable services in the United States over a seven-year period, 2011 through 2017, reveals an unequivocal reliance on such incentives. Those totals are detailed in Table 6.4. At the start of the decade, the basic cable services were well ahead of the broadcast networks in the selection of locations where productions were eligible for incentives. In 2010, 16 of 25 original dramas on those four outlets were eligible for production incentives, 64.0% for the calendar year compared to 47.5% for the broadcast networks during the 2010–2011 season. There was a slight increase in the number of original scripted series at least 40 minutes per episode in the seven years that followed, from 28 in 2011 to 31 in 2017 with a high of 33 in 2015. More significant was the increase in the percentage of original series eligible for state, provincial, and/or federal incentives, from 78.6% in 2011 to 93.5% in 2017. Outside of a slight drop from 2015 to 2016, when there was also a drop in the number of the original series produced from 33 to 28, there were year-over-year increases in the percentage of series eligible for incentives.

There are various trends that emerge in the analysis of basic cable original series over this period to time. One pattern is the prominence of California. The original tax credit program in the State of California, adopted in 2009 with an annual allocation of $100 million, made a specific provision for new "basic cable" series. Three of the selected basic cable services, FX, TNT, and USA, produced at least one series under the California tax credit program from 2011 through 2017, with at least five starting in 2012 and a high of seven series total in 2014, 2015, and 2016. TNT was the most prominent in California, with five or more eligible productions in 2013, 2014, and 2015. A second trend among basic cable series is a reliance on state programs other than the two largest, New York and California. Those states were home to at least

Table 6.4 Original scripted series and miniseries, at least 40 minutes per episode, on selected U.S. basic cable networks – AMC, FX, TNT, and USA – with and without production incentives, 2011 through 2017

	2011	2012	2013	2014	2015	2016	2017
Total Scripted Series	28	28	29	30	33	28	31
State-Level Incentives in the United States	15	16	18	18	20	20	18
National- or Provincial-Level Incentives in Canada	7	7	7	7	7	3	6
Incentives in Other Countries	0	0	0	1	4	3	5
Total with Production Incentives	27 (78.6%)	23 (82.1%)	25 (86.2%)	26 (86.7%)	31 (93.9%)	26 (92.9%)	29 (93.5%)
Total without Production Incentives	6 (21.4%)	5 (17.9%)	4 (13.8%)	4 (13.3%)	2 (6.1%)	2 (7.1%)	2 (6.5%)

seven productions from 2011 through 2017. That total hit a high of ten in 2017, with two each in Georgia, Louisiana, and Texas and one each in Louisiana, New Mexico, North Carolina, and Oregon. AMC was the most prominent in these totals, including at least five series in 2015, 2016, and 2017, with some of its best-known shows produced outside California and New York, including *Breaking Bad* and *Better Call Saul* in New Mexico and *The Walking Dead* in Georgia.

The total value of such incentives is impossible to determine since some states and provinces do not disclose the total tax credits allocated, but these states do provide some insight. In New York, where programs were eligible for 30% credit of eligible costs, the third season of *The Americans* on FX in 2015 received $10,892,183 in tax credits, an average of $837,860 for 13 episodes, while the first and only season of *Public Morals* on TNT in 2015 received $9,596,196, an average of $959,620 for 10 episodes (Empire State Development, 2016). The qualified New York cost for those two series for the 2015 seasons was $68,294,597, an average of $2,969,330 for a combined total of 23 episodes. In California, where series were eligible for 20% credit of eligible costs, 25% for relocating series, six series received tax credits for episodes telecast in 2015, including four on TNT and two on FX. The six programs are listed in Table 6.5. As discussed, California reports the reservation of credits for programs rather than the final allocation, but

Table 6.5 Original scripted series and miniseries, at least 40 minutes per episode, on AMC, FX, TNT, and USA receiving California tax credits in 2015

Production Title	Network	Season	Episodes	Production company(s)	Qualified expenditures	Reservatio of credits
Agent X	TNT	1	10	Turner Original Productions	$26,499,000	$5,300,0
American Horror Story[8]	FX	5	10	Twentieth Century Fox Television	$30,324,167	$7,580,8
Justified	FX	6	13	Sony Pictures Television & Bluebrush Productions	$32,705,000	$6,541,0
Major Crimes[9]	TNT	3 & 4	21	Warner Bros. Television	$39,801,556	$7,960,0
Murder in the First	TNT	2	12	TNT Original Productions	$24,908,000	$4,982,0
Perception[10]	TNT	3	3	ABC Studios	$9,249,667	$1,850,0
Rizzoli & Isles[11]	TNT	5 & 6	18	Warner Horizon Television	$40,157,098	$8,031,6
					$203,644,487	$42,245,5

the comparison is still valuable. Those six series had qualified expenditures of $203,644,487, an average of $2,288,140 for a combined total of 89 episodes (California Film Commission, 2017). Those six series received a total of $42,245,549 in tax credits, an average of $474,669 per episode. *American Horror Story* received the highest per average per episodes, $758,083, qualifying under Film & TV Tax Credit Program 2.0 as a relocating television program eligible for a 25% credit after moving from Louisiana for season five.

Premium Networks and Online Services

The changing state of original series production was most evident on a list of the most expensive one-hour dramas in 2017. Where once the broadcast networks were king, premium cable networks and online services are now bankrolling the most expensive original series. The broadcast drama with the highest per episode cost, *Once Upon A Time*, ranked ninth on the list at $4.5 million per episode (Smith, 2017). The eight programs that cost more than the ABC drama included three from Netflix, two from HBO, two from STARZ, and one from CBS All Access. The most expensive dramas were Netflix's *The Crown*, at an estimated $15 million per episode, and HBO's *Westworld* and *Game of Thrones*, at $10 million per episode. Little wonder that Shonda Rhymes, the creator of *Grey's Anatomy, Scandal*, and others over 15 years at ABC, signed a production deal with Netflix in the spring of 2017.

While premium cable networks and online services were upping the budgets for original dramas, they were also more aggressive in the pursuit of tax credits and production grants. While there might not be significant differences in the percentage of shows eligible for production incentives, there are more shows that receive tax credits from multiple locations for both production and postproduction. The State of California, for example, allocated $12.084 million for the first season of *Westworld*, with another $17.673 reserved for the second season. The series, moreover, acknowledged additional financial support from the State of Utah Governor's Office of Economic Development. Netflix's *Goodless*, a miniseries released in 2017, was a Western that featured the New Mexico landscape, an incentive-rich location, but the credits also acknowledged the Ontario tax credit program and the New York postproduction program. Likewise, HBO's *Big Little Lies* acknowledges locations in Los Angeles and Monterey Peninsula, albeit not under the California program, but also tax credits from the province of Quebec. And no series represents that trend more than *Game of Thrones*, which is known for utilizing locations in Northern Ireland, Iceland, Croatia, and Spain, all of which offer an assortment of national and regional tax credits, not to mention various locations for postproduction and special effects.

There is little question that premium cable networks and online services are competing for viewers, and one could combine the data for these

Table 6.6 Original scripted series and miniseries, at least 40 minutes per episode, on three premium cable services – HBO, Showtime, and STARZ – with and without production incentives, 2011 through 2017

	2011	2012	2013	2014	2015	2016	2017
Total Dramas	15	14	15	18	16	16	18
State-Level Incentives in the United States	6	5	4	7	6	7	10
National- or Provincial-Level Incentives in Canada	2	1	1	1	2	3	4
Incentives in Other Countries	3	3	4	8	7	7	7
Total with Production Incentives	10 (66.7%)	0 (64.3%)	9 (60.0%)	14 (77.8%)	13 (81.2%)	13 (81.2%)	17 (94.4%)
Total without Production Incentives	5 (33.3%)	5 (35.7%)	6 (40.0%)	4 (22.2%)	3 (18.8%)	3 (18.8%)	1 (5.6%)

two groups, but the dramatic rise in the number of original series on online services require that the data of the two are separated. From 2011 through 2017, the number of original series appearing on HBO Showtime and STARZ that were a minimum of 40 minutes per episode has remained more or less constant, ranging from a low of 14 in 2012 to a high of 18 in both 2014 and 2017. At the same time, the percentage of shows eligible for tax credits or other incentives has increased on a steady basis, from less than 70% in 2011, 2012, and 2013 to over 80% in 2015 and 2016 and a high of 94.4% in 2017. Those totals are detailed in Table 6.6.

The need to separate the premium cable services from the online streaming service is necessitated less by the relative percentage of series and miniseries eligible for various incentives than by the dramatic increase in the hour-long originals produced for Amazon, Hulu, and, most significantly, Netflix. Those totals are detailed in Table 6.7. Those three services did not produce any scripted original series fitting the set criteria for this study prior to 2013, when Netflix debuted *House of Cards*, *Orange is the New Black*, and *Hemlock Grove*. All three of those series acknowledged tax incentives in their end credits from Maryland, New York, and Ontario, respectively. Hulu did debut an original scripted series in 2012, a mockumentary titled *Battleground*, but episodes were only 21 or 22 minutes in length. Netflix added two more original scripted series in 2014, *The Killing* and the aforementioned *Marco Polo*. *The Killing* was eligible for tax credits in British Columbia, while the first season of *Marco Polo* acknowledged credits from the Venice Film Fund and National Film Development Corporation of Malaysia as well as support from both the Canadian national program and Ontario provincial program and the New York postproduction incentive program.

The rise in original scripted series since 2013 and 2014 is significant, increasing from 5 in 2014 to 16 in 2015, 33 in 2016, and 41 in 2017. Much of this growth was attributable to Netflix, which went from a total of five original scripted, English-language series a minimum of 40 minutes in length in 2014 to 10 in 2015, 20 in 2016, and 25 in 2017. This, moreover, only tells part of the Netflix stories, as it produced original scripted series in various languages other than English and still others that were 30 minutes or less in length. What is most significant about the Netflix numbers, however, is the percentage of original series eligible for production incentives. Over that three-year period, 2015 through 2017, there was only one hour-long Netflix original series that was not eligible for incentives, *Gilmore Girls: A Year in the Life*. That four-episode miniseries was produced at the Warner Bros. lot in Burbank, the same location as the seven seasons of *Gilmore Girls* from 2000 through 2007.

The other pattern evident in the analysis of Netflix is the number of original series collecting tax credits or other incentives from multiple programs. As noted earlier, the second season of *Marco Polo* received incentives for shooting in Malaysia, Hungary, and Slovakia, but it also

Table 6.7 Original scripted series and miniseries, at least 40 minutes per episode, on three online streaming services – Amazon, Hulu, and Netflix – with and without production incentives, 2011 through 2017

	2011	2012	2013	2014	2015	2016	2017
Total Dramas	0	0	3	5	16	33	41
State-Level Incentives in the United States	0	0	2	3	10	14	21
National- or Provincial-Level Incentives in Canada	0	0	1	3	4	7	10
Incentives in Other Countries	0	0	0	1	2	10	11
Total with Production Incentives	0 (0.0%)	0 (0.0%)	3 (100.0%)	5 (100.0%)	14 (87.5%)	28 (84.8%)	35 (85.4%)
Total without Production Incentives	0 (0.0%)	0 (0.0%)	0 (0.0%)	0 (0.0%)	2 (12.5%)	5 (15.2%)	6 (14.6%)

received postproduction credits in Ontario and New York. The clearest example of that trend is *Game of Thrones*. It is best known for the multiple locations used for filming, but just as significant is the number of different studios used for visual effects. In season seven, there were at least 17 different design studios in at least eight different countries credited, with incentives acknowledged in the end credits in the following locations: British Columbia, Quebec, Australia, New Zealand, Ireland, and Germany. The exact number of locations is difficult to assess, since these studios are now transnational. Pixomondo, best known for producing the dragons on *Game of Thrones*, was founded in Germany and still has studios in Frankfurt and Stuttgart, but it also has studios in Los Angeles, Toronto, Vancouver, Shanghai, and Beijing. The visual effects producer for the show, Steve Kullback, has said that the show will "test two or three hopefuls every year and bring on one or two," and while there are creative considerations, there are also other realities: "we're not immune to the standard business needs of finance. We take seriously the tax advantages available worldwide."[12]

The importance of tax incentives might be most evident with visual effects (VFX), an area of more and more prominence in scripted program production. The advancements in computer-generated imagery (CGI) and the linking of far-flung VFX studios through high-speed transmission lines and shared servers has transformed the production process and allowed media conglomerates to pursue cheaper labor and tax incentives around the world. In the production of *Hugo*, for example, Pixomondo was able to turnaround work at a faster pace, with work being passed from New York to Los Angeles to Beijing and Shanghai to Berlin and Frankfurt to London to Toronto as time zones passed (Seymour, 2011). While this might be a positive step forward for the media conglomerates and their bottom lines, it has had a deleterious impact the visual effects industry. This was most evident in 2013 when Rhythm & Hues won the Academy Award Best Visual Effects for its work on *Life of Pi* weeks after it filed for bankruptcy protection, which led to protests outside the Dolby Theater in Hollywood during the ceremony. This, in turn, has raised ongoing debates about labor issues in the visual effects industry.[13]

Conclusion

The chase for production incentives across the television platforms included in this analysis show one undeniable trend: the major media conglomerates are searching far and wide for tax breaks that will improve their bottom lines. The change is most evident among the broadcast networks, which increased from just under 50% in 2010–2011 to over 80% in 2016–2017. This increase, moreover, occurred during a time period when the broadcast networks were increasing the number of hour-long scripted series and miniseries in production. While that shift is significant, what is perhaps more telling is the high percentage of programs on newer platforms (streaming services in particular) that are utilizing a range of incentives, both for production and postproduction. The number of shows on Amazon, Hulu, and Netflix that met the criteria for this analysis increased from a total of 5 in 2015 to 41 in 2017, but the percentage of those programs eligible for production incentives remained at or above 84.8% in each sample period.

The prominence of Netflix in this discussion is impossible to ignore. In a quarterly earnings call in October 2017, Chief Financial Officer David Wells said that Netflix would increase its budget for content, both original and acquired, from around $6 billion in 2017 to as much as $8 billion in 2018 (Netflix, 2017b). That number far outpaces the investment in scripted programming for the broadcast and cable networks and other streaming services. The data collected for this analysis, moreover, would suggest that Netflix has been aggressive in securing tax credits, with only one English-language original series or miniseries, at least 40 minutes per episode, not acknowledging tax credits in end credits or shot in a location where it would be eligible for such. As noted earlier, that program, *Gilmore Girls: A Year in the Life*, was a reprise of the long-running show on the CW broadcast network that returned to the Warner Bros. lot.

There is another aspect of the Netflix story that is worth considering. Earlier in 2017, Chief Content Officer Ted Sarandos lamented the impact chasing tax credits had on the cast and crew and vowed to do more production in and around Hollywood in an interview with *TheWrap* (Donnelly and Waxman, 2007). He discussed what he saw as an improvement in the writing for HBO's *Veep* once it relocated from Maryland to California, stating that, "Shooting in L.A. is an investment in the quality of the show" (Donnelly and Waxman, 2007). It is important to note that *Veep* moved to California as a relocating series that made it eligible for tax credits, $6.577 million for season five with an additional $13.789 million allocated for seasons six and seven. Netflix, moreover, moved production of just one scripted program at least 40 minutes per episode that debuted prior to January 1, 2018, to California and that program, *The OA*, was allocated $8.202 million in tax incentives. While it might be honest to lament the impact chasing production incentives has on individuals and families, the bottom line remains the bottom line and Netflix had close to $20 billion in debt at the close of 2017, much of that for streaming content obligations. And in an industrialized Hollywood, the bottom line usually wins.

Notes

1 See Tannenwald (2010), Luther (2010), and Robyn and David (2012).
2 See McDonald (2007), McDonald (2011), Lester (2012), Steele (2015), and Christopherson and Rightor (2010).

3 For example, the $18,243,915 credit issued for the first season of *Madam Secretary*, which was broadcast on ABC in the 2014–2015 season, was included in the Empire State Development report issued on September 27, 2017. That same report included the $21,217,413 credit issued for the second season of *Madam Secretary*, which was broadcast in 2015–2016.

4 *Gracepoint* on FOX was eligible for production incentives in British Columbia and postproduction incentives in New York.

5 *Quantico* on ABC was eligible for production incentives in Quebec and postproduction incentives in New York.

6 *Frequency* on CW was eligible for incentives in British Columbia and New York; *Prison Break Resurrection* on Fox was eligible for incentives in British Columbia and Morocco.

7 Episodes of the second season of *Unforgettable* were broadcast in both 2012–2013 and 2013–2014, with seven episodes in the summer of 2013 and six episodes in the winter and spring of 2014. The third season was then broadcast in the summer of 2014. For the purposes of this analysis, the credits allocation for the 2012–2013 season are distributed based on a per episode average, with the total credits for six episodes for season two being combined with the credits for season three.

8 FX aired 10 of 12 episodes of the fifth season of *American Horror Story* in 2015. The totals for qualified expenditures and credits is based on a per episode calculation for the episodes telecast in 2015. Totals do not include credits from the state of Louisiana for the fourth season, which was produced in New Orleans. The first three episodes of season four were telecast in January 2015.

9 The totals for *Major Crimes* include averages for episodes from season three (3) and four (18) that were telecast in 2015.

10 The totals for *Perception* include averages for the final three episodes for season three that were telecast in 2015.

11 The totals for *Rizzoli & Isles* include averages for episodes from seasons five (6) and six (12) that were telecast in 2015.

12 Quoted in Bunish (2017).

13 See Curtin and Vanderhoef (2015).

References

Bunish, C. (2017). "VFX Game of Thrones," *Post Magazine*, July 1. Accessed at www.postmagazine.com/Publications/Post-Magazine/2017/July-1-2017/VFX-I-Game-of-Thrones-I-.aspx.

California Film Commission. (2017). "Film and Television Tax Credit Program 1.0 – Alphabetical Listing of Approved Projects," December 11.

Christopherson, S. and Rightor, N. (2010). "The Creative Economy as 'Big Business': Evaluating State Strategies to Lure Filmmakers," *Journal of Planning Education and Research*, 29:3, 336–352.

Curtin, M. and Vanderhoef, J. (2015). "A Vanishing Piece of the Pi: The Globalization of Visual Effects Labor," *Television & New Media*, 16:3, 219–239.

Empire State Development. (2016). "Film Tax Credit – Quarterly Report. Calendar Year 2016; Second Quarter, June 30.

Donnelly, M. and Waxman, S. (2007). "Netflix Plans to Move Productions to California, 'Invest in Infrastructure,' Ted Sarandos Says," *TheWrap*, April 11, www.thewrap.com/ted-sarandos-netflix-move-production-california-infrastructure/

Ernst and Young. (2009). "Economic and Fiscal Impacts of the New Mexico Film Production Tax Credit," January.

Golding, P. and Murdock, G. (2000). "Culture, Communication and Political Economy," in Curran, J. & Gurevitch, M. (Eds.), *Mass Media & Society* (3rd edition, pp. 72–74). New York: Oxford University Press, 2000.

Goldsmith, B., and O'Regan, T. (2008). "International Film Production: Interests and Motivations", in Wasko, J. & Erickson, M. (Eds.), *Cross-Border Cultural Production: Economic Runaway or Globalization?* (pp. 13–44). Amherst, NY: Cambria Press.

Jones, M. (2002), "Motion Picture Production in California," California Research Bureau (CRB 02-001), March.

Lester, J. (2012) "Tax Credits for Foreign Location Shooting of Films: No Net Benefit for Canada," *Canadian Public Policy*, 39: 3, September, 451–472.

Luther, W. (2010). "Movie Production Incentives: Blockbuster Support for Lackluster Policy," *Tax Foundation*, No. 173, January.

McDonald, A. (2007). "Through the Looking Glass: Runaway Productions and 'Hollywood Economics,'" *University of Pennsylvania Journal of Labor and Employment Law*, 9:4, 879.

McDonald, A. (2011). "Down the Rabbit Hole: The Madness of State Film Incentives as a 'Solution' to Runaway Production," *University of Pennsylvania Journal of Business Law*, 14: 85.

Motion Picture Association of America. (2016). "MPAA Analysis Refutes 'False and Misleading' Study on Film Production Incentives by USC Assistant Professor Michael Thom," *Press Release*, September 14.

Netflix, Inc. (2017a), "Form 10-Q," United States Securities and Exchange Commission, Washington DC, July 19.

Netflix, Inc. (2017b) "Q3 2017 Netflix Inc. Earnings Call," October 16, 2017.

Otterson, J. (2018). "487 Scripted Series Aired in 2017, FX Chief John Landgraf Says," *Variety*, January 5, 2018.

Popp, A.V. and Peach, J. (2008). "The Film Industry in New Mexico and The Provision of Tax Incentives," Arrowhead Center, Office of Policy Analysis, New Mexico State University, August 26.

Robyn, M. and David, H. (2012). "Movie Production Incentives in the Last Frontier," Tax Foundation, No. 199, April.

Seymour, M. (2011). "Hugo: A Study of Modern Inventive Visual Effects," fxguide, December 1. www.fxguide.com/featured/hugo-a-study-of-modern-inventive-visual -effcts/.

Smith, E. (2017). "Budget Battled for 1-hour Drama Series Continue," Economics of TV & Film, SNL Kagan Database, December 1, 2017. Accessed on January 13, 2018: https://platform.mi.spglobal.com/SNL.Services.Export.Service/v2/Export/Retrieve?filename=Html_92bbb7b7-0710-4230-8119-ee37t7843aa2.html.

Smythe, D. (1960). "On the Political Economy of Communications," *Journalism Quarterly*, 37, 564.

Steele, D. (2015). "Rethinking the Focus of UK Film Support: Is Subsiding US Studios a Safe Strategy for UK Film Production in the Coming Decade," *Cultural Trends*, 24:1, 74–79.

Tannenwald, R. (2010). "State Film Subsidies: Not Much Bang for Too Many Bucks," Center on Budget and Policy Priorities, December 9.

Thom, M. (2016). "Lights, Camera, but No Action? Tax and Economic Development Lessons from State Motion Picture Incentive Programs," *American Review of Public Administration* 48:1, 33–51.

Turchiano, D. (2017). "2017 Emmys: 'This Is Us' Brings Broadcast Into the Drama Race," *Variety*, July 13.

Wasko, J. and Erickson, M. (2008). "Introduction," in Wasko, J. and Erickson, M. (Eds.), *Cross-Border Cultural Production: Economic Runaway or Globalization*. Amherst, NY: Cambria Press.

Weiner, J. (2009). "Ernst & Young Analyses of New Mexico and New York State Tax Credits," New England Public Policy Center at the Federal Reserve Bank of Boston, April 2.

7 Old Strategies in the New Paradigm
Web Series and Corporate Control

Mary P. Erickson

The television industry has experienced seismic changes in the last two decades. Broadcast and cable networks, under the umbrellas of powerhouse entertainment companies, have struggled to simultaneously understand and incorporate a new paradigm of online programming distribution that tends to eschew traditional strategies of programming grids, ratings, and restricted releases. Meanwhile, unconventional players like Netflix and Amazon have taken the reins of this new landscape, redefining how content reaches audiences by taking advantage of the functionalities of online platforms.

The web series or serialized content developed for online platforms are a cornerstone of online distribution; this format is seen as a potential holy grail for securing industry dominance. As conventional configurations within the television and film industry are upended, the field has opened up for additional competitors, who are rapidly consolidating their own control and power in order to solidify their position in the industry.

Using a political economic framework, this chapter examines the priorities and objectives of the key corporate platforms producing and distributing web series. Emphasis is placed on the types of strategies used by these platforms for securing maximum control and minimum risk as well as the ways in which these companies may differentiate themselves from more traditional audiovisual entertainment corporations. By engaging in a political economic examination, we can see how the industry approaches the potential of online distribution in search of control in a rapidly changing and unstable media environment.

Web Series and the Growth of an Industry

Web series or serialized content developed for online platforms have been around for about 20 years, although they were few and far between early on given the realities of streaming capabilities in the late 1990s. More online video content was developed in the mid-2000s, utilizing early versions of social media platforms like Friendster and MySpace to deliver content to audiences. YouTube was introduced in 2005, and it became a preferred platform very early on for all kinds of content. As more users joined YouTube, the amount of content exploded, and soon some content creators poured their energies into creating web series.

More experimentation with format, structure, and programming allowed online video content to blossom, with vlogging, sponsored or branded content, one-off digital shorts, and narrative series developing rapidly in the landscape. From the 2010s onward, web series have been an integral part of online content production. Today, the landscape is made of large and small production companies as well as independent individuals, producing and distributing content in a multitude of configurations. Some web series are, for example, replications of traditional narrative television, while others are daily beauty or lifestyle vlogs; still others are instructional or educational documentary style series, branded series that promote companies or products, individuals playing video games, and more. All these types can be recognized as web series, regardless of funding, production team, distribution path, or content.

Web series as objects of analysis are relatively understudied, as is the case with most independently produced media. Over the course of web series' brief history, the format has existed predominantly outside the mainstream industry, and the scholarly attention that does address web series has been primarily focused on instances when they cross into or interrupt the mainstream industry. The most comprehensive study of web series is Aymar Jean Christian's body of work, culminating in his monograph, *Open TV* (Christian, 2018), which provides multiple entry points into how we can understand web series in the contemporary era. Other studies examine online distribution suitability (Peirce, 2010), independent distribution (Moore, 2013), alternative or diverse representation (Monaghan, 2017), fan contributions (Christian, 2011), branded web series (Segarra-Saavedra et al., 2017), and nontraditional funding models (McLeod, 2017).

As more corporate players enter the fray, there is increased interest in understanding how they may be shifting the tenor and potential of web series and streaming functionalities. Netflix is a primary focus, as many scholars consider how the company capitalized on a serendipitous moment of shifting audience viewing habits as well as failures on the part of its competition (see, for example, Keating, 2012; McDonald, 2013). Other studies have emphasized Netflix's strategies for producing desirable content to attract audiences (Jenner, 2014), promotional strategies (Tryon, 2015), brand identity differentiation (Wayne, 2018), and expansion into other territories (Zboralska & Davis, 2017). A handful of other studies have begun to investigate other platforms, including how much of YouTube's content has become increasingly professionally produced (Kim, 2012; Morreale, 2014) and how Amazon uses licensed programming to lure customers (Wayne, 2018).

This study adds to the literature by extending beyond the focus on how newer entertainment companies are innovating the industry; instead, this study investigates whether these companies are replicating strategies that have long been implemented by their veteran competitors. Specifically, platforms such as Netflix, Amazon Prime Video, and Hulu emphasize the expansion of intellectual property, the use of marquee titles and bankable names, and the growth of global markets. These strategies, at their core, ensure that corporate entities can exert economic and distribution control over web series on their platforms in order to maximize profit and minimize risk.

An Overview of Corporate Platforms

Major corporate platforms' relationships with web series are aligned with their corporate objectives. Namely, these companies are geared to minimize risk and maximize profit. Their content production and acquisition strategies emphasize the growth of their respective subscriber bases, accomplished primarily through globally recognizable names and brands, intellectual property expansion, and marquee titles. The three top corporate platforms – Netflix, Amazon Prime Video, and Hulu – are invested in securing the dominant share of the continually growing global audience for streaming content.

Netflix, founded in 1997, has emerged to dominate the digital content distribution market. With 117.5 million members (46% of whom are in the United States) in 190 countries at the end of 2017, Netflix brought in a reported $11.6 billion in streaming revenue (Feldman, 2018; "Number of Netflix Streaming Subscribers," 2018). The company spent approximately $2 billion in marketing in 2017, and anticipated further record-breaking growth for the company in a bid to continue driving up subscriber numbers. Netflix produced top original series such as *House of Cards* (2013–2018),[1] *Orange is the New Black* (2013–2019), and *Stranger Things* (2016–present).

Amazon Prime is a subscription-based service offered by Amazon.com Inc., affording Prime members free shipping on the retail Web site along with access to Prime Video and Music. Prime was launched in 2005, 11 years after the company itself was founded, and rapidly grew to accommodate 90 million subscribers in the United States (as of late 2017), although it is unclear how many of those subscribers use Prime Video. The Prime Video service, available in 240 countries, became available on its own in 2016 as a month-to-month subscriber video-on-demand (SVOD) service, in addition to its availability bundled with Amazon Prime. Prime Video produced award-winning original series such as *Transparent* (2014–present), *Mozart in the Jungle* (2014–present), and *The Marvelous Mrs. Maisel* (2017–present).

Hulu is a joint venture among Disney (30%), Fox (30%), Comcast/NBC Universal (30%), and Time Warner (10%). Disney proposed to acquire 21st Century Fox in 2017, which would give Disney a majority stake in Hulu; this caused a flurry of speculation over the direction of the platform.[2] Founded in 2007, Hulu was originally a platform for the exploitation of TV libraries and evolved into offering licensed content from its parent companies, live content, movies, and its own award-winning original series, such as *The Handmaid's Tale* (2017–present). Hulu's 17 million subscribers either paid $11.99/month for ad-free content or $7.99/month for ad-supported content, which generated approximately $1 billion in advertising revenue for the company in 2017 (Ha, 2018).

Subscribers were not exclusively tied to one platform over another; rather, one market survey revealed that 45% of Netflix subscribers also use Amazon Prime Video, while 60% of Amazon Prime customers also use Netflix (Bary, 2017). Similarly, there was overlap between usage of these two platforms and Hulu as well as with other platforms. As such, it is important to acknowledge other power players in this landscape that are participating in this ecosystem and may help drive the direction of the industry. Apple, YouTube, and Facebook vie for space and viewers, as do, increasingly, more traditional television networks like CBS.

A distant competitor to the top three platforms, yet the largest company globally in terms of market capitalization (Lynley, 2017), Apple began expanding its video-on-demand strategy. It began committing $1 billion to content acquisition in 2018 and hiring television executives from Sony, Amazon, and a production company affiliated with Universal TV. It had already offered content through Apple Music, licensing *Carpool Karaoke* and its original critically panned reality series, *Planet of the Apps*, in 2017 (Ryan, 2017). Industry insiders speculated that Apple would be well positioned to compete effectively with Netflix and Amazon eventually, especially given its preexisting technology for disseminating content: Apple's forays into VOD "could mean that more people stay within its ecosystem," using Apple technologies to access Apple content (Balakrishnan, 2017; Kharpal, 2017).

YouTube, the online video platform, was founded in 2005 and quickly skyrocketed to the forefront of Silicon Valley's awareness. Google acquired the company before the end of the following year for $1.65 billion. The company was primarily built on user-generated content, uploaded around the globe at what became a rate of 300 hours every minute in 2017. Monetization opportunities for this vast spectrum of content initially stumped YouTube, but the platform soon began partnering with advertisers and became a highly profitable revenue stream for parent company Google (Wasko and Erickson, 2009). The rise of the YouTube celebrity marked the platform's legitimization with audiences, and these YouTubers produced web series of some format or another, more often focusing on gameplay or lifestyle vlogs; the most well-paid stars made $10.5–$16.5 million in 2017 (Lynch, 2017). In 2015, the platform launched YouTube Red, a subscription-based service with no advertising. In the early days, the service sought to utilize content producers who had "risen up democratically" in popularity on YouTube and develop new original content to be featured to paying subscribers (Sydell, 2015). Some of these early partners included Felix Kjellberg (better known as PewDiePie) and the Fine Brothers. A year later, the service had 1.5 million paying subscribers, and since then, the platform has turned its attention toward developing content through YouTube Originals, both with homegrown YouTube stars and major studio partnerships. YouTube grew at a consistently rapid pace, and some analysts speculated that the company was worth $75 billion in 2017 (Lovelace, 2017).

Facebook was introduced in 2004 as a platform for college students to connect with each other. As the reach of this platform expanded, hitting two billion monthly active users in 2017 (Constine, 2017), so too did its scope. The company purchased other social networking sites, including Instagram in 2012 and WhatsApp in 2014, as well as companies specializing in artificial intelligence, machine learning, virtual reality, and facial recognition. Facebook also moved to develop its own video streaming platform, Facebook Watch, in 2017, as a feature added on to the Facebook social networking platform. It began pursuing a strategy of partnering with other companies to fund and provide content for Watch, including traditional cable networks such as A+E Networks and National Geographic; individual producers such as Mike Rowe (of *Dirty Jobs* fame); vloggers like Nuseir Yassin; other partners such as Condé Nast Entertainment, Mashable, and The Atlantic; and live sporting events (Spangler, 2017). Moreover, the platform hopes to stretch its reach to fashion itself as a competitor of YouTube, allowing for anyone and everyone to post video content on the site. Facebook Watch's initial financing of content is intended to demonstrate to users the types of desirable content for Watch. "To help inspire creators and seed the ecosystem," Facebook announced in a press release, "we've also funded some shows that are examples of community-oriented and episodic video series" (Danker, 2017). Furthermore, as one Facebook executive notes, "The goal long term is absolutely that the ecosystem will be creating these shows" (Spangler, 2017).

Some of the major Hollywood film and television studios also deal in web series content, distributing both original and licensed series via streaming video-on-demand platforms like CBS All Access, CW Seed, and HBO Now. Disney aims to launch its own streaming service in 2019. Other companies operate platforms for distributing streaming content such as Sony PlayStation Vue and DirecTV Now, but these primarily stream a range of conventional cable networks; Vue offers a combination of channels from local stations as well as broadcast and cable networks.

Content Strategies of Corporate Platforms

In terms of content, the three most dominant services in the industry (Netflix, Amazon, and Hulu) host movies, licensed series, and original series. These companies utilize similar strategies as Hollywood studios in their approach to content production, acquisition, and distribution, emphasizing the scalability of a singular intellectual property into multiple franchise opportunities. As well, the focus on bankable directors and actors provide the platforms with built-in fan followings to tap into. Furthermore, the web series format is more appealing than the feature-length film format for these companies because of the potential long-tail financial returns, fueled by continued audience engagement. "[F]ilms don't build up a continuing audience," notes former Amazon Studios head Roy Price. "Nor do they invite binge viewing…. But in terms of promoting engagement with a video service, there's nothing like a TV series" (Spangler & Setoodeh, 2014). Rob Hayes, from NBC Entertainment's Digital Media segment, concurs: "A series gives you better longevity and better margins" (Spangler & Setoodeh, 2014).

As evidenced by the content strategies of both Amazon Prime Video/Amazon Studios and Netflix, these companies operate at a tier that prioritizes their growth at a global scale. These strategies are inherently incompatible with independent web series production, as they emphasize minimum risk for maximum reward. This includes marquee titles and bankable names, the exploitation of intellectual property to build and expand media universes, and the growth of global markets.

Marquee Titles and Bankable Names

Netflix has been aggressive in producing, adapting, and distributing high-profile projects with recognizable brands and/or names. One of its first series, *House of Cards*, starred Kevin Spacey and Robin Wright Penn, while other marquee series have included a number of adaptations based on Marvel Comics characters such as *Jessica Jones*, *Daredevil*, and *Luke Cage*. The company also backed Baz Luhrmann's *The Get Down* and *Sense8* by Lana and Lilly Wachowski.[3]

With its ever-expanding international audience, the company looked to incorporate more non-English language series into its slate of original programming. *Babylon Berlin*, directed by Tom Twyker (director of *Run Lola Run*), debuted on Netflix in 2018 after a brief run on German and British television. *The Wave*, a German award-winning film about a dangerous social experiment, began development into an original series of the same name in 2018. Turning to high-profile projects in India, Netflix announced its first original series based on an Indian property, *Sacred Games*, in 2018; this series would star a number of well-known Bollywood actors. Another seven series were announced at the same time, one of which was an adaptation of Salman Rushdie's novel, *Midnight's Children*. Netflix targeted Polish writer Andrzej Sapkowski's franchise, *The Witcher*, slated for adaptation in 2019. The Netflix series will undoubtedly draw on fans of *The Witcher*'s popular novels, short stories, and role-playing video game.

As well, the company produced continuations of television series that had previously been canceled such as *Arrested Development, Gilmore Girls, Fuller House, Longmire, Black Mirror, Trailer Park Boys*, and many others. Expanding on preexisting properties, Netflix was able to capitalize on a relatively low-risk endeavor with a guaranteed fan base.

While a formidable force in this landscape, Amazon still struggled in 2017 to build its catalog to compete with Netflix's powerhouse original series. The company spent $4.5 billion on content acquisition that year, yet did not land what it would consider a marquee series like HBO's *Game of Thrones*. "We're increasingly focused on the impact of the biggest shows," notes former head of Amazon Studios Roy Price. "It's pretty evident that it takes big shows to move the needle ... At the end of the day, you only have so many slots. With those slots you have to drive viewership and drive subscriptions" (Littleton and Holloway, 2017). As such, the company continued to chase high-profile series with bankable stars and high production value.

With this objective in mind, Amazon greenlit several high-profile projects for 2018, including *The Romanoffs* from *Mad Men* producer Matthew Weiner; an adaptation of *Jack Ryan*, Tom Clancy's franchise, with John Krasinksi; and a comic book adaptation helmed by Seth Rogan. But Amazon's most visible – and potentially lucrative – deal was its acquisition of global rights to adapt *Lord of the Rings* into a five-season series at a hefty price tag of $250 million, with estimates that the production itself will cost $1 billion or more. Turning Peter Jackson's globally successful film franchise into a serialized version requires a strategy similar to that franchise. Jackson's attorney noted, "I think Amazon is taking a page out of the studios' emphasis on franchises." In order to compete with Netflix, HBO, and others, Amazon has had to ramp up its commitment to developing marquee titles. The attorney continued, "[Amazon is] realizing that with the overproduction of television, you need to get the eyeballs to the screen, and you can do that with franchise titles" (Siegel, 2018).

The arena for content has grown increasingly crowded, with other large companies vying for prestige by adapting high-profile series based on well-known properties. Hulu, for example, adapted *The Handmaid's Tale, Catch-22, The Invisible Man*, and *Less than Zero*. Even YouTube, a platform that built its empire on user-generated content, broadened its scope of content offerings by turning to more traditional fare in the vein of television series. In 2018, YouTube partnered with Sony Pictures TV to produce *Cobra Kai*, a reboot of the *Karate Kid* franchise, complete with original stars Ralph Macchio and William Zabka (Schneider, 2018). The platform also started working with a number of other globally recognizable names, including Ben Stiller, Kevin Hart, Channing Tatum, and

LeBron James. It cannot be overlooked that YouTube celebrities are also globally recognizable names, which gives YouTube a unique cache of talent from which to draw.

The strategy of using marquee titles and bankable names is a familiar one for Hollywood studios, and Netflix, Amazon, and others readily adapt the model. In this way, the companies can more easily locate pre-existing audiences for their programming and thereby ensure a return on investment.

Intellectual Property Expansion

Netflix, Amazon Prime Video, and Hulu each strive to differentiate themselves in order to secure loyal customers. Netflix occupies the power position, transitioning over the 2010s from being strictly a content delivery platform to a producer of original series and films that emulates a Hollywood studio. Its original series, *Stranger Things*, blossomed into a veritable franchise, with two successful seasons, a third season slated for 2019, an aftershow called *Beyond Stranger Things*, and licensing deals for toys and other merchandise that build on the series' nostalgia pull for audiences who grew up in the 1980s. In 2017, Netflix acquired Millarworld, a comic book publisher; the move indicated that Netflix was primed to capitalize on intellectual properties that can bridge television, film, comics, merchandise, and other formats. Moreover, exclusive rights to this intellectual property guarantees Netflix's ability to grow the franchise as it sees fit. Millarworld and Netflix published a comic book, *The Magic Order*, in 2018, and added more comic books to its slate that would also be developed into films or web series. Additionally, Netflix looks to exploit other intellectual properties such as *Carmen Sandiego*, developing a film and animated series based on the 1990s video game; Netflix is also partnering with Houghton Mifflin Harcourt to publish a book series based on the animated series (Rodriguez, 2018).

Early on, Amazon Studios tested the publication of a comic book in hopes of translating it for the screen. *Blackburn Burrow*, based on a script from an amateur screenwriter, was optioned by Amazon in 2012 and released as a four-issue digital comic book for free download. Amazon intended to gauge audience reaction to the material with the comic (Fritz, 2012); the film was never produced, and Amazon didn't delve into comic book publishing again. However, Amazon's foray into the *Lord of the Rings* series signals an eye toward franchise expansion, as industry insiders speculate that the company's adaptation may also include spin-offs.

Hulu brokered a deal to expand on the universe of many of Stephen King's novels in an original series called *Castle Rock*, using Castle Rock, a town that has been featured in a number of King's works, as the hinge. But Hulu's growth strategies have been mostly focused in other directions rather than expanding intellectual property in the ways that competitors like Netflix does.

Netflix has a track record of popular and successful series that are enticing to media partners, and is rapidly turning itself into a juggernaut of the streaming world. As Netflix in particular continues moving toward emulating a conventional studio, it has incorporated many of the conventional strategies that strengthen its market position, which in turn other companies also incorporate. Expanding intellectual property, either as a series or across multiple media types, is yet another tactic to exploit.

Reaching Global Markets

Closely linked to the expansion of recognizable names is the growth of global markets for these major platforms. As Netflix has grown, for example, it has been increasingly involved at the production and financing level in exchange for exclusive global distribution rights. It simultaneously launched streaming services in 130 countries in early 2016, opening the door to audiences across six continents.[4]

In 2017, the company renewed a distribution deal with Adam Sandler to premiere four of his forthcoming films on the platform. Ridiculed by some American industry insiders because of critics' disparaging reviews of Sandler's films, the deal continues Netflix's relationship with Sandler, extending the previous four-picture deal made in 2014 as a way to recruit and retain global audiences. Netflix's Chief Content Officer Ted Sarandos noted, "People love Adam's films on Netflix... His appeal spans across viewers of all ages...not just in the US but all over the world" (Yarow, 2014). The focus on the global market, with a bankable star at the forefront, gives Netflix continued strength in securing more international subscribers. Netflix has also invested in licensing anime series as well as a multi-series partnership with Marvel, whose comic book characters are globally appealing (Barrett, 2016a).

Licensed content is not as easily exported to 190 countries (or, in Amazon's case, 200 countries) as original programming. There are distribution restrictions built into licensing deals in terms of geographic distribution and length of availability, along with possible difficulties in localizing the content. Therefore, Netflix has turned its attention to broadening the global reach of its top-rated programs, producing original shows that, speculates *Wired* magazine, "it thinks the whole world will watch" (Barrett, 2017b). Furthermore, it pays acute attention to localizing content that resonates with audiences in different markets. In the case of *Stranger Things* (2017–present), Netflix provided translations and dubbing for this cult show with a meticulous touch, creating a "show bible" to ensure accurate translations of *Dungeons and Dragons* references and 1980s advertising of Eggo waffles. "After you localize [the programming]," notes Netflix executive Todd Yellin, "you see substantially more growth in those countries" (Barrett, 2017a). What Netflix is also doing here is banking on global audiences' shared cultural understandings of these predominantly American cultural references.

In addition, original programming can provide more opportunity for expansion into regions that lack reliable high-speed internet infrastructures. Licensed content may be restricted not only in terms of regional distribution, but it also may be restricted in terms of online versus offline viewing. In regions with lower internet connectivity, original programming can be offered as downloadable content, so when internet connections are good, users can download content to then be viewed offline at a later time (Barrett, 2016b).

Overall, the direction of the corporate industry emphasizes conventional business strategies that result in economic control in order to maximize profits and minimize risk. Regardless of position in the market, these platforms for distributing content have begun to prioritize the development of original content that ensures they will control the exploitation of this content, and thus control the economic potential of said content. One industry insider sums up the overall intent of these corporate strategies in the context of online programming: "The new world is built on value creation and things that get viewers' attention" (Goldberg, 2017). Tried-and-true tactics such as bankable names, marquee titles, the extension of global reach, and intellectual property exploitation emphasize value creation and viewer attention.

Personnel Strategies of Corporate Platforms

In conjunction with the types of strategies discussed above, these companies hire executives with years of entertainment – and specifically, television – experience to implement said strategies. The personnel strategies of these platforms ensure that the companies do not fly blind in their drive to dominate the industry.

For example, the executives of Amazon Studios, which leads the production division for Amazon Prime Video, mainly come from senior positions in dominant television and film corporations. This includes its CEO Jennifer Salke, who hailed most recently from NBC Entertainment and, prior to that, Twentieth Century Fox Television. Salke's television experience secured her post, as Amazon sought to strengthen the caliber of its executives in order to compete with Netflix and others. Amazon Studios' head of television was another executive drawing on experience in traditional television, having previously worked for Disney in both the ABC and ESPN television divisions as well as Fox's television division. The company's moves to build its executive portfolio have been deemed a move to demonstrate that Amazon is a "real player" within the Hollywood entertainment industry (Koblin, 2018). Even Amazon Studios' corporate offices are located in the Los Angeles area instead of Amazon's headquarters in Seattle, which further confirms its commitment to being a player in the entertainment industry.

Hulu also sought to fortify its production division "by adding new expertise and capabilities to [their] executive ranks," according to its CEO Randy Freer, who came to Hulu from Fox Networks Group. Apple hired "two of the most talented TV executives in the world [who] have been instrumental in making this the golden age of television," according to one of the company's executives (Apple, 2017). Interestingly, the pair of executives, Jamie Erlicht and Zack Van Amburg, both formerly leaders of Sony Pictures Television, were said to have left "traditional media behind" to move into subscription VOD (Andreeva, 2018). Yet their imperative at Apple was to strengthen the company's programming slate to compete with Netflix, Amazon, Hulu, and others.

In contrast, Netflix has placed less focus on building its stable of television executives, continuing instead to keep Ted Sarandos as head of content. Sarandos came to Netflix in 2000 after beginning his career in video store management, and adapted models of home video distribution first to Netflix's home delivery service and then to its streaming service (Keating, 2012). Netflix historically jettisoned the distribution models that defined traditional television (including attention to programming grids, ratings, and incremental release of program episodes), yet it has shifted its emphasis, to a large degree, toward mimicking traditional television content.

The traditional television industry, while less formidable than in previous decades, still holds sway over the ways in which its competitors approach their own growth and stability. While many executives, in working for online distributors, are excited about shaping the direction of the industry, their habits of minimizing risk and maximizing profits are useful in shoring up the strength of these newer companies and shaping the direction of the industry away from the most innovative and groundbreaking methods and toward the methods that spell big profits and lower risk.

Metrics of Success

As we examine how these corporate platforms create value and capture viewer attention, we may turn to the concept of success, which can be defined in vastly different terms depending on the actor. The metrics of success for corporate entities, while not exclusively monetary, are best and most often expressed through financial gain. It is the chief objective of corporations with shareholders and/or investors to demonstrate healthy financial growth. Media companies employ a number of strategies to ensure growth, including synergy, vertical and horizontal integration, franchising, and market expansion into international markets, among others (Wasko, 2003). In doing so, companies actively seek to decrease risk by streamlining their operations; a corollary result is often the flattening of creative content (Croteau & Hoynes, 2006).

The potential for audience growth is another marker that determines success for companies like Netflix, Hulu, and others. While not directly or specifically financial, this growth represents future financial gain for the company, and many strategies are contingent upon the company's ability to harness markets that will shift from potential to actual revenue streams.

Pure financial strength is not the sole gauge for success, however, although this is certainly the most vital component. But there is also, particularly for executives within the audiovisual entertainment industry, the question of critical integrity of web series. To gain respect within the industry, platforms need to have critically acclaimed content; quantity does not (always) define quality. But when one examines "quality," it is often determined, as in the traditional Hollywood-based model, by production budget, bankable stars, and marketing spending. While Netflix, Amazon, and Hulu may be able to introduce other metrics for success, turning, as they say, the control over to the audience, the increased reliance on traditional strategies to determine success do not make for dramatically altered metrics. Rather, they make for a retrenching of traditional business models that prioritize expense, celebrity, and profit.

These are still early days in the overall delivery of online serialized content. There are still methods that can be tested, honed, and copied. There is more currency in audience response than ever before, and Netflix in particular has been at the forefront of developing and perfecting algorithms that assess audience preferences, hoping to truly "give audiences what they want." But as the competition for web series dominance intensifies, the key companies grow increasingly wary of risk, and there is the marked shift to reducing that risk, best achieved through tried-and-true strategies employed for decades by traditional entertainment companies.

Conclusion

The rise of the web series as a standard for industry production has radically altered what television means and which entertainment companies are most secure in the new landscape. In order to maintain the lead, Netflix has first set many of the standards for how streaming video-on-demand would work, and other companies like Amazon joined the fray to upend how audiovisual entertainment reaches audiences.

While Netflix and others have approached the industry with innovative tactics, it is clear that these are not enough to secure a long-term position. In order to maintain their lead, these companies must also incorporate strategies that are inevitably used by traditional entertainment companies, including exploiting intellectual property, expanding global markets, and relying on bankable names and marquee franchises. In order to effectively implement these strategies, the newer companies bring on personnel expertise from traditional entertainment companies. Veteran television executives may perceive their roles as treading new ground for the overall television industry, but the strategies that they have been hired to design and implement tend to replicate the same ones used by their former employers.

The newer companies have moved quickly in order to bolster their position against possible competitors, the most threatening of which would likely be the entertainment behemoths that have generally dominated entertainment for decades. Yet the relatively swift toehold in the industry has been met with relatively slow responses from the more established companies. Disney, for example, just began to develop its own streaming service, slated for launch in 2019, a move that seemed a rather belated response to some of the new guard in the industry (Spangler, 2018).[5]

Where companies like Netflix and Amazon Prime Video stand apart from traditional television is the sheer scope of offerings. Both platforms can host hundreds of series and movies simultaneously; this content is both originally produced as well as licensed, it comes from all over the world, and it is produced by large studios and independent producers. Some of these series have been heralded for giving voice to marginalized populations. Indeed, Amazon and others do have mechanisms for funneling independently produced series into their distribution networks (Amazon Prime Video Direct is one such example). This content is used to expand the platform's range of offerings, and also to identify solidly performing web series that can then be acquired or licensed to maximize profits for the platform. The possibilities engendered by digital technology for the production of independent content are many; however the pipelines for distributing this content run the risk of shrinking because of the intensified focus on the part of major companies to emphasize blockbuster programming. Further research in this area can analyze the role and impact of independent work on these companies.

To remain dominant in the industry as more traditional entertainment powerhouses enter the fray, these (newer) companies find they must resort to the strategies that led traditional companies to become dominant in the first place. No longer can they rely solely on the "power of the people," as it were; the grassroots and unconventional strategies that may have given Netflix its initial lock on the industry are no longer serving the company when its competition now is the behemoths that are finally venturing into this territory. And what we find, then, is that the web series industry and television industry are merging with each other rather than one taking over the other. There is mutual contribution to the growth and primacy of web series as a dominant content format.

Notes

1 *House of Cards*, a Golden Globe and Emmy award winning series, went on hiatus in the middle of its sixth season production in 2017 as star Kevin Spacey was accused of sexual misconduct. The series' final season resumed production in early 2018.
2 As of this writing, Disney's $52.4 billion acquisition of 21st Century Fox still awaits government approval.
3 *The Get Down* and *Sense8* were canceled after one season and two seasons, respectively.
4 Technically Netflix's reach spans all seven continents; someone apparently accessed Netflix in Antarctica to watch *Stranger Things* in 2017. One of the major exceptions to Netflix's reach is its absence in China, a partnership the company continues to pursue.
5 Netflix Chief Content Officer Ted Sarandos commented, "I' don't know what took them so long," with regard to Disney's development of its own streaming service (Spangler, 2018).

References

Andreeva, N. (2018, May 14). Apple's Jamie Erlicht and Zack Van Amburg make moves to shake up SVOD scripted space. *Deadline*. Retrieved from https://deadline.com/2018/05/apple-jamie-erlicht-zack-van-amburg-svod-disruptors-news-1202382963/

Apple. (2017). Jamie Erlicht and Zack Van Amburg joining Apple to lead video programming. *Apple Press Release*. Retrieved from apple.com/newsroom/2017/06/Jamie-erlicht-and-zack-van-amburg-joining-apple-to-lead-video-programming

Balakrishnan, A. (2017). Tim Cook gave a strong hint that Apple will battle Amazon and Netflix in original video. *CNBC*. Retrieved from https://www.cnbc.com/2017/01/31/apple-tim-cook-talks-original-video-content-on-earnings-call.html

Barrett, B. (2016a). Amazon and Netflix look to their own shows as the key to world domination. *Wired Magazine*. Retrieved from https://www.wired.com/2016/12/amazon-netflix-look-shows-key-world-domination/

Barrett, B. (2016b). Netflix just launched in 130 new countries. Like, this morning. *Wired Magazine*. Retrieved from https://www.wired.com/2016/01/netflix-just-launched-in-130-new-countries-like-this-morning/

Barrett, B. (2017a). How Netflix made 'Stranger Things' a global phenomenon. *Wired Magazine*. Retrieved from https://www.wired.com/story/netflix-stranger-things-global/

Barrett, B. (2017b). Want a look at Netflix's future? Follow the anime. *Wired Magazine*. Retrieved from https://www.wired.com/story/netflix-anime/

Bary, E. (2017). Why the Netflix/Amazon debate is already over. *Barrons*. Retrieved from https://www.barrons.com/articles/why-the-netflix-amazon-debate-is-already-over-1491845573

Christian, A. J. (2011). Fandom as industrial response: Producing identity in an independent web series. *Transformative Works and Cultures* 8(1). http://journal.transformativeworks.org/index.php/twc/article/view/250/237

Christian, A. J. (2018). *Open TV: Innovation beyond Hollywood and the rise of web television*. New York: New York University Press.

Constine, J. (2017). Facebook now has 2 billion users…and responsibility. *Tech Crunch*. Retrieved from https://techcrunch.com/2017/06/27/facebook-2-billion-users/

Croteau, D. & Hoynes, W. (2006). *The business of media: Corporate media and the public interest*. Thousand Oaks, CA: Pine Forge Press.

Danker, D. (2017). Introducing Watch, a new platform for shows on Facebook. Facebook Newsroom. Retrieved from https://newsroom.fb.com/news/2017/08/introducing-watch-a-new-platform-for-shows-on-facebook/

Feldman, D. (2018). Netflix has record-breaking fourth quarter in 2017, exceeds $11B in revenue. *Forbes*. Retrieved from https://www.forbes.com/sites/danafeldman/2018/01/22/netflix-has-record-breaking-fourth-quarter-in-2017-exceeds-11b-in-revenue/

Fritz, B. (2012, September 12). Amazon Studios going into comics. *The Los Angeles Times*. http://articles.latimes.com/2012/sep/12/entertainment/la-et-ct-amazon-studios-comic-20120912

Goldberg, L. (2017, November 17). Will Amazon's 'Lord of the Rings' series be TV's most expensive show of all time? *The Hollywood Reporter*. https://www.hollywoodreporter.com/live-feed/will-amazons-lord-rings-series-be-tvs-expensive-show-all-time-1058129

Ha, A. (2018). Hulu reached more than 17M subscribers and $1B in ad revenue last year. *Tech Crunch*. Retrieved from https://techcrunch.com/2018/01/09/hulu-17m-subscribers/

Jenner, M. (2014). Is this TVIV? Netflix, TVIII and binge-watching. *New Media & Society* 18(2), pp. 257–273.

Keating, G. (2012). *Netflixed: The epic battle for America's eyeballs*. New York: Penguin.

Kharpal, A. (2017). Apple could launch video streaming to rival Netflix while Facebook could do pay-per-view analysts predict. *CNBC*. Retrieved from https://www.cnbc.com/2017/11/15/apple-launch-video-streaming-service-rival-netflix-2018-csi-insight.html

Kim, J. (2012). The institutionalization of YouTube: From user-generated content to professionally generated content. *Media, Culture and Society* 34(1), pp. 53–67.

Koblin, J. (2018, June 1). Hello, you must be going: Hulu parts with a top executive. *The New York Times*. Retrieved from https://www.nytimes.com/2018/06/01/business/media/hulu-executive-joel-stillerman.html

Littleton, C. & Holloway, D. (2017). Jeff Bezos mandates programming shift at Amazon Studios. *Variety*. Retrieved from http://variety.com/2017/tv/news/amazon-studios-jeff-bezos-roy-price-zelda-1202552532/

Lovelace, B. (2017). If YouTube were a stock, it would be worth $75 billion, says leading Google analyst. *CNBC*. Retrieved from https://www.cnbc.com/2017/07/25/top-google-analyst-says-youtube-is-worth-75-billion.html

Lynch, J. (2017). Meet the YouTube millionaires: These are the highest paid YouTube stars of 2017. *Business Insider*. Retrieved from http://www.businessinsider.com/highest-paid-youtube-stars-2017-12

Lynley, M. (2017). Apple taps $900B after a blowout fourth quarter. *Tech Crunch*. Retrieved from https://techcrunch.com/2017/11/02/apple-briefly-taps-900b-after-a-blowout-fourth-quarter

McDonald, K. (2013). Digital dreams in a material world: The rise of Netflix and its impact on changing distribution and exhibition patterns. *Jumpcut 55.* http://ejumpcut.org/archive/jc55.2013/McDonaldNetflix/index.html

McLeod, M. (2017). Crowdfunding the web series: A case study in the political economy of new media and the production of a fan following. *The International Journal of the Image* 8(1), pp. 71–79.

Monaghan, W. (2017). *Starting From … Now* and the web series to television crossover: An online revolution? *Media International Australia* 164(1), pp. 82–91.

Moore, C. (2013). Distribution is queen: LGBTQ media on demand. *Cinema Journal* 53, pp. 137–144.

Morreale, J. (2014). From homemade to store bought: Annoying Orange and the professionalization of YouTube. *Journal of Consumer Culture* 14(1), pp. 113–128.

Number of Netflix streaming subscribers worldwide from 3rd quarter 2011 to 1st quarter 2018 (in millions). (2018). *Statista.* Retrieved from https://www.statista.com/statistics/250934/quarterly-number-of-netflix-streaming-subscribers-worldwide/

Peirce, M. (2010). Remediation theory: Analyzing what made *Quarterlife* successful as an online series and not a television series. *Television and New Media* 12(4), pp. 314–325.

Rawson, J. (2014, Sept. 12). The web series is dying – and Netflix and Amazon Prime are responsible. *The Guardian.* Retrieved from https://www.theguardian.com/tv-and-radio/tvandradioblog/2014/sep/12/the-web-series-is-dying-and-netflix-and-amazon-prime-are-responsible

Rodriguez, A. (2018, March 30). Netflix is learning how in the world to play the franchise game with Carmen Sandiego. *Quartz.* Retrieved from https://qz.com/1240867/netflix-is-engineering-a-true-franchise-with-carmen-sandiego/

Ryan, M. (2017). TV review: Apple's 'Planet of the Apps.' *Variety.* Retrieved from http://variety.com/2017/tv/reviews/planet-of-the-apps-apple-gwyneth-paltrow-jessica-alba-1202456477/

Schneider, M. (2018). YouTube's Susanne Daniels on how 'Cobra Kai' signals its evolution. *Indiewire.* Retrieved from http://www.indiewire.com/2018/04/youtube-red-originals-cobra-kai-susanne-daniels-1201958204/

Segarra-Saavedra, J., Tur-Viñes, V., Campos-Domínguez, E., & del-Pino-Romero, C. (2017). Branded web-series as an advertising strategy. The #EncuentraTuLugar case. *Revista Latina de Comunicación Social* 72, pp. 883–896. http://www.revistalatinacs.org/072paper/1198/48en.html

Siegel, T. (2018, April 5). Inside Amazon's $250M 'Lord of the Rings' deal: "It's very much a creature of the times." *The Hollywood Reporter.* Retrieved from https://www.hollywoodreporter.com/live-feed/how-lord-rings-tv-series-landed-at-amazon-not-netflix-1099213

Smith, M. D. & Telang, R. (2016). *Streaming, sharing, stealing: Big data and the future of entertainment.* Cambridge: MIT Press.

Spangler, T. (2017). Facebook wants tons of original shows – But it doesn't want to buy them. *Variety.* Retrieved from http://variety.com/2017/digital/news/facebook-watch-original-shows-content-strategy-funding-1202522193/

Spangler, T. (2018, May 14). Netflix content chief says 85% of new spending is on originals. *Variety*. https://variety.com/2018/digital/news/netflix-original-spending-85-percent-1202809623

Spangler, T. & Setoodeh, R. (2014, April 30). Filmmakers moving where the money is. *Variety*. Retrieved from http://variety.com/2014/digital/news/film-directors-find-its-easier-to-sell-series-than-movies-to-digital-buyers-1201166915/

Sydell, L. (2015). What happens when the price of free goes up? YouTube is about to find out. *Hawaii Public Radio*. Retrieved from http://hawaiipublicradio.org/post/what-happens-when-price-free-goes-youtubes-about-find-out

Tryon, C. (2015). TV got better: Netflix's original programming strategies and binge viewing. *Media Industries Journal* 2(2). https://quod.lib.umich.edu/m/mij/15031809.0002.206/--tv-got-better-netflixs-original-programming-strategies?rgn=main;view=fulltext

Wasko, J. (2003). *How Hollywood works*. London: Sage.

Wasko, J. & Erickson, M. (2009). The political economy of YouTube. In P. Snickars and P. Vonderau (Eds.), *The YouTube Reader*. Stockholm: National Library of Sweden.

Wayne, M. L. (2018). Netflix, Amazon and branded television content in subscription video on-demand portals. *Media, Culture & Society* 40(5), pp. 725–741.

Yarow, J. (2014). Adam Sandler signs an exclusive 4-movie deal with Netflix because 'it rhymes with wet chicks'. *Business Insider*. Retrieved from http://www.businessinsider.com/netflix-signs-adam-sandler-to-a-4-year-movie-deal-2014-10

Zboralska, E. & Davis, C. (2017). Transnational over-the-top video distribution as a business and policy disruptor: The case of Netflix in Canada. *Journal of Media Innovations* 4(1), pp. 4–25.

8 State Monopoly of Telecommunications in Ethiopia

Revisiting Natural Monopoly in the Era of Deregulation

Téwodros W. Workneh and H. Leslie Steeves

This chapter uses the case of Ethiopia to illuminate a question frequently raised in contemporary political economy of media and media globalization scholarship: what is – or could be – the role of the state as media and other markets globalize? Media and communications are major industries and also constitute key components of marketization processes. As the role of the state has been increasingly questioned, we find it valuable to carefully consider relations among multiple sites of power – media, state, and economic – in our research, particularly in outlier instances such as Ethiopia, where state power remains exceptionally strong. Furthermore, we believe that political economy of media analyses must be deeply historical in order to comprehensively address the economic, political, and cultural nuances that lead to each unique outcome.

In this chapter, we first review current debates on the role of the state as globalization expands and on telecommunications as a *natural monopoly* best governed by the state in order to ensure universal service. Next, we present our methodology and map out the historical evolution of the state-owned telecommunication enterprise Ethio-Telecom – the oldest Public Telecommunications Operator (PTO) in Africa. Through document analysis involving close examination of recently declassified financial agreement documents, institutional reports, and policy papers, our chapter chronicles the institutional history of telecommunications in Ethiopia against a backdrop of the tenets of the propositions of natural monopoly. In doing so, it highlights processes and stakeholders involved in state-sponsored telecommunications infrastructure development from 1894 to the present day, with emphasis on the role of the World Bank and, more recently, China.

The Nation-State and Globalization

Numerous scholars have discussed and debated the significance of the nation-state in today's rapidly concentrating global economy (Bullard, 1997; Greenfeld, 2011; Gritsch, 2005; Hankiss, 1999; Miller & Lawrence, 2001; Wasko & Erickson, 2008; Wasko, 2014; Wasko, Murdock &

Sousa, 2011). In his influential *Foreign Affairs* article "Will the Nation-State Survive Globalization?," Wolf (2001) argues that neither distance nor national borders impede economic transactions. He explores the spillover effects of market forces, both predatory and benign, and asks whether governments have become weaker and less relevant.

While many contest Wolf's conclusion, arguing that the nation-state's growing irrelevance is a far-stretched proposition, there is a sense of common understanding that today's global economy has undermined – or at least complicated – traditional notions of sovereignty and autonomy. Today, transnational corporations relentlessly seek to acquire any remaining untapped global markets. Regional economic integrations are commonplace, as evidenced by the likes of the European Union (EU) in Europe, the North American Free Trade Agreement (NAFTA) in North America (now USMCA), and the Economic Community of West African States (ECOWAS) in Africa. Local trade regulations are growingly becoming subordinate to international trade standards set by the likes of the World Trade Organization (WTO).

While the tide of economic globalization may disrupt traditional structures of governance in politically and economically fragile countries in the developing world, the demise of the nation-state is exaggerated. The Horn of Africa nation of Ethiopia, despite its substantial weaker economic position, offers a compelling case on how nation-states have withstood relentless pressures to, per neoliberal directives, privatize/liberalize major pillars of their economies such as telecommunications.

Inevitably, economic policies, especially in developing countries, are rooted in development discourse. The tensions between the interventionist policies of the Ethiopian government and the free market doctrines of the World Bank (and later the International Monetary Fund), for example, are best illustrated by the suspension of financing by the latter over the reluctance of the Ethiopian government to deregulate the telecommunications sector. The Ethiopian state rationalizes its refusal to liberalize telecommunications by arguing that this sector constitutes a vital driver of not only economic development, but also *equitable* growth. Central to this argument is that the notions of universal access and universal service in telecommunications are critical to collective economic development. Market forces, state officials argue, by virtue of their profit-driven ethos, will only seek the affluent and the privileged, marginalizing and further disenfranchising the poor (Workneh, 2016). Significantly, though not explored in this chapter, Ethiopia's rhetoric of universal access generally considers economic class only and seldom other related divides that could further disadvantage citizens such as gender, ethnicity, age, and religion (for example, see Steeves & Wasko, 2001).

The Ethiopian state's hard line on state monopoly of telecommunications is particularly compelling, given the sector's global metamorphosis from a state-controlled organ to private enterprise in the last three decades. Until the latter part of the 20th century, telecommunications was generally considered a natural monopoly with the state as the only capable entity to govern critical infrastructure. However, widespread privatization and liberalization policies that accompanied neoliberal shifts in the United States and Britain changed this line of thinking. The subsequent adoption of legislation like the Telecommunications Act of 1996 in the United States that "let anyone enter any communications business" and "let any communications business compete in any market against any other" opened the telecommunication market for private ownership (Federal Communications Commission, 1996). As with other neoliberal policies, these trends in the global north had a significant influence on telecommunications governance elsewhere. A rare exception to this practice, Ethiopia's telecommunications industry is characterized by a vertically integrated market run by a state-owned enterprise outside the realm of competition.

Natrual Monopoly, Universal Access, and Universal Service

A monopoly represents a condition where all sales in a given industry or market are dominated by a single firm or service provider. A natural monopoly is a characteristic of an industry or market where it is believed the presence of a single firm is more efficient, since it involves the lowest production costs. Baumol (1977), one of the pioneers in the modern theorization of natural monopoly, defines the concept as a condition that exists when "an industry in which multiform production is costlier than production by a monopoly" (p. 810). Traditionally, natural monopolies have occurred when there was a need for a vast bedrock infrastructure to start a business operation (Liebowitz & Margolis, 1998). Put simply, a natural monopoly emerges when competition involving multiple producers causes higher prices for consumers. As a result, some sectors, including transportation, communication, and postal networks, have historically been singled out by economists to operate more efficiently via natural monopoly arrangements. Competition may result in duplicative facilities that in turn could drive prices up as participating firms attempt to recover their investments. For this reason, these sectors have historically enjoyed special privileges and protections to become government franchise industries with the aim of reducing long-term costs.

Early scholarship associated natural monopoly with a sole service provider or a business operator. Such monopolistic industry design is not a result of deliberate enforcement by regulation; rather, these industries emerge because of limited resources such as talent and location (Mosca, 2008). In this sense, a natural monopoly "does not refer to the actual number of sellers in a market but to the relationship between demand and the technology of supply" (Posner, 1969, p. 548). However, Carlton and Perloff (2004) argue, "when total production costs would rise if two or more firms produced instead of one, the single firm in a market is called a 'natural monopoly'" (p. 104). Natural monopolies are also associated with supply-demand characteristics, where the product or service supplied must be essential; the products must be non-storable; and the supplier must have a favorable production location (Sharkey, 1982).

The neoliberal critique of natural monopoly dismisses the notion as counterproductive to free market ideals. As Rothbard (2006, p. 93) highlights, "any designation of a few industries as 'public utilities' is completely arbitrary and unjustified." This is consistent with proponents of market fundamentalism who see the notion of universal access/service – a commonly cited rationale by government-controlled natural monopolies – through state intervention detrimental to innovation in telecommunications. They argue that markets can and should *take care* of access concerns, and that "market failures" do not exist. Market fundamentalists argue deregulation and consequent competition will solve problems of access (Faulhaber, 1997; Pilati, 1999). Others contend that market failures exist, but they contend intervention is not the answer (Hart, 1998; Neu & Scanlan, 2000; Shuler, 1999; Xavier, 1997). Intervention, they suggest, alters technological neutrality and slows down innovation. As Faulhaber (1997) remarks, innovation would be hampered should "the invisible hand of the market be replaced (whether intended or not) by the visible one of the government" (p. 5). According to Garnham (1997):

> Such an acceleration [of universal service] is likely to lead simply to highly inefficient patterns of investment with a large amount of fixed plant earning unacceptably low rates of return; the result of this will either delay long-term network development and traffic growth, by asking existing subscribers to pay more than they otherwise would for this excess capacity, or by diverting tax revenue from where it could be spent more efficiently.
>
> (p. 211)

Conversely, protagonists of universal service recognize the reality of market failures and argue for intervention, justifying state-sanctioned natural monopolies. "Latent" proponents of universal service admit the need for public intervention, although they also argue that intervention should be minimalized. This bloc advocates for restricted universal service obligations that are explicitly focused on solving identified problems (Gillett, 1994; MacKie-Mason, 1998; Mansell & Steinmueller, 1996; Murroni, 1997; Noam, 1993; Wolak 1996). "Manifest" proponents of universal service view telecommunications as a public or merit good. Consequently, intervention is justified to distribute telecommunication services optimally for all (Burgelman, 1996; Gómez Sáenz de Hermúa, 2000; Hadden & Lenert, 1995; Parker, 2000; Shields et al., 1993). A third group, universal access/service "fundamentalists," proposes strong equity arguments and essentially perceive access to telecommunications service as a right. For this group, calculations in cost and pure economic efficiency are marginal priorities. They contend government has the obligation to provide the service to everyone, regardless of any economic or even technological considerations (Bar & Munk Riis, 1997; De Reuck & Joseph, 1999; Forestier, Grace, & Kenny, 2002; Latzer, 2000).

Methodological Considerations

We approach this study via the analysis of historical documents. Specifically, in attempting to interrogate a century of state monopoly of telecommunications in Ethiopia, this chapter relies on document analysis of secondary resources. World Bank documents were especially useful, as the World Bank was the most important actor in financing Ethiopian telecommunication development prior to the 1990s. Access to these documents was partially made possible by the Bank's implementation of a new Open Access policy, effective July 1, 2012.[1] We focused on the more comprehensive and rich "Documents and Reports" section of the World Bank database, which holds more than 145,000 documents online. The preliminary search of relevant documents was conducted with the key words "Ethiopia" and "telecommunication." The search yielded 164 results. This was followed by a manual survey of the contents of each document. In the end, 15 documents produced between 1951 and 1993 were selected for careful examination based on their direct concern over the Ethiopian telecommunications sector. These documents mainly included project appraisal and credit recommendation reports.

Although state control of telecommunications in Ethiopia has historically been justified along natural monopoly narratives, the current rationale in continuing this practice is largely attributed to policy (Workneh, 2018). In other words, the state monopoly of telecommunications today is directly related to the political program and the economic policies of the ruling party of Ethiopia for the past 27 years, the Ethiopian People's Revolutionary Democratic Front (EPRDF). Subsequently, in addition to World Bank documents, Poverty Reduction Strategy Papers (PRSPs)[2] and the Growth and Transformation Plan (GTP) of the Federal Democratic Republic of Ethiopia (FDRE) are considered for analysis.

Historicizing State Monopoly of Telecommunications in Ethiopia

The IBRD and IDA Years (1958–1992)

Although the origin of telecommunications in Ethiopia dates to 1894, it wasn't until the Imperial Board of Telecommunications of Ethiopia (IBTE) was established in October 1952 that major structural reforms were put in place in response to the growing demand of communication infrastructure. A key player in IBTE's expansion scheme was the International Bank for Reconstruction & Development (IBRD), which provided the financial impetus. After the completion in 1956 of the reconstruction and expansion project mostly financed by IBRD, IBTE continued to add new facilities out of retained earnings. However, it was soon realized that the demand for IBTE's services caught up with capacity. It was estimated that between 1962 and 1965, the demand for telephone and telegraph services from IBTE would increase by 10% and 9%, respectively, a burgeoning market the sector couldn't accommodate (IBRD, 1962). In addition to the demand-supply problem, the services provided by the IBTE were suffering from frequent interruptions. The urban, interurban, and international telephone and radio-telephone services experienced increased outages due to rainy seasons, maintenance problems, and strong atmospheric static over the eastern Africa region (IBRD, 1962).

As a result, the Ethiopian government launched the Second Telecommunications Project of 1962–1964. IBTE, by now endowed with the authority to negotiate and secure loans independently,[3] approached IBRD for a loan of about $ 2.9 million to cover most of the foreign exchange cost (IBRD, 1965a). Upon approval of the loan, the project aimed to upgrade the existing capacity of IBTE for urban telephone, interurban telephone, and telegraph services. When combined with other costs in land, buildings, broadcasting services, vehicles, and tools, the total cost of the project was estimated at $6.244 million (IBRD, 1965b).

In 1965 negotiations between the Ethiopian government and IBRD began in Washington, D.C., for a loan of $5.6 million to finance the Third Telecommunications Project (1965–1967) of the IBTE, although, in the end, Ethiopia settled for $4.8 million (IBRD, 1965a). Between 1962 and 1965, demand for IBTE's services accelerated by 19% per annum, which is more than double earlier estimates of 9%. In fact, the ratio of 0.07 telephones per 100 people was one of the lowest compared to other African countries at the time (IBRD, 1965b).[4] To respond to this demand, the Third Telecommunications Project aimed to install 13,200 additional lines of new automatic exchange equipment, about 10,000 by the financial arrangement made between IBTE and Swedish telecom company Telefonaktiebolaget LM Ericsson (IBRD, 1965b).

One of the conditions set by IBRD in this and the previous loans was for IBTE to hire expatriates for key managerial and technical positions. As a result, it was agreed that the Swedish Telephone and Telegraph Administration should continue supplying personnel to IBTE. The positions of General Manager, Network Planning Advisor, Transport & Workshop Advisor, and other key positions were held by Swedish and Norwegian nationals (IBRD, 1965b).

The Fourth Telecommunications Project aimed to increase the capacity of the urban telephone lines by 29,000, and expand long-distance communication facilities that included installation of microwave and very high frequency (VHF) systems and automatic trunk exchanges. Telegraph, telex, and international communication facilities were also part of the expansion program (IBRD, 1965a). Even with this expansion rate, the proposed program would only satisfy demand for services in line with a growth rate of 12% a year, a rather conservative figure compared to the actual growth rate of 17% that was registered between 1960 and 1965 (IBRD, 1965a). When the Fourth Telecommunications Project was completed, 343 cities and towns were connected through IBTE's telephone network. Total subscriptions for telephone and telex reached 47,263 and 271, respectively, and the number of telephone sets totaled 63,689 (Tsigie & Feyissa, 1999).

It was not long before IBTE approached IBRD and its member institution, the International Development Association (IDA), for what would become the Fifth Telecommunications Project (1974–1978). What was unique about this program compared to the previous projects was its separation into two overlapping phases – the first between 1974 and 1977 and the second between 1975 and 1978 – due to "shortage of IDA resources" (IDA, 1973, p. 10). IBTE was confident of its creditworthiness, given its increase in its share capital from $8 million to $16 million between 1967 and 1973 (IDA, 1973).[5] The cost of the first phase of the project, $37.1 million, was once again split between IBTE and IBRD. From the total, IDA supplied $21.4 million (58%) to cover the foreign exchange requirement exclusive of certain facilities worth $1.4 million, which IBTE has already contracted to other vendors. The remaining 42% of the financing came from internal sources (IDA, 1973). The Fifth Telecommunications Project included the addition of 39,800 automatic and 4,500 manual exchange lines, four new microwave systems, expansion of the telex network, and, for the first time in the history of telecommunications in Ethiopia, an earth satellite station that boosted capacity in international communication (IDA, 1973). With the exception of the satellite station, IBTE was in charge of all facets of the project, including preparation of bidding documents, bid evaluation, and engineering.

Administratively, one of the loan conditions between IBTE and the Bank involved the organizational restructuring of IBTE, especially in the areas of planning and accounting. To this end, on November 1, 1972, IBTE appointed a Manager of Planning reporting directly to the General Manager. The Bank was insistent on the transfer of planning staff in the Engineering Department to the newly established office of the Manager of Planning. This remained a point of contention between IBTE and the Bank for some time, as the latter constantly declared its dissatisfaction with the understaffing of the newly appointed planning position (IBRD, 1973; IDA, 1973, 1975a, 1975b).

Between 1973 and 1975, the Fifth Telecommunications Project had lapses in effective execution because of a series of political instabilities in the Ethiopian Empire and popular uprisings across the country. After a period of civil unrest, the Emperor was removed from his position in 1974 and was replaced by the Provisional Military Administrative Council (PMAC), or simply referred to as *Derg*. The monarchy was formally abolished in May 1975, and Marxism-Leninism was proclaimed the ideology of the state. This was followed on January 1, 1975, by a decree that nationalized the financial sector, including banks, insurance companies, and savings associations. Similar measures were taken against manufacturing and distributing firms that were privately owned by Ethiopians and foreign nationals (IDA, 1975a). Imperial names of public institutions were soon revised consistent with the new order. As a result, the Imperial Board of Telecommunications of Ethiopia was provisionally renamed Board of Telecommunications of Ethiopia (BTE) by the PMAC (IDA, 1975a).

The credit for the first phase of the project became effective on August 1974, approximately six months behind schedule due to a six-month delay caused by labor disturbances. Although political stability was yet to be realized, the transition didn't seriously affect the official business of the government. The civilian cabinet and the Ethiopian bureaucracy continued to function reasonably well allowing ongoing development projects to resume with acceptable efficiency (IDA, 1975b). In the meantime, BTE remained a government-owned commercial corporation under the auspices of the Ministry of Communications. Despite changing political and economic developments of Ethiopia that were frowned on by international financial institutions, the IDA declared its satisfaction "that the project is still of a high priority and is economically, technically and financially justified in the changed circumstances" (IDA, 1975b, p. 12).

The 1974 revolution brought significant challenges to the Ethiopian Telecommunications Authority (ETA).[6] A significant number of senior staff left, causing setbacks in technological development and operational efficiency. As a result, ETA was busy filling its vacant positions for the next six years. This meant less priority for infrastructure development and network expansion in a company that barely kept up with demand. Moreover, the tenacity with which the PMAC executed extreme socialist reforms in nationalizing manufacturing companies and banks previously owned privately was not popular with the World Bank. This affected the Ethiopian telecommunications sector significantly, as its momentum in expanding to meet increased demand was held back by at least five years because of loan delays to the Sixth Telecommunications Project (1984–1988). This was evident when ETA, upon preparing a telecommunications development program for the period 1981/1982–1985/1986, found out IDA rejected its credit application on June 30, 1981 (World Bank, 1984a). IDA's reluctance to fund the project was a hard blow to ETA because it scared off other potential sources of financing. The disruption of the expansion project, although provisional, had enduring costs to the Ethiopian telecommunications sector, as ETA was left behind during a time of rapidly changing technology, computerization, and service diversification globally.

Although PMAC identified the expansion of the telecommunications sector as a priority in its economic program, unrelenting internal and external factors left little room for undeterred development to occur. Externally, PMAC's political and economic ideology was unpopular with Western lenders, limiting loan possibilities and tightening conditions. Furthermore, Ethiopia was dragged into a costly war with neighboring Somalia when the latter invaded the southeastern part of the country in July 1977. Internally, immediately after the war against Somalia, the *Derg* was engaged in a brutal fighting against ethno-nationalist groups, including the Eritrean People's Liberation Front (EPLF) and the Tigrayan Peoples' Liberation Front (TPLF), and other groups that ranged from the conservative and pro-monarchy Ethiopian Democratic Union (EDU) to the far leftist Ethiopian People's Revolutionary Party (EPRP) (Bahru, 2002).

When seen against this backdrop of political and economic instability, ETA's challenges in performance optimization were unsurprising. Regardless, attempts were made to reinvigorate ETA to overcome its financial, institutional, and operational problems. Structurally, ETA retained its share company façade, though it was fully owned by the government and established by proclamation. Like its predecessor, ETA was administered by a Board of Directors (World Bank, 1984b). The Board of Directors, nominated by the government, had the Minister of Transport and Communication (MOTC) as its *ex officio* chairman.

After its initial attempt in 1981 to finance its Sixth Telecommunications Project was rejected by IDA, PMAC's second revised loan application was accepted in 1983 with the understanding that the implementation period would fall between 1984 and 1988 (World Bank, 1984a). The loan negotiations for the Sixth Telecommunications Project were long and complicated as they involved multiple stakeholders, including PMAC, IDA, the African Development Bank (AfDB), the Government of Italy, and the Government of Sweden. In the end, it was agreed that the cost of the project, $151.8 million, would be covered by a parallel cofinancing to the amount of $40 million from IDA, $25 million from the government of Italy, $12 million from the Government of Sweden, and $ 26.4 million from the AfDB. The remaining $48.4 million, the majority of the financing (31.9%), was covered by ETA's internal coffers (World Bank, 1984a, 1984b). The average 12% annual interest of the loans was very high – more than two times of the previous loans – which probably is an indication of how PMAC was limited and cornered in its financial options, particularly at a time when the country was facing severe foreign currency shortages.

Consolidation of a State Monopoly and the Localization of Financing (1992–2009)

The 1980s and 1990s saw the majority of telecommunication operators across the developed world embracing liberalization and privatization. The divestiture of AT&T in the United States, the privatization of Nippon Telegraph and Telephone (NTT) in Japan, and British Telecommunications (BT) in the United Kingdom in 1984 signaled the end of the global telecommunication sector as a natural monopoly (Abbott & Brady, 1999). By the early 1980s British and American governments, joined by large segments of the media and Hayekian intelligentsia, declared that free markets could do nearly everything better than government, leading to the popularity of deregulation and privatization as the flagship ethos of the Organization for Economic Co-operation and Development (OECD) states and global financial institutions (Comor, 1994). More importantly, the fate of global telecommunications as a private entity was sealed when 69 members of the WTO signed an agreement on February 15, 1997, to provide market access to their basic telecommunications services. The WTO Agreement on Telecommunications Service became the first global pact on the deregulation of basic telecommunications service. At the time, the countries that signed the agreement accounted for about 93% of the global market in basic telecommunications service (Forestier, Grace, & Kenny, 2002).

These new developments in the global economy in general and in the telecommunications sector in particular made deregulation the cornerstone of loan conditions. This was a challenging proposition for EPRDF, the ruling party of FDRE since 1991, given its unwavering insistence on consolidating state monopoly of the telecom sector and fending off external and internal pushes toward deregulation. Consequently, it became apparent that traditional financial sources like the World Bank were reluctant to provide loans to Ethiopia as long as it insisted on state monopoly of the telecom sector. It was partly because of this ideological tension between the Ethiopian government and Western financial institutions that the Seventh Telecommunications Project was rescheduled for implementation between 1992/1993 and 1996/1997 from its original plan of implementation between 1990 and 1994.

The initial cost of the Seventh Telecommunications Project was estimated at $250 million, a figure that far exceeded any of the prior six telecommunication projects (Table 8.1). From this amount, ETA was looking to secure the foreign exchange component of the investment ($170 million) from external sources. Despite several attempts, ETA's effort for favorable terms and conditions for loans fell short. until it finally obtained $64 million from the AfDB (AfDB, 2006). However, this was still an amount that fell short of ETA's plans. Eventually, both AfDB and the World Bank ceased financing the Ethiopian telecommunications

Table 8.1 Summary of all telecommunication expansion projects until 1993

Project	Year of loan approval	Total cost	Internal financing	External Loan	Lender	Status	Closure date
First Telecommunications Project	1951	1.5		1.5	IBRD	Completed	12/31/56
Second Telecommunications Project	1962	6.24	3.34	2.9	IBRD	Completed	12/31/65
Third Telecommunications Project	1965	10.8	3.5	4.8 1.6 09	IBRD USAID L.M. Ericsson	Completed	12/31/69
Fourth Telecommunications Project	1969	25		4.5 4.5 1.1 2.8	IBRD SIDA L.M. Ericsson IBRD	Completed	12/31/79
Fifth Telecommunications Project	1974 (Phase I) 1975 (Phase II)	60.6		17.4 16.0	IDA IDA	Completed Completed	06/30/81 06/30/83
Sixth Telecommunications Project	1984	151.8	48.4	40.0 25.0 12.0 26.4	IDA Italy Sweden AfDB	Completed	06/30/88

Adapted from International Bank for Reconstruction & Development (1962, 1965a, 1965b, 1969a, 1969b, 1973); International Development (1973, 1975a, 1975b); World Bank (1984a, 1984b, 1993).

sector, forcing the Government of Ethiopia (GoE) to look internally for funds, mostly through credit from commercial banks and selling bonds. Between 2004 and 2005 alone, the sector raised $615 million through the sale of bonds (AfDB, 2006).

In the meantime, the EPRDF-led government found it necessary to restructure ETA to separate regulatory branches from operational entities. Accordingly, two separate bodies, the ETA and the Ethiopian Telecommunications Corporation (ETC), were established by Proclamation No. 49/1996 on November 1996 (ETC, 2009). The separation of regulatory and operational activities was consistent with international trends in telecommunications management structure, as the number of independent regulators increased dramatically from 13 in 1990 to 140 in 2005. Established under the then Ministry of Transport and Communications, the new ETA was tasked "to ensure the implementation of government policy, to create a conducive atmosphere for private investment in the telecom sector as well as to set standards for services and types of communication equipment-imported, assembled or locally" (ETC, 2009, p. 23).

Upon its establishment in 2002, ETA granted ETC monopoly rights that provided the latter with fixed-line, mobile, Internet, and data communications services and related training services. Audited by the Audit Services Corporation (ASC), ETC as a state-owned company had management autonomy, a separate legal personality, a supervising authority, and a management board (ETC, 2009). Its responsibilities included design of the telecommunications network, procurement of telecommunications equipment, construction, installation, and maintenance of the equipment and provision of telecommunications services to the public (ETC, 2009).

In previous years, the Ethiopian government's investment on telecommunications infrastructure had been increasing steadily, to the extent that it comprised nearly 10% of the country's GDP. The majority of ETC's investment went to fixed wireless and mobile network infrastructure, including third-generation (3G) mobile technology as well as a national fiber optic backbone. ETC streamlined its development strategy with the Plan for Accelerated and Sustained Development to End Poverty (PASDEP) that served as FDRE's guiding strategic framework for the five-year period 2005/2006–2009/2010. PASDEP defined the nation's overall strategy for development during the course of the five years. The PASDEP program aimed to reinforce telecommunications development propositions laid out by the previous Sustainable Development and Poverty Reduction Program (SDPRP), including: the provision of broadband, multimedia, and Internet services; laying underground fiber optics cables covering extensive areas; conversion of hand-operated, semi-automatic telecommunication centers into digital systems; undertaking preliminary preparations to implement rural telecommunication expansion projects; extending telephone services at the *qäbäle*[7] level; major expansion of telephone coverage, from about 400,000 lines at the beginning of SDPRP to over 1 million by the end of 2004/2005; reductions in the cost of international calls and of Internet connections; and corporate reforms of Ethiopian Telecommunication Corporation (ETC) to increase efficiency (MoFED, 2006).

PASDEP aspired to deploy "a world-class backbone and connectivity network" that included a full digitized national transmission microwave and switching system; 4,000 km of fiber along the major national route and 122+ interconnecting stations; 1,200+ broadband Very Small Aperture Terminal (VSAT) nationwide; a broadband multimedia Internet Protocol/Multi Protocol Label Switching (IP/MPLS) core network nationwide; a broadband Internet network with points of presence nationwide; and wireless Code Division Multiple Access (CDMA) to 5,000 rural villages (MoFED, 2006, p. 41).

The operationalization of PASDEP's proposal was mainly carried out through a vendor credit agreement the GoE signed with Chinese telecom provider and infrastructure development giant ZTE in 2007 to the amount of $1.5 billion. The ZTE project resulted in the rollout of 10,000 km backbone fiber optics cable across the country, enabling successful deployment programs like SchoolNet and WoredaNet. The project also created a mobile network capacity of over 30 million subscribers and a CDMA wireless network covering rural areas (MoFED, 2006).

While SDPRP had outlined and executed some lofty schemes in the infrastructure development of ICTs, particularly in laying a nationwide backbone of fiber optics, coverage of telecommunications in Ethiopia was still among the lowest in the world, with approximately five lines per 1,000 persons, and 87% of the rural population living more than 5 km from the nearest telephone service facility by 2006 (MoFED, 2006). PASDEP's end goal was to increase fixed telephone subscribers from 620,000 to over 3.23 million, cellular mobile subscribers from about 410,000 to over 6.76 million, and Internet connectivity from 17,000 to 0.193 million. It also aspired for the percentage of population with access to telecommunications within 5 km to reach 100% (MoFED, 2006).

Rebranding, Outsourcing, and the Chinese Influx (2010–Present)

With the expiration of the PASDEP in 2010, the GoE introduced the GTP that set the nation's economic and development agenda between 2010 and 2015. The GTP included a lofty communication infrastructure development program that aimed to intensify the need-based network expansion work and increase the rural universal telecommunication access program. In addition, the GTP aimed at improving and maintaining the quality of fixed line, mobile phone, Internet, and data service provision. Finally, it laid the framework for a conducive environment for using the latest telecommunication technologies, for fair and economical utilization of national frequencies, telecommunication numbers and IP addresses, and for increasing the revenue from these services (MoFED, 2010).

In order to execute the GTP's telecommunications infrastructure schemes, GoE found it crucial to revamp ETC administratively, operationally, and structurally. In November 2010, Ethio-Telecom was established under Proclamation 197/2010 under the Council of Ministers with a capital investment of 40 billion Ethiopian Birr (ETB).[8]

Today Ethio-Telecom has the monopoly over fixed, mobile, Internet, and Value Added Services (VAS) like Domain Name registration and distribution over .et country code top-level domain (ccTLD),[9] the Domain Name System, Web hosting, and Internet Protocol Address Service (Ministry of Communication, n.d.). It offers dial-up Internet, CDMA 2000 wireless Internet, Asymmetric digital subscriber line (ADSL), and wireless Internet using AIRONET, VSAT, and Enhanced Voice-Data Optimized (EVDO). Only a few facets of Ethio-Telecom are available for private sector participation like the resale of airtime vouchers and Internet services through cyber cafés. Since the establishment of Ethio-Telecom, mobile telecommunications subscribers surged from 1.2 million to 23.7 million between 2007 and 2013. According to the Ministry of Communication and Information Technology (MCIT), voice communication geographic coverage has reached 64% with the fixed telecommunciation network comprising 790,188 subscribers, a figure that represents 1% of the population (MCIT, n.d.).

Administratively, Ethio-Telecom's management was outsourced to France Telecom-Orange for a two-year contract in 2010 for a fee of $ 40 million. Under France Telecom's management between 2010 and 2012, Ethio-Telecom's customer base reached 18.28 million subscribers, nearly a 60% increase from 2010 (Abiye, 2013). Mobile services, which constituted the vast majority of the customer base, passed the 20 million mark and fixed line numbers reached 805,000 – 81.4% of the projected performance target.

Financially, Ethio-Telecom's overall gross revenues by the end of France Telecom's tenure reached $ 690 million, with two-thirds coming from mobile services. This accounted for 70% of the $980 million of the target set in the agreement between France Telecom and GoE. By the end of 2012, Ethio-Telecom's net profits, the money actually earned after taxes and other fees, amounted to $ 495 million, a profit margin that fell short of the $600 million they hoped to net (Yewondwossen, 2012). Almost one-quarter (22.4%) of Ethio-Telecom's profits came from international traffic, with the rest primarily coming from fixed telephone lines. France Telecom's contract, which had a potential to be extended if certain goals were met, was not renewed after MCIT announced the former's tenure would end on December 13 and Ethiopian staff would take over the management of the state-owned monopoly (Yewondwossen, 2012).

In 2013 Ethio-Telecom made a landmark agreement between Chinese telecom giants Huawei and ZTE for a nationwide telecommunications infrustructure development, with a $1.6 billion vendor credit arrangement involving the EXIM Bank of China (Essa, 2013).

Conclusion

This chapter explored the historical development of the Ethiopian telecommunications sector from the introduction of the first telephone apparatus in 1894 to the present day. We emphasized major telecommunication infrastructure development projects between 1952 and 1992 that were made possible by financial arrangements secured with the IBRD, IDA, and the World Bank. With the Ethiopian government's refusal to liberalize the telecommunications sector in the 1990s against the rising tide of laissez faire economics, traditional financial sources were reluctant fund further infrastructure development projects. As a result, the EPRDF-led Ethiopian government was forced to localize its funding sources for investing in the telecommunication sector until the emergence of Chinese vendor-financing schemes in the past decade.

Until the privatization tide that swept the global telecommunication industry in the last quarter of the 20th century, the regulated status of telecommunications as a state enterprise in Ethiopia was consistent with natural monopoly arguments for minimizing consumer service costs by protecting state-owned expensive bedrock infrastructure investment from duplicative competition. In recent years, framing the Ethiopian telecommunication industry's state proprietorship has probably transcended natural monopoly arguments to incorporate other development policy rationales. In defending its monopolistic approach, Ethiopian policymakers argue first that market forces work contrary to the government's goal of achieving universal access and universal service in telecommunications. Market forces, the Ethiopian government contends, have "imperfections" that call for state intervention so that equitable distribution of resources can be realized. Second, GoE has repeatedly characterized the telecommunications sector as a "cash cow" that generates huge amounts of revenue for the state, which, in turn, is used to finance the expansion of the sector and other infrastructure projects. Third, the current ruling party, while resolutely dismissing foreign proprietorship, believes the telecommunications sector in Ethiopia cannot be liberalized because of the absence of a potent local private sector that can invest on the industry (for details, see Workneh 2018).

Critics of the monopolistic arrangement today argue that state control of telecommunications promotes inefficiency and stalls growth. Ethiopia's previous financers such as the World Bank contend that state monopoly of the telecommunications sector affects the supply of capital in local banks, as government borrowing for investment in telecommunications infrastructure development dries up financing that the private sector could use. They also argue the monopoly arrangement is also less appealing for foreign direct investment that brings know-how and financing to these projects.

One of the remaining few countries to exercise state monopoly of telecommunications, Ethiopia provides rare insight into the promises and challenges of a counter-neoliberal arrangement of infrastructure development and service delivery. Notwithstanding Ethiopia's posture against profit-driven pressures of global capitalism in the form of deregulation, challenges of universal service and universal access remain in the midst of a rapidly changing telecom industry. In this sense, it can be argued that the emergence of a multipolar world with alternative financing options such as China offers a unique opportunity for the Ethiopian government to sustain its vision of telecommunications as a public utility. However, it is also true that the technological and innovative volatility of the sector poses an uncertain future for the existing model as evidenced by the Ethiopian parliament's recent ratification of a bill to deregulate the telecommunications sector as of 2019 (Endeshaw, 2019). Finally, we note that while the ideals of universal access and service seem great in theory, questions remain about systemic bias by intersecting social divisions beyond economic class, including gender, ethnicity, age, religion, and geographic location. These are areas for future study.

Notes

1 The first phase of the World Bank's open-access policy was launched in 2012, with an Open Knowledge Repository that adopted a set of Creative Commons copyright licenses. As a result, anybody is free to use, reuse, and redistribute most of the Bank's knowledge products and research outputs for commercial or noncommercial purposes.

2 PRSPs are prepared by member countries in broad consultation with stakeholders and development partners, including the staffs of the World Bank and the IMF. Updated every three years with annual progress reports, they describe the country's macroeconomic, structural, and social policies in support of growth and poverty reduction as well as associated external financing needs and major sources of financing.

3 Proclamation No. 170/60 (June 22, 1960) established the authority of IBTE to borrow funds required for operation and expansion, with the limitation that the outstanding debt should not exceed three times the paid-up share capital and with the proviso of government's ratification of each loan. The proclamation also increased IBTE's capital to $3.1 million.

4 In comparison, other African countries had the following figures of telephones per 100 people by 1965: Nigeria 0.15; Tanganyika (Tanzania) 0.18; Liberia 0.20; Uganda 0.21; Kenya 0.49; and South Africa 6.02 (International Bank, 1965).

5 Proclamation No. 246/67 (June 27, 1967) declared the share capital of IBTE to increase from $4.9 million to $8 million. This share capital was increased to $16 million by Proclamation No. 319/73 (Tsigie & Feyissa, 1999).

6 After shortly changing its name to the Provisional Military Government of Socialist Ethiopia Telecommunications Service, BTE was soon renamed again as the Ethiopian Telecommunication Authority (ETA) (ETC, 2009).
7 *Qäbäles* are municipalities. They are the smallest administrative division in Ethiopia.
8 On December 2010, 1 USD = 16.636 ETB.
9 A country code top-level domain (ccTLD) designates a top-level domain assigned for a country or a sovereign state. In the hierarchy of the Domain Name System of the Internet, a top-level domain (TLD) contains the highest level and is found at the root zone of the name space. For example, consider the domain name of Ethio-Telecom, www.ethiotelecom.et. In this case, the top-level domain is et.

References

Abbott, A., & Brady, G. (1999). The liberalization of the telecommunications sector: A rent-seeking perspective. *European Journal of Law and Economics,* 8(1), 63–77.

Abiye, Y. (2013, May 18). MPs lambast Debretsion over Ethio-Telecom's "poor service." *The Reporter.* Retrieved from http://www.thereporterethiopia.com/index.php/news-headlines/item/500-mps-lambast-debretsion-over-ethio-telecom%E2%80%99s-%E2%80%9Cpoor-service%E2%80%9D

Africa Development Bank Group. (2006). *Ethiopia: Review of Bank Group assistance to the public utility sector.* Tunis: Operations Evaluations Department (OPEV). Retrieved from http://www.afdb.org/fileadmin/uploads/afdb/Documents/Evaluation-Reports/10090246-EN-ethiopia-bga-to-the-public-utility-sector.pdf

Bahru, Z. (2002). *A history of modern Ethiopia, 1855–1991.* Oxford: James Currey.

Bar, F. and Munk Riis, A. (1997). From welfare to innovation: Toward a new rationale for universal service, *Communications & Strategies,* 26, 185–206.

Baumol, W. J. (1977). On the proper cost tests for natural monopoly in a multi-product industry. *The American Economic Review,* 67(5), 809–822.

Bullard, N. (1997). The nation-state confronted with globalization: Asian perspectives. *Development,* 40(4), 31–35.

Burgelman, J.C. (1996). Service universel, service public et souci de diversité: le débat sur les autoroutes de l'information, *Réseaux,* 78, 41–52.

Carlton, D. W., & Perloff, J. M. (2005). *Modern industrial organization.* Boston: Pearson/Addison Wesley.

Comor, E. A. (1994). *The global political economy of communication: Hegemony, telecommunication, and the information economy.* New York: St. Martin's Press.

De Reuck, J. and Joseph, R. (1999). Universal service in a participatory democracy: A perspective from Australia, *Government Information Quarterly,* 16(4), 345–352.

Endeshaw, D. (2019, June 7). Ethiopia plans to issue telco licenses by year-end. *Reuters.* Retrieved from https://www.reuters.com/article/ethiopia-telecoms/update-1-ethiopia-parliament-to-approve-telecoms-liberalisation-law-idUSL8N23E25Q

Essa, E., (2013, July 01). Measuring China's motivations in Africa. *Alja-zeera*. Retrieved from http://www.aljazeera.com/indepth/features/2013/07/20137110258606419.html

Ethiopian Telecommunications Corporation. (2009). *Corporate profile*. Addis Ababa: ETC.

Faulhaber, G.R. (1997). Public policy for a networked nation. *The University of Florida Journal of Law and Public Policy, 8*, 219–242.

Federal Communications Commission. (1996). *Telecommunications Act of 1996*. Retrieved April 30, 2014, from http://transition.fcc.gov/Reports/tcom1996.pdf

Forestier, E., Grace, J., and Kenny, C. (2002). Can information and communication technologies be pro-poor?, *Telecommunications Policy, 26*(11), 623–646.

Garnham, N. (1997). Universal service. In W.H. Melody (Ed.), *Telecom reform: Principles, policies and regulatory practices* (pp. 207–212). Lyngby: Den Private Ingeniørfond, Technical University of Denmark.

Gillett, S.E. (1994). *Technological change, market structure, and universal service*. 22th Telecommunications Policy Research Conference. Alexandria, 1–3 October.

Gómez Sáenz de Hermúa, M. (2000). *El servicio universal: presente y futuro*. XIII Biennial Conference of the International Telecommunications Society (ITS). Buenos Aires, 2–5 July. Retrieved from http://www.its2000.org.ar/conference/saenzhermua.pdf

Greenfeld, L. (2011). The globalization of nationalism and the future of the nation-state. *International Journal of Politics, Culture, and Society, 24*(1–2), 5–9.

Gritsch, M. (2005). The nation-state and economic globalization: Soft geopolitics and increased state autonomy? *Review of International Political Economy, 12*(1), 1–25.

Hadden, S.G. and Lenert, E. (1995). Telecommunications networks are not VCRs: The public nature of new information technologies for universal service. *Media, Culture and Society, 17*(1), 121–140.

Hankiss, E. (1999). Globalization and the end of the nation state? *World Futures, 53*(2), 135–147.

Hart, T. (1998). A dynamic universal service for a heterogeneous European Union. *Telecommunications Policy, 22*(10), 839–852.

International Bank for Reconstruction & Development. (1962). *Imperial Board of Telecommunications appraisal of the 1962–64 expansion program*. Washington, DC.

International Bank for Reconstruction & Development. (1965a). *Appraisal of the Imperial Board of Telecommunications third telecommunications project Ethiopia*. Washington, DC.

International Bank for Reconstruction & Development. (1965b). *Report and recommendation of the president to the executive directors on a proposed loan to the Imperial Board of Telecommunications of Ethiopia*. Washington, DC.

International Bank for Reconstruction & Development & International Development Association. (1973). *Report and recommendation of the president to the executive directors on a proposed credit to the Empire of Ethiopia for the fifth telecommunications project*. Washington, DC.

International Development Association. (1973). *Imperial Board of Telecommunications of Ethiopia: Appraisal of a telecommunications project.* Washington, DC.

International Development Association. (1975a). *Ethiopia: appraisal of a telecommunications project.* Washington, DC.

International Development Association. (1975b). *Report and recommendation of the president to the executive directors on a proposed credit to Ethiopia for a telecommunications project.* Washington, DC.

Latzer, M. (2000). Toward an integrated universal services policy for the 'mediamatics' sector. In E. Bohlin, K. Brodin, A. Lundgren and B. Thorngren (Eds.), *Convergence in communications and beyond* (pp. 301–312). Amsterdam: Elsevier Science.

Liebowitz, S.J. and Margolis, S.E. (1998). Network effects and externalities. In P. Newman (Ed.), *The new Palgrave's dictionary of economics and the law* (pp. 671–675). London: MacMillan.

MacKie-Mason, J.K. (1998). *Layering for equity and efficiency: A principled approach to universal service policy.* Report of the Department of Economics and School of Information, University of Michigan. Retrieved from http://www-personal.umich.edu/~jmm/papers/aol-rpt-feb98.pdf

Mansell, R. and Steinmueller, W.E. (1996). *Regulation and policy for advanced communication technologies and services.* FAIR, Forecast and Assessment of Socio-Economic Impact of Advanced Communications and Recommendations, Working paper N. 5. Sussex: The SPRU Publications Office.

Miller, T. and Lawrence, G. (2001). Globalization and Culture. In T. Miller (Ed.), *A Companion to Cultural Studies.* Blackwell Publishing Ltd, Malden, MA. doi: 10.1002/9780470998809.ch28

Ministry of Communication and Information Technology. (n.d). *ICT sector development in Ethiopia.* Retrieved from http://www.mcit.gov.et/web/english/information-by-topic/-/asset_publisher/E65Wf2Nkdm5u/content/ict-sector-development-in-ethiop-1;jsessionid=C20C76951729A95D7606FE43D2AE9661

Ministry of Finance & Economic Development. (2006). *A plan for accelerated and sustained development to end poverty (PASDEP).* Retrieved from http://www.afdb.org/fileadmin/uploads/afdb/Documents/Policy-Documents/Plan_for_Accelerated_and_Sustained_(PASDEP)_final_July_2007_Volume_I_3.pdf

Ministry of Finance & Economic Development. (2010). *Growth and transformation plan: Policy matrix.* Retrieved from http://www.mofed.gov.et/English/Resources/Documents/GTP%20Policy%20Matrix%20(English)2.pdf

Mosca, M. (2008). On the origins of the concept of natural monopoly: Economies of scale and competition. *European Journal of the History of Economic Thought, 15*(2), 317–353.

Murroni, C. (1997). Universal service in liberalised telecommunications markets. In *The Economics of the Information Society* (pp. 109–116). Luxembourg: Office for Official Publications of the EC.

Neu, W. and Scanlan, M. (2000). *Study on the re-examination of the scope of universal service in the telecommunications sector of the European Union, in the context of the 1999 review.* Study for the European Commission DG Information Society. WIK, Bad Honnef. Retrieved from http://europa.eu.int/ISPO/infosoc/telecompolicy/en/wikuso2.pdf

Noam, E.M. (1993). *NetTrans accounts: Reforming the financial support system for universal service in telecommunications.* Columbia Institute for Tele-Information, Discussion Draft. New York: Columbia University. Retrieved from http://www.vii.org/papers/nettrans.htm

Parker, E.B. (2000). Closing the digital divide in rural America, *Telecommunications Policy, 24*(4), 281–290.

Posner, R.A. (1969). Natural monopoly and its regulation. *Stanford Law Review, 21,* 548.

Pilati, A. (1999). A chi piace il servizio universale?, *Beltel, 4*(6), 7–8.

Rothbard, M.N. (2006). *Power & market: Government and the economy.* Auburn: Ludwig von Mises Institute.

Sharkey, W.W. (1982). *The theory of natural monopoly.* Cambridge: Cambridge University Press.

Shields, P., Dervin, B., Richter, C. and Soller, R. (1993). Who needs 'POTS-plus' services? A comparison of residential user needs along the rural-urban continuum. *Telecommunications Policy, 17*(8), 563–587.

Shuler, J.A. (1999). A critique of universal service, e-rate, and the chimera of the public's interest. *Government Information Quarterly, 16*(4), 359–369.

Steeves, H.L. & Wasko, J. (2001). Feminist theory and political economy: Toward a friendly alliance. In E. Meehan and E. Riordan (Eds.), *Sex and money: Intersections of feminism and political economy in media* (pp. 16–29). Minneapolis: University of Minnesota Press.

Tsigie, A. & Feyissa, G. (1999). Ethiopia: Past, present, and future. In E.M. Noam (Ed.), *Telecommunications in Africa* (pp. 51–78). New York: Oxford University Press.

Wasko, J. (2005). Studying the political economy of media and information. *Communição e Sociedade, 7:* 2–48.

Wasko, J. (2014). The study of the political economy of media in the twenty-first century. *International Journal of Media & Cultural Politics, 10*(3), 259–271.

Wasko, J. & Erickson, M. (eds.) (2008). *Cross-border cultural production: Economic runaway or globalization.* Amherst, NY: Cambria Press.

Wasko, J., Murdock, G., & Sousa, H. (2011). Introduction: The political economy of communications: Core concerns and issues. In J. Wasko, G. Murdock & H. Sousa (eds). *The handbook of political economy of communications.* Oxford: Wiley-Blackwell. doi:10.1002/9781444395402.ch

Wolak, F.A. (1996). Can universal service survive in a competitive telecommunications environment? Evidence from the United States consumer expenditure survey. *Information Economics and Policy, 8*(3), 163–203.

Workneh, T. W. (2016). Chinese multinationals in the Ethiopian telecommunications sector. *Communication, Culture & Critique, 9*(1), 126–147.

World Bank. (1984a). *Staff appraisal report, Ethiopia: Sixth telecommunications project.* Washington, DC.

World Bank. (1984b). *Report and recommendations of the president of the international development association to the executive directors on a proposed credit in an amount equivalent to SDR 38.7 million to Ethiopia for a sixth telecommunications project.* Washington, DC.

World Bank. (1993). *Project completion report, Ethiopia: Sixth telecommunications project.* Washington, DC.

Wolf, M. (2001). Will the nation-state survive globalization?. *Foreign Affairs*, pp. 178–190.

Xavier, P. (1997). Service universel et accès public dans une société de l'information. *STI Revue*, 20, 141–179.

Yewondwossen, M. (2012, December 4). France Telecom's contract ends. *Capital*. Retrieved from http://www.capitalethiopia.com/index.php?option=com_content&view=article&id=2093:france-telecoms-contract-ends&catid=35:-capital&Itemid=27

9 Through Being Cool

The Critical Political Economy of iTunes

David Gracon

Introduction

Lang and Hughes (2003) claim that nearly all aspects of modern music experiences are driven by the intersection between technological innovations and the social impacts of those innovations. From the way music is created, produced, and recorded; to the way it is distributed, to its portability and consumption – technology drives the music ecosystem. As this essay will reveal, this was the case with the Apple corporation and its iTunes Store between 2003 and 2012.

Murnane (2017) and Friedlander (2017) note that the Nielsen Soundscan and Recording Industry Association of America (RIAA) figures concluded that digital music streaming services have eclipsed music downloading sales for the first time in 2016. Streaming services such as Spotify, Pandora, Google Play, Apple Music, and YouTube currently dominate the music retail (although music *renting* would be more apt today as one doesn't own anything) market. Before this recent fluctuation in the market, Apple's iTunes Store monopolized the music industry and it was the primary venue to purchase and consume paid-for music. Between 2003 and 2012, Apple's iTunes Store was the dominant force in music retail, as the integration of the paid-for MP3 and the iPod music player allowed Apple to monopolize music retail. At the same time, with the absence of physical CD printing and packaging costs, and by cutting out middlemen such as physical distributors, one-stops and brick and mortar retailers, Apple along with record companies retained more revenues on download sales.

For some, Apple has secured a cult status, and their diehard customers have been referred to as an "army of evangelists" (Cuneo et al., 2003, p. 2). The Apple brand is a contemporary embodiment of the seduction of commodity fetishism. Their sleek gadgetry, such as smartphones, tablets, and laptop computers (and the relatively defunct iPod, as it is no longer manufactured), and iTunes Store masks the real conditions as well as policies and practices that brought the iconic technology corporation incredible market dominance. Underneath the flashy advertising spectacle and sleek minimalist design of the Apple brand lays an intricate web of institutional corporate power that enabled and secured their position as the top retailer of recorded music in the United States and the global market.

The aim of this essay is to reveal and critique the true conditions behind Apple's economic dominance; to unpack exactly how the corporation came to dominate music retail, an industry they previously were not associated with, and how they ultimately reshaped the music industry from 2003 to 2012. This study entails a critical analysis of the economic arrangements, policies, and practices at the monopolistic core of Apple and the iTunes Store.

The theoretical framework by which the policies and practices of the iTunes Store are examined is the political economy of communication. In brief, Peters (2017) claims that "the term political economy is used in communication studies to refer to a wide-ranging set of questions regarding recursive relationships between communication technologies, media industries, market structures, labor relations and government regulatory policies" (p. 152). Hardy (2017) adds that the core of critical political economy envisions a more culturally diverse and democratic communications, but realizes that capitalism places significant structural limitations on the ability to realize such visions in a manner compatible with widening social justice, equity, and empowerment. This critical framework applies to music retail, and as Sirois and Wasko (2011) assert, "a strong distribution network will ensure that an album will end up at retailers and then finally in consumers hands. Therefore, control over distribution leads to control of the market and the industry" (p. 349). This essay is thus a snapshot of Apple's control of the market and eventual monopolization of music retail between 2003 and 2012.

Apple deployed specific policies and concrete practices to manifest market control. These patterns included vertical integration, the monopoly practice of merging the iTunes Store with Apple hardware; digital rights management (DRM) as a protector of intellectual property rights and market control; Apple's collusion with the major record labels in terms of digital licensing and distribution rights; the barriers to digital entry for independent retailers; product synergies and multimedia convergence in the iTunes media ecology; product placement and exclusive only offers; pricing practices and privacy issues; and last, the exploitative labor practices behind Apple's hardware. This analysis was accomplished by examining the industry trade literature such as *Billboard* and *Variety*, Apple's financial reports, journalistic sources, and secondary research and studies as well as related data from my dissertation on independent music retail.

This essay fills a gap within music retail literature under the umbrella of the political economy of communication by analyzing and exposing the underlying economic and monopolistic policies and practices of Apple and iTunes. Let's first examine vertical integration and DRM.

Vertical Integration and Digital Rights Management

> Jobs always wanted Apple to create its own unified utopia, a magical walled garden where hardware and software and peripheral devices worked well together to create a great experience, and where the success of one product drove sales of all the companions.
>
> (p. 405).—Walter Isaacson, author of *Steve Jobs* (2011)

Likewise, Apple's "unified utopia" and "walled garden," as Isaacson (2011) notes, ostensibly facilitated and cornered a new market while deploying profitable methods to consuming music commodities. For example, Apple's vertical integration between their hardware (iPod and iPad) and musical content available on the iTunes Store was a primary factor for their prolonged market dominance between 2003 and 2012. Vertical integration is where elements of the supply chain are united through common ownership. For example, Apple manufactures hardware and sells these commodities in their stores, both virtual and brick and mortar. Along the line, they incorporate the integration of Apple software (i.e., the iTunes Store) and serve as a content provider, all of which fuels the sale of hardware. This unified "walled garden" becomes mutually reinforcing and economically profitable. This relates to Brabazon, Cull, Kent, and McRae's (2005) claim that "movements in musical technology create new markets, new audiences and new ways of consuming product." Vertical integration has economically driven the iTunes Store, which had been directly correlated to the massive popularity and market dominance of the iPod portable music player. Arthur (2012) asserts the iPod had continually been the number one portable music player in terms of both volume and value sales, and Apple benefitted enormously by cornering this market.

From a $.99 song purchased on iTunes, Apple earned about $.10 per sale, which many in the industry considered to be akin to a loss leader, whereas the true economic profiteering resulted from the sale of hardware products, in particular, the iPod. The iTunes Store later fostered additional hardware sales with the iPad, iPhone, and personal computers (both laptop and desktop), all of which automatically came equipped with the iTunes Store software. As Sirois and Wasko (2011) claim, "Indeed, recorded music itself is actually becoming a secondary commodity; that is, much as in the early 1900s, recorded music is being used to sell hardware and other commodities" (p. 352). We can see this in practice as Isaacson (2011) notes, "Jobs realized that there was yet another advantage to the fact that Apple had an integrated system of computer, software and device. It meant that sales of the iPod would drive sales of the iMac personal computer" (p. 392). Creeber and Martin (2009) add that the growth and sale of large hard drives to store music as another example of hardware related to the increased portability of digital music.

Since the unveiling of the iTunes Store in 2003, music files purchased through the retailer could only be played on corresponding Apple hardware, in particular, the iPod. This practice continued until 2009. This deliberate proprietary collusion between the musical content sold through the iTunes Store and Apple hardware effectively curbed the competition in terms of the portable music player market as well as the digital online retail market. Customers were forced to use the iTunes Store if they owned an iPod. A consumer who purchased a competing portable digital music player such as the Microsoft Zune or Creative Labs Zen during this time couldn't purchase or store iTunes' content (in October 2003, the iTunes store crossed over to Windows; however, the use of an iPod was still required). As the iTunes Store increasingly became a key player in the paid-for digital download market, consumers had little choice but to utilize iTunes. As Knopper (2009) claims, "the iTunes Store capitalized on this by essentially forcing consumers to purchase more iPods at $300 to $500 apiece" (p. 178). He adds, "in the fourth quarter of 2003, iPods generated about 7% of Apple's $1.7 billion in revenue—$121 million overall" (p. 178). Isaacson (2011) notes that some record companies wanted a royalty from each device sold, as Apple profited from the use of their recorded content.

The control between musical content purchased from the iTunes Store and the iPod were solidified by the DRM technology. As a form of corporate doublespeak, Apple called this technology *FairPlay*. All tracks purchased from the iTunes Store were encoded with the *FairPlay* technology. Knopper (2009) claims that pressure for DRM came from the record labels that ostensibly wanted to protect their intellectual property holdings. Roth (2007) adds, "probably the most significant aspect of iTunes is that it addresses online music piracy and provides a new revenue option by selling copyrighted music over the Internet" (p. 524). Copyright allows entrepreneurs to have a monopoly and control over their products. For example, DRM gives copyright holders the right to control the making of copies by incorporating technology with use restrictions (Roth, 2007, p. 522). Other non-Apple portable music players conveniently did not support *FairPlay* encoded tracks. Thus, Apple effectively locked or created a "walled garden" with the musical content and their hardware. The popularity of the iPod skyrocketed in conjunction with the increased market dominance of the iTunes Store, which allowed Apple to dominate two markets as a result of vertical integration – the digital retail market and the portable music player market. Holahan (2007) adds that labels were violating antitrust agreements by using DRM to prevent music from being sold by a variety of retailers, thereby stifling competition that could have otherwise kept prices down. Roth continues, "the close link that DRM encoded music creates between iTunes and the iPod triggers anti-trust concerns," as seen through evidence of increased prices and excluded competition imply the existence of market power

(p. 525). As a result of obtaining an iTunes subscription, consumers were willing to tolerate higher prices for iPods as a result of the increasing cost of switching online music providers (p. 532). Apple's offense began when it filtered the purchase of music through iTunes and they restricted how it could be played. Roth continues, "Barring the purchase of other portable music players by iTunes subscribers reflects a willful scheme to acquire and maintain monopoly power" (p. 535).

In 2009, Apple dropped the DRM technology. Post DRM, music tracks were known as iTunes Plus as the sound quality of the files had significantly improved. However, for the tracks purchased before 2009, to upgrade to iTunes Plus an additional upgrade fee was assigned per track, thus further commodifying files already purchased through iTunes, which was the case for most tracks. Breen (2011) claims the fee for this conversion was an additional $.30 per track or $3 per album (the entire back catalog of Bob Dylan and U2 would've cost about $500 for the upgrade). Bockstedt, Kauffman, and Riggins (2005) reinforce this logic as companies "create value with digital assets and are able to re-harvest them in an infinite number of transactions" (p. 82). It is important to note that without the iTunes Plus upgrade, iTunes's music purchased prior to 2009 could only be played on an iPod.

This additional conversion fee in conjunction with technological change is a common trope in the evolution of music formats. As music formats change with time, it is not only extremely lucrative for the record labels, but also for the technology companies that manufacture the corresponding hardware. For example, when the CD format was released, many consumers purchased the same albums they already owned on vinyl on the new and more expensive CD. This also drove the sale of CD players. Thus, this logic is nothing new.

What brought about the 2009 change in policy? One possible reason is that Apple was increasingly being accused of violating antitrust laws with the integration of iTunes, DRM, and their proprietary hardware. In 2006 Norway, Sweden, and Denmark launched a common open letter to Apple regarding the restrictions of the DRM technology. According to *CNN* (2013) German and French consumer groups joined forces with Norway and Finland and their goal was to create a united European front against iTunes. The Apple 2012 financial report notes, "The Apple iPod iTunes Antitrust Litigation" (formerly Charoensak v. Apple Computer, Inc. and Tucker v. Apple Computer, Inc.) is currently pending stateside. The plaintiffs allege various claims, including the unlawful tying of music purchased on the iTunes Store with the purchase of iPods and unlawful acquisition or maintenance of monopoly market power under the Sherman Act and other anti-monopoly laws.

According to various press and PR statements, Apple was in favor of removing DRM and had always insisted the major labels required the technology. Regardless, Apple benefitted economically from this vertical integration and effectively cornered the market in terms of digital music sales and the portable music player market.

iTunes and the Major Labels

Bettig and Hall (2012) assert that the music industry follows the logic of capitalism, resulting in specific structures and practices. The authors claim, "The commodification of music and music video content affects what is produced and the industry reflects the overriding tendency within capitalism towards concentration and oligopoly" (p. 115). As a result of these tendencies, it is vital to examine the power arrangements between iTunes and the major record labels.

In the post-Napster wake of the early 2000s, there was no legitimate paid-for music delivery service with widespread consumer appeal and the major labels were hesitant and late to enter the digital download market. Kernfeld (2011) notes that the major record labels took nearly two years before launching the first subscription services, Pressplay and RealOneMusic, in early 2002. Both were unsuccessful and quickly failed. However, the digital download market was eventually monetized. Arthur (2012) claims, "the music industry has fallen back on an old strategy, well rehearsed in its industrial history, of resistance to disruptive technologies, which gives way to experimentation and dalliances, and then finally to their subversion or takeover" (p. 127). The author continues, "The music industry hopes to choke off the radical potential of open networks and replace them with closed, proprietary systems" (p. 128). Enter Apple and their "walled garden."

Apple CEO Steve Jobs was able to convince and sign licensing deals with the major record labels, a feat that radically altered the paid-for market for digital distribution. At the time, the "big five" major record labels included EMI, Universal, Warner, Sony Music Entertainment, and BMG – a powerful oligopoly of labels that owned and distributed a vast majority of music in the United States and the world (in the subsequent years, it should be noted that thousands of independent record labels also contributed music licenses to the iTunes Store). Apple harnessed the major labels into licensing their music, thus creating an immensely powerful relationship between a developing technology corporation and the major label system. Apple was increasingly able to legitimize and dominate the paid-for digital download market, which was largely reinforced by the booming iPod and hardware market, all contained within their closed proprietary system. As a result of these arrangements, the iTunes Store became an online one-stop megastore, the primary platform to purchase digital songs and albums.

Bettig and Hall (2012) claim that while much has changed in the music industry over the last ten years, certain features of the industry haven't changed as it pursues the same goal as most U.S. media, which is to make a profit by selling cultural commodities. The intersection between Apple and the major labels was significant because the labels controlled and promoted vast quantities of music that reached mass audiences. According to Campbell, Martin, and Fabos (2017), the U.S. and global music business still constitutes a powerful oligopoly, a business situation in which a few firms control most of an industry's production and distribution resources. The authors continue, "This global reach gives these firms enormous influence over what types of music gain worldwide distribution and popular acceptance" (p. 126). Furthering this thread, Scherzinger (2005) notes, "Media cross ownership and joint ventures tend to reduce competition, lower risk and increase profits. This, in turn, has forced musical production to succumb to the advertising, marketing, styling, and engineering techniques of increasingly uniform and profit driven criteria" (p. 24). While the iTunes Store contains much depth in terms of musical variety (significantly more than the brick and mortar days of Walmart and other chain stores), they primarily promoted and pushed the most popular and profitable musical acts associated with the major label system.

In 2013, only three major music corporations remained due to the continued consolidation of the music industry. These labels included Universal Music Group, Sony Music Entertainment, and Warner Music Group. Campbell, Martin, and Fabos (2014) assert that these three companies controlled nearly 90% of the recording industry market in the United States at the time. Although their revenues had eroded over the past decade, the major music corporations still continued to wield great power, as they controlled when and how their artists' music will be licensed to play on new distribution services, such as iTunes, as opposed to other independent distribution outlets. As Burkart (2005) notes, "the major labels rely on maintaining cultural rents by restricting access to online music distribution by exerting anti-competiveness throughout its traditional distribution bottlenecks" (p. 498). Thus, it comes as no surprise the top selling music within the iTunes Store regularly consisted of music primarily from the three major labels on the content provider with the most market power. Such arrangements simultaneously led to numerous multimedia synergies, privileged placement on the iTunes storefront as well as exclusive only offers that exasperated commodification and monopolistic tendencies.

Barriers to Digital Entry

Considerable barriers to enter the paid-for digital download market existed during Apple's reign of power. Burkart and McCourt (2004) note, "The rationalization and vast extension of intellectual property rights in the US preserved the content industry's competitive advantages in the commercial distribution of digital media" (p. 350). Due to the collusion between Apple and the major record labels noted in the previous section, there were considerable barriers to enter the digital download market for independent retailers. In fact, it was virtually impossible. This was because the iTunes Store, Amazon, Walmart (their MP3 download store that eventually failed), and Napster (the legitimate Napster owned by Best Buy) are massive corporations with the necessary capital and resources to construct and maintain massive digital download stores. *Billboard's* Deidu (2013) notes that operating and maintaining the iTunes Store consumed nearly $3.5 billion per year, thus making it extremely cost prohibitive for start-ups and competitors.

The major corporate retailers (iTunes, Amazon) had significant leverage with substantial financial backing and could better forge relationships with the major record labels by procuring the costly intellectual property rights to license and distribute digital music. The same complicated process had to be accomplished with each of the major labels in order to offer a complete inventory of recorded music. Without all the major labels on board, there would be significant gaps in terms of content, and this would have undoubtedly affected the popularity of the content provider. As a result, it was essential to have the rights and access from all the major record labels.

Small (2012) asserts that music licensing is a highly complex and arduous process. It requires arrangements from the rights holders of the composition copyright, which typically includes music publishing companies, and rights holders of sound recordings, which typically includes record labels. To make matters more complex, a number of record labels and publishing companies can claim ownership to a particular song. In terms of being a start-up, Small suggests, "The answer is by having an existing committed customer base that can guarantee future cash flows. Therefore, a large-scale corporate retailer has a significant advantage in negotiating with rights holders over an entrepreneurial firm starting from scratch" (p. 56). It was more efficient and cost effective for the major labels to streamline their massive catalogs to a small number of corporate content providers, in particular iTunes and Amazon. It made economic sense to collude their economies of scale with large-scale corporate content providers as opposed to a fragmented market of scattered independent retailers who lack the financial means to participate. Because of these arrangements, there were few opportunities to enter the paid-for digital music market. In Gracon's (2010) dissertation on the political economy of the independent record store, Terry Currier, the owner of Music Millennium, a brick and mortar retailer based in Portland, Oregon, claimed:

> You can't just do digital delivery. Working with lawyers from the digital side of all these different record labels and record distribution companies trying to work out deals to be able to do so. There is cost

involved, there are legal things involved, and not anybody off the street can go make this happen.

(p. 263)

Small (2012) notes that maintaining the necessary licenses requires significant human resources to track down and maintain relationships with rights holders. It also requires a large number of relationship managers, publishing experts, and lawyers to maintain and accumulate a catalog. Small continues, "The scale required, in terms of human resources, makes the prospects for a start up firm extremely daunting" (p. 57). As a result, iTunes and Amazon benefitted from these barriers to entry as the competition was effectively stifled. Arthur (2012) adds that Apple dominated the music download world with 63% of the market, while Amazon was second with 22%. This meant that 85% of the digital download market was highly concentrated in the hands of two corporate content providers.

The corporate concentration of digital music retail effectively closed the door on independent retailers wanting to enter the market. The barriers to entry effectively reproduced extreme market concentration and the independents were effectively shut out of the market.

Pricing Issues

Pricing in the iTunes Store raised some additional concerns. Campbell, Martin, and Fabos (2014) claim iTunes sold songs with variable pricing at $0.69–$1.49; however the typical track costs $.99 (p. 145).[1] The authors noted that a $1.29 track generated about $.0.40 for iTunes (iTunes received 30% of every song sale) and a standard $0.09 mechanical royalty for the song publisher and writer, leaving about $0.60 for the record company. Artists with a royalty rate of about 15% would get $0.20 from the song download. Bockstedt, Kauffman, and Riggins (2005) claim, "for single song transactions the service provider will net a.03 loss to a.02 profit, assuming there are no costs for providing the music" (p. 9), as the true profiteering occurred through the sale of hardware. However, as noted earlier, running and maintaining the iTunes Stores cost $3.5 billion annually.

With no physical CD printing and packaging costs and no middlemen such as physical distributors, one-stops and brick and mortar retailers, record companies could retain more of the revenue on download sales. In *Rolling Stone*, Knopper (2011) notes that this model was not only more profitable for the record labels, but within the digital distribution model there were significantly fewer laborers involved with a digital store, as opposed to the chain of labor associated with physical distributors and retail workers in brick and mortar stores. Bockstedt, Kauffman, and Riggins (2005) claim, "manufacturers and distributers are becoming obsolete as record labels, producers, and artists can go directly to digital music retailers without producing physical product, bringing the music supplier and the consumer closer together" (p. 17).

A second issue in terms of pricing involved the labor of the artists themselves. Some artists who sold their music through iTunes may not have had provisions in their contract for digital distribution sales, as their contract predated this era. In this case, there were instances where the major labels retained all the profits from the sale of digital tracks and albums on iTunes and the artist received nothing – a clearly exploitative practice. Similarly, Bettig and Hall (2012) add:

> Mechanical royalties for the use of a song are paid to songwriters and publishers, not the artists. Mechanical rights were not extended to digital downloads, ringtones and other services until 2008, based on a ruling by the Copyright Royalty Board that set rates for permanent digital downloads at 9.1 cents a track, the same for physical recordings.
>
> (p. 137)

Bettig and Hall (2012) continue, "By treating music downloads as so-called new media/technology, the record companies paid artists a lower rate than for physical music while still charging a packaging fee" (p. 137). The artists continued to be exploited for their musical labor as the digital world developed and formats evolved. As Thompson (2011) notes, artists needed to sell 12,399 songs at $.99 per day to earn the equivalent of minimum wage (with a monthly minimum wage of $1,160). As a result of these arrangements, few artists earned the equivalent of minimum wage for their musical labor.

A third issue with pricing was its fixed nature, which was historically set by Apple. The major labels complained for years that Apple had too much control setting prices. Since Apple retained a dominant foothold in the digital retail market and had little competition, this arrangement effectively stifled the competition and deflated innovation (similar arguments can be made with the cornering of the iPod market). Because there was little competition in the digital download market, Apple had significant control in terms of setting prices. More competition would have equaled a greater variety of pricing.

When digital albums typically sold for $9.99 and physical CDs sold for $12–14, we saw how the digital world propagated by the iTunes Store cannibalized the CD market. They also cannibalized physical brick and mortar retailers, thus further eliminating retail competition. In 2006 Tower Records closed down. Between 2003 and 2006, Gracon (2010) observes, "800 independent record stores closed their doors for good" (p. 124). Fewer independent stores meant less competition for iTunes, as it also reinforced the move away from tangible music formats. Knopper

(2009) adds that sales of iTunes singles surged, while old-fashioned album sales and major label revenues dropped considerably since the inception of the iTunes Store in 2003. Although this shift was great for consumers (one could purchase the tracks they desired as opposed to a whole album), it was simultaneously negative for the record companies and the artists. Digital music wasn't as profitable as CDs. Knopper continues, "in the post-iTunes world, labels would lay off thousands of people and cut all but the obvious big selling acts from their artist rosters" (p. 181).

Farrell (2011) commented on how the iTunes monopoly was criticized by Mike Lang, the CEO of Miramax, for "effectively strangling the industry" (news.techeye.net [retrieved July 6, 2013]). Because the music industry had allowed too few content providers, it was suffering, as there wasn't enough diversity in distribution. The major labels felt that Apple had too much power (in terms of pricing and product integration) and had taken over the entire music business and worked the labels into a bad business model. Grover and Burrows (2007) noted in *Businessweek* that Doug Morris (Music Chief at Universal Music) realized he and his fellow music executives had ceded too much control to Jobs and Apple. "We got rolled like a bunch of puppies" (www.businessweek.com [retrieved July 9, 2013]).

Other Issues

Some miscellaneous issues and concerns remain with product synergy, music placement/exclusive material, privacy issues, and exploited labor in terms of the production of Apple hardware.

As Burkart (2005) notes, transnational entertainment corporations, which promote music as an ever-expanding series of revenue streams, record sales, advertising revenues, movie tie-ins, and streaming audio are no longer tied to a particular sound carrier. He continues, "Music releases have developed into components of larger media franchises, used for cross promotion and branding across corporate divisions" (p. 492). Network power and synergy mobilizes resources, digital assets, business intelligence, capital, and products in a common digital domain shared by music, publishers, video and film producers, broadcasters, TV programmers, portal operators, advertisers, and social media. These companies play major roles in moving music from the wireless Internet to portable players, Smartphones, video games, and social media platforms while making money at every stage in the chain (p. 111).

Such synergistic practices are evident with the iTunes Store. As the iTunes Store evolved, it developed beyond music sales. The iTunes store was one of the first online "media hubs," a cross-platform multimedia retailer with music, movies, television shows, movie rentals, podcasts, books, and later Apps. This convergence of media forms into one unified digital retail space provides countless opportunities for cross-promotion and product synergy, where the hyper commodification of media was mutually reinforcing. For example, soundtracks for movies (rented or sold) can be instantly purchased through the iTunes Store, thus integrating film and music sales. The store offers hundreds of movie trailers and music videos to additionally boost music sales. With the Apple Music streaming service, there are opportunities to purchase tracks and albums directly through the iTunes Store.

There was cross-promotion with Pepsi (bottle caps with free music downloads) and similar campaigns with Coco-Cola, 7–11, and the Gap (consumers obtained a free song by trying on a pair of jeans), and a U2 branded iPod containing the bands entire back catalog, an Apple exclusive. In the mid-2000s, due to its licensing arrangements with the Disney Corporation, the iTunes Store predominantly featured Disney films and television programming from its ABC holdings. Isaacson (2011) claims, by 2011 an important new business had emerged where people trusted their online identity and payment information which allowed Apple to sell, for example, a magazine subscription through its online store. Apple hosted branded live concerts at the iTunes Festival in London that included Justin Timberlake, Coldplay, and Jack White. The performances were live or on-demand via iTunes and U.K. fans could win tickets by using the iTunes festival app. In sum, these colluding corporate synergies enhanced cross-platform commodification in the iTunes media hub while reinforcing the promotion and proliferation of various corporate media forms. The synergistic online media hub of iTunes has played a foundational role in the paradigm shift in the multifarious ways contemporary digital culture has embraced new methods of commodification (often in ways that are ambiguous to most consumers) that warrants further investigation by political economists.

How music was positioned in the iTunes storefront was significant in terms of exposure and download sales. Apple didn't take payments for premium placement; however, bands and labels obtained prime placement by providing exclusive material to iTunes. Sometimes the music was provided to iTunes weeks before other retailers could access it. This allowed iTunes to monopolize exclusive content. Gracon (2010) notes, Maggie Vail at the independent label Kill Rock Stars explained:

> Because it's so hard to get placement on iTunes, and often times you give them the record two weeks before stores get it, and the mom and pops get real upset at that, if you continuously do that. Because it's undercutting their sales. For some records, iTunes is 70% of their sales. Certain bands sell so much that you have to give them the best placement. So you might end up giving it to them a week early. We did this for two Deerhoof records in a row, I think, with iTunes. And the second time, Lesley, who used to run the retail stuff

at Touch and Go (formally an independent distributor/label) called and said, 'The stores are so upset. You can't do this again.' I hadn't even thought of it. I didn't think of them as necessarily competing, but they are.

(p. 263)

This exclusive only retail practice undercut sales at independent record stores. With both physical and on-line retailers, it forced consumers to shop at the iTunes' Store to obtain exclusive content. It also reinforced the paradigm of on-line digital music consumption, use of the iTunes store, and potentially encouraged consumption/integration with Apple hardware such as the iPod (especially between 2003 and 2009 when the DRM technology was still in place). Getting premium placement on iTunes essentially entailed undercutting other independent retailers and playing the music retail game according to the rules of Apple. Knopper (2008) notes, Bob Dylan, U2, and Eminem had all provided exclusive tracks over the years. Other non-iTunes retailers didn't have access to the sale of this musical content – a blatant form of market control. These were monopoly practices and another lucid example of Apple's "walled garden."

The eventual market dominance of the iTunes Store raised additional questions regarding the definition of independent music. Traditionally, the definition of independent music was based on the label of release and the distribution channel (both being independent and not of the big three major labels). In the profile sharing era, it was less complicated in terms of making this independent/major label distinction. However, iTunes effectively harvested the independent music market, as thousands of indie labels were essentially forced to sell through Apple because of their market dominance and monopoly practices. As a result, if an "independent" artist distributed their work through iTunes, were they still in fact independent? This becomes increasingly murky. However, indie labels tend to follow a market logic, despite the politics of "independence" and resistance to corporate culture. With so few content providers, the labels were forced to utilize iTunes, which further solidified their monopoly status in the industry. As a result of this, political economists must rethink the definition and implications of independent media in the era of digital distribution. What does independent media mean under such arrangements?

There was also privacy concerns associated with iTunes. Soon after the launch of iTunes Plus in 2009, reports surfaced that the DRM-free *Fair-Play* tracks sold by iTunes contained identifying information about the customer. This information included the embedding of the purchasing account's full name and e-mail address as metadata in the file; however, this information had always been in iTunes downloads both with and without

FairPlay DRM. According to Frith (2012), privacy groups expressed concerns that this data could be misused if possessions carrying the files were stolen and potentially wrongly incriminate a user for copyright infringement. Burkart and McCourt (2004) claim, "registration policies and end-user license agreements allow the portal networks to profile the identities of users, merge and enrich profiles with extra user information, and establish brand loyalties that would encourage these users to return again and again" (p. 353). Apple's Customer Privacy Policy (2010) contends that Apple updated its general privacy policy and revealed that it could collect real-time, location-based information on users aged 13 and over. The revised policy stated that Apple reserved the right to share this information with third parties who provided services to the customer, including advertisers, promotion services, and in some legal cases, governmental authorities. In the event of a corporate reorganization or merger, Apple had the ability to transfer any and all personal information collected to the relevant third party. Such practices were an early digital incarnation of what Kuhn (2018) refers to as a society of mass surveillance, where personal user information and big data is harvested by governments and social media corporations for political and economic gain – all of which have grave implications for democratic societies.

Last, I briefly discuss the labor issues with Apple. The *New York Times* (2012) noted in 2011 that Apple CEO Tim Cook earned more than $570 million. The 230,000 employees who worked for China's massive factory plant in Foxconn City, where the iPhone and iPod (the very hardware that allowed iTunes to monopolize the music industry) was assembled, earned about $1.50 per hour. This labor stratification was a result of Apple's global exploitation of workers which allowed the corporation to further maximize profits at the expense of basic human rights. There were numerous labor issues in terms of the manufacture of Apple hardware. In 2006 *The Washington Post* noted that over 200,000 workers that lived and worked in the factory regularly worked more than 60 hours per week. The article also reported that workers made about $100 per month and were required to pay for rent and food from the company, which generally amounted to a little over half of workers earnings (Musgrove, 2006). Malone and Jones (2010) claim that after a number of suicides in the Foxconn facility, workers were forced to sign a legally binding document guaranteeing that they would not kill themselves. Malone and Jones (2010) continue by noting that Apple admitted that its suppliers' child labor practices in China had worsened. For Apple to operate in China and earn billions in profits, the workers were not treated as human beings nor were they paid fairly. It is vital to recognize how, where, and by whom Apple hardware products are manufactured and how the iPod and the iTunes Store was inherently complicit in the global exploitation of labor.

Conclusion

This essay revealed and unpacked various monopolistic policies and practices that reinforced the economic dominance of Apple's iTunes Store between 2003 and 2012. From the collusion of the iPod with music files with DRM technology, to the harnessing of the major record labels, to the insurmountable corporate barriers to enter the market, to the shady pricing practices, the surveillance of consumer information and the at times deadly exploitation of labor through hardware production in China, Apple actively utilized these methods to monopolize and ultimately reshape the music industry for financial gain.

Holt (2011) claims:

> it is our duty as citizens, consumers, and educators to cultivate awareness about the dynamics of regulatory practice, political discourse, and the nexus of technological and institutional convergence that will shape the future of entertainment empires and the vitality of our media.
>
> (p. 177)

Likewise, the critical aim here was to disrupt the spectacle of the Apple brand by revealing its true nature as an exploitative tenet of late capitalism. This essay also promotes media literacy, evokes critical discussion, and promotes future research on the political economy of the music industry, in particular, retail. At the end of the day, if one wants to resist such tenacious corporate practices, we must consider the alternatives. Go to a local brick and mortar independent record store and purchase an independent vinyl record instead.

Note

1 All figures in U.S. dollars unless otherwise noted.

References

Apple Customer Privacy Policy. (2010, June 21). *Apple.com.* Retrieved August 12, 2013, from http://www.apple.com/privacy/0201

Apple Inc. (2012). *Apple form 10-K, October 31, 2012.* Retrieved July 10, 2013, from http://investor.apple.com/financials.cfm

Arthur, C. (2012). *Digital wars: Apple, Google, Microsoft and the battle for the internet.* London: Kogan Page.

Bettig, R. & Hall, J.L. (2012). *Big media, big money: Cultural texts and political economics.* Lanham, MD: Rowman & Littlefield Publishers, Inc.

Bockstedt, J.C., Kauffman, R.J., & Riggins F.J. (2006). The move to artist-led online music distribution: A theory-based assessment and prospects for structural changes in the digital music market. *International Journal of Electronic Commerce.* 10(3, Number 3, Spring), 7–38.

Brabazon, T., Cull, F., Kent, M., & McRae, L. (2005). Jingling the single: The iPodification of the music industry. *Australian Quarterly.* 77(3), 26–36.

Breen, C. (2011, June 6). First look: iTunes in the cloud. *Macworld.* Retrieved July, 15, 2013, from http://www.macworld.com/article/1160339/itunesncloud.html

Burkart, P. (2005). Loose integration in the popular music industry. *Popular Music and Society.* 28 (4, October), 489–500.

Burkart, P. & McCourt, T. (2004). Infrastructure for the celestial jukebox. *Popular Music.* 23(3), 349–362.

Campbell, R., Martin, C., & Fabos, B. (2014). *Media and culture: Mass communication in a digital age.* Ninth Edition. New York, NY: Bedford/St. Martin's.

Campbell, R., Martin, C., & Fabos, B. (2017). *Media and culture: Mass communication in a digital age.* (11th ed.). New York, NY: Bedford/St. Martin's.

Creeber, G., & Martin, R. (2009). *Digital cultures.* Maidenhead: Open University Press.

Cuneo, A.C., Elkin, T., Kim, K., & Stanley, T.L. (2003, December 15). Apple transcends as lifestyle brand. *Advertising Age.* 74(50), S-2.

Deidu, H. (2013, May 4). What is iTunes today? *Billboard Magazine.*

Farrell, N. (2011, October 6). iTunes threatens music industry more than piracy: Miramax warns about digital monopolies. *Techeye.net.* Retrieved July, 6, 2013, from http://news.techeye.net/internet/itunes-threatens-music-industry-more-than-piracy

Friedlander, J. (2017). News and notes on 2016 RIAA shipment and revenue statistics. Retrieved October 15, 2017, from https://www.riaa.com/u-s-sales-database

Frith, D. (2012, June 6). Privacy problem for iTunes plus. *Australian IT.* Retrieved July, 13, 2013, from http://web.archive.org/web/20070714071829/http://australianit.news.co m.au/story/0,24897,21874643-39525,00.html

Gracon, D. (2010). *Exiled records and over-the-counterculture: A cultural political economic analysis of the independent record store.* Unpublished doctoral dissertation, University of Oregon.

Grover, R. & Burrows, P. (2007, October 21). Universal music takes on iTunes. *Businessweek.* Retrieved July, 9, 2011, from http://www.businessweek.com/stories/2007-10-21/universal-music-takes- on-itunes

Hardy, J. (2017). Money, (co)production and power: The contribution of critical political economy to digital journalism studies. *Digital Journalism.* 5(1), 1–25.

Holahan, C. (2007, January 5). Taking action against digital rights. *Business Week,* 7.

Holt, Jennifer. (2011) *Empires of entertainment: Media industries and the politics of deregulation 1980–1996.* New Brunswick, NJ: Rutgers University Press.

Isaacson, W. (2011). *Steve Jobs.* New York, NY: Simon & Schuster.

Kernfeld, B.D. (2011). *Pop song piracy: Disobedient music distribution since 1929.* Chicago, IL: University of Chicago Press.

Knopper, S. (2009). *Appetite for self-destruction: The spectacular crash of the record industry in the digital age.* New York, NY: Free Press.

Knopper, S. (2011, October 25). The new economics of the music industry: How artists really make money in the cloud – or don't. *Rolling Stone.* Retrieved July, 8, 2013, from http://www.rollingstone.com/music/news/the-new-economics-of-the-music-industry-20111025#ixzz2bbkqnHjF

Kuhn, K. (2018, April 16). There's a bigger brother watching you—and profiting from it. *Newsroom*. Retrieved April 16, 2018, from https://www.newsroom.co.nz/2018/04/15/104919/theres-a-bigger-brother-watching-you-and-profiting-from-it

Lang, K. & Hughes, J. (2003). If I had a song: The culture of digital community networks and its impact on the music industry. *Journal on Media Management*. 5(3), 180–189.

Malone, A. & Jones, R. (2010, June 11). Revealed: Inside the Chinese suicide sweatshop where workers toil in 34-hour shifts to make your iPod. *Mail Online*. Retrieved July, 10, 2013, from http://www.dailymail.co.uk/news/article-1285980/Revealed-Inside- Chinese-suicide-sweatshop-workers-toil-34-hour-shifts-make- iPod.html#ixzz2bnHBbQge

Murnane, K. (2017). The US music industry crossed a threshold in 2016. Retrieved October 15, 2017, from https://www.forbes.com/sites/evinmurnane/2017/01/18/the-us-music-industry-passed-a-milestone-in-2016/#6069c5d15a90

Musgrove, M. (2006, June 16). Sweatshop conditions at iPod factory reported. *Washington Post*. Retrieved, July, 16, 2013, from http://www.washingtonpost.com/wpdyn/content/article/2006/06/15/AR2 006061501898.html

Peters, M.A. (2017). Media, markets, and political economy: Examining and analyzing power, in Cotter, C., & Perrin, D. (Eds.) *The Routledge Handbook of Language and Media* (pp. 151–163). London: Routledge.

Roth, M. (2007). Entering the DRM-free zone: An intellectual property and antitrust analysis of the online music industry. *Fordham Intellectual Property, Media and Entertainment Law Journal*. 18(2), 515–540.

Scherzinger, M. (2005). Music, corporate power, and unending war. *Cultural Critique*. 60, 23–67.

Sirois, A. & Wasko, J. (2011). The political economy of the recorded music industry: Redefinitions and new trajectories in the digital age, in Wasko, J., Murdock, & G. Sousa, H. (Eds.). *The Handbook of Political Economy of Communications* (pp. 331–357). Chichester, West Sussex: Wiley-Blackwell.

Small, O. (2012). Reshaping the music distribution model: An iTunes opportunity. *Journal of Media Business Studies*. 9(4), 41–68.

Thompson, D. (2011, November 30). How musicians really make money in one long graph. *The Atlantic*. Retrieved June, 22, 2013, from http://www.theatlantic.com/business/archive/2011/11/how-musicians-really-make-money-in-one-long-graph/249267/

10 In Practice and Theory? Scholarship on Wikipedia's Political Economy

Randall Livingstone

Wikipedia, the free online encyclopedia, is the fifth most visited website globally, and it has been ranked in the top 10 most trafficked sites for over a decade (Alexa, 2017). The other top sites are familiar names – Google, YouTube, Facebook, Baidu, Yahoo, Amazon – yet Wikipedia stands out for a number of reasons. Wikipedia is not a search engine, not advertising supported, and not e-commerce. The site is the only non-profit of the group (and further still, the only nonprofit in the top 50 most trafficked sites), funded by an educational organization, the Wikimedia Foundation (WMF), which employs less than 300 people (Alexa, 2017). And the site's policies, procedures, and content are self-governed and user-generated, and with the software it runs on open source. Unlike its familiar Internet peers, Wikipedia offers something unique – openness, transparency, and decentralization – that harkens back to an early Internet ethos.

Indeed, Wikipedia has found success by operating within the dueling ideologies of postindustrial capitalism and the open-source technology movement, each of which has shaped the site in various ways. As former WMF Executive Director Sue Gardner (2011) pointed out:

> The Wikimedia Foundation is a weird organization, full of contradictions and ambiguity and messiness. We are deeply rooted in the free software / free culture movement, which is still generally perceived as 'fringe' and 'radical,' and yet we operate one of the world's most popular websites. We share attributes with large cultural and educational institutions and also with Silicon Valley start-ups.

Many new media scholars have championed the idealism of Wikipedia as a pursuit of knowledge and openness (Benkler, 2006; Jenkins, 2006a; Shirky, 2008), but understanding the reality and implications of the project, sometimes said to work "in practice, not in theory" (Ayers, Matthews, & Yates, 2008, p. 458), requires a more critical analysis, including that of the project's political economy.

Writing at the onset of the social media era, Mansell (2004) argued, "The relative neglect of political economy analysis in research on new media means that the overall social and economic dynamics of the production and the consumption of new media continue to be subjects of speculation" (p. 96). Some critical researchers have answered this call (Fuchs, 2012; Mosco, 2011; Wasko & Erickson, 2009), digging into the economic and institutional forces that that have influenced the swift ascension of digital media. Often these analyses explore how new media organizations and formations fit within or diverge from established Marxist critiques of the media industries, from the Frankfurt School's notion of the cultural industries (Horkheimer & Adorno, 1947), to Murdock and Golding's (1973) ownership structures, to Smythe's (1977) audience as commodity; as such, the focus is often placed on commercial media enterprises like Google and Facebook. But in the past decade, a solid body of literature and critical scholarship has been established on the political economic forces that in many ways have influenced the development, structure, and operation of Wikipedia, the most notable nonprofit playing in a corporate playground. Concerns related to digital and immaterial labor, mass collaboration, ownership and governance, gift economies, cognitive commodities, and the materiality of the Internet have all been explored in the context of Wikipedia. Journals like *tripleC: Communication, Capitalism, and Critique, Journal of Peer Production*, and *New Media & Society* stand out for publishing this vein of research, while organizations like the Institute of Network Cultures and the International Association for Media and Communication Research produce anthologies and hold conferences exploring important, critical points of view.

Through reviewing some of the major scholarly work on the political economy of Wikipedia, this chapter explores the major tensions that emerge from critical analysis of the project. While there are numerous ways to structure such a review, this work is organized around two central concerns of digital political economy: materiality/immateriality and ideologies challenging capitalism. Throughout, the chapter explores how major thinkers in this area consider Wikipedia's place in our current system of postindustrial consumer capitalism and potential to resist its trappings. As Wasko (2014) reminds us:

> The study of political economy of the media and communications continues to grow and evolve [...] a careful analysis of capitalism, its structures, the consequences of those structures and the contradictions that abound is more than ever relevant and needed.
>
> (p. 268)

Materiality/Immateriality

Mosco (2011) writes, "If, as Dallas Smythe (1977) famously remarked, communication is the blind spot of western Marxism, then labor remains a blind spot of western communication studies, including the political economy tradition" (p. 358). From Marx (1867) through Braverman (1998), critical political economists have explored the exploitation of physical labor at the hands of capitalism, and now in the digital age, scholars are examining the use and abuse of cognitive, intellectual, and immaterial labor (Dyer-Witheford, 1999; Fuchs, 2015; Terranova, 2004). Understanding these forms of labor is particularly key to an analysis of Wikipedia, as nearly all of the work done on the site is furnished by volunteers who give up any ownership claims to the work. In addition, exploring the immaterial labor and material infrastructures that maintain and propel the project help us identify and consider new blind spots in this networked digital media.

Hardt and Negri (2004) popularized the notion of *immaterial labor*, which they define as "labor that creates immaterial products, such as knowledge, information, communication, a relationship, or an emotional response" (p. 108). Immaterial labor in the form of communication is necessary for the function of society, and is therefore a public "common" that would ideally be cooperatively owned by society; however, under capitalism this labor is exploited and converted to surplus value by the corporate class (Hardt and Negri, 2004). More so than the traditional audiences of legacy media, users of digital media are often content producers as well as consumers, an added dynamic of media convergence (Bruns, 2008; Jenkins, 2006). Lessig (2006) and Zittrain (2008), among others, argue that the Internet is organically a communications common and the virtues of free, open information and unrestricted participation drive its development. But many Internet sites have become what Andrejevic (2002) calls a "digital enclosure," where communication data and personal data become the private property of the site, only to be fed back to the users in the form of advertising.

Immateriality is an important factor in considering the political economy of Wikipedia, especially when considering labor on the site. A growing body of literature has investigated the role of software robots ("bots") and automated tools on the project (Geiger, 2011; Geiger & Ribes, 2010; Niederer & van Dijck, 2010; Livingstone, 2012, 2014, 2016). Across all language versions of the project, nearly one quarter of edits are made by bots, and on some smaller language versions, the majority of edits are made by bots (Livingstone, 2014). Niederer and van Dijck (2010) argue that "To understand Wikipedia's collaborative process, we need to unravel not simply Wikipedia's human agents, but the specificities of its technicity" (p. 1384). Geiger (2011) traces the politics at play when bots take on roles in a social context on the project, sometimes upsetting human contributors who expect traditional bureaucratic processes. Other work by Geiger and Ribes (2010) highlights how bots and semiautomated tools create a system of distributed cognition that allows human and software editors to more productively fight vandalism on the site. They conclude that "semi- and fully-automated tools constitute an information infrastructure that makes possible the quick and seamless processes of valuation, negotiation, and administration between countless editors and issues" (Geiger & Ribes, 2010, p. 2).

Popular culture scholars like Jenkins (2006a, 2006b) have documented many instances of the digital labor pervading the Internet, even suggesting that fan communities and content producers use their collective intelligence to push back against the traditional culture industries and ultimately have a say in the market economy. Terranova (2004) also identifies collective intelligence as a key trait of online immaterial labor, though her analysis is from a more critical political economic perspective:

> As a collective quality of the labor force, immaterial labor can be understood to pervade the social body with different degrees of intensity. This intensity is produced by the processes of 'channeling' of the capitalist formation which distributes value according to its logic of profit ... music, fashion, and information are all produced collectively but are selectively compensated. Only some companies are picked up by corporate distribution chains in the case of fashion and music; only a few sites are invested in by venture capital. However it is a form of collective cultural labor which makes these products possible even though the profit is disproportionately appropriated by established corporations.
>
> (p. 84)

Both Terranova (2004) and Murdock (2010) argue that the digital economy is really a moral economy where state, capital, and civil interests converge; the result is a space that exhibits both a market-driven compulsion and a gift economy reminiscent of tribal cultures. To understand digital labor, then, the political economist must investigate the relationship between these contrasting logics and the power dynamics that emerge. Terranova (2004) writes that "neither capital nor living labour want a labour force which is permanently excluded from the possibilities of immaterial labor," but ultimately, capital is unwilling to cede control "over the unfolding of these virtualities and the processes of valorization" (p. 84). Murdock (2010) agrees, finding capital too exploitative for this relationship and, similarly to Lessig (2004), he calls for the establishment of a digital commons to preserve the openness of digital labor and to keep public and cultural knowledge and artifacts free and accessible.

Labor is a unique element to understanding the political economy of Wikipedia, as the site runs on the work of a small number of paid staff at the WMF and a vast sea of volunteer contributors. Each group is of concern to political economists, but more attention has been given to the mass of "editors" who write the content and embody the community on the site. Wikipedia has over 100,000 monthly contributors who create and maintain the site's content, which ranges from traditional encyclopedia entries to articles on obscure topics (Wikipedia, 2018). The site's cofounder Jimmy Wales has been quoted as respecting the full autonomy of the site's volunteers: "Wiki is not paper, and [contributors'] time is not owned by us. We can't say, 'Why do we have these employees doing stuff that's so useless?' They're not hurting anything. Let them write" (as cited in Gleick, 2011, p. 381). Unlike the contributor base on other digital projects, including social media sites and Free/Libre Open Source Software (FLOSS), Jemielniak (2014) points out that Wikipedia contributors have no economic incentive to contribute, as their work on the project has virtually no exchange value outside of the project (i.e., the work is not a resume builder and does not help with future employment prospects, as FLOSS programming in fact could). Loveland and Reagle (2013) agree that any social capital accrued on the site "is of limited value outside Wikipedia, unlike the wages paid to other encyclopedists" (p. 1298). The lack of both wages and other forms of extrinsic capital stands out in the history of encyclopedic projects:

> While not all encyclopedists before the time of Wikipedia were motivated by money, the vast majority were, even if this motive existed alongside more idealistic ones. Many made a living as encyclopedists. By contrast, few people are paid to write articles for Wikipedia – and most of these people do so discreetly as their promotional efforts are counter to Wikipedia's policies on neutrality and conflict of interest. Furthermore, authors are unable to take full credit for authorship of an article – an enticement that drew unpaid contributors to prestigious printed encyclopedias – since articles in Wikipedia are open to revision and collaboration.
>
> (Loveland & Reagle, 2013, p. 1298)

Indeed, the lack of credit or authorship stands out from a market capitalist system where individual efforts are leveraged against competitors. The pseudonymous/anonymous nature of Wikipedia contributions suggests what Firer-Blaess and Fuchs (2014) describe as an "info-communist" system (described more in the next section).

Some authors have proposed new terms and concepts for understanding the labor positions that digital media contributors on sites like Wikipedia occupy. Bruns (2007, 2008), Bruns & Schmidt (2011) who has written extensively on Wikipedia and early Web 2.0 platforms, offers "produsage," a portmanteau of "producer" and "usage" that "encapsulates the paradigm shift towards user-led forms of collaborative content creation which are proving to have an increasing impact on media, economy, law, social practices, and democracy itself" (Bruns, 2007). His creation of a new term for this type of online engagement is an effort to further distinguish the logic of industrial mass society and its methods of production from the logic of postindustrial society and its production, as Manovich (2001) highlighted earlier. Further, Tapscott and Williams (2006) have advanced the term "wikinomics" to describe a system where traditional capitalist enterprises can benefit from user-generated content and Web 2.0 ideologies, while others have written of "participatory culture" and "participatory media" as our current state of affairs (Jenkins, 2006; Rheingold, 2008). Van Dijck and Nieborg (2009) were early voices in critically interrogating these concepts of digital collaboration. Of "wikinomics" and business-centric Web 2.0 manifestos, they argue that "by celebrating a perfect match between producers and users, commerce and commons, creativity and consumerism, the authors smoothly turn the alignment of countercultural ideals with mainstream business interests into a hegemonic ideology supported by the masses" (Van Dijck & Nieborg, 2009, p. 860). Lund (2017b) supports this criticism, writing that "wikinomics" "appears as a superficial statement about our time where class struggle is a toned-down phenomenon (at least in the West) and does not appear as an important dimension to focus attention on" (p. 279), and other recent political economists concur (Fuchs, 2013; Tkacz, 2015).

Both Firer-Blaess and Fuchs (2014) and Lund (2017b) reference the famous "to hunt in the morning, fish in the afternoon" passage from Marx (1845) to describe the emancipatory potential that Wikipedia's model of contributions opens up, but Lund (2017b) challenges a idealistic understanding of the project's nature:

> There is an assumed core in the project where the motive for involvement is centred on the creation of an encyclopedia, but there are also activities that are mainly social (or even antisocial), and activities that are primarily focused on the individual economic interest, present.
>
> (p. 12)

Wikipedia is sometimes the site of largely unauthorized work by public relations firms (Arthur, 2013; Blue, 2012; Lund, 2017b), and likely also the site of other professional work by academics and other organizations. The financial relationship between the parent WMF, local chapters, and external institutions and donors also complicates the perception that Wikipedia is a complete system of free volunteer labor (Lund, 2017b). In addition, Lund and Venalainen (2016) point out that:

> some of the paid positions related to Wikipedia, such as the 'Wikipedian in Residence' scheme tailored for museums, libraries, and other non-profits, are almost universally accepted within the editing community, while others, such as working for a public relations agency, are fiercely contested.
>
> (pp. 78–79)

These tensions reflect a core belief within the site's volunteer community and the WMF, which amended the project's Terms of Service in response to paid-editing scandals that contributions should be made with full transparency and be free of profit-driven motives.

Benkler (2006) popularized the notion of commons-based peer production, a system of production particularly information production that distinguishes itself from traditional managerial production systems. With commons-based peer production, work is distributed rather than hierarchical and lacks a traditional profit motive, as the products of the labor are jointly shared and contribute to a public commons rather than becoming a private good. Benkler (2006) discusses Wikipedia as a case study for this type of peer production, and reflecting on Wikipedia's 10th anniversary, he wrote that "the biggest gift that Wikipedia has given to us [is] a vision of practical utopia that allows us to harness the more sociable, human aspects of who we are to effective collective action" (Benkler, 2011).

Benkler's (2006) seminal work is highly cited in the academic literature on information technology in general and projects like Wikipedia in particular. While some agree with his dissection of the principles that make Wikipedia a system of peer production (Rigi, 2012, 2013; Shirky, 2008), others are more critical of the realities of work on Wikipedia being understood in this manner. Tkacz (2015) writes that Benkler's (2006) (and other proselytizers of peer production) claim that Wikipedia is nonhierarchical is incorrect, and that in fact this collaborative work "is not spontaneous, not based on individual merit, not without durable hierarchies" (p. 50). Through tracing controversies on the project, including the presence of artwork depicting the Islamic prophet Muhammed, he argues that the ideology of openness and commons-based peer production actually constrains its own propositions in some ways by creating "frames" that determine what should and should not be contributed. "This is not to suggest that such exclusion is necessarily bad," Tzacz (2015) claims, "just that it is necessary: the same frame that makes a coherent thing like Wikipedia possible does so by sorting out what is the other" (p. 86). Overall, Tzacz (2015) challenges the purity of terms like "openness" and "collaboration" when understanding the project, as they carry ideological baggage that doesn't always match the reality of work on the site.

Other Internet scholars and critics have debated the nature of a "digital commons" on Wikipedia. Lanier (2006) famously criticized the current of emancipatory speculation around the project during its early years, characterizing it as an "online fetish site for foolish collectivism." But extreme evaluations in either direction are "hyperbolic," according to Loveland and Reagle (2013), who write:

> while it is novel that hundreds of thousands of contributors have worked directly and interactively on Wikipedia in its first decade of

life, claiming Wikipedia is the work of either an 'elite' or a 'mob' is simplistic; it is both and more.

(p. 1298)

Firer-Blaess and Fuchs (2014) also call into question the reality of commons-based peer production in action on Wikipedia, pointing out how the demographic constitution of the community should shape our perception of the project. Surveys have found that the Wikipedia contributor base is largely white, male, Western, and educated (Wikimedia Foundation, 2011), similar to other early Internet and digital projects. As such, considerations of a democratic commons on the site needs to be tempered and contextualized: "[Wikipedians'] narrow specificity as a labor segment reflects the general stratification patterns in global capitalism and shows that a truly info-communist mode of production requires a communist society in which free time, skills, and material wealth become universal" (Firer-Blaess & Fuchs, 2014, p. 91).

The focus of this section so far has been labor, but the material infrastructure that makes the idealism of Wikipedia possible (or any Internet enterprise for that matter) should not be discounted or ignored. And yet Lund and Venalainen (2016) argue that the material technological infrastructure as well as the funding structure "have too often been overlooked in the discussions on the commons and peer production (p. 79). They elaborate:

> At the surface level, the operational logic of Wikipedia seems markedly detached from commercial dependencies and openly unsympathetic towards them: after all, Wikipedia is an "encyclopaedia that anyone can edit"—a free service hosted by a non-profit foundation. It is based upon encyclopaedic ideals not so dissimilar to the ones of scientific research: communalism, universalism, disinterestedness and organized scepticism (Merton 1973). However, even Wikipedia cannot completely rule out the realm of the prevailing monetary economy. While the digitalized knowledge itself might be free and open, the material structures of its production and reproduction are still largely governed by the ordinary laws of the market.
>
> (Lund & Venalainen, 2016, p. 82)

Lund and Venalainen (2016) dig in deeper to what they label "the two tiers of Wikipedia's gift economy": donations of money and donations of work time (p. 82). Their original analysis of WMF financials as well as secondary analysis of labor time on the site suggests "the economic value of the unpaid work (if it were to be purchased from the market) is almost ten times the sum of Wikimedia Foundation's annual income" (Lund & Venalainen, 2016, p. 84). In terms of the material infrastructure necessary for Wikipedia to exist and succeed, Tkacz (2015) states that inventorying "the materiality of Wikipedia is not an easy task":

> It obviously includes the project's many servers, various forms of software and code of which MediaWiki is probably the most important, as well as the physical space of the Wikimedia Foundation and national Wikipedia chapters. But perhaps it also includes the personal computer, mobile devices, screens, keyboards, navigation devices, operating systems, and web browsers that are necessary conditions for contributing to the project. And what of the fiber-optic and copper cables, wireless networks, Internet protocols, and indeed energy grids required to make these other things function?

Indeed, despite remaining an ultra lean operation in comparison to other major websites, the WMF and local chapters need to maintain an infrastructure to support 14.5 billion page views per month (Zachte, 2017).

Challenging Capitalism

In Wasko's (2014) recent overview of the political economy of media in the 21st century, she highlights a number of recent developments in the field that directly relate to Wikipedia, including a return to the idea of the commons and a focus on new digital technologies. Wasko (2014) also points out that "many scholars these days are calling for a reinvigoration of Marxist analysis" (p. 267). Indeed, framing an understanding of both the macro and micro levels of Wikipedia around Marxist philosophy has both highlighted new and potentially emancipatory aspects of the project as well as contradictions within its system. This section reviews some major threads in considering Wikipedia from a Marxian perspective.

Marx (1861) conceives a "mode of production" as encompassing both the productive forces (labor, tools) and the relations of production (between owners and workers) of an enterprise. An early episode in Wikipedia's history, the Spanish fork, demonstrates the complexity and possibility of a noncapitalist mode of production for digital media. Indeed, the concept of forking (Famiglietti, 2011; Tkacz, 2011) highlights the confluence of material and immaterial infrastructure concerns on Wikipedia that were discussed previously.

In software development, a fork is a splitting of the project where the source code is copied to a new location, which then begins independent development to create a new and distinct software. This process is largely unique to open-source and open-content projects like Linux and Wikipedia, as issues like copyright prevent the full duplication of content on other projects, and Tkacz (2011) outlines the larger connection to economy:

> From an economic perspective, forking directly contravenes the law of scarcity and seemingly the very basis of value under capitalism. This also means that forking is generally not considered applicable to 'material things,' such as hardware and traditional institutions, that satisfy the scarcity criteria.
>
> (p. 95)

Wikipedia experienced a notable fork after only a year of existence, as contributors to the Spanish Wikipedia grew alarmed at the possibility of advertising appearing on the site. In protest, these contributors copied the full content of the Spanish Wikipedia to another project, the Encyclopedia Libre Universal en Espanol (Enyedy & Tkacz, 2011). This forked project still exists today, though at a much smaller size than what the Spanish Wikipedia grew to be.

The idea of forking is sometimes romanticized, as it indicates a decentralized project nature where anyone can challenge the authority of bureaucracy and break away without the loss of value or what Tkacz (2011) describes as a "so-called exit with benefits" (p. 106). This goal of decentralization was supported by many early Wikipedians, and even prior, by free software activist Richard Stallman, who imagined "a distributed network of individually owned computers" hosting a free encyclopedia (Famiglietti, 2011, p. 297). But as the case of the Spanish fork indicates, starting a new project is complicated by the material and immaterial resources of both the original and the new site. As Enyedy and Tkacz (2011) recount, access to the servers and content of the early Wikipedia was difficult for both bureaucratic and technical reasons, and setting up a new server for the forked content required finding and implementing new hardware and excessive time copying content. The fork, which seemed in principle a reasonable check against an unacceptable direction the original project might take, turned out to be a difficult maneuver to implement.

Tkacz (2011) assesses that a true fork of Wikipedia is not possible, as the project is much more than the encyclopedic content:

> Not only is the source itself not forkable, but it also cannot be seen as the essence of a project. The contributors are part of the project, as is the unique logo, but so too is the domain, the hosting, and the servers.
>
> (p. 100)

And this has implications for how we should understand Wikipedia's peer production and structure. Famiglietti (2011) writes, "Despite its influence, the ideal of decentralized production does not accurately describe Wikipedia's current condition. Yet this ideal has shaped the policies and practices of Wikipedia as users negotiate with the owners of Wikipedia's server space" (p. 306). Instead of holding on to "inaccurate and harmful ideologies" of decentralization and individuality, he continues, we should consider the project "a community of users negotiating a shared space" (p. 306).

Fuchs (2012, 2013, 2015) has written extensively over the past decade on the political economy of digital media and the Internet, considering various digital services and corporations, including Facebook, Twitter, and Google. His analysis approach often applies Marxist and critical theory to understand the material and cultural conditions of production and consumption of digital media. With collaborator Firer-Blaess, Fuchs (2014) argues that Wikipedia should be considered a communist project and is, more specifically, an example of "info-communism," which they define as "an informational mode of production [...] a dialectic connection of social relations and information technology-based productive forces that create informational goods and services" (p. 90). Info-communism offers an alternative to the capitalist information economy that focuses on private property by means of copyright and artificial scarcity. Firer-Blaess and Fuchs (2014) discuss three dimensions of production (subjective, objective, and effect), of which Wikipedia stands out for its communist tendencies. First, the system of decision-making on the site, which utilizes debate, consensus, and participatory democracy, signals cooperation, which is the subjective dimension of production and a principle highlighted in many of Marx' writings. Second, the project's system of funding via donations, governance through the non-profit WMF, and commons-based distribution of content and software through copyleft licensing signals common ownership of the means of production, a central concern of Marx's vision of communism. Third, Wikipedia offers the potential for autonomy and self-determination, as contributors generally participate for the pleasure of intellectual work and cooperation rather than personal positioning in the labor market; this signals the communist ideal of a well-rounded, self-determined workforce. Of course, Wikipedia is not a purely communist enterprise, as Firer-Blaess and Fuchs (2014) point out in their analysis (for example, Wikipedia content can be commodified by third party enterprises that use this content in their services, thus creating surplus value and exploiting the content creators; and Wikipedia contributors are often those with the luxury of time, wealth, and knowledge, thus creating class distinctions that privilege an elite population). They conclude that the "free knowledge production by Wikipedians is a force that is embedded into capitalism, but to a certain degree transcends it at the same time [...] Wikipedia is the brightest info-communist star on the Internet's class struggle firmament" (Firer-Blaess & Fuchs, 2014, pp. 99–100).

Lund (2017a, 2017b) has extensively considered the ideological and material dimensions of Wikipedia's peer production and funding in recent work, with much analysis around two conceptual formations: the communism of capital and the capitalism of communism. The communism of capital, explored at the turn of the 21st century by Virno (2004), encapsulates the way that capitalism has taken up and integrated certain communist concerns. More critically, Beverungen, Murtola, and Schwartz (2013) characterize this as "capital hijack[ing] ideas traditionally considered communist and morph[ing] them into something recognisable yet uncanny" (p. 485). This can take the form of the benevolence of wealthy capitalists, the integration of communism symbols and icons into market mechanisms (like advertising), and the reliance on peer production and free intellectual labor (Beverungen, Murtola, & Schwartz, 2013). This latter form encapsulates Wikipedia's role in this formation, as the project's nonprofit organization, open licensing, and volunteer collaboration often position it as the foil to other tech behemoths. Lund (2017b) argues that the communism of capital formation, along with a Silicon Valley-inspired California Likeness Ideology that prizes individualism and neoliberalism, dominate considerations of communist potentials on Wikipedia at the expense of other formations.

The other formation explored in this vein is the capitalism of communism, discussed in the work of Lund and Venalainen (2016) and Lund (2017b). This is a model more close to Marxist ideals of the commons and the struggle away from the traditionally capitalist system of economics and exploitation, a model where peer production is understood as a viable structure toward a communist goal. Lund and Venalainan (2016) look at the structure of funding that maintains the Wikimedia projects as well as examples and controversies around paid editing on the site in exploring how the project at large (as well as the project's community) understands its relationship to capitalism. They argue that the project's financial model, reliant on small donations from a dispersed community more so than large gifts from capitalist firms and organizations, "is a strong factor" in the capitalism of communism (Lund & Venalainan, 2016, p. 89). Along with recent examples of crowdfunding and digital currencies, Wikipedia represents:

> a latent stream of capitalism of communism [that is] a principally emancipatory force that has some serious obstacles ahead of it, but [one that] can be made more sustainable through the inclusion of a[sic] anti-capitalist critique of [...] ideological formations.
> (Lund & Venalainan, 2016, p. 90)

One line of critique is to interrogate the idea of the digital commons as "immaterial," as Lund and Venalainan (2016) do; instead of immateriality, they propose a focus on the "monetary materialities" of both the commons and the commoners who maintain it, which includes at the macro level, systems of funding and governance, and at the micro level, individual actions like paid editing and the community's opinions of and response to controversies such as paid editing. The authors conclude:

> All in all, we are witnessing increasing attempts to contain and control the commercial influence on Wikipedia and to direct business activities to the advantage of the project. This is not a sign of a less radical community within the peer production, but rather an example of a capitalism of the commons (Bauwens and Kostakis 2014, pp. 356–361), or as we put it, a capitalism of communism.
>
> (Lund & Venalainan, 2016, pp. 92–93)

Conclusion

The radical openness and transparency of Wikipedia as a content platform has provided an abundance of data for empirical researchers to mine for more than a decade. The big data via complete data dumps of article changes, talk page interactions, and user contributions has provided insight for data scientists into how the project works at a macro level. At the same time, qualitative researchers have sought to understand how and why its contributors provide their time and expertise to the world's largest encyclopedia. Amongst the broad and expanding canon of scholarship on Wikipedia, though, the work of critical political economists cannot be overlooked. This chapter sought to highlight work that interrogates the nature of materiality, labor, infrastructure, and ideology on a site that provides information to a large portion of Internet users. Critical perspectives on such a prevalent and important site grow in urgency as the news and information milieu of our current period increasingly breaks down into misinformation and propaganda, and thus this chapter will end with suggestions for additional inquiry.

The WMF continues to grow in size and funding. Its 2016–2017 Annual Report listed over $87 million in donations from 6.1 million donors, with 17 donors at the $50,000 level or higher (Wikimedia Foundation, 2018a). Major Gifts (>$1,000) totaled $10.2 million, about 12% of all donations, of which the WMF writes: "Large donations help the Wikimedia Foundation diversify our revenue stream, and they give high-capacity donors a chance to make a significant positive impact on our mission" (Wikimedia Foundation, 2018b). Additionally, grants from the Alfred P. Sloan Foundation ($3 million) and the Craig Newmark Foundation ($500,000) were earmarked for project work on free licensing educational media and anti-harassment initiatives, respectively

(Wikimedia Foundation, 2018b). The WMF, led by a board of trustees, and local Wikimedia chapters make up a vast bureaucracy of governance and control to collect and distribute this funding. Board members come from both corporate and academic posts, with Jimmy Wales perennially holding the "founder's seat." While some work (Jemielniak, 2014; Lund & Venalainen, 2016; Lund, 2017b) has considered the organizational and funding structures that keep the lights on for Wikipedia, continued and deeper attention should be given to the charitable network of powerful organizations that the WFM depends on and the agendas they set.

Critical work should also continue challenging the inequality in the project's contributor base and its implications for the content of Wikipedia. The gender gap and demographic imbalances of editors have been addressed in some scholarship (Firer-Blaess & Fuchs, 2014; Lam et al., 2011) and is a constant concern of the WMF, which has launched initiatives in the past to improve representation, only to fail at reaching their goals (Bosch, 2012; Guo, 2018; Paling, 2015). Political economists must continue looking at the informational power dynamics and consequences of the white, male, and privileged authorship on cross-gender and cross-cultural subjects.

Finally, it is important for political economists to understand the vision and the mission of the WMF, both in theory and practice, for as Firer-Blaess and Fuchs (2014) point out, the Wikipedia projects may represent a new mode of production, one that "is embedded into capitalism, but to a certain degree transcends it at the same time" (p. 99). The WMF's vision statement asks us to "Imagine a world in which every single human being can freely share in the sum of all knowledge" (Wikimedia Foundation, 2009), while its mission endeavors to "empower and engage people around the world to collect and develop educational content under a free license or in the public domain, and to disseminate it effectively and globally" (Wikimedia Foundation, 2017). While other organizations, including media and Internet companies, purport to further education, free collaboration, and digital literacy goals, they do so with an underlying (or outright) profit motive that corrupts any emancipatory potential. As outlined in this chapter, Wikipedia offers another way, one that somewhat frees the organization and millions of its contributors from the entrenched influence of capitalist production. Political economists need to follow, understand, critique, and when possible, realize the potential of the free content movement that Wikipedia represents, for as Wasko (2014) reminds us, a crucial element of political economy work is praxis and "scholars [should] incorporate issues related to policy and activism in their research, as well as [work] outside academic settings to promote media change" (p. 268). Wikipedia, despite some shortcomings, offers avenues for this important work.

References

Alexa. (2017). The top 500 sites on the web. Retrieved from https://www.alexa.com/topsites

Andrejevic, M. (2002). The work of being watched. *Critical Studies in Media Communication, 19*(2), 230–248.

Arthur, C. (2013, November 21). Wikipedia sends cease-and-desist letter to PR firm offering paid edits to site. *The Guardian.* Retrieved from https://www.theguardian.com/technology/2013/nov/21/wikipedia-cease-and-desist-pr-firm-offering-paid-edits

Ayers, P., Matthews, C., & Yates, B. (2008). *How Wikipedia works: And how you can be a part of it.* San Francisco, CA: No Starch Press.

Benkler, Y. (2006). *The wealth of networks: How social production transforms markets and freedom.* New Haven, CT: Yale University Press.

Benkler, Y. (2011, January 15). Yochai Benkler on Wikipedia's 10th anniversary. *The Atlantic.* Retrieved from https://www.theatlantic.com/technology/archive/2011/01/yochai-benkler-on-wikipedias-10th-anniversary/69642/

Beverungen, A., Murtola, A., & Schwartz, G. (2013). The communism of capitalism? *Ephemera: Theory & Politics in Organization, 13*(3): 483–495.

Blue, V. (2012, September 18). Corruption in Wikiland? Paid PR scandal erupts at Wikipedia. *CNet.* Retrieved from https://www.cnet.com/news/corruption-in-wikiland-paid-pr-scandal-erupts-at-wikipedia/

Bosch, T. (2012, July 13). How Kate Middleton's wedding gown demonstrates Wikipedia's woman problem. *Slate.* Retrieved from http://www.slate.com/blogs/future_tense/2012/07/13/kate_middleton_s_wedding_gown_and_wikipedia_s_gender_gap_.html

Braverman, H. (1998). *Labor and monopoly capital: The degradation of work in the twentieth century.* New York, NY: Monthly Review Press.

Bruns, A. (2007). Produsage: Towards a broader framework for user-led content creation. In Proceedings of the 6th ACM SIGCHI conference on Creativity & Cognition, Washington, DC.

Bruns, A. (2008). *Blogs, Wikipedia, second life, and beyond: From production to produsage.* New York, NY: Peter Lang.

Bruns, A., & Schmidt, J. (2011). Produsage: A closer look at continuing developments. *New Review of Hypermedia and Multimedia, 17*(1): 3–7.

Dyer-Witherfork, N. (1999). *Cyber-Marx: Cycles and circuits of struggle in high-technology capitalism.* Champaign, IL: University of Illinois Press.

Enyedy, E., & Tkacz, N. (2011). 'Good luck with your wikiPAIDia': Reflections on the 2002 fork of the Spanish Wikipedia. In G. Lovink & N. Tkacz (Eds.), *Critical point of view: A Wikipedia reader* (pp. 78–93). Amsterdam, NL: Institute of Network Cultures.

Famiglietti, A. (2011). The right to fork: A historical survey of de/centralization in Wikipedia. In G. Lovink & N. Tkacz (Eds.), *Critical point of view: A Wikipedia reader* (pp. 78–93). Amsterdam, NL: Institute of Network Cultures.

Firer-Blaess, S., & Fuchs, C. (2014). Wikipedia: An info-communist manifesto. *Television & New Media, 15*(2): 87–103.

Fuchs, C. (2012). The political economy of Facebook. *Television and New Media, 13*(2), 139–159.

Fuchs, C. (2013). *Social media: A critical introduction.* Thousand Oaks, CA: Sage.

Fuchs, C. (2015). *Culture and economy in the age of social media.* New York, NY: Routledge.

Gardner, S. (2011). Sue Gardner's blog: About. Retrieved from https://web.archive.org/web/20110809192652/suegardner.org/about

Geiger, R. S. (2011). The lives of bots. In G. Lovink & N. Tkacz (Eds.), *Critical point of view: A Wikipedia reader* (pp. 78–93). Amsterdam, NL: Institute of Network Cultures.

Geiger, R. S., & Ribes, D. (2010). The work of sustaining order in Wikipedia: The banning of a vandal. *Proceedings from the 2010 ACM Conference on Computer Supported Cooperative Work,* Savannah, GA.

Gleick, J. (2011). *The information: A history, a theory, a flood.* New York, NY: Pantheon Books.

Guo, E. (2018, January 8). Inside the fight to change Wikipedia's gender problem. *Inverse.* Retrieved from https://www.inverse.com/article/39999-wikipedias-women-editors

Hardt, M., & Negri, A. (2004). *Multitude: War and democracy in the age of Empire.* New York, NY: Penguin Books.

Horkheimer, M., & Adorno, T. W. (1947). *Dialectic of enlightenment.* New York, NY: Herder and Herder.

Jemielniak, D. (2014). *Common knowledge? An ethnography of Wikipedia.* Stanford, CA: Stanford University Press.

Jenkins, H. (2006a). *Convergence culture: Where old and new media collide.* New York, NY: New York University Press.

Jenkins, H. (2006b). *Fans, bloggers, and gamers: Exploring participatory culture.* New York, NY: New York University Press.

Lam, S. K., Uduwage, A., Dong, Z., Sen, S., Musicant, D. R., Terveen, L., & Riedl, J. (2011). WP: clubhouse?: An exploration of Wikipedia's gender imbalance. *WikiSym '11: Proceedings of the 7th International Symposium on Wikis and Open Collaboration.* Retrieved from https://dl.acm.org/citation.cfm?id=2038560

Lanier, J. (2006, May 29). Digital Maoism: The hazards of the new online collectivism. *Edge.* Retrieved from https://www.edge.org/conversation/jaron_lanier-digital-maoism-the-hazards-of-the-new-online-collectivism

Lessig, L. (2004). The creative commons. *Montana Law Review, 65*(1): 1–13.

Lessig, L. (2006). *Code: Version 2.0.* New York, NY: Basic Books.

Livingstone, R. M. (2012). *Network of knowledge: Wikipedia as a sociotechnical system of intelligence* (Doctoral dissertation). Retrieved from Proquest (ED551305).

Livingstone, R. M. (2014). Immaterial editors: Bots and bot policies across global Wikipedia. In P. Fichman & N. Hara (Eds.), *Global Wikipedia: International and cross-cultural issues in online collaboration.* Lanham, MD: Scarecrow.

Livingstone, R. M. (2016). Population automation: Rambot's work and legacy on Wikipedia. *First Monday, 21*(1).

Loveland, J., & Reagle, J. (2013). Wikipedia and encyclopedic production. *New Media & Society, 15*(8): 1294–1311.

Lund, A. (2017a). A critical political economic framework for peer production's relation to capitalism. *Journal of Peer Production,* (10). Retrieved from http://peerproduction.net/issues/issue-10-peer-production-and-work/peer-reviewed-papers/a-critical-political-economic-framework-for-peer-productions-relation-to-capitalism/

Lund, A. (2017b). *Wikipedia, work, and capitalism: A realm of freedom?* London: Palgrave Macmillan.

Lund, A., & Venalainen, J. (2016). Monetary materialities of peer-produced knowledge: The case of Wikipedia and its tensions with paid labour. *tripleC, 14*(1): 78–98.

Manovich, L. (2001). *The language of new media.* Cambridge, MA: MIT Press.

Mansell, R. (2004). Political economy, power, and new media. *New Media & Society, 6*(1): 96–105.

Marx, K. (1845). *The German ideology.* Retrieved from https://www.marxists.org/archive/marx/works/1845/german-ideology/ch01a.htm

Marx, K. (1861). *Grundrisse.* Retrieved from https://www.marxists.org/archive/marx/works/1857/grundrisse/

Marx, K. (1867). *Capital: A critique of political economy.* Retrieved from http://www.marxists.org/archive/marx/works/1867-c1/

Merton, R. K. (1973). *The sociology of science: Theoretical and empirical investigations.* Chicago, IL: University of Chicago Press.

Mosco, V. (2011). The political economy of labor. In J. Wasko, G. Murdock, & I. Sousa (Eds.), *The handbook of political economy of communications* (pp. 358–380). West Sussex: Wiley-Blackwell.

Murdock, G. (2010, March 30). *The return of the gift: Participation and exploitation on the Internet.* SOJC Communication and Society Annual Lecture, Eugene, OR.

Murdock, G. & Golding, P. (1973). For a political economy of mass communications. In J. Wasko, G. Murdock, & I. Sousa (Eds.), *The handbook of political economy of communications* (pp. 345–366). West Sussex: Wiley-Blackwell.

Niederer, S., & van Dijck, J. (2010). Wisdom of the crowd or technicity of content? Wikipedia as a sociotechnical system. *New Media & Society, 12*(8), 1368–1387.

Paling, E. (2015, October 21). Wikipedia's hostility to women. *The Atlantic.* Retrieved from https://www.theatlantic.com/technology/archive/2015/10/how-wikipedia-is-hostile-to-women/411619/

Rheingold, H. (2008). Using participatory media and public voice to encourage civic engagement. *Civic Life Online: Learning How Digital Media Can Engage Youth.* Cambridge, MA: MIT Press.

Rigi, J. (2012). Peer to peer production as the alternative to capitalism: A new communist horizon. *Journal of Peer Production,* (1). Retrieved from http://peerproduction.net/issues/issue-1/invited-comments/a-new-communist-horizon/

Rigi, J. (2013). Peer production and Marxian communism: Contours of a new emerging mode of production. *Capital & Class, 27*(3): 397–416.

Smythe, D. (1977). Communications: Blindspot of western Marxism. *Canadian Journal of Political and Social Theory, 1*(3), 1–20.

Shirky, C. (2008). *Here comes everybody: The power of organizing without organizations.* New York, NY: Penguin Press.

Tapscott, D., & Williams, A. D. (2006). *Wikinomics: How mass collaboration changes everything.* New York, NY: Portfolio.

Terranova, T. (2004). *Network culture: Politics for the information age.* London: Pluto Press.

Tkacz, N. (2011). The politics of forking paths. In G. Lovink & N. Tkacz (Eds.), *Critical point of view: A Wikipedia reader* (pp. 94–109). Amsterdam, NL: Institute of Network Cultures.

Tkacz, N. (2015). *Wikipedia and the politics of openness.* Chicago, IL: University of Chicago Press.

Van Dijck, J., & Nieborg, D. (2009). Wikinomics and its discontents: A Critical analysis of Web 2.0 business manifestos. *New Media & Society, 11*(5), 855–874.

Virno, P. (2004). *A grammar of the multitude: For an analysis of contemporary forms of life.* New York, NY: Semiotext(e).

Wasko, J. (2014). The study of the political economy of the media in the twenty-first century. *International Journal of Media & Cultural Politics, 10*(3): 259–271.

Wasko, J. & Erickson, M. P. (2009). The political economy of YouTube. In P. Snickars & P. Vonderau (Eds.), *The YouTube reader* (pp. 372–386). Stockholm, SW: National Library of Sweden.

Wikimedia Foundation. (2009). Vision. Retrieved from https://wikimedia foundation.org/wiki/Vision

Wikimedia Foundation. (2011). Editor survey report. Retrieved from https://commons.wikimedia.org/wiki/File:Editor_Survey_Report_-_April_2011.pdf

Wikimedia Foundation. (2017). Mission statement. Retrieved from https://wikimediafoundation.org/wiki/Mission_statement

Wikimedia Foundation (2018a). Wikimedia Foundation 2016–2017 annual report. Retrieved from https://annual.wikimedia.org/2017/index.html

Wikimedia Foundation (2018b). 2016–2017 fundrasing report. Retrieved from https://wikimediafoundation.org/wiki/2016-2017_Fundraising_Report

Wikipedia. (2018). Wikipedians. Retrieved from https://en.wikipedia.org/wiki/Wikipedia:Wikipedians

Zachte, E. (2017, October 16). Wikipedia traffic analysis report. Retrieved from https://stats.wikimedia.org/wikimedia/squids/SquidReportPageViewsPerCountryOverview.htm

Zittrain, J. (2008). *The future of the Internet and how to stop it.* New Haven, CT: Yale University Press.

Part III
New and Enduring Challenges

11 Bribe and Journalism

Jörg Becker

Over roughly the last half century, the threat to journalism has been a central topic of social scientists and political economists. Whether from the rise of public relations, of digital technologies like Facebook and Twitter, or from a variety of other forces, the political economy of journalism has been an area of concern around the world. These concerns are not new, however, particularly not the concerns over the impact of private ownership and its attendant profit motive.

As this chapter will show, the implications of private ownership of journalistic media have been well understood for more than 150 years, predating and predicting the modern concerns over media consolidation and its impacts. By looking to three literary pieces from around the world, the concerns and implications of privately owned, for-profit journalism are recontextualized into a longer, more troubling history.

The 19th century: German Novelists and Journalists

In 19th-century Germany, there was considerable overlap between literature and the rise of journalism and between journalism and State-controlled power structures. Not only was Johann Wolfgang von Goethe court poet to his friend Karl August, Grand Duke of Saxe-Weimar-Eisenach, he was also the latter's war minister. As a journalist and war correspondent, he described the military campaign by German princes against Jacobin France in a text titled *Kampagne in Frankreich 1792* (*Campaign in France 1792*) that was published in 1822 (Cf. Wohlleben, 1981).

One of the most important German novelists of the 19th century also worked as a journalist and war reporter: Theodor Fontane, who had penned the well-known best-selling novels *Jenny Treibel*, *Effi Briest*, and *The Stechlin*, also went to war in France some 50 years after Goethe (Cf. Krings, 2007). In the years 1873–1876 he put to paper his own memories of this German war of aggression against France in three volumes entitled *Der Krieg gegen Frankreich 1870–1871* (*The War against France 1870–1871*). Fontane's 1858 war poem "Das Trauerspiel in Afghanistan" ("The Tragedy of Afghanistan") is also noteworthy in this context. Incidentally, the end of Fontane's ballad parallels the outcomes of the current Western military interventions: "Die hören sollen, sie hören nicht mehr, vernichtet ist das ganze Heer, mit dreizehntausend der Zug begann, einer kam heim aus Afghanistan" ("Those who should listen, they no longer do, the entire army destroyed, the campaign began with thirteen thousand men, just one came home from Afghanistan").

The overlap between literature and journalism held true for a number of others as well: dramatist Heinrich Kleist as publisher of the *Berliner Abendblätter*, poet Ludwig Börne and his radical-democratic essays, poet Heinrich Heine as foreign correspondent of *Augsburger Allgemeine Zeitung*, poet Karl Gutzkow with his feature articles in the Frankfurt newspaper *Phönix*, and dramatist Georg Büchner and his *Hessischer Landbote*.[1] The writer Gustav Freytag, who spent the final years of his long life working exclusively as a journalist in Wiesbaden, was also part of this very same dual tradition.

Gustav Freytag's comedy Die Journalisten (1852)

When the writer Gustav Freytag took his comedy *Die Journalisten* to the theater stage in 1852, the extensive and lengthy disputes surrounding press censorship and freedom of the press had already been settled (Cf. Freytag, 2010, p. 61). However, while freedom of press had been guaranteed in the Constitution of the German Empire of March 28, 1849, the reality looked somewhat different, especially in the major German states of Prussia and Austria. Moreover, press freedom had been considerably curtailed by new laws passed in 1854. Leaflets, magazines, newspapers, flyers, and visual depictions were now only allowed to be published under two conditions: First, the publisher had to apply for a state license for his trade, and second, he had to provide authorities with a copy of his print material before each publication was issued.

The press, then, was one of the most politically delicate and hotly contested topics of the day. Freytag knew this only too well. He was thus well advised to publish his thoughts on the topic in the form of a burlesque and a farce. A different choice such as romantic Realism as employed by fellow poet Heinrich Heine, 20 years Freytag's senior, for instance, or the socio-critical Naturalism favored by French writer Émile Zola, who was 20 years younger, would have cost Freytag his job, his reputation, and royalties. Dressed up as a comedy in four acts, his *Die Journalisten* is a highly ironic tale of two romantic relationships. Two beautiful women fight for their respective lovers, whom at the beginning of the play they are unable to marry for reasons of social class. The tale has a happy ending and both couples are jubilant. In terms of literary genre, Freytag's theatrical burlesque resembles an opera buffa, with mistaken identities, hide-and-seek, and an element of the absurd (Figure 11.1).

Figure 11.1 Gustav Freytag Monument in Wiesbaden, Germany.
Source and Copyright: Uli Bingel, Wiesbaden.

The political rivalry between two local newspapers during an election campaign in a small German town forms the backdrop to the action. The liberal newspaper is called *Union*, the conservative *Coriolan*. And it is precisely with the name "Coriolan" that Freytag plays an ironic game. Named after a Roman hero in a Shakespearean tragedy and an overture by Beethoven created 45 years earlier, Freytag confronts his newspaper *Coriolan* with German small town fuddy-duddies, political corruption, money, and the power cravings of old male has-beens. After the politically troubled Vormärz era and Heine's fierce attacks on the idealistic German Classical period, Gustav Freytag could only see virtues and sense in the "free spirit of the German nation" with derisive eyes. Such values had become hollow for him, the opposite of courageous action (Freytag, 2010, p. 61). And of course the name of the other newspaper, *Union*, was likewise full of irony, given that the central dilemma of the German Constitution of 1848 had been that a union between all the small German states had proven impossible to achieve. It is the liberal

newspaper *Union* that comes off especially badly. That which constituted the fighting spirit of a forward-thinking liberalism in the Vormärz
era had in 1852 degenerated into a newspaper "with a bad spirit and
full of recklessness" (Freytag, 2010, p. 58). Freytag turns someone, who
in his younger years was presumably a fierce journalist of this paper,
into a gluttonous bohemian, an "eccentric" with an "irregular" lifestyle,
someone who "runs up debts," who lives "quite freely, very wildly, im-
morally and without dignity" (Freytag, 2010, pp. 14–17, 24).

Freytag does not hold journalism in very high esteem. One of his female protagonists quips: "A newspaper ruins the character!" She further
speaks of "the evil spirit journalism," and journalists are described as
"hasty, restless and absent-minded" people. It is commonplace for journalists to want to change from one paper to another simply for a bigger
paycheck. It is also seen as typical for politically spiteful attacks to be
published under a pseudonym, or that those who complain about journalism want to exploit it for their own benefit, or that being a journalist
by trade is regarded as a serious obstacle to marriage (Freytag, 2010,
pp. 35, 59, 62, 81).

Entirely in keeping with the anti-Semitic spirit of the 19th century,
the most opportunistic journalist in Gustav Freytag's theater play
is a German Jew. He is at the bottom of the hierarchy at the paper
Coriolan. His liberal boss treats him like dirt, does not want him anywhere near him, and labels him "vulgar" in conversation with others, "hates" and "despises" him (Freytag, 2010, pp. 10 and 38). This
character does not speak proper High German and replies to questions
with counterquestions – something that is seen as being "[stereo]typi-
cally Jewish." In the play's constellation of characters he represents the
epitome of the evil world. His view of journalistic work is cynical and
shaped by (stereotypically Jewish) avarice: "My misfortune is just that
I am in a bad branch of business. I have to make sure I get out of literature"[2] (Freytag, 2010, p. 79).

This *Coriolan* journalist, who writes both to the left and to the right
as required and has no true personal conviction, bears the surname
Schmock. Following Freytag's burlesque, the name Schmock became
synonymous with opportunistic journalists in the German language,
with someone who was happy to take whichever view he would be paid
most handsomely for. For a long time he represented the opposite of a
journalist who felt an obligation to the truth and objectivity. He was the
unprincipled rogue, the hack, and pen pusher. As late as 1902 Wolfgang
Madjera gave a dreadful journalist named Schmock in his play "Helden
der Feder" ("Heroes of the Pen") the sobriquet "characterless scribbler."
(Madjera, 1902). Somewhat similar to Schmock is the figure of the Jewish merchant Veitel Itzig, a character in Gustav Freytag's best-selling
novel *Debit and Credit*, published in 1855. He is portrayed in Mani-
chean comparison to the virtuous German trader Anton Wohlfahrth.

The fact that journalists are seen as morally despicable opportunists is made clear by the confession by Schmock: "[My editor] taught me to write in all directions. I wrote to the left and then to the right again. I can write in whichever direction" (Madjera, 1902, p. 39). Or: "Make up your own stories, what are you a journalist for?" (Madjera, 1902, p. 18). This line by Schmock was left out of some late 19th-century productions, as a Jewish journalist's opportunistic lack of character would have appeared as obedience to his German-Aryan boss's orders (Cf. von Zur Mühlen, 2016). I shall return to journalistic opportunism as well as to the sentence "It is fashionable now that everything should be pleasant for the readers" later in this essay (Cf. von Zur Mühlen, 2016, p. 79).

Thus, in 1852 an opportunistic Jewish journalist like Schmock served as a prelude to what would become the official, systematic regime logic in Nazi Germany from 1933 onwards, namely journalistic anti-Semitism and fascist agitation against Jewish media companies. Adolf Hitler had already written of the press being a "weapon in the service of Judaism" in *Mein Kampf*, and so went about bringing it under his control with "all tenacity and ingenuity" (Hitler, 1933, p. 345). This undertaking was followed in the Nazi era of the early 1940s by anti-Semitic sentences written by the young journalist Elisabeth Noelle, or anti-Semitic torrents of hate against Jewish press enterprises spewed by the doctor of law Hans Theodor Froehlich, who was the contact person at the Nazi propaganda ministry for Elisabeth Noelle's dissertation (Cf. Becker, 2013, pp. 240ff). In 1943 he published an essay of almost 60 pages of pernicious anti-Semitic polemic in the United States under his pseudonym Theodor von Bipen, including calling the journalist Walter Winchell one of the "worst representatives of the Jewish gutter press," accusing him of "slimy ambiguity," speaking of "[the American press] being infiltrated with Jews," and calling New York "the biggest city of Jews worldwide, [where] newspaper publishers are entirely dependent on the goodwill and cooperation of their Jewish newspaper sellers."[3]

Society and literature under Napoleon III in France

In France, as in Germany, political reaction was more firmly assured in the second half of the 19th century following the revolutionary upheavals of the early years. Under Napoleon, internal repression in France corresponded with imperial adventures abroad (Franco-Austrian War, Crimean War, French troops in Mexico). At the same time, the second half of the century saw an enormous, steep, and increasingly dynamic increase in the development of the productive forces. Railway and telegraph became symbols of incessant technological advancement. The latter also resulted in the rise of a rapidly growing mass of proud and pugnacious industrial workers that formed powerful unions and large socialist parties.

In contrast to German Romanticism, French Romanticism of the early 19th century did not involve the complete internalization and depoliticization of its literary heroes. This meant that in France, the transition from Romanticism (Hugo, Lamartine) to the social criticism of Naturalism (Maupassant, Zola) and Realism (Stendhal, Flaubert, Balzac, Verne) was smoother and easier. The concept of Enlightenment, won in bloody and difficult battles in the French Revolution, was preserved throughout Romanticism, Naturalism, and Realism.[4] France knew "committed" literature long before Sartre coined the term in 1945. In France, literature is and always has been a representative of "l'opinion publique."[5] It therefore makes sense for French sociology to be rooted in literary criticism – public arguments, qualitative analysis, and social theory – and precisely not in the philosophical pragmatism and functionalism that was bound to force American sociology into a quantitative positivism. What is telling in this respect is that a Realist writer such as Balzac saw himself as a doctor of the social sciences. The angry article "J'accuse" by writer and journalist Émile Zola, which led to the decisive political turn in the anti-Semitic Dreyfus affair of 1898, is thus not a lapse of French literary history, but one of its consistent high points.

Émile Zola's Novel L'Argent (1891)

Émile Zola was able to publish *L'Argent* (*Money*), based on the much-read book *Le manuel du spéculateur à la bourse* (*The Manual of the Stock Exchange Speculator*), issued by the anarchistic socialist Pierre-Joseph Proudhon in 1853 as one of his last great novels in 1891.[6] By this time Zola had turned himself into a novel-writing machine – from 1871 onwards, he published a novel per year – and his writing had made him both rich and famous. *L'Argent* was the penultimate work of his 20-volume cycle of novels *Les Rougon-Macquart*, which he subtitled *A Natural and Social History of a Family under the Second Empire*.

In *L'Argent*, Zola traces the rise and fall of the large French bank "Union Générale" under the leadership of its director Eugène Bontoux. In the novel, he is called Saccard. He is an ingenious planner, who wins his fortune through daring gambling on the stock exchange. With the help of the financial establishment he has founded, Saccard wants to economically conquer the Middle East for France. Zola introduces the financier Gundermann – based on the banker James de Rothschild – as Saccard's antagonist. Gundermann ultimately manages to bring Saccard's bank to its knees, causing him and all his enterprises in the Orient to go bankrupt. Here Zola references the real bankruptcy of the "Union Générale" in 1882, which shook the entire European financial world and, incidentally, also led many other writers to pen novels about the stock exchange.

Zola's novel begins at the "Bourse," – the French stock exchange – and ends with the two words "love" and "life"; the plot of the novel, while extensive, exists between these two poles. Saccard proclaims his loyalty to finance, telling us, "There is nothing like stolen money to yield a profit" and "men devour those around them for fear lest they should themselves be devoured."[7] Zola describes a roguish world of finance and banking with speculation "under cover of a man of straw" and the "high fever of speculation." "Ah! money, money the King, money the deity," Zola has his character proclaim apodictically (Zola, 2007, pp. 199, 240, 227). Zola does not engage in personalizing; he is aware of the fact that, both in practical and theoretical terms, there are social structures behind the individuals. This becomes clear when he has the intellectual Sigismond Busch observe that our "existing society [is] based upon the capitalistic system" (Zola, 2007, p. 296).

When reading sentences such as Saccard's utterance that:

> Poisonous and destructive money became the ferment of all social vegetation, served as the necessary compost for the execution of the great works [...] From this force, which was the root of all evil, there also sprang everything that was good.

We are reminded of economist Joseph Schumpeter's well-known dictum of the destructive force of economic progress (Zola, 2007, pp. 232–233). And not only Schumpeter comes to mind, but also the Marxist economist Rudolf Hilferding, who made us all aware of the immense economic importance of the financial markets and monetary capital for productive capital in his book *Finance Capital* as early as 1910.

Zola was familiar with the work of socialist Pierre-Joseph Proudhon and was, of course, also aware of the ideas of the brothers Emile and Isaac Péreire, who not only founded their industry-oriented bank "Crédit Mobilier" on November 18, 1852, but, leaning on the notions of early socialist Henri de Saint-Simon, also dreamt of an industrialization supported by banks leading to a socialist society. And naturally Zola was also familiar with the work of his contemporary Karl Marx, seeing that as in *L'Argent* he mentioned the initial publication of Marx's *Capital* in September 1867 (Zola, 2007, p. 296). Yet even if Zola envisaged merely a radical-democratic and republican revolution and not a socialist one,[8] he does rise above the image of individual bourgeois rebel of his earlier novels in his 1885 novel *Germinal*, in which the collective revolutionary is the working class.

While such economic interrelationships surrounding Zola's work may be common knowledge, Zola's novel *L'Argent* is first and foremost also extremely convincing in its author's detailed knowledge of the French press at the time and its social conditions and functions. The banker

Saccard is acutely aware of the fact that he will only succeed in establishing a new bank empire listed on the stock exchange with very active media involvement because he wants to motivate small savers, the rural poor, and farmers and workers in particular to buy shares. Rather than holding background talks with opportunistic journalists, he simply buys a newspaper, which henceforth belongs to the bank: *L'Espérance*, a "Catholic journal in distress," with Saccard becoming its publisher and director (Zola, 2007, p. 182). He establishes an advertising fund under the wing of the bank, aiming to "devote all available money to it" (Zola, 2007, p. 122). The "daily campaign" led by his editor in chief Jantrou is colossal; Saccard puts up posters across all of Paris, issues brochures, buys several small financial papers, and an additional daily newspaper (Zola, 2007, p. 184).

Yet Zola was familiar with other tricks of the media: Jokes are consciously made of public relations work, adversarial journalists are paid hush money, favorable reporting is ensured by gifting journalists bank shares, and there were even "fashionable women who [...] allow advertisements to be tattooed on their persons" (Zola, 2007, p. 195). The editor Jantrou offers Saccard his services for the newspaper *L'Espérance* with the following words:

> Every morning there would be a page reserved for you, articles that would sing your praises, or paragraphs reminding people of you, with allusions to you in contributions altogether foreign to financial matters—in short, a regular campaign, in which, *à propos* of everything and nothing, you would be incessantly exalted on the slaughtered bodies of your rivals.
>
> (Zola, 2007, p. 122)

Jantrou ends his journalistic proposition with the words: "Have a paper, it is a power" (Zola, 2007, p. 123).

Literature and Society in 1950s Peru

The leap from a postrevolutionary Germany of 1852 to the Peru of 1952 is shorter than one might think. In the Latin American country with the highest percentage of indigenous population, whose native language is not Spanish, the revolutionary spirit of optimism after the end of World War I was bound to bring about a literary indigenism that was at the same time intimately linked to social questions. Exceptional examples of the genre are Ciro Alegría's two novels *Los perros hambrientos* (*The Hungry Dogs*) published in 1938 and *El mundo es ancho y ajeno* (*Broad and Alien Is the World*) published in 1941, both revolving around the indigenous people's struggle against hunger, exploitation, and land barons. During this time, José Carlos Mariátegui also fought for a Peruvian indigenism with his socialist theories of an agrarian socialism. He was supported by the French economist Louis Baudin in the latter's 1942 book *Essais sur le socialisme. Les Incas du Pérou.* The writer and journalist Ciro Alegría was still a member of the "Alianza Popular Revolucionaria Americana" (American Popular Revolutionary Alliance or APRA), which was founded in 1924 but was already somewhat outdated by the early 1950s. The Mexican "Partido Revolucionario Institucional" (PRI), founded in 1929, faced a similar situation. By the 1950s, both APRA and PRI had left all revolutionary verve behind them and instead represented the interests of the urban middle classes.

Mario Vargas Llosa set the plot of his 1977 novel *La tía Julia y el escribidor* (*Aunt Julia and the Scriptwriter*) in the 1950s when the APRA was a persecuted party in Peru and military dictator General Manuel Apolinario Odría Amoretti was president.[9] While the novel is not part of the Peruvian revolutionary fight against the misery in which the country found itself at the time of its setting, it does breathe a postrevolutionary pathos as a picaresque novel – an ironic "revolution light" for a now affluent bourgeoisie of the second generation after the revolutionaries of the 1920s and 1930s.

Like Gustav Freytag, Vargas Llosa is concerned with the political role of the mass media. However, in this case the focus is not on newspapers, but on the radio. Indeed, this was this medium which in the early 1950s stood at the vanguard of modernization strategies owing to the forced modernization of peripheral capitalism in Latin America originating from the United States. This held true in the reality of an aggressively wild private radio landscape as well as in the communication and development research conducted under the aegis of communication experts such as Daniel Lerner or Wilbur L. Schramm working for organizations, including the Central Intelligence Agency (CIA), Project Camelot, the United States Information Agency (USIA), or later the Peace Corps.

Mario Vargas Llosa's Novel La tía Julia y el escribidor *(1977)*

The professional designation "escribidor" in the title of the novel marks the book's critical thrust in the direction of radio journalism. In contrast to the Spanish word "escritor," the Spanish word "escribidor" is a slightly derogatory term for a bad writer or hack. In this case, it is also a matter of writing in order to earn money rather than for the sake of art. Pedro Camacho, the "escribidor" of radionovelas, is set in contrast to the first-person narrator, an "escritor," and thus a writer – a character who is also a radio journalist and who is revealed at the end of the novel to be a young Mario Vargas Llosa. However, the autobiographical novel does not just revolve around the difference between "escribidor" and "escritor," but more importantly between fact and fiction and kitsch and reality. While the "escribidor" Pedro Camacho asserts time and again that his radionovelas give a true account of reality, but ultimately he is so drawn into the vortex of his own fictional world that he ends up going crazy.

Vargas Llosa's novel gives a very precise account of the content of the radionovelas, sometimes with a touch of mischievousness. They are about "a stream of adultery, suicide, passions, encounters, inheritances, adorations, coincidences and crimes" and "colossal, heartrending dramas" (Vargas Llosa, 1988, pp. 12 and 96). Vargas Llosa also sees the social function of these radio offerings very clearly: Their listeners:

> loved radio drama serials because they were entertaining, sad or dramatic, because they distracted them, allowed them to dream and experience things that were impossible in real life, because they called attention to certain truths or because they were always a little romantic.
> (Vargas Llosa, 1988, p. 97)

In order to carry his tongue-in-cheek irony to the extreme, at the end of his novel Vargas Llosa writes that Pedro Camacho's radio drama serials were so successful that even the stones listened to them (Vargas Llosa, 1988, p. 251). In fact, Odría, Peru's military dictator, never missed one of the daily episodes either (Vargas Llosa, 1988, p. 176). The importance of radionovelas in the 1940s and 1950s Latin America can be seen by the example of the life story of Eva Perón, whose enormous popularity – especially among poor and common people – was thanks to her first job as a speaker for a radio drama serial.

As Vargas Llosa emphasizes in his novel several times, Cuba played an exceptional role in the production of radionovelas. In the story, radio dramas by the station CMQ compete with the cheap local productions of Pedro Camacho. Cuba with its radio offerings is described to be like a "brothel," with CMQ behaving like a "shark" in it (Vargas Llosa, 1988, p. 360). And indeed, Cuba was the most successful Latin American country in the radio drama sector. The serial "El collar de lágrimas" ("Necklace of Tears") by José Sánchez Arcilla ran for many years, totaling 965 episodes.

Vargas Llosa's novel serves as a congenial literary mirror to the genre of the radionovela. The radionovela – together with its television follow-up, the telenovela – sometimes draw from real-life events to critique journalism in particular and the media in general. The genre of radionovelas and its reincarnation as telenovelas have originated in Latin America, and are now part of a global and highly lucrative business known as the content industry.[10]

Theoretical Conclusions: Journalism, Money, and Power

While the three novels considered come from three different historical as well as national and cultural contexts, their commonalities outweigh their differences. It should also be noted of course that Freytag, Zola, and Vargas Llosa all simultaneously worked as journalists and writers – and all were considerably wealthy. But within the novels, all three foreground similar concerns over the connections between journalism, money, and power. Whether a conservative like Gustav Freytag in 1852 Germany, a radical-democratic bourgeois like Émile Zola in 1891 France, or the wealthy upper middle-class Mario Vargas Llosa from 1977 Peru, all provide a similarly critical and distrustful assessment of the relationship between media, money, and power via three broad themes: journalists versus novelists, money's impact on journalism, and journalism as a mechanism of power.

Journalists versus Novelists

One obvious commonality between the novels is that they pit a journalist, who is "bad" because he is opportunistic, against a "good" novelist. The first is paid well, but "has no morals," while the second may be morally lofty but makes no money. This dichotomy rests not only on the perhaps stereotypical views of the three authors in question, but also on lived experience and an understanding of historically evolved forms of divisions of labor between these professions, which are different in each case. The mid- to late 19th-century markets for books evolved, which were large enough to ensure a popular author had enough readers for his texts. This meant that authors were able to distinguish themselves from journalists in terms of a division of labor and in some cases make a living as freelance professionals. In this respect, the 19th century saw journalists and writers freed of the yoke of the feudal patriarchy of earlier centuries. They enjoyed an additional new degree of freedom, albeit as servants of a capitalist free market. As such, it seems there may be only a clear division of labor between journalists and novelists that starts around the turn of the 20th century. Because of this, it should not be surprising that union cooperation between writers, journalists, and printers have been troubled in spite of apparent linkages.

This division of labor is further threatened by a rise in public relations employment at the same time as a decrease in journalistic employment. In Germany, for example, in 2018 there are approximately 200,000 PR jobs compared to only 100,000 in journalism. This development parallels what is happening elsewhere, particularly in the United States. Moreover, the rise of the commercial privatized advertising machine exemplified by Facebook, Twitter, Instagram, individual bloggers, and online portals, which have no qualitative journalistic filters, only exacerbates this problem. In light of this, concerns that the age of journalism, which has lasted around 150 years thus far, might end within a few decades seem warranted, though it may result in a small elitist journalistic remainder that shift back into being writers, much as it was in the early 19th century

Journalism and Money

Where affirmative thinkers speak of competition and pluralism of the media, these writers know better. In Vargas Llosa's book, two seemingly rival radio stations belong to one and the same family; in Freytag's play, a newspaper simply buys another newspaper it appears to be in competition with; and Zola's bank director buys newspapers and financial papers en masse in order to assimilate them into his corporation in a streamlined fashion. Interestingly, private and business-related concerns are intermingled in a highly risqué way in Freytag's play: the acquisition of one newspaper by the other for a sum of 20,000 thalers is also linked to the "purchase" of wives and daughters, in order to prevent a marriage from interfering with business interests – a set of circumstances true to life.

Vargas Llosa has a sound grasp of contemporary developments in his political-economic observations of the radio sector in the early 1950s. He does not simply address the remuneration of journalists working for radio stations; instead, his sights are on the commercial machinery of private broadcasting. Even in relation to the early 1950s, he points out – while ironically emulating the genre of the picaresque novel – that in their use of audience research and survey data, private broadcasting companies and their allied advertising agencies are concerned with nothing other than increasing their revenue from commercials. Vargas Llosa's language is quite dramatic in this regard. He calls Cuba with its radio station CMQ a "brothel," the station a "shark," and cites the possibility of turning a quiz program into a "new gold mine" (Vargas Llosa, 1988, pp. 360, 371). Can one even put more succinctly the naked truth of a broadcaster's interest in profit than Vargas Llosa when he writes that "the radio dramas from Cuba were sold according to weight, as this was less risky than selling them according to the number of pages or words" (Vargas Llosa, 1988, p. 12).

When an author like Zola criticizes the nature of the financial markets, he is of course much more critical (and also more topical) than one Freytag or Vargas Llosa, even though the former's novel is set back in the late 19th century. Zola addressing the role and function of the financial markets for the media in his analysis of the development of capitalism makes total sense. He is no longer concerned with the financial corruption of individual journalists, but with an internationally operating banking consortium that also runs a media conglomerate. Zola calls it an advertising fund with newspapers, financial papers, and a poster producer. Such an advertising fund may be sold back and forth depending on stock price. What Zola describes here is also an accurate portrayal of today's Reuters PLC, an internationally active financial service provider and near-monopolist with an affiliated press agency which generates less than 10% of the group's overall turnover.

Journalism and Power

Questions of power concerning internal and external relations arise in connection with journalism. All three writers are more than aware of the journalist's financial situation and his dependency on newspaper publishers or radio proprietors. Vargas Llosa's supposedly so successful writer of radionovelas, Camacho, lives in a shabby rear-courtyard apartment because he cannot afford to live anywhere else; Zola's unsuccessful journalist begs others in vain for a small loan so he may survive, while Freytag's journalist Schmock complains about his meager pay and the repeated editing by his superiors. His paltry remuneration of "1 line for 5 pfennigs" certainly seems analogous to the click economy currently emerging in journalism, without employment contracts or social security.[11]

But the authors are well aware of journalists' dependency in terms of editorial responsibility concerning content. For example, Freytag has a journalist say: "I can write in all directions" (Freytag, 2010, p. 79). And in Vargas Llosa's work, a protagonist likewise contemptuously calls journalism "the prostitution of the pen" (Vargas Llosa, 1988, p. 130). Indeed it appears that with power relationships within journalistic editorial departments being as they are, all thoughts of a journalist's freedom or of the freedom of the word turn out to be nothing but ideological prattle.

While there have been numerous discussions in communication studies concerning the internal power relations between different journalistic actors, in Germany it was only in the 1960s and 1970s that a protracted and controversial debate took place on this so-called internal freedom of the press. It culminated in 1970 with the magazine *Der Spiegel* setting so-called editorial regulations, according to which the editors, documentary journalists, and employees of the publishing house are partners with a 50% share in the magazine, and a publisher is thus unable to force individual journalists to express the one or other opinion. Such a situation is still the exception rather than the rule.

All three writers are likewise acutely aware of the fact that the freedom of the media is also massively threatened by the lack of an external freedom of the press. All three works of fiction are thus swarming with senior politicians. Freytag has a local journalist run for the office of delegate of the city parliament, while Vargas Llosa's president not only listens to every episode of the radionovelas each day, but the father of the first-person narrator is also a friend of the labor minister. Furthermore, in Vargas Llosa's book the government bribes a newspaper with advertising commissions if they "attack certain persons and defend others" (Vargas Llosa, 1988, p. 385). In the end the Argentinian ambassador even protests against the radionovelas on the grounds that they insult Argentina.

Zola is the analytically sharpest of the three authors when it comes to politicians' abuse of power in relation to the press. Zola's book sees senior politicians exercise control and wield power in the corporate sector. The brother of banker Saccard is a minister, and a member of parliament sits on his bank's supervisory board alongside proponents of "the entire French nobility" (Zola, 2007, p. 173). Much the same holds true for the major bank of his competitor Gundermann, whose power is described as all-encompassing, effecting "a swallowing-up of the public wealth," with Gundermann "the true master, the omnipotent king, feared and obeyed by Paris and by the world" (Zola, 2007, p. 90). While Zola has his character proclaim "Have a paper, it is a power" with good reason, a journalist in Freytag's text seconds him with the following words: "My first toast is to the great power that brings forth delegates: the newspaper" (Zola, 2007, p. 123; Freytag, 2010, p. 83). Yet it is precisely with this topic of power that the three writers, Freytag, Zola, and Vargas Llosa, enter an arena that could and should rightly be called a systematic blind spot, both in empirical and theoretical communication studies. Power is the anathema of middle-class communication theories.[12]

The Historical Political Economy of Journalism in Germany

While there has been a longstanding battle between the political economy and cultural studies in the English-speaking world, this controversy must be regarded with a certain sense of bafflement from a German perspective. This German bewilderment can be elucidated among other things by way of a historical flashback.

Around the same time Gustav Freytage wrote *Die Journalisten*, the German social philosopher Karl Marx was also considering the connection between economy and media. We need think only of his famous sentence of 1842 that "the first freedom of press is not to be a business" (Thomas, 2013). Even at the time both were writing, this was rarely the practice, however. An empirical look at the press landscape of 19th-century Germany reveals that most newspapers consisted of more than 90% commercial advertisements. This holds true for the *Nachrichten für die Oberamts-Bezirke Calw und Neuenbürg*, for example. The second issue of 1848 contained the following advertisements: sales announcements for plots of land, wood, real estate, houses, meadows, wine, beer, baked goods, hair balm, auctions of inheritances, etc. It is only on the last of the newspaper's eight pages that we find editorial content, namely a political end-of-the-year review of 1848. Naturally, in this revolutionary year of 1848 there were also newspapers published in Germany such as *Die Reform. Ein Communal= und Bürgerblatt*, issued in Hamburg, which did not include a single advertisement but only radical-democratic essays. However, in a political-economic analysis of the press in the 19th century, the newspaper from Calw is more important than the example from Hamburg, in so far as we see with the aid of the former that a free press can also result from a fight for economic freedom and not just in the fight against press censorship and for political freedoms. Editorial content may then merely constitute additional income alongside advertising – as seen in the example from Calw.

Against this historical background, we may then point out that free journalism is both a result of economic freedom and at the same time its servant, as under capitalist ownership structures freedom is inevitably turned into servitude. In other words, the failed revolution of 1848 in Germany was a bourgeois rather than a socialist revolution. Moreover, from the beginnings of German communication studies, the connection between press and economy was very clear to many researchers.

In 1892 Karl Bücher, a professor of political economics at the University of Leipzig, was the first to comment. He critically remarked that the newspaper operator:

> does not intend, as many naïve people think, to represent public interests [in the newspaper], but to profit by selling advertising space. The editorial content of the newspaper is nothing but a cost-increasing means to this end, and it is among the most striking aspects of the civilized world that it continues to endure this state of affairs.
>
> (Bücher, 1981, p. 146)

This position was echoed by Hermann Diez in 1910 with his booklet *Das Zeitungswesen* (*The Press*) in a popular science series issued by the publishing house Teubner-Verlag. Diez was not an academic, but was a practicing journalist working for a news desk, and from 1912 onwards worked for the Wolff news agency. He noted, "The existence of modern newspapers is financially entirely dependent on advertisement sales" (Diez, 1910, p. 139). Arguing further, he explained:

> As of a certain threshold a much-read paper will by necessity become bad, because it no longer concerns itself with the importance of things, nor even with the reader's desires and needs, but simply with advertisers and the price of paper.
>
> (Diez, 1910, p. 142f)

Based on these tendencies, he argued for concerns over monopoly potential for the media, saying "The conclusion of the characteristic development of our current circumstances relating to the press would be a monopoly status of the large capitalist newspaper enterprises of just a few capital cities" (Diez, 1910, p. 141).

What is remarkable is not just the radical nature of Diez's thinking; his everyday experience in the newspaper and news agency business evidently corresponds with the political-economic analysis of critical academics. Both are aware of the economic basis of their media analyses and both agree on there being systemic conflicts between culture/press and economy. It is also worthy of note in relation to two of Diez's quotes that he rightly understands a homogenization of newspaper content to result from circulation numbers and market size. That which Freytag still superficially describes as a "fashion," namely writing content that is "pleasant for the reader," Diez sharply and analytically identifies as a function of the economy (Freytag, 2010, p. 79).

Finally, the aforementioned Dieter Paul Baumert follows in these critical footsteps with his doctoral thesis in political science on the history of journalism in Germany published in 1928. While Bücher and Diez had avoided the concept of a capitalist system in their writing, Baumert titles his last chapter "Journalism and capitalism." The central sentence in this chapter reads:

> Both the capitalist structure of the newspaper business in general and the link between newspaper and advertising contracts in particular have made a threat to the intellectual work in the press appear acute, and have given rise to demands geared for the most part towards a fundamental reorganization of the newspaper business.
>
> (Cf. Baumert, 2013, p. 167)

Baumert's analysis was compatible with the *Institut für Sozialforschung* (Institute for Social Research) founded in 1923 in Frankfurt and the critical theory developed there. This critical theory was to be interdisciplinary, to link economics, culture, musical, and literary theory, psychology, and social philosophy. Economists Kurt Albert Gerlach, Richard Sorge, Felix Weil, and Friedrich Pollock conducted interdisciplinary research at the institute in Frankfurt.[13] However, in that critical theory, the economic analysis of society increasingly gave way to a social and cultural philosophical mindset, which resulted in the economic-materialistic analysis of media production coming up short, even in concepts like Horkheimer and Adorno's "culture industry," as described in their 1944 work "Dialectic of Enlightenment." Armand Mattelart leveled this very criticism at the concept of the culture industry as early as 1982 in a UNESCO publication, and it still holds true today (Mattelart & Piemme, 1982).

But, as is well known, German fascism brutally interrupted all critical social science and the proponents of the Frankfurt School were driven into exile. The critical alternative line to the mainstream of the study of the press, namely Bücher–Diez–Baumert–Frankfurt School, was brought to an abrupt halt. An entirely uncritical humanistic study of feuilletons and newspapers was thus able to break ground. Anchored as it was in an individualistic German Romanticism and a *völkisch* nationally oriented historical scholarship, this science was easily usurped by fascism;

this type of feuilleton study gladly made a pact with German Nazism. The shared root of German fascism and a study of feuilletons and newspapers oriented on a history of ideas based in German idealism – this tradition of thought continued into the postwar period and wasn't successfully challenged until the late 1960s, positing a different role for writers and scholars.

Conclusion: The Writer as Scholar

There have been innumerable authors who simultaneously worked as journalists. In Latin America they include, alongside Peruvian Vargas Llosa, Gabriel García Márquez from Columbia, as well as José Martí from Cuba, Luis Sepúlveda from Chile, and Mario Benedetti from Uruguay. For Latin America in particular it would be important to systematically evaluate the many novels in which the media play a central role. This would encompass, for example, the role of cinema for pubescent adolescents from the slums of Mexico City in Oscar Lewis' ethnological study *The Children of Sánchez. Autobiography of a Mexican Family* of 1961 and the film novels by Manuel Puig such as *La traición de Rita Hayworth* (*Betrayed by Rita Hayworth*) of 1968 or *El beso de la mujer araña* (*Kiss of the Spider Woman*) of 1976.

In Germany, the most notable of all exceptional novels written on the media would be Heinrich Böll's novel on the unbearable agitation by the tabloid newspaper *Bild-Zeitung* against left-wing students in the 1970s. This book, published in 1974 under the title *Die verlorene Ehre der Katharina Blum oder Wie Gewalt entstehen und wohin sie führen kann* (*The Lost Honour of Katharina Blum, or: how violence develops and where it can lead*), was Böll's most successful novel and was translated into over 30 languages.

The sociologist Leo Löwenthal was the most important literary theorist at the Institut für Sozialforschung. It is by no means coincidental to the self-conception of German critical theory that he was able to publish his epochal essay "Zur gesellschaftlichen Lage der Literatur" ("On the Social Situation of Literature") in the institute's first volume of the first year of issue, 1932. His struggle against an idealistic literary history and for a materialistic analysis of society through literary analysis led him to the following ideas on the social function of the novel: according to Löwenthal, this function lay in "studying the effect of the law of competition on the private fate of human beings, and tracing it even into those spheres which seem to evade the immediate sway of public life, market operations and class struggles" (Löwenthal, 1975, p. 16). With these kinds of reflections and demands, the methodology of ideology critique thus found its way into critical social theory.

With the turn from critical theory to constructivism, systems analysis, and cultural studies, and the associated turn from ideology critique to discourse analysis in the early 1990s, there is currently no ideology critical engagement with literature. The writer Émile Zola said of his work that he was practicing "practical sociology" in his novels, and that he was teaching "the bitter science of life" through them and an "important lesson of the real."[14] In French, the old meaning of "belles lettres" is "beautiful knowledge." In the French language, belles lettres or books of fiction often combine literary criticism and social analysis. This essay is thus an homage to this French understanding of qualitative social theory.

Notes

1 The following collection of essays provides a good introduction to this topic: Pöttker, H., & Stan'ko, A. I. (2016). *Mühen der Moderne: Von Kleist bis Tschechow-deutsche und russische Publizisten des 19. Jahrhunderts = Usiliiâ᷉ èpokhi moderna: Ot Kleĭsta do Chekhova: Publitsĭsty Germanii i Rossii 19 veka* (Öffentlichkeit und Geschichte; 9). (Köln: Herbert von Halem Verlag).

2 Literature here pertains to "the written world," which includes journalism.

3 See Bipen, Theodor von, "Presse und Judentum," in: Schönemann, F., Halfeld, A., & Kegel, F. (1943). *Kultur in USA die Wirklichkeit eines Massenwahns* (Nazi propaganda literature; NCY-1806.1). (Berlin: Junker and Dünnhaupt), pp. 318–374; here: pp. 320, 321, 325, and 363 (trans.).

4 For a detailed analysis on this topic cf. Fontius, Martin, "Literaturkritik im 'Zeitalter der Kritik,'" in: Schröder, Winfried et al. (eds.), *Französische Aufklärung. Bürgerliche Emanzipation, Literatur und Bewusstseinsbildung* (Leipzig: Reclam, 1974), pp. 346–402.

5 The expression "l'opinion publique" was first used in the Dictionnaire de l'Académie of 1798. It is thus a term of the revolutionary struggle and could not have originated from feudal Germany. The German term "öffentliche Meinung" is a late loan translation from the French. In the French tradition, a "homme de lettres" is a highly regarded "man of letters." This even made it possible for a conservative politician such as de Gaulle to publicly pay respect to the communist Sartre as a "homme de lettres."

6 In general on this novel cf. Winklehner, Brigitte, "Das Finanzwesen der Gründerzeit im Spiegel von Émile Zolas 'L'Argent,'" in: Winklehner, Brigitte (ed.), *Literatur und Wissenschaft. Begegnung und Integration. Festschrift für Rudolf Baehr* (Tübingen: Stauffenburg, 1987), pp. 123–135.

7 See Zola, E. (2007). Money [1891]. *Trans. Ernest Alfred Vizetelly* (New York: Mondial), available online at https://archive.org/details/moneylargent00zola (last accessed March 22, 2018), pp. 179 and 336.

8 As Wolfgang Klein correctly argues in *Der nüchterne Blick. Programmatischer Realismus in Frankreich nach 1848* (Berlin: Aufbau, 1989), pp. 236ff.

9 In general on this novel cf. Prieto, Rene, "The two narrative voices in Mario Vargas Llosa's 'Aunt Julia and the Scriptwriter,'" *Latin American Literary View*. Vol. 11, no. 22/1983, pp. 15–25.

10 Cf. by way of example on this Boyd-Barret, Oliver & Thussu, Daya Kishan, *Contra Flow in Global News. International and Regional News Exchange Mechanisms* (London: Libbey, 1992).

11 For more details cf. Fuchs, C. (2014). *Digital Labour and Karl Marx* (Taylor and Francis).

12 The sociologist Frieder Naschold cited power as the most important variable
of communication studies early on, adding however that it did not come into
effect in the mostly idealistic approaches. Cf. Naschold, Frieder, "Kommunikationstheorien," in: Aufermann, Jörg et al. (eds.) *Gesellschaftliche Kommunikation und Information*, vol. 1 (Frankfurt: Fischer Athenäum, 1973),
pp. 11–48.
13 Cf. in more detail on the economic tradition of critical theory Erazo Heufelder, Jeanette, (2017). *Der argentinische Krösus. Kleine Wirtschaftsgeschichte der Frankfurter Schule* (Berlin: Berenberg).
14 Cited in Klein, W. (1989). *Der nüchterne Blick: Programmatischer Realismus in Frankreich nach 1848* (Berlin: Aufbau Taschenbuch Verlag Gmbh).

References

Baumert, D. P. (2013). *Die Enstehung des deutschen Journalismus: eine sozial-
geschichtliche Studie/hrsg. und eingel. von Walter Hömberg* (Vol. 11). Baden-
Baden: Nomos.

Becker, J. (2013). *Elisabeth Noelle-Neumann: Demoskopin zwischen NS-
Ideologie und Konservatismus.* Paderborn: Verlag Ferdinand Schöningh.

Boyd-Barrett, O., & Thussu, D. K. (1992). *Contra-flow in Global News: International and Regional News Exchange Mechanisms* (Acamedia Research
Monographs; 8). London: J. Libbey.

Bücher, K. (1981). *Auswahl der publizistikwissenschaftlichen Schriften* (Vol. 1).
Bochum: Studienverlag Brockmeyer.

Diez, H. (1910). *Das Zeitungswesen.* Leipzig: Teubner.

Fontius, M. (1974). Literaturkritik im 'Zeitalter der Kritik', in. Schröder, W.
ua (Hg.), *Französische Aufklärung. Bürgerliche Emanzipation, Literatur und
Bewusstseinsbildung.* Leipzig: Reclam, 346–402.

Freytag, G. (2010). *Die journalisten; lustspiel in vier akten.* Contumax. (Original work published 1905).

Fuchs, C. (2014). *Digital Labour and Karl Marx.* New York: Taylor and Francis.

Heufelder, J. E. (2017). *Der argentinische Krösus: Kleine Wirtschaftsgeschichte
der Frankfurter Schule.* Berlin: Berenberg Verlag GmbH.

Hitler, A. (1933). *Mein Kampf,* (61st edition). Munich: Eher Verlag.

Klein, W. (1989). *Der nüchterne Blick: programmatischer Realismus in Frankreich nach 1848.* Berlin: Aufbau Taschenbuch Verlag Gmbh.

Krings, D. (2007). Theodor Fontane als Journalist. *Die Journalismustheorie
Theodor Fontanes und sein journalistisches Werk am Beispiel seiner The-
aterkritiken, Diss., Dortmund.*

Madjera, W. (1902). *Helden der Feder.* Vienna: Ronagen Verlag.

Mattelart, A. & Piemme, J. (1982). "Cultural Industries: The Origin of an
Idea," *Cultural Industries: A Challenge for the Future of Culture.* Paris: Unesco, 51–61.

Naschold, F. (1973) "Kommunikationstheorien," in: Aufermann, Jörg et al.
(eds.), *Gesellschaftliche Kommunikation und Information: Forschungsrich-
tungen und Problemstellungen: Ein Arbeitsbuch zur Massenkommunika-
tion.* Frankfurt: Athenäum Verlag, pp. 11–48.

Prieto, R. (1983). The Two Narrative Voices in Mario Vargas Llosa's "Aunt
Julia and the Scriptwriter". *Latin American Literary Review,* 11(22), 15–25.

Schönemann, F., Halfeld, A., & Kegel, F. (1943). *Kultur in USA die Wirklichkeit eines Massenwahns* (Nazi propaganda literature; NCY-1806.1). Berlin: Junker and Dünnhaupt.

Thomas, M. L. (2013). Marx and the Freedom of the Press. *Socialist Review* (376, January). http://socialistreview.org.uk/376/marx-freedom-press (last accessed March 19, 2018).

Vargas Llosa, M. (1988). *Tante Julia und der Kunstschreiber: Roman.* Frankfurt am Main: Suhrkamp.

von Zur Mühlen, B. T. (2016). *Gustav Freytag: Biographie.* Göttingen: Wallstein Verlag.

Winklehner, Brigitte, "Das Finanzwesen der Gründerzeit im Spiegel von Émile Zolas, L'Argent,'" in Winklehner, Brigitte (ed.), *Literatur und Wissenschaft: Begegnung und Integration: Festschrift für Rudolf Baehr* (Vol. 6). Tübingen: Stauffenburg, pp. 123–135.

Wohlleben, J. (1981). *Goethe als Journalist und Essayist* (Europäische Hochschulschriften. Reihe 1, Deutsche Literatur und Germanistik; Bd. 419). Frankfurt am Main; Bern: Lang.

Zola, E. (2007). Money [1891]. *Trans. Ernest Alfred Vizetelly.* New York: Mondial.

12 Labor in the Age of Digital (Re)Production*

Gerald Sussman

Introduction

> The more production comes to rest on exchange value, hence on exchange, the more important do the physical conditions of exchange – the means of communication and transport – become for the costs of circulation. *Capital by its nature drives beyond every spatial barrier. Thus the creation of the physical conditions of exchange – of the means of communication and transport – the annihilation of space by time – becomes an extraordinary necessity for it* – Karl Marx (1973, italics added)

> "We Are All Workers" – Levi's ad

The prodigious writings by Janet Wasko, including many important contributions dealing with media labor, have been a great inspiration to me and other critical communication scholars. Moreover, she has been part of a growing cohort of scholars, including several of her own students, who have formed the bridgehead of international political economic research in communications. Her publications on the movie industry (listed elsewhere in this book) and on the largest financial, arguably most influential, mass cultural institution in the world, the Disney Company, is required reading for understanding the political economy and worldwide ideological power of Hollywood. My own academic career and long-standing interest in labor issues is, in fact, closely tied to the efforts of this critical intellectual who opened several doors to me in my early years in the academy. Professor Wasko is well known as a generous mentor and academic leader, but her commitments to the rights of working people have always been at the forefront of her research. It is therefore with great appreciation and respect that I offer this chapter on conceptualizing new forms of labor power in an age of digital (re)production.

---

* This article originally appeared under the title "Systemic Propaganda as Ideology and Productive Exchange" in *tripleC: Communication, Capitalism, and Critique*, available at www.triple-c.at/index.php/tripleC.

As a living praxis, one of the critical tasks of marxism[1] is to apply its incisive logic to interpreting the current conditions in the labor process and in the modern production of surplus value. Reflecting on the influence of capitalist state power and ideology on popular consciousness and on labor resistance, this essay argues that marxist media studies is a tool not only for understanding communications as an infrastructure of capitalist production, but also in explaining its increasingly penetrative applications as systemic propaganda. Media are centrally important in reproducing the ideological preconditions underpinning state legitimacy at home and abroad and, a fatal contradiction, in deepening the abstraction, alienation, and dehumanization of labor, ultimately destroying the very basis of its legitimacy. The accumulation, coercion, and cultural functions of mainstream media in support of the capitalist mode of production – within what has become *a promotional economy* – have intensified and yet are increasingly transparent, making hegemonic (i.e., ruling class) ideology, the grand narrative behind propaganda, considerably more vulnerable to challenge and disruption. If anything, the internationalization and automation of production enabled through digital technology has only strengthened the marxian approach as a way to understand the radical changes in capital accumulation and work life (Dyer-Witheford, 1999, pp. 5–6).

In this essay, I look at formal marxist interpretations of *ideology* from four principal sources of that discussion – Marx and Engels, Lukács, Gramsci, and Althusser – and apply their thinking to present-day revisionist marxian analyses of *labor* to build on the critical intersection of the two. I argue that the neoliberal transformation of the economic system, with particular focus on the United States, from one based on manufacturing employment (now down to below 10% from 16.5% in 1987 and an even starker decline in its share of GDP: 11% in 2010 from 25% in the early 1980s) to one built on services, including financial and information services, has altered the political and ideological culture. In this context, promotion and ideology-based propaganda[2] have risen to central *factors of production* – while directly influencing the casualization, informalization, and precarity of labor.

This essay draws in part on the work of the Italian Autonomistas and their "social factory" thesis, in which distinctions between formal and informal labor and producer and consumer continue to break down.[3] To this I add the importance and *organic role* of systemic propaganda in reducing the status of citizens to individuated consumers and of citizenship to spectatorship. I start with core ideas regarding base and superstructure to set up the marxian framework and proceed to a general discussion of the uses of propaganda in the contemporary production process, the neoliberal economic context, ideology and class consciousness, and the relationship of ideology and propaganda to the informalization of labor in the social factory.

Propaganda and Ideology as Base and Superstructure

In his Preface to *A Contribution to a Critique of Political Economy* (1859), Marx distinguished the realm of the social relations of production (the base) from that of the ideological (legitimating) institutions (the superstructure) that help to maintain the political order:

In studying such transformations (leading to revolution), it is always necessary to distinguish between the material transformation of the economic conditions of production, which can be determined with the precision of natural science and the legal, political, religious, artistic, or philosophic – in short, ideological forms in which men become conscious of this conflict and fight it out.

That men (sic) would fight it out makes clear that what Marx had in mind about ideology is that while it is dominated by the institutions of capital, it is nonetheless contested terrain over which conflict continuously resurfaces, and not simply a predictable sphere predetermined by virtue of the control of the productive forces.

However, capital is never complacent about the risks associated with ideology. In its relentless and ever-expanding drive toward totalizing power over people and nonhuman resources and over time and space, late capitalism has mapped out consciousness as its final frontier. This involves a deeper order of production and continuous reproduction of ideology and public persuasion necessitated by the service character of the digital economy and aimed at cultivating passivity, the promotion of desire, and the construction of materialist identities. What do I mean by *propaganda*? To begin with, propaganda refers to organized doctrinal texts communicated throughout the voice, print, and audio/visual media in the service of state and corporate interests (and of aspiring power interests). *Systemic propaganda* means the penetration of promotional activities into almost every sphere of public life: the conduct of domestic politics and foreign affairs, the selling of public policy, the marketing of goods, services, and public and private institutions, and the profusion of consumption within the "culture-ideology of consumerism" (Sklair, 2001), with social psychological inducements to self-commodification (adoption of the insignia, habits, and discursive practices of the commodity culture) and an informalized "prosumer" labor force. It is also found in the wholesale infomercialization of news and spectacularization of mass media, joined by intensified subterranean and subliminal advertising, the commercialization of public space and public events, and in the promotion of self-promotion (via websites, Facebook, blogs, Twitter, etc.). The range and depth of promotion throughout the cultural and political life of the United States and other countries has led to what a group of critical scholars have termed a "propaganda society" (see Sussman, 2011). By *promotion* I mean a lower-level regular employment of advertising, marketing, direct marketing, public relations (PR), and other direct selling initiatives on behalf of the more prosaic objectives of both elites and non-elites and performed by those trained as active promotional and self-promotional agents.

On the question of *ideology*, I first turn to Marx and Engels. In *The German Ideology*, they start with the universal structure of the commodity, which is the material embodiment of the social relations of production reified within capitalist ideology as a relationship not among workers but among things. The reification takes the form of what Marx (1967) referred to as the "commodity fetish," the objectification of the commodity dwelling on the outward appeal of a thing without reference to the intrinsic exploitative conditions of labor and unpaid "externalities" that brought such a thing into existence and the circuit of exchange. Representations of an independent character of commodities, orphaned from their direct producers, are thus made to appear natural. The "superstructure" is a realm of consciousness-molding (ideology), a range of activities produced by institutions (e.g., education, church, media, courts, corporate self-promotion) acting as the legitimating, sometimes oppositional, agents of/against the capitalist "base" (sphere of production) to provide a culture of compliance with (or resistance to) the hegemonic designs and values of the ruling class.

Where does the marxist concept of ideology fit into an explanation of contemporary societal conditions? Marx and Engels clearly understood the power of ideology to indoctrinate the working class and to redirect their attention from the system of exploitation:

> Morality, religion, metaphysics, all the rest of ideology and their corresponding forms of consciousness, thus no longer retain the semblance of independence. They have no history, no development; but men, developing their material production and their material intercourse, alter, along with this their real existence, their thinking and the products of their thinking... generally speaking, the ideas of those who lack the means of mental production are subject to it. The ruling ideas are nothing more than the ideal expression of the dominant material relationships, the dominant material relationships grasped as ideas.
>
> (Marx and Engels, 1845)

For Marx and Engels (1845), "language is practical consciousness," and we can interpret "language" to cover a broad swath of communication(s), including advertising and marketing, in the reproduction of hegemonic ideology and the materialist realm from which it springs. In the material universe that Marx inhabited, his emphasis was understandably placed on the central importance of communications as an infrastructure of capitalist production inasmuch as communications was confined to servicing the production and circulation of basic necessities of 19th-century life. The hegemonic power (cf. Gramsci) of ideological state apparatuses (cf. Althusser) in his era was at an early phase of the emerging consciousness industries (cf. Enzensberger). Marx died before the takeoff of the modern advertising agency and the onset of mass marketing that eventually established consumerism as a dominant way of life and as one that supervised a more efficient circuit of production-consumption. The velocity of circulation in the late 19th century could not compare to the contemporary speed with which capital, especially finance and other *immaterial* forms of capital (advertising, fashion, cultural activities, software, data files, works of art, photography, and the like) are moved around the world.[4] "Brand value" is an immaterial form of value creation – the socialization of capital – in which consumers identify with the (fetishized) lifestyle ideas associated with the commodity (Arvidsson, 2005). As Hardt and Negri (2000, p. 24) noted: "Biopower... refers to a situation in which what is directly at stake in power is the production and reproduction of life itself."

Marx generally regarded ideology as a construct of dominant repressive regimes, writing in *The German Ideology* (1845) the familiar epigraph, "The ideas of the ruling class are in every epoch the ruling ideas...," expressing the interests and dominant material relationships of the state, whereas his intellectual progeny have tended to view ideology as a necessary function of any state, capitalist, theocratic, or socialist. Indeed, within the Soviet Union, the uses of agitation and propaganda (agitprop) were regarded as means to educate the masses about socialism and to animate and activate them in the pursuit of social rectification. Marx, however, primarily regarded ideology as the means by which the interests and dominant material relationships of the capitalist state and a mythical understanding of capital are naturalized in public consciousness, a theme critically elucidated by Antonio Gramsci.

Marx thus associated "ideology" with the *false consciousness* spread by the ruling class, a superstructural project intended to enjoin the obedience of the working class (the function of legitimation). For that reason, Marx devoted little attention to ideology as an *alternative* form of consciousness that could prepare workers to embrace socialism, though he did describe the moment in the class struggle when the proletariat turn from a class "in itself" (*an sich*) to a class "for itself" (*für sich*) (Marx, 1971). For Gramsci, the domination of classes (hegemony)[5] in capitalist societies is more ideological and cultural than physically coercive. The task of working class liberation, he argued, rests with educated radicals, the organic intellectuals (members of the working class who articulate a practical understanding of repression and struggle through active counter-ideology) capable of seeing through the miasma of bourgeois propaganda.

Althusser as well regarded ideology in dialectical terms and treated it as a formative aspect of class identity, though he attributed its power more in structural terms (*infra*). For Althusser, ideology establishes ways of thinking and acting. As he observed:

> the reproduction of labour power requires not only a reproduction of its skills, but also, at the same time, a reproduction of its submission to the rules of the established order, i.e. a reproduction of submission to the ruling ideology for the workers, and a reproduction of the ability to manipulate the ruling ideology correctly for the agents of exploitation and repression, so that they, too, will provide for the domination of the ruling class "in words".
>
> (Althusser, 1994, p. 104)

Althusser argued that under capitalism it is principally the education system that reproduces the culture of compliance; in an earlier era, the Middle Ages, it was the Church. These days the dominant (mainstream) media perhaps exercise even greater hegemony over the minds of working people than do formal educational institutions, a point made by the Frankfurt School theorists, particularly Herbert Marcuse (1964), who regarded media-driven consumerism as a totalitarian ideology for pacifying the working class. As a practice, propaganda relies on ideological understandings to effect its intended results.

In the workplace, ideology operates at each stage of production. Workers must be prepared to lend their power to the production process. They must also internalize the discipline in the workplace needed for its smooth operation. Ideology next assumes a critical function in the circulation of commodities (the role of advertising, marketing, branding, and other promotional activities are critical here). And finally ideology is central to the conversion of commodities at the point of sale where they are transformed into money for sellers and into consumption for buyers (Kjøsen, 2010). In the production of digital commodities, the points of production and consumption are nearly coterminous, annihilating space by time and permitting capital to rapidly increase the velocity of circulation and the entire circuit of production-consumption.

Raymond Williams (1973), however, argued that ideology should not be construed as merely instrumentalist or reductionist:

> For if ideology were merely some abstract imposed notion, if our social and political and cultural ideas and assumptions and habits were merely the result of specific manipulation, of a kind of overt training which might be simply ended or withdrawn, then the society would be very much easier to move and to change than in practice it has ever been or is.

Rather, ideology is constructed through interplay between base and superstructure, between culture, including its residues of earlier cultural epochs, and the reflexive practices of cultural, social, and political economic institutions. Capitalist ideological reproduction is achieved not through the repression of dissent as much as its *appropriation* within commodified confines of protest, stripped of spontaneous or revolutionary impulses. Capital takes no prisoners in its assault on all manifestations of cultural resistance.[6] In one of the more explicit consumerist efforts to wipe out memories of revolutionary thought, Macy's logo, a five-pointed red star, 60 years ago would have brought its executives before the House Un-American Activities Committee. Saks Fifth Avenue uses designs that are stylized in the form of Constructivist state-run department store ads in the 1920s Soviet Union (Wilson, 2009). Ads for Fortune 500 company Levi Strauss, produced by the Wieden & Kennedy PR firm, sell jeans with such slogans as: "We Are All Workers," "Made Strong for the New Work," and "Everybody's Work is Equally Important." It wasn't a quote from Marx, when an ad called "2011 Jeep Grand Cherokee Manifesto Commercial" (Chiger, 2010) ran with the slogan, "Things We Make, Make Us," but it sounds as if it were.

Capitalism repeatedly draws on revolutionaries for its self-aggrandizing inspirations, a tribute of sorts to the irrepressible character of radical leaders and working people. But it repackages and commodifies radical movements without any reference to the original sources or contexts. True radical ideas and representations are never patented, but once stolen by capital they are converted to property. Perhaps even sections of the *Communist Manifesto* may one day be copyrighted, with infringement suits directed at anyone who dares to publicly recite its passages – similar to Time Warner's ownership of the ubiquitous happy birthday song.

In the digital informational era, the promotional (circulation) aspects of production take on a higher order of importance, a centrality of discursive and symbolic persuasiveness and general valorizing and non-valorizing social practice, inasmuch as the manufacturing base has been relocated en masse to low wage (third world) industrial zones of the new international division of labor. This leaves Western economies the task of selling and consuming the commodities produced offshore. In the United States, where shopping has long been the most important personal activity outside of work and sleep, circulation has become the most critical aspect of wealth creation – the circulation of that which is affectively produced in the first place (in effect the circulation of circulation) –and within that reality immaterial promotion efforts are key to the maintenance of the capitalist mode of production, the overarching ideological sphere, and the unending waging of class warfare and pursuit of cultural hegemony over workers, wherever they may cluster.

Propaganda and the Mode of Production

Where does contemporary commercial ideology fit into Marx's superstructure thesis? In the 19th century, communications came into its own as a means of supporting industrialization, urbanization, and mediatization of the leading industrial cities and states. Marx was among the most prescient observers of the power of communications to speed up the process of commodity production and circulation and in the spreading profanity of a capitalist ideology that, as he and Engels put it, "batters down all Chinese walls" (Marx and Engels, 1848). For the most part, however, Marx looked at communications, most especially the telegraph, as an instrument serving the production sphere – in contrast to the dominant ideology then and now that construes technological history within traditional hagiographic renderings of Morse, Bell, Edison, and others and a genealogy of their "inventions" (see Sussman, 1997, especially Chapters 3 and 4). With the advancement of communications in commerce[7] (the facilitating role of telegraphy in newspapers, newspapers in radio, radio in television, and the like), later marxists such as Gramsci and Lukács took a deeper interest in and appreciation of the ideological functions of communications.

Since the Second World War, the state increasingly has exercised ideological control over the accumulation, coercion, and legitimation processes with the aid of advanced technology and the sweeping presence of (*pace* Althusser) Repressive State Apparatuses and the less blunt instruments of Ideological State Apparatuses. State legitimacy rests in part on its capacity to represent and internalize in the consciousness of its citizens its *raison d'etre* and its policies and manner of administration as natural, just, and in the best interests of the populace. Ideology is stored propaganda (and vice versa), employed toward specific state and commercial objectives and ratified through the general beliefs, values, assumptions, and received ideas that propagate its cultural power. In the sphere of material culture, propaganda is central to the production of commodities, in the manufacture of desire (without use value, there is no exchange value), and in the broader ideology of consumption as a way of life (*consumo, ergo sum*).

As Mike Wayne suggests, to update Marx we need not only to consider formal marxist categories of analysis but to review them in light of a changed world that takes into consideration the "increasing importance of culture, communication, the exchange of ideas, feedback systems, data analysis and so forth, in the production process" (2003, p. 45). In a *promotional economy*, the forces of production are dedicated to circulating domestically or foreign-made products and require a system of surveillance and information processing to fuel its steady stream of propaganda. It also involves a systematic violation of norms of privacy of millions of people on whose lives it relies for its data harvesting and valorization – constituting in effect an "identity labor" force. This panoptic power in turn rests on a heightened fetishizing of commodity culture that induces workers and consumers (and intermediary "prosumers" – see *infra*) to submit not just their knowledge but their personal profiles to the labor process and commodity value formation.

In his widely cited discussion of audience as labor, Dallas Smythe (1977, 1981) anticipated a future in which sections of capital would deepen the range of its efforts toward the commodification of consciousness and a closer reliance on the value-producing consumer (*prosumer*). Smythe focused on advertising and the "work" of audiences, which he understood to be a demographic, in the watching of ads. Thus the audience, acting as a "labor force," a deviation from the orthodox marxist view of surplus value creation (what he saw as a "blindspot" in its communication research), is itself treated as a commodity. But what he did not live long enough to witness were the advanced scientific methods by which advertisers watch the watchers. His most important insight was that promotion breaks down the separation between producers and consumers, between work and leisure, and between use value and exchange value. Advertisers pay for audiences' TV and print media watching (or radio listening) time to sell them not only specific commodities, but also the habit of consumption, and they are happy to pay for audiences' attention, particularly those audiences with the propensity to consume their products.[8]

Corporate ideology reifies and universalizes false consciousness by concealing the exploitative nature of the commodity, as if it were something other than the labor and labor conditions embedded in its materialization, and through identification with possession of those commodities (I am what I own). In this way the object becomes the subject and the subject becomes the object. Indeed, capitalism could not operate without attending to the molding of what Lukács called a "unified structure of consciousness" amongst the workforce – as producers (engaged in exchange value), as consumers (engaged in use value), and as administrators of the system of production. "Bureaucracy implies the adjustment of one's way of life, mode of work and hence of consciousness to the general socioeconomic premises of the capitalist economy" (Lukács, 1971).

The propaganda and promotional functions of the state, particularly when the success of the economy depends on the sales effort, have never been more critical to its survival. Apostles of neoliberal doctrine, particularly in the United States, seek to bring the remainder of nature and independent social life into the circuit of production and consumption through a revised international division of labor, segregating the manual from mental and creative from robotic aspects of work. As U.S. manufacturing industries and agriculture have been shrinking, services have come to represent more than 80% of the GDP, with information services representing the largest share of value added GDP and 59% of the U.S. workforce by 2000 (Apte, Karmarkar, and Nath, 2007, pp. 2, 4). The promotional activities, including advertising, marketing, public relations, branding, and sales management, are crucial to the circulative aspects of production in the U.S. economy, which, with only 4% of the world population, consumes a quarter of global energy output and a third of the world's paper and plastic; the average American as of 2000 consumed 53 times more than the average Chinese person (Tilford, 2000), though that ratio is certainly changing with China's developing consumer economy.

Both the growth and concentration of the U.S. promotional economy is astounding. Just 100 advertisers (of nearly 40,000 firms) represent 41% of the country's total advertising expenditures (Wood, 2008). Advertising alone was an estimated 2.6% of the GDP in 2007 or $153.7 billion (TNS Media Intelligence, 2007), while worldwide spending on advertising reached close to $500 billion in 2008 (Mullaney, 2009). And although advertising momentarily slowed during the start of the recession, 2008–2009, PR has continued to expand. Total U.S. spending on communications in 2008 was estimated at $923.91 billion, a 5.4% growth over the previous year (IT Facts, 2008). This staggering figure is close to Australia's entire GDP and larger than all but 13 (out of 210) other countries. The infrastructure for propaganda and promotion has never been more permeative.

The promotional culture reaches into all phases of political, economic, and social life. The phrase "public space" is fast losing its meaning, as one is confronted by a visual spectrum in American cities that are filled with advertising and commercial logos. High school stadiums bear the imprint of commercial advertising, while soft drink companies compete for school "pouring rights." Street cars and bus stops are branded with corporate identities as are professional sports stadia and even theater tickets. Probably as many people watch the Super Bowl for its 30-second ads, each of which in 2012 cost on average $3.5 million, as those interested in the game itself.[9] Personal websites, blogs, and Facebook accounts and e-book readers come with conspicuous commercial advertising. With the help of a compliant Supreme Court, which in 2010 ruled in favor of permitting nearly unlimited spending by "super PACs" (*Citizens United v. Federal Election Commission*), American federal elections are expected to cost over $8 billion in 2012. Most of this spending will end up as 30-second TV political spots, for which political media consultants will collect a 15% commission (for a longer discussion of corporate branding, see Sussman, 2011).

Neoliberalism, Ideology, and the Informalization of Living Labor

Traditional propaganda normally was employed in the service of *specific* policy or project outcomes of the state; *systemic propaganda* derives from a generalized and globally integrated strategy of development rooted in neoliberal political economy and supportive technological infrastructure. One can date the transition to systemic propaganda to the beginning of "deindustrialization,"[10] deregulation, and flexible accumulation starting in the 1970s. Aided by digital communications technology, boundaries – economic and moral, public and private – that long stood intact to that point began to crumble like the Berlin Wall. With the shift from fordism to a more flexible mode of production, capital is able to capture "larger pools of social and cultural knowledge" (Terranova, 2000, p. 38), which it transforms into commodities and private wealth. Despite the severe crisis of the 1970s, capitalism was anything but finished and was not about to yield to a crisis of confidence, a legitimation crisis – what Jimmy Carter sermonized at the time as a national "malaise." The neoliberal project acquired a political leadership with Reagan and Thatcher that reinvigorated capitalist expansionism. However, Althusser (1994) argued that the capitalist state does not depend for its vitality on innovations in the technological sphere or on particular individuals but does require a recharging of its ideological channels: "*To my knowledge, no class can hold State power over a long period without at the same time exercising its hegemony over and in the State Ideological Apparatuses*" (italics in original, p. 112).

Indeed, with its grounding more firmly embedded in services than manufacturing and with greater emphasis on individuated consumption, neoliberalism is marked by increased investments in cultural production and in the proliferation of signs (Goldman, 1992) that permeate every sphere of society. The selling of commodities, material and immaterial, is now intrinsic to the corporate capitalist state's mode of economic, political, and cultural (re)production, such that the consumerist life becomes the norm of a corporatist state society, making propagandists of those engaged in this collective effort to convert citizenship to spectatorship. The promotional (capitalist) economy is the most predatory of all forms of industrial economies, as it is designed to colonize not only the bodies of its workers, as in the manufacturing system, but also their consciousness, identity, and personality – as well as the leadership of the state. Well over half the members of the U.S. Congress become lobbyists, lawyers, or executives of corporations once they formally leave their government posts, normalizing business practice as an extension of government service.[11]

In the promotional economy, the consciousness of the workforce is "atomized" for the segmented tasks of commodity production, through which workers become alienated from any sense of their independent productive capacities and further marginalized as remote appendages to machine production. The logic of such development and the resources employed for its implementation, including digital technology and objectified labor, are spread out over time and space. The relatively stable conditions of work that once existed vanish from mainstream public discussion, and the life of uncertainty, instability, and precarity becomes the general social norm. That is to say, within a specific mode of development,[12] all life is organized under a regime and discipline of understanding (ideology) and a division of labor assigned to the main tasks of that regime.

The transition from a fordist regime to what Harvey (2007) calls one of "flexible accumulation" necessitated a deeper level of worker discipline that could expand capitalist control over the spatially dispersed and disaggregated workplace. Time-motion methods of managing workers in the manufactory offered lessons for tertiary sector jobs, such that standardized, routinized, regimented, repetitive tasks could be instituted in service practices, in effect creating not a postindustrial as much as a *hyperindustrial* society (Sussman, 2011, pp. 11–12). Workers' subjectivity, seized and surveilled as serviceable in the production-consumption circuit, becomes the veritable *property* of capital. Informal identity labor is integrated with formal labor, with the predominant form of work rooted in informational services and the promotional industries.

Fordist (routinized) labor, meanwhile, is effectively expanded through the collapsing and convergence of job descriptions or expectations in which promotional performance is appended to jobs that in the past did not include them, such as the scripted speech of chain store cashiers ("Did you find everything you were looking for?"), customer relations employees, technical support and other call center operators, and wait staff who in their transactions with consumers suggest additional purchasing options ("Would you like a drink with that order?" and the like). Similarly, TV sportscasters and radio talk show hosts are now expected to plug products on-air. Promotional behavior under the new work requirements is intended to increase exchange value, thus enabling an intensification of exploitation (the surplus value appropriated and valorized under such ultra-commodified "labor power").

In the neoliberal promotional economy, with the infrastructural support of digital technology, capital has undergone a major restructuring, driven by both organizational and technological opportunities and necessities – and characterized by deregulation, privatization, deterritorialization, cutbacks in government social spending, technological and institutional convergences, union busting, erosion of the public sphere, manufacturing and service sector outsourcing, and a deepening of consumerist ideology. When not long ago one could still imagine the separation of the workplace and home life, work and leisure, public and private space, producer and consumer, formal and informal labor, today with corporate capital at the forefront of social and political changes, these and other such dichotomies are converged and subsumed under a corporate aegis. Both inside and outside the formal workplace, workers submit their identity data, voluntarily and involuntarily, via institutionalized and often covert surveillance as a central factor in the production and marketing of goods and services. In such surplus value-generating opportunities, "prosumers" are employed consciously or unconsciously as free informal labor,[13] undertaking such labor using their own equipment and software (computers, programs, and internet connections). The intensification of labor extraction in a system in which informational aspects of production have become increasingly possible and necessary has led to a changing form and composition of labor in material and immaterial goods production.[14]

Creative industries also regularly announce, usually online, the outsourcing of problem-solving activities to amateurs or specialists willing to participate without standard pay, perhaps in hopes of a prize or status of some sort, in finding solutions that profit the company – a system of free or very modestly compensated labor the industry calls "crowdsourcing".[15] Inasmuch as such work contributes to the creation of exchange value, people at large and outside the formal workplace have come to constitute a major source of informal labor (in the crowdsourcing example via the liberal use of their knowledge for software production). As one study noted, "the co-creation economy is about experimenting with new possibilities for value creation that are based on the expropriation of free cultural, technological, social, and affective labor of the consumer masses" (Zwick, Bonsu, and Darmody, 2008, p. 166). The principal form of labor involved in commercial crowdsourcing or surveillance is promotional in character, reinforcing the appeal and ideological aspects of the consumerist economy. Businesses want to know how to better design, market, and brand their products and look to audiences for that knowledge.

Such new forms of labor, compelled by speedup in a promotional economy, one in which the space between production and circulation is potentially reduced to zero (Kjøsen, 2010, p. 83), generates a greater reliance on mental over physical labor. This "immaterial labor," writes Tiziana Terranova, a critic from the Autonomista persuasion, "involves a series of activities that are not normally recognized as 'work' – in other words, the kinds of activities involved in defining and fixing cultural and artistic standards, fashions, tastes, consumer norms, and, more strategically, public opinion" (Terranova, 2000, p. 41), but which are nonetheless part of the "process of valorization" (Lazzarato, 1996, pp. 132–133). That is to say, consumers help to produce the value of a commodity, even if only within a narrow range of resources that such labor is able or willing to invest in a given commodity creation.[16]

The traditional categorical boundaries between production and consumption have thus begun to wither. In a parallel manner, the distinction between traditional media products and advertising has also begun to disappear in the age of mega-media, the "infomercial," product placement, news plugola (the marketing of parent or affiliated network assets as part of the news agenda; see Higgins and Sussman, 2007), and numerous other forms of commercial crossover that shift the construction of commodities from direct and formal to more indirect and informal sources of production. As one critical technology scholar comments, "the direct exploitation of labor is becoming less important as a source of profit and the private exploitation of social knowledge is becoming more important" (Tessa Morris-Suzuki, cited in Arvidsson, 2006, p. 9). Surveillance is also normalized at the level of popular media culture. The journalist Chris Hedges notes how "'Big Brother' and 'Survivor' glamorize the intrusiveness of the surveillance state" to draft voyeuristic impulses of audiences in the project of self-commodification (Hedges, 2009, p. 39).

In the selling economy, greater importance is given to the circulation of commodities, which makes both its promotion and the larger culture of consumerism (ideology) central to the creation of surplus value. There is a separate sphere of activity, which can be called the production of consumption, involving the various promotional activities (advertising, marketing, public relations, sales management, branding, and the like), which are industries in and of themselves. The mobilization of people as prosumers in the promotional economy leads to what Mario Tronti (see Cleaver, 1992) identified as the "social factory" – the production of all by all, a deeper level productive and ideological penetration integrating the social relations of production and consumption. Within the social factory, where capital focuses more of its attention on cultural production, the consumer imagines her/himself to have a communitarian identity through access to the commodity. Raymond Williams (1973), concerned with the prevailing ideology of capitalism, urged that "we should look not for the components of a product but for the conditions of a practice.... the point of departure, in practical and theoretical work, within an active and self-renewing marxist cultural tradition."

Hyperindustrialization of work routines is typical in retail sales, telemarketing, automobile service, clerical jobs, and other low-wage, nonprofessional occupations, often organized with precise automated pavlovian signaling systems (e.g., buzzers and flashing lights in fast food restaurant kitchens, predictive dialing technology at call centers) that pace the responsive output of workers. Though there is now a more geographical spread of manual and mental labor, the conveyor belt method of production looks very much the same for the millions of workers tied to checkout counters, call centers, and fast food assembly lines as it does in the manufactory setting. Even medical clinic physicians are paced by the clock and pressured to treat patients as processing units with taylorist regularity.

With new forms of immaterial capital and an informalized labor pool, there are no speed limits to the circulation of immaterial commodities. The reproduced value of commodities in digital format is potentially immense, as there are no added production costs associated with each retransmission, hence superexploitation of those who produce but do not own the prototype. Capital in fact must withhold the release of digital commodities in order to prepare for its circulation (advertising, marketing, etc.) (Kjøsen, 2010, p. 83). Once released, however, it is elatively easy for others to reproduce and recirculate items on a shareware basis. File sharing practices is known as "copyright infringement" from the capitalist standpoint, but could just as easily be regarded as redistribution of compensation in kind for the appropriation of labor value that went into the production of commodities – better than access to software would be broader, more beneficial social benefits, such as single payer national healthcare, free higher education, and the guarantee of decent housing.

All the King's Horses and All the King's Men Couldn't Put Humpty Together Again": The Coming Collapse of State Legitimacy?

Under neoliberalism and the digital communications system, the consumer has become far more integrated not only as an end user of production (consumption) but as a *factor* of production – the *prosumer*. In the promotional economy, in which surveillance and communications in general are now vital aspects in perfecting the circuit of production, from the sweatshops in China to the Internetshops in America to final consumption, there are no longer well-defined boundaries to what constitutes labor (those who create exchange value). Far from undermining the marxist theory of value and the related precepts of exploitation and alienation, the idea of promotional labor places marxism at the center of understanding the new global economy. The biggest change in the past 35 years or so is the rise of the promotional economy in which the central economic (and cultural, political, and ideological) activity is selling, whether it be tangible commodities, largely produced offshore, or public policies.

With the system of production so entwined in the system of consumption, the ensemble of the "social factory," the present assignment of ownership of production knowledge to the capitalist class is fundamentally disputable. Value creation in the promotional economy makes conspicuous the fact that commodity production derives from socially constructed knowledge (Virno, 2001) – what Marx (1973) called the "general intellect." Capital relies on the general intellect to increase productivity and sustain its rate of profit. In the social factory, the scope of the general intellect on which capital can directly draw is vastly enlarged through the means of digital contact, surveillance, knowledge expropriation, and the promotion of desire. But as Negri (2006), Žižek (2009), and others have argued, capitalism has *privatized* the general intellect, the result of which is an "increase of surplus labor time [that] *prevents* more and more people from enjoying the free time of creative learning and experimentation that would lead the general intellect to flourish" (Smith n.d., p. 5; italics in original).

The increasing use of informalized labor in the form of surveys, polling, crowdsourcing, focus groups, Web use, media subscription, credit card surveillance, cookies, "cool-hunting," and myriad other ways of employing identity labor of consumers as value producers (prosumerism) makes virtually everyone a bona fide shareholder in the production of goods and services. That is, the capitalist system has converted the society as a whole into a production "factory" and into what has become a system of socially organized consumption (Lazzarato, 1996), with labor functions extended throughout the matrix of personal, social, and work life. The system of patents, trademarks, and copyrights, always an ideological and legal as much as a property instrument for the control of production and regulation of society by the capitalist class, has become an anachronistic residue of a belief system that has no relationship to how production is actually constituted.

In a production system conceived as a reification of the "general intellect," the appropriate form of ownership would be collective. Of course the name given to a system in which ownership is signed to the whole society is socialism. Is socialism possible? In the promotional economy, it is all the more transparent that the working class as a whole[17] produces the wealth of nations, ergo here has never been a more compelling justification for workers to claim political power on that basis. The creative designs of communications to manage capitalist society can also be employed and are being employed to undermine it (Wikileaks exposés, growing distrust of the mainstream media, media "piracy" and hacking, anti-advertising movements, growing uses of alternative media, Occupy social networking, and other on-the-ground and mediated forms of resistance). There are clear signs of rupture in U.S. domestic ruling ideology, but physical conditions will have to deteriorate before a counter-ideology based on collectivist thinking can take shape and produce propaganda in line with radically different notions of social progress, teleology, and the role of the individual.

What forms of opposition and resistance are presently feasible and how can they rejuvenate a sense of class struggle? In a digital informational environment, mental labor is indeed difficult to keep proprietary, and there appears to be an unrelenting grassroots effort to maintain the principal information sharing and social networking system, the Internet, as a system of free exchange. No democratic state worthy of the name can exist without a vibrant communication system that provides citizens with the means to make informed and rational political and personal choices. There cannot be a complete negation of all that has evolved under capitalism, but there can be a reappropriation of the promotional means of production toward the cultivation of a harmonious work life, with far less emphasis on consumption and far more value placed on planetary coexistence with all life forms. It is important for social activists to fight for an open Internet system and at the same time for recovery of the airwaves. The Occupy Movement needs to include local and network TV channels as targets for occupation, because they still represent the principal sources of "news," information, propaganda, and ideology for most Americans. Their constant stream of misinformation, ideological distortion, and destructive consumerism and imperialist jingoism has been lethal to the prospects of a more democratic society.

An active and enlightened source of free exchange on the Web, based on principles of inclusiveness and social justice, can contribute to a wakening and reawakening of the spirit of the commons and to deep challenges by the working class as a whole (the social factory) to state institutional repression and the fatuousness of its class-centered rationalizations. This level and *consciousness* of collective agency in turn can form the alternative of cooperative labor and the radical deconstruction of and reflexivity of refusal toward corporatism and the erosion of its hegemonic ideology and propaganda, the formation of socialist political institutions, and the gradual elimination of the many forms of exploitation and alienation and class reproduction itself. When the conditions are right and with the aid of digital media designed for other promotional purposes, a *tsunami* of revolt, like that witnessed in the "Arab Spring," will spread across the shores of the United States and its corporate capitalist world system allies, cancelling the grand imperialist theft of worker knowledge and creativity and substituting collectivization for privatization in the common interest of citizenship and human survival.

Notes

1 I use the lower case for marxism, marxist, and marxian to assert its assimilation as a worldwide framework of analysis, equivalent to putting capitalism and socialism in lower case.
2 The general distinction I make between promotion and propaganda is that promotional activities are individuated acts on behalf of specific products and policies, whereas propaganda (which incorporates promotion) is undertaken for the broader purpose of constructing ideological hegemony over the whole society. On the distinction between ideology and propaganda, the former is a worldview (a way of making sense), while the latter is a set of discursive and symbolic practices derived from a particular form of ideological sense-making.
3 There is an intensive debate about whether the Automistas are indeed marxists. That debate is beyond the scope of this paper. I wish only to infer that what constitutes labor has changed with the intensification of capitalist relations of production within the digital informational mode of development and the relocation of production from the factory to the social factory.
4 By 2010, the volume of daily currency trading worldwide reached $4 trillion (Watts, 2010).
5 The hegemonic culture is one in which the values of the bourgeoisie become the "common sense" values of the whole society, where the working class identifies its own interests with that of the bourgeoisie and thereby desist from resistance or rebellion.
6 Among the many examples of such appropriation of dissent are the fashion of "convict" pants; clothing bearing names like Ideology, Propaganda, and Revolution; Das Kapital and Che Guevara t-shirts; "The Body Shop" capitalizing on the ideology of the environmental movement; Mercedes Benz

car ads ripping off the eponymous song title lyrics of Janis Joplin; corporate polluters greenwashing themselves (to which culture jammers like Adbusters retaliate); the PR industry's "astroturfing" and "guerrilla marketing"; corporate tycoons assuming the pose of global philanthropists; Apple Computer marketing its identity as rebellious, even while it brutally exploits its workers in China to the point of inciting active rebellion (Harris, 2012).

7 Telegraphy was also crucial in the development of financial markets and in consolidating the power of Wall Street over national capital.

8 To this farsighted analysis, Jhally and Livant (1986) offered the more nuanced explanation of the coproduction of "watching time" by networks that purchase the "watching power" of audiences and sell it to advertisers.

9 The amount of actual ball-in-play time for an average 185-minute televised National Football League game comes to just 11 minutes; the rest is advertising (a third), replays, huddling, and just shots of players standing around (Biderman, 2010). This calculation of TV advertising time doesn't include the visual space covered by corporate logos adorning player uniforms and stadium billboards, fences, green screens, and merchandise.

10 The term "deindustrialization" is somewhat contentious, depending on whether one views economy in national or global terms. If the latter, one can argue from a world systems perspective that manufacturing, although spatially decentered, remains centralized in terms of control and that the overseas transnational corporate workforce is constituted as part of a common labor formation with the design, R&D, promotional, and sales workers that are employed in the core countries.

11 According to the Center for Responsive Politics (2012), of those members of the 111th Congress (2009–2011), 52% went to become lobbyists or clients of lobbyists; an additional 5.2% worked for political action committees; and 22.1% of the rest became executives of private organizations.

12 Manuel Castells (1996) uses the term "mode of development" to refer to the digital media of production and exchange. He regards the digital informational mode of development as akin to the centralizing force of electricity in the making of the industrial world a century earlier.

13 One form of crowdsourcing is local television stations' use of their websites, blogs, Facebook, Twitter, YouTube, and special apps for soliciting news tips, photos, video, and feedback from prosumer audiences, in some cases on an exclusive (quasi-contractual) basis. Certain high-end cameras are marketed as "prosumer" quality.

14 The formal workplace is not by any means the sole locus of value creation. There is in fact a presumption of free labor that now prevails in many spheres of daily life: self-checkout at shopping centers, submission to various kinds of polling and consumer surveys, consumer data profiling created through "cookies" and credit card surveillance, registration for the use of websites, the use of ATM machines instead of tellers, and many other, often inconspicuous, acts that convert consumer behaviors and information into factors of production, further mystifying (fetishizing) the nature of the commodity.

15 The willingness of workers to supply their free intellectual labor to a private entrepreneur represents the power of reification of commodities disassociated from their social relations of production. Informal labor that contributes aesthetic, social, or affective appeal to commodities or that helps establish their marketable potential is in most instances free labor, not wage labor, sometimes offered voluntarily, more often captured by stealth. It demonstrates what Hardt and Negri (2001) have argued about the intensification of capital's internalized direction, though, I would contend, this does not mean that capital has abandoned its spatially aggrandizing ambitions.

16 The Autonomistas, including Terranova, Lazzarato, Tronti, and others, are sometimes placed between orthodox marxists and anarchists, though they embrace notions of class in ways that anarchists do not. The principal difference between orthodox and autonomist marxism on the question of class is that the former take a broader view of what and who constitutes a class formation. In the context of a state, where factory labor has greatly diminished in scale and where work is increasingly embedded in immaterial forms of production, it would appear appropriate to reconsider class constituency, although the concept of the social relations of production is as valid as ever.

17 Hardt and Negri (2000) choose to refer to the class of noncapitalists as the "multitude," a somewhat vague description of the "99%." Even if Marx's term "petty bourgeoisie" (those with capitalist administrative functions, such as lawyers, accountants, corporate scientists and engineers, and others) is out of fashion, his concept of class stratification is more substantial than the undifferentiated notion of "multitude." However, both Hardt and Negri and Marx use terminology, whether multitude or proletariat, which tend to wash over cultural and practical distinctions based on race, ethnicity, and gender.

References

Althusser, L. (1994). Ideology and Ideological State Apparatuses (Notes Toward an Investigation). In *Mapping Ideology*, Slavoj Žižek (Ed.), London: Verso, pp. 100–140.

Apte, U. M., Uday, S. K., and Hiranya, K. N. (2007). *Information Services in the US Economy: Value, Jobs and Management Implications*. Accessed January 15, 2012. www.ifm.eng.cam.ac.uk/ssme/references/Karmarkar_ref2_cambridgessme07.pdf

Arvidsson, A. (2005). Brands: A Critical Perspective. *Journal of Consumer Culture* 5 (2): 235–258.

Biderman, D. (2010). 11 Minutes of Action. *Wall Street Journal,* January 15. Online edition.

Brabham, D. (2011). The Myth of Amateur Crowds. *Flow TV Website.* January 15. Accessed January 15, 2012. http://flowtv.org/2011/01/the-myth-of-amateur-crowds/

Castells, M. (1996). *The Rise of the Network Society: The Information Age: Economy, Society and Culture*. Cambridge, MA: Blackwell.

Center for Responsive Politics. (2012). Revolving Door: Former Members of the 111th Congress. *Open Secrets.Org Website.* Accessed March 1, 2012. www.opensecrets.org/revolving/departing.php?cong=111

Chiger, B. (2010). In Want of Things We Can Touch. *Anidea Website.* Accessed February 3, 2012. http://anidea.com/strategy/inwant-of-things-we-can-touch/

Cleaver, H. (1992). The Inversion of Class Perspective in Marxian Theory: From Valorisation to Self-Valorisation. In W. Bonefeld, R. Gunn, and K. Psychopedis (Eds.), *Essay on Open Marxism: Theory and Practice*, Vol. 2. London: Pluto Press, pp. 106–144.

Dyer-Witheford, N. (1999). *Cyber-Marx: Cycles and Circuits of Struggle in High-Technology Capitalism*. Urbana, IL: University of Illinois Press.

Fleming, P. and Sturdy, A. (2011). "Being Yourself" in the Electronic Sweatshop: New Forms of Normative Control. *Human Relations* 64 (2): 177–200.

Goldman, R. (1992). *Reading Ads Socially*. New York: Routledge.

Gramsci. A. 2007. *Prison Notebooks*, Vol. 3. Trans. by Joseph A. Buttigieg. New York: Columbia University Press.

Hardt, M. and Negri, A. (2000). *Empire*. Cambridge, MA: Harvard University Press.

Harris, P. (2012). Apple Hit by Boycott Call over Worker Abuses in China. *The Observer*, January 28. Online edition.

Harvey, D. (2007). *A Brief History of Neoliberalism*. New York: Oxford University Press.

Hedges, C. (2009). *Empire of Illusion: The End of Literacy and the Triumph of Spectacle*. New York: Nation Books.

Higgins, C. L. and Sussman, G. (2007). Plugola: News for Profit, Entertainment, and Network Consolidation. In T. A. Gibson and M. Lowes (Eds.), *Urban Communication: Production, Text, Context*. Lanham, MD: Rowman & Littlefield, pp. 141–162.

IT Facts. (2008). Telecom Spending to Reach $923.91 Bln in 2008. Accessed February 29, 2012. www.itfacts.biz/telecom-spending-to-reach-92391-bln-in-2008/11091

Jhally, S. and Livant, B. (1986). Watching as Working: The Valorization of Audience Consciousness. *Journal of Communication* 36 (3):124–143.

Jubas, K. (2007). Conceptual Con/Fusion in Democratic Societies: Understandings and Limitations of Consumer- Citizenship. *Journal of Consumer Culture* 7 (2): 231–254.

Kjøsen, A. M. (2010). An Accident of Value: A Marxist-Virilian Analysis of Digital Piracy. Master's thesis, University of Western Ontario. Accessed January 14, 2012. http://uwo.academia.edu/kjosen/Papers/387636/An_Accident_of_Value_A_Marxist-Vi rilian_Analysis_of_Digital_Piracy

Lazzarato, M. (1996). Immaterial Labor. In Paolo Virno and Michael Hardt (Eds.), *Radical Thought in Italy: A Potential Politics*. Minneapolis: University of Minnesota Press, pp. 132–146.

Lukács, G. (1971). *History and Class Consciousness: Studies in Marxist Dialectics*. Cambridge, MA: MIT Press.

Marcuse, H. (1964). *One-Dimensional Man: Studies in the Ideology of Advanced Industrial Society*. Boston: Beacon Press.

Marx, K. (1859). Preface: *A Contribution to a Critique of Political Economy*. Accessed December 18, 2011. www.marxists.org/archive/marx/works/1859/critique-pol-economy/preface.htm

Marx, K. (1967). *Capital*. Vol. 1. New York: International Publishers.

Marx, K. (1971). *The Poverty of Philosophy*. Moscow: Progress Publishers.

Marx, K. (1973). *The Grundrisse*. Trans. M. Nicolaus. New York: Penguin. Accessed December 12, 2011. www.marxists.org/archive/marx/works/1857/grundrisse/ch10.htm

Marx, K. and Engels, F. (1845). *The German Ideology*. Accessed December 14, 2011. www.marxists.org/archive/marx/works/1845/german-ideology/ch01b.htm

Marx, K. and Engels, F. (1848). *Manifesto of the Communist Party*. Accessed December 13, 2011. www.marxists.org/archive/marx/works/1848/communist-manifesto/ch01.htm

McInerny, V. (2003). Presenting a New Ideology. The Clothing Line aims for Style and Quality Without Designer Prices. *The Oregonian*, April 29, C-1.

Mullaney, T. (2009). Global Ad Spending to Fall in 2009, Forecasters Say. *Bloomberg News.* Accessed January 13, 2012. www.bloomberg.com/apps/news?pid=newsarchive&sid=aZ2ysU0uRIYo&refer= home

Negri, A. (2006). Goodbye Mr. Socialism: *In Conversation with Raf Valvola Scelsi.* New York: Seven Stories Press.

Sklair, L. (2001). *The Transnational Capitalist Class.* Malden, MA: Blackwell.

Smith, T. (n.d.). The 'General Intellect' in the *Grundrisse* and Beyond. Accessed March 23, 2012. www.public.iastate.edu/~tonys/10%20The%20General%20Intellect.pdf

Smythe, D. W. (1977). Communications: Blindspot of Western Marxism. *Canadian Journal of Political and Social Theory* 1 (3): 1–27.

Smythe, D. W. (1981). On the Audience Commodity and Its Work. In *Dependency Road: Communications, Capitalism, Consciousness, and Canada.* Norwood, NJ: Ablex, pp. 22–51.

Sussman, G. (1997). *Communications, Technology, and Politics in the Information Age.* Thousand Oaks, CA: Sage.

Sussman, G. (2011). Introduction: The Propaganda Society. In Gerald Sussman (Ed.), *The Propaganda Society: Promotional Culture and Politics in Global Context.* New York: Peter Lang, pp. 1–21.

Terranova, T. (2000). Free Labor: Producing Culture for the Digital Economy. *Social Text* 18 (2): 33–58.

Tilford, D. (2000). Why Consumption Matters. *Sierra Club.* Accessed February 12, 2012. http://www.sierraclub.org/sustainable_consumption/tilford.asp

Virno, P. (2001). *General Intellect.* Trans. Arianna Bove. Accessed January 18, 2012. www.generationonline. org/p/fpvirno10.htm

Watts, W. L. (2012). Daily Foreign-Exchange Turnover Hits $4 Trillion. *Market Watch.* Accessed January 22, 2012. www.marketwatch.com/story/daily-currency-trading-turnover-hits-4-trillion-2010-09-01

Wayne, M. (2003). *Marxism and Media Studies.* London: Pluto Press.

Williams, R. (1973). Base and Superstructure in Marxist Cultural Theory. Accessed December 15, 2011. www.rlwclarke.net/courses/LITS3303/2008-2009/04CWilliamsBaseandSuperstructureinMarxistCulturalTheory.pdf

Wilson, E. (2009). Consumers of the World Unite. *New York Times.* Online edition, January 7.

Wood, D. J. (2008). *Hanon McKendry Buys into Alternative Media Firm for Online Advertising Growth.* Accessed January 22, 2012. www.rapidgrowthmedia.com/devnews/mndscpe1002.aspx

Žižek, S. (2009). *First as Tragedy, Then as Farce.* London: Verso.

Žižek, S. (2012). The Revolt of the Salaried Bourgeoisie. *London Review of Books,* 9–10. January 26.

Zwick, D., Bonsu, S. K., and Darmody, A. (2008). Putting Consumers to Work: "Co-Creation" and New Marketing Govern-Mentality. *Journal of Consumer Culture* 8 (2): 163–196.

13 Power Under Pressure
Digital Capitalism in Crisis*

Dan Schiller[1]

Massive and sustained corporate investment around ICTs developed in response to the economic downturn of the 1970s, within a multi-faceted attempt to renew profitable growth. Five core components of this encompassing response were financialization, militarization, wage repression, transnationalization, and accelerated commodification. Yet these axes of a developing digital capitalism eventually converged on a new and deeper financial-economic crisis. May we expect this sector to reprise its earlier role in renewing the accumulation process? How may geopolitical-economic forces be rebalanced?

The past year has been one of great accomplishment in the economic field, wrote the Secretary of Commerce four years into the slump:

> We find almost every major indicator of business conditions moderately above the level of a year ago ... There is much evidence that the Recovery program will proceed progressively, that our remaining problems will be slowly but surely surmounted.

("Roper Projects," 1934)

That calming message came on New Year's Day – 1934. What we now call the Great Depression still had years left to run.

Today, the predicate of booming corporate profits has been millions of layoffs, with no end in sight for high unemployment (Harding, 2011; Powell, 2011; Sum & McGlaughlin, 2010). Housing prices continue to stagger; commercial real estate is stressed (Kapner, 2010). Consumer demand remains iffy, with record-setting inequality adding to the burden (Clifford, 2011). The U.S. Federal Reserve Chairman (Bernanke) noted in November 2010 that the level of output in the advanced economies overall was about 8% below its long-term trend. European sovereign debt crises, rocketing grain prices (Cookson, 2011), and the outbreak of what the Brazilian finance minister called (Jacque, 2010) a "currency war" engendered other reverberating instabilities. The director of the International Monetary Fund (IMF) allows (Strauss-Kahn, 2011) that

---

* This article originally appeared in the *International Journal of Communication*, available at https://ijoc.org/index.php/ijoc.

"It is a recovery beset by tensions and strains—which could even sow the seeds of the next crisis." *Financial Times* journalist Martin Wolf (2010a) was more forthright: "This crisis is far from over," he wrote six months ago. How long the crisis may last is an open question.

The concept of digital capitalism offers a way of clarifying the profoundly important role of communications and information in this global slump (Schiller, 1999). I developed this concept at a sharply different moment, during the late 1990s, as a corrective to the triumphalism then circulating around the so-called "New Economy." Capital, I argued, remained at the center of the political economy even as the market system was restructured to accept a profitable information-intensive orientation.

This remains true today. But circumstances have altered decisively. For the first time in 75 years, the world is mired in a downturn that originated in the developed market economies – the slump's epicenter is the historical hub of information and communications technology (ICT) innovation (McNally, 2011; Walker, 2010). The theory of digital capitalism now must ask: How is the political economy's escalating reliance on communications and information linked to today's crisis? And moving from there: How may communications and information figure in its eventual resolution, as the global market system reorganizes?

Information and Communications in Capital's Spatial–Temporal Fix

Our starting point is the 1970s. Responding to what was then the most severe downturn of the postwar era, U.S. elites sought to restore profitable market growth by developing what David Harvey (2003, pp. 87–88) calls a "spatio-temporal fix." Within the many-sided and contingent process of reconstruction that followed, information and communications played an axial role.

Consider first the 40-year flood of capital into finance. The roots of this financialization encompass more than bankers' avarice. The crumbling of the postwar international financial order supplied the enabling context. Judith Stein (2010, p. 296) explains how, after the United States abandoned the fixed peg of the Gold Standard, transnational corporations (TNCs) doing business in multiple national markets and currencies sought means of hedging risks arising from newly volatile exchange rates. Meanwhile, overcapacity and growing competition in the manufacturing industry placed pressure on corporations' existing accumulation strategies, motivating a flight into financial vehicles. Stagnating wages, finally, stimulated household demand for credit and a willingness to take on debt (Harvey, 2010; Reich, 2010). Financialization emerged as an overarching economic syndrome (Brenner, 2009; Foster & Magdoff, 2009).

Finance, in turn, became a site of massive ICT investment, to support both networked services and mathematically complex product innovations. From the late 1960s' remake of *Wall Street* around computerized trading and Citibank CEO Walter Wriston's (1979) subsequent encomiums to the "information standard," we may trace an unbroken line to the present. Financial services companies constitute the second largest sectoral source of demand for ICTs, following the communications industry (U.S. Census Bureau, 2010). And big banks may lavish greater resources on technology than tech companies themselves. In 2008, Citigroup employed 25,000 software developers and spent an estimated $4.9 billion on ICT (Guerrera, 2009).

With the deregulation and increasing interlinkage of global finance, the new tools and products allowed risk to be repackaged and spread across the world. This dispersal of individual risk turned out, however, to spread systemic risk: When the crisis erupted in an obscure corner of the U.S. market for mortgage-backed securities, networked cross-border financial chains circulated its lethal impulse outward instantaneously (IMF, 2009; Tett, 2011).

A second crucial means of restoring profitable growth stemmed from the federal government and, in particular, from the U.S. Department of Defense. Coming out of World War II, corporate capital had allied with military agencies to launch what became a sustained technological revolution in information processing and communications. Project SAGE and the DEW Line were formative examples. A decade or so later, the Vietnam War engendered new visions around the so-called "electronic battlefield" (Klare, 1972); visions of "net-centric warfare" became successively more grandiose. President Reagan's "Star Wars," or Strategic Defense Initiative (Mosco, 1989), of course catapulted weapons spending into the Internet era.

ICTs have become intrinsic elements in the machinery of war (Schiller, 2008). Here is the Deputy Secretary of Defense (Lynn, 2010, p. 98) writing in a recent issue of *Foreign Affairs*:

> Information technology enables almost everything the U.S. military does: logistical support and global command and control of forces, real–time provision of intelligence, and remote operations. Every one of these functions depends heavily on the military's global communications backbone, which consists of 15,000 networks and seven million computing devices across hundreds of installations in dozens of countries. More than 90,000 people work full time to maintain it.

In one estimate, the defense department's 2011 information technology (IT) budget exceeds $36 billion, approaching half of the federal government's overall spending on IT (IT Dashboard, 2010). The contradiction between this lethal high-tech apparatus and humanity's need for peaceable reconstruction remains acute.

The third and fourth vectors of ICT growth ran together as, in the wake of the 1970s' profit squeeze, capital also broadly reorganized the system of production. One was directed at cutting labor costs. Crucial here was the innovation of "lean production" practices, in which IT-heavy but employee-light systems were introduced in an expanding series of work settings (Moody, 1997). Real wages in the United States dropped by 10% between 1978 and 1983 and, beginning in 1979, the value of U.S. labor power fell for the remainder of the century (McNally, 2011, pp. 36, 48). Contributing to the decline were concurrent attacks on unions, reduced government support for social services, downsizing, outsourcing – and a rapidly growing foreign direct investment (FDI).

Attempts to reduce labor costs succeeded beyond the imagination of corporate leaders during the Nixon era. The flooding of the global market for labor power with a couple of billion people – throughout China, the old Soviet Bloc, and other parts of what was once a more independent Third World (Prashad, 2007) – marks an outstanding feature of our times. Harvey (2010) underlines the profoundly contradictory result: Its success in pursuing wage repression means that capital must now contend with flagging consumer demand. Like financialization, however, newly accelerated FDI came about not only because of capital's power but also because of its vulnerability. Renewed inter-capitalist competition and deepening excess capacity *drove* capital to seek out new investment outlets for the surplus that was the crushing result of its own prior successes.

Big companies had long been purchasing factories, offices, mines, and plantations outside the U.S. domestic market (Appel, 2007). The motivations varied case by case: cheapened labor power, enhanced market access, new sources of natural resources. The near-instant doubling of the world's wage labor supply, however, gave strong new priority to corporate efforts to reorganize their production systems.

TNCs began to set up integrated cross-border supply chains to sell into multiple national markets – including the United States. "As recently as 30 years ago," writes the director general of the WTO (Lamy, 2011), "products were assembled in one country, using inputs from that same country." No longer. "Today the concept of country of origin is obsolete … No car or commercial jet could now be built with inputs from just one country." Manufacturing of the iPhone, which has been well documented, links nine companies in seven countries (Asian Development Bank, 2010). In March 2011, Japan's triple catastrophe – earthquake, tsunami, and nuclear reactor meltdown – swiftly engendered knock-on effects as it began to interfere with "just-in-time" global supply chains in automobile and electronics production (Tett, 2011).

Corporate information systems were repeatedly reengineered, in light of shifts in strategy, public policy, and networking technology. This internationalization of production (UNCTAD, 2010, p. xviii), however, remained hinged to ICT. Corporate or enterprise networks indeed account for the lion's share of all network-related spending (Parker & Taylor, 2010). A trade association reports (WITSA, 2010, p. 15) that consumer spending on ICTs comprises merely one-third of the total market; business and government accounted for more than two-thirds.

The consumer market, however, was and remains vital as a springboard into new territories of profit, in Gary Fields' (2004) term. It accordingly constituted a fifth key site of change in response to the crisis of the 1970s. What I have called "accelerated commodification" (Schiller, 2007, pp. 34–57) propelled a series of changes in and around communications, starting from a spectacular buildup of investment to upgrade and extend liberalized network infrastructures.

Communications and the Enlargement of Commodity Culture

Liberalization began in the giant U.S. domestic market, but quickly moved beyond it. What had been a welfarist, typically government-operated service was reorganized into a corporate-commercial function. Between 1988, when Chile privatized its incumbent telecommunications operator, and 2005, more than 80 less developed countries underwent privatization (World Bank, 2006, p. 7). Enormous system build-outs followed as surplus investment funds surged into the sector.

Within countries where it had been prohibited or substantially restricted by the state, a major new outlet for transnational capital was secured. FDI flowing into the less developed countries' telecommunications systems increased tenfold during the decade after 1990 (World Bank, 2006, p. 7). Networks drew more investment in developing countries – hundreds of billions of dollars – than any other industry (Verizon, 2010, p. 8). FDI became a major – perhaps the major – driver of system development, and this tendency persisted after 2000, as Greenfield projects replaced privatizations as the major growth nexus (World Bank, 2006, p. 17, 2010).

The Internet, as it became popular, both built on and further stimulated this investment. A continuing cascade of new Internet-enabled services and distribution channels has generated unprecedentedly wide-ranging market destabilization. One notable example is voice-over Internet protocol (VOIP). In a mere five years, Skype has become the world's largest supplier of cross-border voice communications. "Cross-border traffic routed by Skype ... is projected to grow by an astonishing 45 billion minutes in 2010—more than twice the volume added by all of the world's phone companies, combined" (TeleGeography, 2011). Another is the market shocks around wireless applications, as subscriptions approach

4.5 billion (Pignal, 2010), so that mobiles can function as a strategic platform – a third screen – alongside televisions and computers.

The mythology of creative destruction overshadows a more fundamental feature: the unleashing of a rampant impulse to commodification. Consider fee-based cultural commodities. Here a small group of companies, led by Apple, Amazon, Google, and Facebook, has muscled in on long-entrenched oligopolies over musical recording, books, games, and film (Naughton, 2011; Tabuchi, 2009; Waters, 2011). The interlopers have built new distribution systems around new software platforms and often proprietary equipment – iPhones, iPads, Kindles, XBoxes. As compact disc markets collapse, the handful of conglomerates whose music subsidiaries channel the lion's share of global recording have had to cede profits to Apple. These conglomerates' film subsidiaries still control traditional movie distribution, but now they must contend not only with dwindling DVD sales and illegal file sharing, but also with Netflix's streaming service. These conglomerates' publishing subsidiaries dominate the U.S. book trade; but this staid industry is now witnessing especially vicious struggles. Traditional publishers and bookstores must try to contend not only with Walmart, but also with Amazon's killingly low retail prices and bullying tactics. Google's cutthroat strategy (now facing an unexpected judicial reverse and a counteroffensive by way of a proposed digital public library of America) has been predicated on the plunder of millions of volumes tended on behalf of the public by academic libraries and librarians (Auletta, 2009; Darnton, 2009a, 2009b, 2011; Helft, 2011; Vaidhyanathan, 2011). Fee-based cultural commodities are recomposing as new products, sold via new distribution systems, as a new set of big owners emerges.

A similar phenomenon is evident around advertiser-dependent media services. YouTube, Google's TV unit purchased five years ago for $1.65 billion, may be leading a transition away from conventional television, but it is distinctly not transcending advertiser patronage; indeed, YouTube has undergone an obsequious redesign in order to bring it more fully in line with advertisers' expectations (Schiller & Sandvig, 2010a; Stross, 2010). Facebook, too, is hard at work rebuilding its hugely popular service around the sales function. Facebook, noted the *Financial Times* just last year, "is desperate to attract ... brand advertisers" (Bradshaw, 2010a, 2010b). That was then. Although uncertainties remain as to whether deeply engaged users will break the magic spell in order to absorb advertisements, marketers are stampeding onto Facebook (Bradshaw, 2011). ComScore (2011) reported in January that "Social networking sites, which now account for more than one–third of all display ad impressions, were a significant driver of growth in the display ad market in 2010."

Market news fixes on these corporate struggles to master the commodity logic of a turbulent communications industry. The juggling of business models is intense as companies scurry to reorder and stabilize their revenue sources – a trend aggravated by the slump.[2] The churn of new product announcements and the endless effort to calculate how market changes will impact on share prices crowd out other considerations. Will Amazon's Kindle keep pace with Apple's iPad? Will an iPhone-enabled Verizon overpower AT&T? Is Facebook led by a nice man?

We may take better measure of this recomposition process by remembering that there are essentially three private options for launching and financing communications products and services: investment capital, advertising, and direct fees – whether they be subscriptions, licenses, or rental charges. The rebuilding of the communications system around new technologies is overwhelmingly a story of how different enterprises and whole industries are casting about between these three models. Commodification – often, recommodification – is in one form or another the common denominator.

There are casualties. The travails of print journalism, which have been building for decades, supply an instructive point of reference. Print ad revenue decreased by nearly half between 2000 and 2009, while newspapers' online revenue makes up for just a fraction of the shortfall (Li, 2010; Peers, 2010). As online competition intensified, the downturn hit; strategic planning then gave way to emergency measures (Bradshaw, 2009). Journalists were laid off in droves and the overall investment in newsgathering was radically cut. A grave threat is posed to original reporting.[3] During 2010, for example, a few dozen full-time U.S. foreign correspondents attempted to cover all of China (Bollinger, 2010). I dare not even ask how many of them speak Mandarin.

This is where we might remember that a fourth possible revenue model – government support – has been ubiquitously deployed throughout the crisis. The United States has thrown trillions of dollars at banks, insurance companies, and automakers; and it will spend billions more to underwrite broadband service nationwide. Yet it has spent nothing at all to try to ensure the functioning of effective journalism.

Why should it be a heresy to suggest that journalism merits public funding? An instinctual answer is that government financial support threatens press freedom. One must always take seriously the threat posed by executive power to civil liberties. But whose freedom of expression is endangered by government support? The majoritarian right of the public to access wide-ranging news and opinion? Or the property right of media owners to pursue commodification as they may choose? Accountability will attach to federal funding, and accountability in turn will encroach on the sanctity of proprietary accumulation by media conglomerates. In the historical source and current center of digital capitalism, such a transgression is deemed unacceptable.

As this discussion suggests, the commodity logic of a restructured communications industry ramifies far beyond the cut-and-thrust of clashing business strategies. There are also other ramifications. Notably, does the crisis signify that the dynamism of digital capitalism is now exhausted?

Renewed Growth Around Information and Communications?

David Harvey (2010) makes an essential point:

> Crises are, as it were, the irrational rationalisers of an always unstable capitalism... .We have always to ask: What is it that is being rationalized here and what directions are the rationalizations taking, since these are what will define not only our manner of exit from the crisis but the future character of capitalism?
>
> (p. 71)

In this connection it is again crucial, though Harvey doesn't do so, to revisit the role of communications and information. As it took shape, digital capitalism gave a fresh impulse to accumulation and – especially during the 1990s – encouraged a fetishistic belief in information as a growth zone and detoxifying agent (Mosco, 2004). This enthusiasm, to be sure, did not resolve capitalism's crisis tendencies – as has now been amply demonstrated. Yet perhaps the sector continues to harbor a rejuvenating potential. May information and communications still act as a pole of growth, in a reprise of their role a generation ago? Will the crisis develop or be managed in such a way as to unleash this value-creating potential?

In the United States, declining annual per capita expenditures on home video, music, newspapers, and magazines have been more than compensated for by increased spending on cable TV and news media, so that overall consumer media spending increased from $740 in 2003 to $901 in 2009 (U.S. Census Bureau, 2011, Table 1130, p. 711). Similarly, while residential telephone service expenditures dropped sharply between 2001 and 2008, cell phone service outlays more than tripled, so that total household telephone service expenditures still grew, from $914 to $1,127 (U.S. Census Bureau, 2011, Table 1147, p. 720). One admittedly self-interested market actor (ComScore, 2011) has called 2010 "a very positive year" for consumer Internet services.

At the bottom of the downturn, Cisco held a stash approximating $20 billion; Microsoft, $19 billion; Google, $16 billion; Intel, $10 billion; and Apple, $26 billion (Vance, 2008; Waters, 2009). These hoards, which have since grown much larger, afford a measure of liquidity – of maneuverability – that eludes capital based in less fortunate economic segments and geographic regions. Undoubtedly, "some of these funds will go toward acquiring struggling competitors" (Vance, 2008). Might the growth of these gigantic hoards, however, also signify a lack of profitable investment opportunities even in the information sector?

Blockages assuredly exist, but, as I argued (Schiller, 1999, 2007) in *Digital Capitalism*, radical political-economic change may yet transform activities historically provided mostly as social services into profitable commodities. This sector's prospective investment and profit potentials indeed have not been fully tapped.

One helpful indicator pertains to the continuing modernization of network systems. Capital expenditures on information processing equipment and software have been on an upward course for decades (Bureau of Economic Analysis, 2011),[4] growing impressively as a proportion of all nonresidential fixed investment in equipment (as opposed to structures) between 1970 and 1990. During the 1990s, IT investment increased by an "astounding" 18% per year, before falling after the Internet bubble popped (Council of Economic Advisors, 2010, p. 127). U.S. annual private investment in information processing equipment and software reportedly doubled between 1995 and 2009, growing 2.5 times faster than other U.S. private fixed investment (Council of Economic Advisors, 2011, p. 65). At $296 billion, according to the Census Bureau's 2008 Information Communication and Technology Survey (the latest year for which reliable data are available), capital investment in ICT, including commercial software, accounted for some 36% of overall corporate spending on equipment (U.S. Census Bureau, 2010).[5]

The crisis has not eliminated the need by all industry segments, from manufacturing to finance to communications, for a continually modernized information infrastructure; and investment in information-processing equipment and software remains a driver of overall economic growth, especially as capital investment has been diverted into finance (Council of Economic Advisors, 2011, pp. 21, 37). "Communication infrastructure investment," the Organization for Economic Cooperation and Development (OECD) (2009, p. 13) tells us, "Plays an increasingly important role in total investment within a country."

Network investment not only undergirds surging international Internet traffic – by 55% in 2008, 60% in 2009, and a projected 56% in 2010 – but also significantly ahead of the trend prior to the downturn (TeleGeography, 2009, 2010a, 2010b). In a less exact but more encompassing sense, network systems and applications also permit powerful corporate and state actors to prepare great tracts of sociocultural practice – notably, education – for private investment and to remake other sectors such as medicine, and agricultural biotechnology, and energy distribution, and road transport (Cookson, 2010; Council of Economic Advisors, 2011, pp. 66–69) around a comparable profit impulse. In principle, fresh cycles of accumulation are feasible within this still expansionary zone. We must therefore look for signs, within the evolving crisis, of efforts to hasten and secure these extensions of the accumulation process.

But how may this "rationalization" take shape? One thing is certain: it will be no mere mechanical exercise. International developments underline that communications are becoming an arena of intensifying struggle to reshape the world political economy.

The collapse of Soviet socialism, China's embrace of capitalism, and a concurrent acquiescence to U.S.-originated neoliberal policies by elites throughout the least developed countries. The scale of capital's search for profitable sites of surplus absorption is now planetary: The universal market discussed 40 years ago by Harry Braverman (1974) has been actualized.

The dominance of U.S. capital throughout the process merits emphasis. The transnational supply of corporate routing equipment is led by Cisco, search engines and online video by Google, social networking by Facebook, and totemic smartphones and other consumer appliances by Apple; Intel dominates semiconductors; Oracle, business software; Microsoft, desktop operating systems. U.S.-based companies are not only the leaders in supply, but also in demand and use: From Walmart to General Electric, U.S. corporations' integration of Internet-based systems and applications set a global standard (Council of Economic Advisors, 2011, p. 65; Mann, 2006, p. 1).

U.S.-based new media have defined and occupied much of the newly global capitalist political economy, quickly attaining a scale that begs comparison. While there exist problems of measurement and valid comparison, consider that Skype's free Internet phone service claimed 560 million users in the year to June 30, 2010 (Gelles, 2010; TeleGeography, 2009). Midway through 2010, Facebook drew 500 million users; Microsoft, 789 million; Yahoo, 633 million (Waters, 2010). Google obtained more than a billion searches each day by 2009 (Kuhn, 2009). There is pronounced unevenness, requiring careful elaboration. But Facebook is visited by 92% of the Internet population in Turkey, 87% in Indonesia, and (merely) 67% in the United States (Waters, 2010). This goes far to explain how the company could be valued in January 2011 at $50 billion (Sorkin & Rush, 2011). These numbers compare favorably with those garnered by the very largest global television networks and, in addition, Web services gain a competitive advantage through their unrivaled capacities for audience measurement and tracking (Chester, 2007). U.S.-based companies have built up transnational media platforms that aspiring rivals will find difficult to dislodge.[6]

U.S.-based capital and the U.S. state have mounted an offensive to retain dominance over this strategic pole of profitable growth (Schiller & Sandvig, 2011). But this is a struggle. New sites of economic dynamism and market strength have emerged. Geopolitical power is less concentrated than it was in the aftermath of the Soviet Union's collapse. There is fresh maneuvering room because the United States, already overextended, has been additionally weakened by the crisis. Disagreements are intensifying over how the world political economy should be overhauled to resolve today's crisis. This lends a keen edge to the competition for mastery of the coveted sources of above-average profitability, notably communications and information.

Developments in the People's Republic of China possess exceptional interest in this respect. Chinese leaders have succeeded in reserving their own national market in communications for homegrown, often state-affiliated, companies (Han, 2011; Hong, 2011; Zhao, 2008, 2010). Domestic suppliers and service providers are market leaders: from gaming site 4,399 and game publisher Shanda to CCTV and Shanghai Media Group, from e-commerce giant Alibaba to social network sites Renren and Kaixin, to microblogger site Weibo, to online video site Youku, to network operators China Mobile and China Telecom, to news agency Xinhua, to PC manufacturer Lenovo and search engine Baidu. It is symptomatic that the top four Web portals – Sohu, Sina, Tencent, Netease – claimed nearly three quarters of the sector's revenue in 2009 (Deibert et. al., 2010, p. 453). Although it would be profoundly mistaken to view China as an autarky and although advertising in particular exhibits substantial outside investment and influence, U.S. transnationals' have been kept at arm's length from service provision and many applications.

The nature of this achievement should be specified. Chinese capital is not on a par with the U.S.-, European-, and Japanese-based companies that in many markets have already built up transnational production and distribution chains (Nolan & Zhang, 2010).[7] Only exceptionally have Chinese extraterritorial groups such as the network equipment vendor Huawei become global leaders (O'Brien, 2009). Yet China's success in reserving its own national market in communications is remarkable in its own right. It constitutes a pronounced exception to the post-World War II historical pattern, in which national communications markets and audiovisual spaces – even in such countries as Brazil and France – came to be dominated by TNCs. As well, it is occurring in the world's second largest economy. China, furthermore, continues to enjoy high growth, even as stagnation and fiscal crisis persists throughout Europe, North America, and Japan; and, finally, China may be poised to use economic policy to spur domestic consumption. China's sizzling communications market only adds to the allure; at latest count, the country boasted 450 million broadband users and 584 million wireless subscribers (TeleGeography CommsUpdate, 2011a, 2011b). For this reason, developments in China's domestic market command outsized extraterritorial importance.

Conflict over access to Chinese markets has therefore duly escalated (Schiller & Sandvig, 2010b). On one side, we see a major executive branch initiative to push forward the longstanding U.S. policy of free flow of information (Schiller & Sandvig, 2011). On the other side, we see newly assertive efforts by Chinese party-state leaders to build a transnational communications industry and impressive (though so far unsuccessful) attempts by network vendor Huawei to gain entry into the U.S. market for advanced communications systems and service (Kirchgaessner & Hille, 2011).

Giuseppe di Lampedusa's (2007, p. 18) fictional formulation in *The Leopard* famously captured the kind of dominative logic that applies today: "If we want things to stay as they are, things will have to change." Still, this is not a sufficient end point. Movement within the political economy encompasses more than a mechanistic capital logic, however much of this logic may be revised to foreground digital sites of accumulation. We are living through a process of change whose character is both contingent and contested, and whose outcomes will be determined by the balance of social forces within particular societies and across the world.

In order for digital capitalism to be reconstituted, there will, as David Harvey (2010) concludes:

> … have to be wrenching and painful shifts in the geographical and sectoral locus of capitalist class power. The capitalist class cannot, if history is any guide, maintain its power without changing its character and moving accumulation on to a different trajectory and into new spaces (such as East Asia).
>
> (pp. 215–216)

Efforts will be made to impose additional concessions on already hard-pressed populations in lower-growth regions such as the United States and Western Europe – in living standards and in democratic liberties. Today, the offloading of debt from private financial institutions to government is being used as a basis for inflicting "austerity" budgets in Western Europe and the United States. As these exactions bite more deeply into social experience, there is every reason to forecast that popular opposition to capital's class project may intensify, as indeed we have seen recently in Wisconsin and other Midwest states.

That communications and information remains a pole of growth in itself gives little cause for celebration. Digital bits do not break free of social pathways, and digital capitalism thus develops as its forbear did – through episodes of crisis and boom – and, as the people of the Middle East have been attempting to remind us, of opportunities for reconstruction along different lines.

Notes

1 Thanks to Susan G. Davis, Shinjoung Yeo, and Yuezhi Zhao for their help with this text.
2 During the worst period to date – the first half of 2009 – ad spending, a half-trillion dollar global outlay, fell by more than 10% in many developed countries (Pfanner, 2009). Sales of books by members of the Association of

American Publishers dropped beneath their long-term sales trend line (Association of American Publishers, 2009).

3 Newspapers consumed 8% of Americans' collective media time in 2008, but received 20% of total advertising; the Internet garnered 29% of our media time, but attracted only 8% of advertising. Commercial air is being let out of one section of the apparatus of selling and pumped into another (Auletta, 2009, p. 261). Newspaper executives' decisions to rely ever more on advertising support looks, in this context, to have been a fundamental error.

4 Grateful thanks to Valerie Strang, Chief of the Business Investment Branch, Company Statistics Division, U.S. Census Bureau, and David Wasshausen, Chief of the Capital Stock Branch, Bureau of Economic Analysis, both of the U.S. Department of Commerce, for assistance in helping me to use these statistics. Neither of these individuals bears any responsibility for the uses to which I put their comments.

5 The statistics supplied by a different agency of the Commerce Department are even larger, chiefly because they include in-house production of software for in-house use (Bureau of Economic Analysis, 2011). Bureau of Economic Analysis, U.S. Department of Commerce, National Economic Accounts, National Income and Product Accounts Table, Table 5.3.5. Private Fixed Investment by Type, Last Revised January 28, 2011. Retrieved February 4, 2011, from www.bea.gov/national/nipaweb/TableView.asp?SelectedTable=145&ViewSeries=NO&Java=no&Request3Place=N&3Place=N&FromView=YES&Freq=Year&First-Year=2008&LastYear=2010&3Place=N&AllYearsChk=YES&Update=Update&JavaBox=no#Mid.

6 Communications and media thereby exemplify a larger trend. Between the 1970s and the 2000s, Nolan and Zhang (2010, pp. 98, 107) show across a wide range of industries that "the 'commanding heights' of the world economy became occupied chiefly by large companies from the advanced economies," the most successful of which "vastly expanded their international investment, building production networks across the globe" and attaining unprecedented scale and market power. Peter Nolan and Jin Zhang, "Global Competition After the Financial Crisis," NLR 64, July–August 2010, pp. 97–108.

7 Growing Chinese FDI is occurring from a very modest base and, as Nolan and Zhang (2010) have underlined, these efforts to transnationalize are taking place in a field crowded with formidably entrenched corporate behemoths.

References

Appel, T. (2007, August 9). Overseas profits provide shelter for U.S. firms. *The Wall Street Journal*, pp. A1, A11.

Asian Development Bank. (2010). *How iPhones are produced*. Retrieved March 16, 2011, from www.adbi.org/working-paper/2010/12/14/4236.iphone.widens.us.trade.deficit.prc/how.iphones.are.produced

Association of American Publishers. (2009). *Industry Statistics 2009*. Retrieved March 9, 2011, from www.publishers.org/main/IndustryStats/indStats_02.htm

Auletta, K. (2009). *Googled: The end of the world as we know it*. New York: Random House.

Bernanke, B. (2010, November 19). *Rebalancing the global recovery*. Speech at the Sixth European Central Bank Central Banking Conference, Frankfurt, Germany.

Bollinger, L. C. (2010, July 14). Journalism needs government help. *The Wall Street Journal*, p. A19.

Bradshaw, T. (2009, March 23). Ad agencies struggle to sell early recovery. *Financial Times*, p. 14.

Bradshaw, T. (2010a, June 24). Facebook on a charm offensive to pull in brand advertisers. *Financial Times*, p. 16.

Bradshaw, T. (2010b, September 22). Twitter looks to tweak service so advertisers can target users. *Financial Times*, p. 16.

Bradshaw, T. (2011, February 22). Facebook ad potential puts fledglings in frame. *Financial Times*, p. 22.

Braverman, H. (1974). *Labor and monopoly capital: The degradation of work in the twentieth century*. New York: Monthly Review.

Brenner, R. (2009). *What's good for Goldman Sachs is good for America: The origins of the current crisis*. Center for Social Theory and Comparative History, Institute for Social Science Research, UCLA. Retrieved March 12, 2011, from http://escholarship.org/uc/item/0sg0782h

Chester, J. (2007). *Digital destiny: New media and the future of democracy*. New York: New Press.

Clifford, S. (2011, January 7). Sales in December were weaker than expected. *The New York Times*, B3.

ComScore. (2011, February). The 2010 U.S. digital year in review. [*Press release*.] Retrieved February 13, 2011, from www.comscore.com/Press_Events/Presentations_Whitepapers/2011/2010_US_Digital_Year_in_Review

Cookson, C. (2010, August 20). Signal manoeuvre. *Financial Times*, p. 5.

Cookson, C. (2011, January 25). Low-cost era is over, warn researchers. *Financial Times*, p. 8.

Council of Economic Advisors. (2010). *Economic Report of the President 2010*. Retrieved March 9, 2011, from www.whitehouse.gov/administration/eop/cea/economic–report–of–the–President/2010

Council of Economic Advisors. (2011). *Economic Report of the President 2011*. Retrieved March 10, 2011, from www.whitehouse.gov/administration/eop/cea/economic–report–of–the–President

Darnton, R. (2009a). *The case for books*. New York: Public Affairs Press.

Darnton, R. (2009b). Google and the future of books. *New York Review of Books, 56* (8).

Darnton, R. (2011, March 23). A digital library better than Google's. *The New York Times*, p. A31.

Deibert, R., Palfrey, J., Rohozinski, R., & Zittrain, J. (2010). *Access controlled: The shaping of power, rights, and rule in cyberspace*. Cambridge, MA: MIT Press.

Fields, G. (2004). *Territories of profit: Communications, capitalist development, and the innovative enterprises of G.F. Swift and Dell Computer*. Stanford: Stanford University Press.

Foster, J. B., & Magdoff, F. (2009). The great financial crisis: Causes and consequences. *Monthly Review Press*.

Gelles, D. (2010, August 10). Skype begins move to list on NASDAQ. *Financial Times*, p. 1.

Guerrera, F. (2009, May 22). Citigroup ramps up tech cuts. *Financial Times*, p. 13.

Han, D. (2011). *Copyrighting Chinese media: Cultural commodification in a global context* (Unpublished doctoral dissertation), University of Illinois at Urbana-Champaign.

Harding, R. (2011, January 8–9). U.S. jobs report an 'utter mess.' *Financial Times*, p. 3.

Harvey, D. (2003). *The new imperialism*. Oxford: Oxford University Press.

Harvey, D. (2010). *The enigma of capital*. Oxford: Oxford University Press.

Helft, M. (2011, March 23). Federal judge rejects Google's negotiated deal to digitize books. *The New York Times*, pp. B1, B2.

Hong, Y. (2011). *Reading the twelfth five-year plan: China's communication-driven mode of economic restructuring* (unpublished manuscript).

International Monetary Fund. (2009). *World economic outlook, April*. Retrieved March 7, 2011, from www.imf.org/external/pubs/ft/weo/2009/01/index.htm

IT Dashboard. (2010). *Your window into the federal IT portfolio*. Retrieved March 7, 2011, from http://it.usaspending.gov

Jacque, L. (2010). The Currency Wars. *Le Monde diplomatique*. December, p. 1.

Kapner, S. (2010, December 30). Spike in foreclosures despite talk of recovery. *Financial Times*, p. 1.

Kirchgaessner, S., & Hille, K. (2011, February 15). Huawei in challenge to U.S. *Financial Times*. Retrieved March 12, 2011, from www.ft.com/cms/s/0/f7d582f0–393a–11e0–97ca–00144feabdc0.html#axzz1GI8WCm8M

Klare, M. (1972). *War without end: American planning for the next Vietnams*. New York: Vintage.

Kuhn, E. (2009, December 18). Google unveils top political searches of 2009. *CNN.com*. Retrieved April 18, 2011, from http://politicalticker.blogs.cnn.com/2009/12/18/google-unveils-top-politicalsearches-of-2009

Lampedusa, G. (2007). *The leopard*. New York: Pantheon (orig. 1960).

Lamy, P. (2011, January 25). 'Made in China' tells us little about global trade. *Financial Times*, p. 11.

Li, K. (2010, August 3). *NYT* broadens digital licensing push. *Financial Times*, p. 17.

Lynn, W. J. (2010, September–October). Defending a new domain. *Foreign Affairs*, 89(5), 97–108.

Mann, C. (2006). *Accelerating the globalization of America: The role for information technology*. Washington, DC: Institute for International Economics.

McNally, D. (2011). *Global slump: The economics and politics of crisis and resistance*. Oakland: PM Press.

Moody, K. (1997). *Workers in a lean world*. London: Verso.

Mosco, V. (1989). *The pay-per society*. Toronto: Garamond Press.

Mosco, V. (2004). *The digital sublime*. Cambridge, MA: MIT Press.

Naughton, J. (2011, March 6). Forget Google—It's Apple that is turning into the evil empire. *The Observer*. Retrieved March 12, 2011, from www.guardian.co.uk/commentisfree/2011/mar/06/john–naughton–apple–dominates–market

O'Brien, K. J. (2009, November 30). Upstart Chinese telecom company rattles industry as it rises to number 2. *The New York Times*. Retrieved March 10, 2011, from www.nytimes.com/2009/11/30/business/global/30telecom.html

Parker, A., & Taylor, P. (2010, July 19). Tough calls are queuing up for AT&T's chief executive. *Financial Times*, p. 18.

Peers, M. (2010, July 29). Mixed ad message from newspapers. *The Wall Street Journal*, p. C12.

Pfanner, E. (2009, September 2). The outlook is murky for media advertising. *The New York Times*, p. B2.

Pignal, S. (2010, August 23). Mobile operators expect app sales to outweigh call revenues in 2013. *Financial Times*, p. 13.

Politi, J., Harding, R., & Demos, T. (2011, January 8–9). U.S. new jobs data hit recovery hopes. *Financial Times*, p. 1.

Powell, M. (2011, January 8). Profits are booming. Why aren't jobs? *The New York Times*, p. Wk 4.

Prashad, V. (2007). *The darker nations: A people's history of the Third World.* New York: New Press.

Reich, R. (2010). *Aftershock: The next economy and America's future.* New York: Knopf. Roper Projects Gradual Revival. (1934, January 1). *The New York Times*, p. 38.

Schiller, D. (1999). *Digital capitalism: Networking the global market system.* Cambridge, MA: MIT Press.

Schiller, D. (2007). *How to think about information.* Urbana: University of Illinois Press.

Schiller, D. (2008). The militarization of U.S. communications. *Communication, Culture & Critique, 1*, 126–138.

Schiller, D., & Sandvig, C. (2010a, March 13). Is YouTube the successor to television—or to LIFE Magazine? *Huffington Post.* Retrieved March 8, 2011, from www.huffingtonpost.com/dan–schiller/is–youtube–the–successor_b_497198.html

Schiller, D., & Sandvig, S. (2010b, April 5). Google v. China: Principled, brave, or business as usual? *Huffington Post.* Retrieved March 9, 2011, from www.huffingtonpost.com/dan–schiller/google–v–china–principled_b_524727.html

Schiller, D., & Sandvig, C. (2011, March 4). Free flow of information and profit. *Huffington Post.* Retrieved March 5, 2011, from www.huffingtonpost.com/dan–schiller/free–flow–of–information–_b_831419.html

Sorkin, A. R., & Rusli, E. M. (2011, January 3). Facebook deal puts its value at $50 billion. *The New York Times*, p. A1.

Stein, J. (2010). *Pivotal decade: How the United States traded factories for finance in the seventies.* New Haven: Yale University Press.

Strauss-Kahn, D. (2011, February). The right kind of global recovery. *Speech presented to Monetary Authority of Singapore.* Retrieved February 5, 2011, from www.imf.org/external/np/speeches/2011/020111.htm

Stross, R. (2010, May 29). YouTube wants you to sit and stay awhile. *The New York Times*, p. B3.

Sum, A., & McGlaughlin, J. (2010). *How the U.S. economic output recession of 2007–2009 led to the great recession in labor markets: The role of corporate job downsizing, work hour reductions, labor productivity gains, and rising corporate profits.* Boston: Center for Labor Market Studies, Northeastern University.

Tabuchi, H. (2009, September 26). To win, beat the apps. *The New York Times*, pp. B1, B4.

TeleGeography. (2009, March 24). CommsUpdate: Skype's share of the long-distance pie on the increase. Available at www.telegeography.com/products/commsupdate

TeleGeography. (2009, September 15). CommsUpdate: What recession? Internet traffic surges in 2009. Available at www.telegeography.com/products/commsupdate

TeleGeography. (2010a, April 28). CommsUpdate Recession? What recession? Available at www.telegeography.com/products/commsupdate

TeleGeography. (2010b, September 16). CommsUpdateInternational Internet traffic soars, while prices tumble. Available at www.telegeography.com/products/commsupdate

TeleGeography. (2011, January 6). CommsUpdate: International long-distance slumps, while Skype soars. Available at www.telegeography.com/products/commsupdate

TeleGeography. (2011a, January 21). CommsUpdate: Trio report year-end KPIs. Available at www.telegeography.com/products/commsupdate

TeleGeography. (2011b, January 24). CommsUpdate: 457 million netizens and counting. Available at www.telegeography.com/products/commsupdate

Tett, G. (2011, March 16). Japan's supply chain risk reverberates across the globe. *Financial Times*, p. 22.

United Nations Conference on Trade and Development. (2010). *World Investment Report 2010*. New York & Geneva: United Nations.

U.S. Bureau of Economic Analysis, Department of Commerce. (2011). *National Economic Accounts* (National Income and Product Accounts Table, Table 5.3.5). Retrieved February 4, 2011, from www.bea.gov/national/nipaweb/TableView.asp?SelectedTable=145&ViewSeries=NO&Java=no&Request3Place=N&3Place=N&FromView=YES&Freq=Year&FirstYear=2008&LastYear=2010&3Place=N&AllYearsChk=YES&Update=Update&JavaBox=no#Mid

U.S. Census Bureau. (2010). *Census Bureau reports 11 percent increase in U.S. business spending on information and communication technology in 2008.* (CB10–17). May 20. Retrieved April 18, 2011 at www.census.gov/newsroom/releases/archives/economic_surveys/cb10-71.html

U.S. Census Bureau. (2011). *Statistical abstract of the United States 2011.* Retrieved March 9, 2011, from www.census.gov/compendia/statab

Vaidhyanathan, S. (2011). *The Googlization of everything (And why we should worry)*. Berkeley: University of California Press.

Vance, A. (2008, November 14). Tech companies, long insulated, now feel slump. *The New York Times*. Retrieved March 9, 2011, from www.nytimes.com/2008/11/15/technology/15tech.html

Verizon. (2009, December 6). *Global free flow of information on the Internet: Hearing before the Department of Commerce*, Docket No. 100921457–0457–01.

Walker, R. (2010). The Golden State adrift. *New Left Review*, 66, 5–30.

Waters, R. (2009, January 26). Tech groups hold on to cash cushions in uncertain times. *Financial Times*, p. 19.

Waters, R. (2010, July 22). Facebook on course to reach 1 bn users. *Financial Times*, p. 15.

Waters, R. (2011, March 10). Media will be forced to play by the Internet's rules. *Financial Times*, p. 15.

Wolf, M. (2010, July 14). Three years on, fault lines threaten the world economy. *Financial Times*, p. 7.

World Bank. (2006). *Information and communications for development: Global trends and policies*. Washington, DC: World Bank.

World Bank. (2010). *Private participation in infrastructure database.* Retrieved February 7, 2011, from http://ppi.worldbank.org/explore/ppi_exploreSector. aspx?sectorID=1

World Information Technology Services Alliance. (2010, June). *Digital Planet 2010, executive summary.* Retrieved March 7, 2011, from www.witsa.org

Wriston, W. B. (1979, June). *Information, electronics and gold.* International Monetary Conference. Retrieved March 6, 2011, from http://dca.lib.tufts. edu/features/wriston/works/speeches.html

Zhao, Y. (2008). *Communication in China.* Lanham: Rowman & Littlefield.

Zhao, Y. (2010). China's pursuits of indigenous innovations in information technology developments: Hopes, follies, and uncertainties. *Chinese Journal of Communication, 3*(3), 266–289.

14 Minutes to Midnight

Capitalist Communication and Climate Catastrophe

Graham Murdock

> We would not find, in the span of almost two hundred years, the earthquakes, pollutions of the air...or the incredible careers of tyrants.
> Herodian of Antioch 1.1.4 (translated by Edward Echols, 1961)

> What economists proclaim as progress ecologists recognise as ruin.
> (Monbiott, 2018)

Slouching Toward Doomsday

In 1947, concerned nuclear scientists involved in the Manhattan Project to build the first atomic bomb launched an annual calculation of how close humanity had come to the prospect of total annihilation. Using the immediately understandable image of a clockface and the countdown to an atomic explosion, they devised the Doomsday Clock to express the risk in terms of minutes away from the zero hour of midnight. Originally designed to assess the likelihood of a nuclear exchange, it now also includes the escalating threats posed by global warming. In 2018 the clock was reset at two minutes to midnight, the closest to zero in its history, based in part on a deeply pessimistic assessment of climate change. As the authors noted:

> Despite the sophisticated disinformation campaign run by climate denialists, the unfolding consequences of an altered climate are a harrowing testament to an undeniable reality. The science linking climate change to human activity—mainly the burning of fossil fuels that produce carbon dioxide and other greenhouse gases—is sound. The world continues to warm as costly impacts mount, and there is evidence that overall rates of sea level rise are accelerating—regardless of protestations to the contrary.
> (Bulletin of the Atomic Scientists, 2018)

In 2015, representatives from 95 nations met in Paris to address this crisis. The resulting Agreement committed the signatories to limiting global temperature rises this century to 1.5° C above preindustrial levels.

The landmark research by Michael Mann and his colleagues demonstrates conclusively that after millennia of relative stability, punctuated by periodic volcanic eruptions and other natural disasters, earth temperatures rose sharply with the development of industrial capitalism and have continued on an upward trajectory through successive decades (Mann, Bradley, & Hughes, 1998). The lesson is crystal clear. The Paris Agreement's goal can only be achieved by fundamentally transforming the current organization of capitalism and the animating assumptions on which it rests.

The basic science of global warming is straightforward. The sun continually bombards the earth with heat. About a third is immediately directed back into space from ice, snow, and other reflective surfaces. The rest is absorbed by the oceans, land, and atmosphere, which, as they heat up, produce thermal radiation that is, in turn, returned to space. This natural cycle creates an equilibrium avoiding extremes in most parts of the planet and keeping average temperatures at a level that ensures a livable and self-reproducing human habitat. At the same time over eons, natural processes of photosynthesis in plants, algae, and bacteria have cumulatively laid down underground and undersea deposits of coal, oil, and natural gas containing energy-rich stores of carbon. When combined with air or oxygen and burned, these fossil fuels, as they are collectively known, generate ready supplies of not only heat and energy, but also carbon dioxide (CO_2). This acts like a blanket preventing heat escaping back into space, creating a greenhouse effect that is further compounded by emissions of the other main "greenhouse gas" – methane.

The cumulative increase in temperature since the emergence of modern capitalism has been driven by two fundamental shifts. The first has been the progressive move away from local and self-sufficient food production to the intensive forms of farming needed to provision an expanding urban population, whose tastes have been reorganized around more meat- and dairy-intensive diets. Servicing this expanding market has required forests and woodlands to be converted to pasture, progressively reducing the size of the green cover that acts as a vital carbon "sink" absorbing significant amounts of the CO_2 (Gibbard et al., 2005). At the same time, intensive farming substantially increases the volume of methane released into the atmosphere from livestock's natural emissions. The second shift, and the more fundamental and far-reaching in its impacts, has been the move away from the renewable sources of energy provided by wind, water, and human and animal traction to reliance on fossil fuels to power the key machineries of industrial capitalism.

Communicative Capitalism and Climate Crisis

Communication systems are central to the effective organization of capitalist economies and social relations, and have contributed to the accelerating climate crisis in three fundamental ways. First, as the dominant symbolic spaces and arenas in which images, narratives, information, and misinformation about climate change are presented and contested, they play a central role in shaping public understandings and action. Second, as the major platforms for the advertising linking production to social demand, the commercially organized media are primary drivers of a culture of hyper consumption that makes unsustainable and increasingly destructive calls on natural resources and energy supplies. Third, the production, maintenance, use, and dismantling or disposal of the proliferating array of dedicated communications infrastructures and devices imposes escalating costs on the environment in their own right.

There is a widespread assumption that the consolidation of industrial capitalism in the mid-19th century saw communication separating from transportation. On the one side, steam-driven railways and shipping replaced human, animal, and wind power transforming the movement of tangible goods and materials. On the other, the telegraph system enabled messages to be dematerialized and transmitted through wired networks as pulses of electricity. Communications no longer needed a physical envelope. The pollution generated by railway engines and steam ships was visible. Smoke poured out of funnels adding to the emissions from factories using coal-fired steam engines to drive production. In contrast, the telegraph appeared to be an eminently clean technology since wires and cables produced no visible emissions. This perception failed to note several obvious features: that the materials required to build the network were obtained through environmentally damaging practices; that the system relied for its operations on electricity was mostly generated by coal-fired power plants; and that delivering printed telegraphic messages to customers required physical carriage. There was never a sharp separation between communication and transportation. They were bound together at every stage of production and distribution. This essential integration has been repeated with broadcast transmissions using the radio spectrum and now with the Internet. As David Morley (2017) has pointed out, mobile phones and container ships occupy the same economic and ecological space and are both fundamental to sustaining a contemporary capitalist system that is more dependent than ever on intensified and environmentally destructive consumption and disposal.

Research has identified a marked acceleration in average temperatures in the years between 1950 and 1973 (Steffen, Grinevald, Crutzen, & McNeil, 2011, p. 850), with later work pointing to a further acceleration in the years since 1970 (Gaffney & Steffen, 2017, p. 4). This pattern is not accidental.

The years between 1950 and 1970 saw the consolidation of a mass consumer society in the United States and, after a period of recovery and reconstruction after World War II, in the advanced capitalist societies of Western Europe. Rising real wages and new payment by installment systems enabled increasing numbers of households to purchase a range of "big ticket" consumer items that promised convenience, mobility, and pleasure. Automobile ownership grew rapidly and communication devices proliferated, as households acquired domestic telephones and installed television sets and record players alongside radios at the center of an increasingly home-centered organization of leisure. This privatization of social life had major environmental consequences. It took far more petroleum to fuel 50 cars transporting a lone individual on the way to work than to operate a bus or coach carrying 50 or more people. The energy required to mount a cinema screening for 500 people was eclipsed by the energy needed to service multiple media in 500 homes. The mass production of transistors introduced new portable media, typified by the transistor radio, further multiplying the communications devices in circulation and the demands on resources and energy.

Alongside this expansion of mediated consumption, however, the years between 1947 and 1977 also saw a significant extension of publicly funded cultural facilities supported by progressive taxation and a regulatory system organized around conceptions of the public interest that placed limits on corporate power. This expansion of public cultural and communicative resources had contradictory environmental impacts. On the one hand, the collective facilities provided by public libraries, museums, galleries, and educational institutions were relatively energy efficient. On the other, the rapid growth of public service television broadcasting to individual households imposed additional pressures.

This welfare variant of capitalism and the countervailing power to commercial domination it underwrote was comprehensively undermined by the structural crisis of profitability that developed from the mid-1970s onwards. This opened the way for champions of neoliberal economics to blame government spending and intervention and argue for maximizing the operation of markets as the only viable solution. The governments of Margaret Thatcher in the United Kingdom and Ronald Reagan in the United States translated this recommendation into an array of practical policies which they pursued with dedicated enthusiasm. Public funding was cut. Public cultural assets were sold to private investors. Protected markets were opened to new entrants. The rates of tax levied to corporations and high earners were cut. Public interest regulation designed to deliver cultural resources for participatory citizenship were discontinued and regulatory regimes reoriented around issues of competition and consumer protection. The bargaining power of organized labor was curtailed by attacks on trade union rights and the replacement of regular employment with precarious and intermittent labor.

This reorientation of capitalism around corporate interests provided a basic template that has been implemented to varying degrees across the globe forging a new neoliberal international order. Digital media emerged at precisely the moment when this new order was being cemented and their development has been shaped in fundamental ways by its reassertion of the primacy of corporate interests. They have enjoyed four major benefits: the free transfer of the fruits of public research and investment in fundamental technological innovation; governmental sanctioning of increased corporate concentration; regulatory failure; and a taxation system that allows unprecedented accumulations of personal wealth.

As Mariana Mazzucato has demonstrated, it was public investment in fundamental research that developed the core technologies on which digital media depend (Mazzucato, 2018). Apple and the other major digital appliance companies piggybacked on government willingness to fund blue skies research into a raft of essential innovations that includes the Internet, GPS, touch screens, and voice activation, taking them up only after they had been tried and tested. As Mazzucato notes, "Apple incrementally incorporated in each new generation of iPods, iPhones and iPads technologies that the State sowed, cultivated and ripened" (Mazzucato, 2018, p. 182), but as she notes has paid no royalties to the public purse for their use. On the contrary, it has enjoyed a free ride.

The loosening of curbs on corporate ownership has concentrated control over digital media in a steadily shrinking number of hands. In response to the increasingly blurred line between broadcasting and telecommunications, the 1996 Telecommunications Act in the United States relaxed the standing rules on media cross-ownership, accelerating and extending the trends toward concentration and conglomeration that was already well underway in the established media sectors. The floodgates appeared open. In December 2000, in the largest merger in U.S. history, America Online's (AOL) bid to acquire Time-Warner was formally approved. At the time, AOL was the largest Internet service provider in the United States while Time-Warner commanded a fifth of the nation's cable television customers together with substantial magazine and film production interests. The expected benefits of integration and synergy failed to materialize, however, and in 2009 AOL was spun off. This setback has not stopped the drive to integrate, and in an ironic twist of fortune in June 2018, Time-Warner was acquired by AT&T, which until its original holdings were broken up in 1982 in a drive to open protected markets to competition had been the regulated monopoly supplier of domestic telephone services in the United States. Integrating carriage and content has been central to the expansionist strategies pursued by the major Internet companies. In November 2006, Google, which was establishing a dominant position in internet search, acquired the video sharing site YouTube as a platform for user-generated material. Facebook, which had opened to the general public two months earlier, has pursued a concerted policy of buying up rivals that threaten its dominance of social media, acquiring the photo sharing site Instagram in 2012 and the mobile messaging system WhatsApp in 2014. Both companies have also been active in establishing major stakes in the next generation of communication technologies. Google's holding company, Alphabet, owns Deep Mind, a leading force in artificial intelligence, and

NestLabs, makers of smart home appliances central to the Internet of things. Facebook has invested in speech recognition, augmented virtual reality, and blockchain technologies.

Despite hosting huge volumes of content, both Facebook and Google have benefitted from the regulatory exemption introduced in the 1996 Communications Decency Act, passed at the same time as the Telecommunications Act. In response to lobbying from Internet service providers, Section 230 of the Act classified them in the same way as telephone services, as carriers not publishers, and therefore not liable for the material posted by users. This released them from the statutory and voluntary regulations governing representations in the established press and broadcast media.

The unprecedented freedom of action accorded to the digital majors has resulted in de facto monopolies or duopolies across the range of popular Internet uses. Google dominates search. Facebook dominates social media. Amazon dominates online retail. Apple and Google dominate smartphone operating systems. They all take full advantage of low rates of corporate taxation and the legislative loopholes that permitted multiple legal devices for tax avoidance allowing them to retain most of the huge profits they generated. The result is a massive transfer of wealth from the public purse to the captains of digital industry. Four of the ten men listed in the *Forbes* 2018 audit of the world's richest men were digital entrepreneurs: Jeff Bezos of Amazon (ranked 1st), Bill Gates of Microsoft (ranked 2nd), Mark Zuckerberg of Facebook (ranked 5th), Larry Ellison of Oracle (ranked 10th), with Larry Page and Serge Brim of Google's parent company Alphabet at 12th and 13th (Kroll & Dolan, 2018).

To connect the ascendency of the digital majors to the escalating climate crisis, we need to retrieve the pivotal role they have played in re-engineering the consumer system. The capitalist crisis of the mid-1970s was in part a crisis of consumption, since by then households had acquired the major items on their wish list and were not replacing them. Addressing the crisis required a new array of desirable consumer objects, an accelerated rate of replacement and disposal, and the promotion of commodities as indispensable extensions of the self and markers of social identity. Digital media met all three requirements, making a fundamental contribution to the climate crisis, first by installing accelerated rates of product replacement at the center of its own business strategies and second by hosting new forms of general product promotion.

Disposable Digitalization

The corporate promoters of digitalization and their political supporters presented it as a permanent revolution, a continuous process of innovation with each new or upgraded product or service promising increased convenience and performance. Previous technologies were rendered obsolete at an accelerating rate. Digital photography decimated the market for cameras using roll film. Vinyl discs and tape recordings were replaced by digital discs and then by streaming as the main mode of personal access to recorded music. Flexible access to films and television shows shifted from video tapes to digital discs to on-demand streaming services. Storage of personal computer data migrated from digital discs and flash drives held by the user to corporately managed cloud facilities. But the most fundamental disruption came with the arrival of smartphones and iPads and the comprehensive integration of separate media into portable devices with formidable computer power.

Previous media devices offered a single function, playing records, making telephone calls, watching television, accessing the Internet, and despite increasing portability, many remained confined to the home and were used only intermittently. Smartphones and tablets integrated multiple functions into a single device and could be used anywhere there was a connection to the Internet, at any time, rapidly installing them as indispensable supports for everyday living.

This radical integration and individualization of media access has significantly multiplied the number of communication devices in circulation and intensified their use. By 2014 there were already more mobile devices than people globally. Recent calculations estimate that by 2021 there will be 1.5 devices for each person, three-quarters of which will be "smart" appliances with computer capacity generating 13 times more traffic than a non-smart device, the bulk of which will be energy and bandwidth hungry video transmissions (Cisco, 2017).

Devices used in 2021 are unlikely to be retained from previous years, however, since maintaining continued profit expansion requires an accelerated cycle of replacement as manufacturers aggressively promote minor modifications and extensions – improved camera facilities, fingerprint security, foldable screens – as indispensable innovations. The result is escalating calls on energy supplies and mounting volumes of waste. These impacts will intensify further with the next generation of digital communication devices organized around smart machines and the Internet of things.

In addition to exacerbating the environmental crisis in their assembly, transportation, use, and disposal, mobile phones have become the central arena for the product promotion that supports a destructive general culture of hyper consumption.

Advertising The Self

The resurgence of market centered economic policies had already opened significant new arenas for advertising, as the monopolies previously enjoyed by public or state television broadcasters across Western Europe and the former Soviet satellites and the emerging economies of India and

South Korea were swept away by the rapid expansion of commercial television channels. But it was the 1996 U.S. Decency Act that laid the basis for the novel business model that has enabled Facebook and Google to capture an increasing share of total advertising spending. Where product promotion on commercial television remained subject to a range of restrictions, the new social media platforms allowed advertisers much greater freedom of operations. The associations between brands, personal image, and lifestyle could be cemented through product placement and other forms of "native" advertising. Users could be enlisted as brand ambassadors and their social networks mobilized to disseminate word-of-mouth endorsements. But the major advantage lay with Facebook and Google's core business model, which offered users free access to their platforms in return for monopoly rights to harvest and commodify the personal data generated by their online activities. Analyzing this data provides advertisers with multiple maps of consumer niches and taste culture facilitating ever more finely tuned and personalized appeals. It is a radically asymmetric distribution of power that has created an intensified variant of surveillance capitalism in which the major digital corporations reserve the right to gather, store, and exploit increasingly comprehensive profiles of users while concealing the operation of the algorithms that interrogate this data with legally enforceable appeals to commercial privilege.

Moral Economies and Moral Ecologies

All economies are moral economies, in the sense that any transaction we enter into links us, whether we acknowledge it or not, to the lives of all whose labor has created the products and services we use. We are similarly linked to the communities living on the lands containing the natural materials and energy sources employed in their production and use and to the sites where we dump our unwanted machines. Market models of capitalism focus relentlessly on the moment when commodities are presented for purchase and champion individual freedom expressed through consumer choices as the preeminent value. The systematic exploitation of the workforce and the despoliation of the environment slide conveniently out of sight. The critical tradition in the political economy of communications retrieves these "hidden abodes" and places them at the center of analysis. Where market economics equate social progress with continued economic growth and looks to dismantle barriers to the ever upwards trajectory of accumulation, critical political economists seek to identify the essential conditions that will guarantee the equitable and environmentally sustainable distribution of the resources required to live with dignity and presents opportunities for self-actualization, not as a competition for personal advantage, but as contributions to a shared endeavor to build a common future.

The current climate crisis presents a number of urgent challenges for public policy, but on the basis of the available research evidence, there is an overwhelming case for prioritizing an immediate halt to all further fossil fuel extraction and redirecting investment and subsidies to supporting renewable energy sources. The fossil fuel industries however continue to spend huge sums on political donations, lobbying, and public relations to block this transition and present their business priorities as synonymous with national economic interests and even the human spirit.

Reliable sources of energy are essential in ensuring that communication systems and devices operate without interruptions and support the full range of possible uses. Some emerging applications are adding significantly to calls on energy supplies. When the energy used in transmitting data is added to the demands imposed by data storage and processing, research reveals that persuading users to give up their flash drives and deposit their data in major public cloud facilities consumes more energy than simply using personal computers (Baliga, Jayant et al., 2011). Or to take another example: the peer-to-peer computer networks that validate bitcoin transactions already consume enough energy each day to supply the island of Haiti with electricity for a year and more annually for more than 150 countries (Holthaus, 2017). Plans to apply bitcoin's underlying blockchain technology to a range of other areas will compound both the unequal distribution of potential benefits and the pressures on energy supply.

Despite the projected growth in renewal sources for electricity generation and industrial processes, fossil fuels are still expected to supply three-quarters of world energy in 2040. Oil is estimated to contribute 28% with a doubling of road vehicles from 1 billion to 2.4 billion, making significant contributions, of which only 720 million will be electric on the most optimistic projections (OPEC, 2019). Coal, which powered the early phase of industrialization in the West, will also continue to make a significant contribution, accounting for almost a fifth (22%) of the global total (U.S. Energy Information Administration, 2017). Demand is likely to come primarily from India and emerging economies in Asia, but recent events suggests that coal still holds a powerful economic and symbolic attraction for politicians in mature capitalist economies. A closer look reveals the strength of the barriers standing in the way of concerted action to address the climate crisis with the urgency it requires.

Old King Coal

Addressing a mineral industry dinner in May 2014, Tony Abbot, the then leader of the Liberal Party in Australia, one of the primary emitters of CO2 among mature capitalist economies, declared that nothing would do "more danger to our future than leaving coal in the ground," and later that year, in October, hailed the opening of the $4.2 billion Caval Ridge mine as a "great day for the world" since "coal is good for humanity" (Chan, 2014). His wish for new mine openings to be "up and up in the years and decades to come" is being enthusiastically pursued by the current Liberal administration, with the construction of the huge Adani coal mine complex in Queensland, despite mounting evidence of substantial environmental damage and concerted popular opposition.

Poland offers another example. Opening the 24th annual United Nations' conference on climate change held in Katowice in the center of the country's coal mining region, in December 2018, the Polish President proudly boasted that "Experts point out that our supplies run for another two hundred years and it would be hard not to use them" (Berendt, 2018). In a surreal touch, delegates charged with devising practical steps toward meeting the goals of the Paris Agreement, who in the conference rooms poured over the latest evidence of a worsening climate crisis, were regaled outside the sessions with invitations to purchase coal-based cosmetics that promised benefits to both body and soul.

But in Donald Trump, the advocates of extractive business as usual have found a vocal defender who commands the world's leading capitalist economy and presides over a system of production and consumption that emits more CO_2 per capita than any other country (European Commission, 2018).

The First Time as Farce. The Second Time as Tragedy

On December 2, 1851, the anniversary of Napoleon Bonaparte's coronation, his nephew Louis Napoleon followed his uncle's example, suspending the French Republic and declaring himself emperor, prompting Marx's caustic observation that while Hegel had rightly noted that "all the great events of world history occur, so to speak twice. He forgot to add: the first time as tragedy, the second as farce" (Marx, 1973, p. 146).

Watching President Trump's televised broadcast from the White House rose garden on June 1, 2017, announcing that the United States was withdrawing from the Paris Agreement on climate change mitigation suggests that in this case we need to turn Marx on his head and see the first iteration of history as farce.

Farce is characterized by mistaken assumptions leading to ludicrously inappropriate actions. Trump's climate policy, based as it is on an adamant denial of the scientific evidence, is, in this sense, truly farcical. In a broadcast interview on *Fox and Friends* in 2016, he claimed to "know much about climate change" and to be in line for "environmental awards" (quoted in Marcin, 2017), a boast comprehensively undermined by his every statement and action. He has consistently pointed to incidents of very cold weather as disproving the scientific consensus, as in his typical tweet from 2014: "coldest weather years. Is our country still spending money on the Global Warming HOAX" (quoted in Marcin, 2017). This cavalier dismissal ignores the research demonstrating that extreme weather events, including periods of intense cold, are a consequence of the disruptions to natural cycles caused by global warming. In a radio interview at the end of 2016, he made it very clear that he did not accept the scientific consensus that average temperatures had risen steadily and irreversibly with the expansion of industrial capitalism, commenting: "I believe there's weather. I believe there's change, and I believe it goes up and it goes down, and it goes up again depending on years and centuries, but I am not a believer." This truculent denial has major policy consequences. He remarked in the same interview: "Obama thinks it's the number one problem in the world today. And I think it's very low on the list" (quoted in Lewis, 2016). For Trump, meeting corporate demands for greater freedom of action, particularly from the fossil fuel interests that supported his bid for the presidency, takes priority.

During his Presidential campaign, he was often photographed at rallies surrounded by banners declaring "Trump Loves Coal." "Clean coal" is a contradiction in term, since when burned, all coal produces CO2; but in his Paris Agreement withdrawal speech, he welcomed its future development and lauded the "big opening in two weeks-a brand new mine. It's unheard of. For many, many years that hasn't happened" (White House, 2017b).

Endorsing the continuing centrality of fossil fuels in the energy mix was at the heart of Trump's rationale for withdrawing from the Paris Agreement. Signing up, he argued, would effectively place America's abundant coal, gas, and oil resources "under lock and key, taking away the great wealth of our nation" and cutting "production for coal [by] 86% [and] natural gas [by] 31%," leading to mass joblessness and poverty (White House, 2017a). They would also, he argued, support a global trading regime he has consistently presented as operating to the disadvantage of "the United States [and] to the exclusive benefit of other countries" led by China (White House, 2017b).

The global competition with a resurgent China has been a recurrent motif in Trump's pronouncements on climate change. In 2012 he claimed that "the concept of global warming was created by and for the Chinese in order to make US manufacturing uncompetitive." Elaborating of this theme in his 2016 *Fox and Friends* interview, he insisted that because the Chinese "burn everything you could burn [and] … their standards are nothing … they can undercut us on price," since U.S. companies are required to comply with multiple environmental restrictions and regulations (Marcin, 2017). This assertion avoids two inconvenient truths.

China's rapid industrialization since the introduction of economic reforms has indeed been powered primarily by coal, generating an annual volume of gross CO2 emissions that is now greater than the United States, which remains in second place. The statistics for CO2 emissions per capita, however, reveal that U.S. citizens contribute more than twice as much CO2 as their Chinese counterparts – 16.07 tons as against 7.73 tons on 2015 calculations, the most recent available (European Commission, 2018). Unlike the figures for gross emissions by country, these calculations take account of both differential population sizes and average disposable income, and point to levels and modes of personal consumption as a significant contributor to global warming.

We also need to note that CO2 remains in the atmosphere for a considerable time. Even if all further emissions ceased today, it would take around 50 years for around half of the already accumulated stocks to disperse and 300 years to reach an 80% reduction. According to one calculation, the remaining residue of 20% could last "tens if not thousands of years before being removed" completely (Hausfather, 2010). The primary responsibility for these historical stocks of CO2 lies with the capitalist economies, led by the United Kingdom, the major European nations, and the United States, which industrialized first and have built economies around mass personal consumption. Trump refuses to acknowledge this history and the primary responsibility it imposes on "first mover" countries to take the lead in addressing the problem.

In a campaign speech in 2015, he deftly combined his dismissal of the scientific evidence with the claim that regulation imposed an unfair burden on tax payers, declaring "global warming...It's a tax. It's a hoax. It's a money making industry" (quoted in Marcin, 2017). Cancelling regulations, cutting public subsidies for essential scientific research, and opening up new areas for coal, gas, and oil extraction have been central planks of the Trump presidency's systematic demolition of the environmental protections introduced by his predecessors.

In March 2017 he issued an executive order instructing all relevant agencies to review existing regulations and take immediate steps to reduce all "regulatory burdens that unnecessarily encumber energy production, constrain economic growth and prevent job creation" (White House, 2017b). Primary responsibility for implementing this instruction has fallen to two agencies: the Interior Department and the Environmental Protection Agency, both headed by new appointees with close ties to fossil fuel interests. The Interior Department administers the National Parks and public lands that make up a fifth of all land in the United States and decides who will have access to the oil and gas deposits they contain. Under Trump's appointee Ryan Zinke, the Departmental ethos shifted decisively from environmental stewardship to fossil fuel exploitation. As another new appointee, Timothy Williams, explained, whereas before "Anything you want to do on public land they want to see what the carbon footprint is and what the social cost is...we're not looking at this" (quoted in Tobias, 2018). In pursuit of the resulting reorientation, millions of acres of public land has been leased to oil and gas companies and the protected areas around the national monuments at Bears Ears and Grand Staircase Escalator in Utah drastically reduced in size to open new fields for commercial exploration and extraction. The Environmental Protection Agency under its first appointee as director, Scott Pruitt, a former fossil fuel lobbyist, has significantly widened the discretion allowed to the oil, gas, and coal industries by cancelling or reducing a raft of regulations restricting air and water pollution.

The end result of the Trump administration's militant disregard for the scientific evidence is entirely predictable. After previous years of progressive decline, CO2 emissions rose sharply in 2018 by 3.4% (Rhodium Group, 2019). When presented with authoritative research demonstrating that far from ensuring future employment and economic growth, continued promotion of fossil fuels will have exactly the opposite effect, Trump remained adamant in his denial. In November 2018 the expert body mandated by Congress to produce periodic assessments of the impact of climate change delivered a stark warning, insisting that "without substantial and sustained reductions in global greenhouse gas emissions," "rising temperatures, sea level rises, and changes in extreme events" are "expected to cause substantial net damage to the US economy [with] annual losses is some economic sectors projected to reach hundreds of billions of dollars by the end of the century" (U.S. Global Change Research Program, 2018, p. 12). When asked to comment, Trump was typically both boastful and dismissive, claiming that "people like myself, we have very high levels of intelligence but we're not necessarily such believers. As to whether or not it's man-made or whether not the effects that you're talking about are there, I don't see it" (quoted in Cole, 2018).

Against a background of extreme weather events around the globe and confirmation that the last decade has seen the world's warmest years on record, in October 2018 the Intergovernmental Panel on Climate Change, the United Nations' expert body responsible for collating the available scientific evidence, published a landmark report: *Global Warming of 1.5 degrees C* (IPPC, 2018). It concluded that there were only 12 years left to ensure that global temperatures were kept to the Paris Agreement's goal of 1.5° above preindustrial levels, and that an increase of even half a degree above that would have devastating consequences with more frequent droughts, floods, and extreme weather, with the most severe effects being felt by the hundreds of millions of people living in vulnerable low-income regions in the southern hemisphere. Trump responded by attacking the report's evidential base and by extension the integrity of the authors, remarking that "I want to look at who drew it. You know, which group drew it. Because I can give you reports that are fabulous, and I can give you reports that aren't so good" (quoted in Bump, 2018). "Fake" science joins "fake" news as a catchall description of any information that raises awkward questions and uncomfortable choices

Stopping the Clock

Trump speaks for a constellation of fossil fuel interests, but he does not speak for the American people. In his address rejecting the Paris Agreement, he claimed to have been elected to represent the citizens of Pittsburg not Paris. It was an unwise choice. Pittsburg, an old steelmaking center and previously one of the most polluted cities in the United States, is an active member of the *We are Still In* coalition of 280 cities and countries and 10 states across the country committed to delivering on the Paris Goal. They are joined by an array of universities and cultural institutions, representatives of the native peoples whose lands have been progressively despoiled by mining and drilling, and by over 2,000 business investors who are moving their money out of fossil fuel companies ("We Are Still In," 2018). They are tapping into a rising current of popular unease in the United States, with 69% of respondents to a recent Yale University poll saying that they were now "somewhat worried" about global warming and 29% claiming to be "very worried," the highest level since the poll was launched a decade ago (Leiserowitz et al., 2019). The increased incidence of extreme weather events has translated global warming from an abstract and remote risk to a tangible and immediate threat.

Around the globe, we see popular mobilizations. Mining and drilling sites are picketed and barricaded. School children are marching, demanding a livable future. I have argued here that because communication systems have become increasingly indispensable to the organization of contemporary capitalism at every level, from global trade to intimate life, their dominant modes of operation are making substantial contributions to exacerbating climate change. This centrality imposes a particular responsibility on scholars of media and communications to enter the debate on how to address the current climate crisis and stop the doomsday clock from moving farther toward midnight

Since its resurgence in the 1970s, critical political economy has set out to specify the conditions that will ensure an equitable distribution of the full range of cultural resources that support humans flourishing and foster respect and care for strangers. It has interrogated the unaccountable corporate power of owners and advertisers, detailed the changing role of governments, states, and international organizations, examined the shifting organization cultural labor, and investigated the alternatives offered by public funding and voluntary and peer-to-peer initiatives. Against a backdrop of unparalled levels of corporate concentration, unprecedented saturation of the cultural landscape by product promotions, increasing casualization and insurity of cultural work, and the intensification of mediated surveillance, these defining concerns are more relevant than ever not only to established struggles for full and equal social and political participation, but also to addressing the climate crisis.

There is now mounting criticism of the digital majors and their operations. Proposals for change that were formerly confined to the margins of debate have moved steadily to the political center, with increasing demands for tougher regulation of the majors' unprecedented economic reach and abuses of communicative power. As a recent British parliamentary report concluded, "the big tech companies must not be allowed to expand exponentially without constraint or proper regulation" (DCMSC, 2019, p. 7). There are calls for their de facto monopolies to be broken up, for the algorithms that direct their operations to be made public, and for rigorous external regulation and oversight of the material, including the advertising, posted on their sites, with appropriate sanctions for violations. More radical proposals, which directly confront their core business model, call for an end to their exclusive right to harvest and exploit user data and its ownership to revert to individual users or be transferred to a communal depository to be used for democratically decided interventions that improve the quality of social life.

These proposals go some way to addressing the distortions and abuses in dominant digital markets, but intervention designed to reverse the damage done by decades of neoliberal economics also needs to restore the public domain and establish a comprehensive digital commons that operate outside the market and provide a robust countervailing power to communication deployed in the service of accumulation (Murdock, 2018a). If, as I have argued here, the culture of hyper consumption is a significant contributory factor in exacerbating the climate crisis, it is essential to reestablish a comprehensive cultural arena that does not carry advertising and which addresses users not as consumers but as citizens and communards, whose opportunities for self-realization are inextricably bound up with the quality of collective life. Building this new collective space will require concerted struggles to reclaim the Internet as a public utility, revivify the range of public cultural institutions, and renegotiate the relations between expert knowledge and professional practice and popular participation. It will also require substantial public funding. Closing the tax loopholes that have allowed the Internet majors to retain almost all of their profits, and imposing an additional levy on their advertising income, offers a solution that addresses the unequal exchange that gave these companies free access to the publicly financed fundamental research on which they have built their businesses. As Mariana Mazzucato notes, "had the State earned back just 1% from the investments it made in the Internet, there would be much more today to invest" (Mazzucato, 2018, p. 201).

Reconstructing a countervailing public communicative space is an essential intervention, but it is no longer enough. It is now clear that a comprehensive approach to addressing the impact of communications on climate change must also confront the social and environmental costs incurred at every stage in developing and using infrastructures and devices. It needs to investigate the operations of the extraction industries that provide the foundational resources and minerals they depend on, interrogate the organizations of their manufacture and transportation, and calibrate the costs of the energy they use and the waste and pollution generated in their disposal. Any future proposal for change must take each of these moments in the communications chain fully into account. Public communication institutions need to be in the vanguard of demonstrating the viability of alternatives to a continuing reliance on environmentally damaging materials and fossil fuels, accelerated cycles of obsolescence, and polluting practices of disposal. Proposals for alternatives that do not place the materiality of media at the center of their strategies remain part of the problem (Murdock, 2018b). Critical political economy has a central role to play in detailing the social and environmental benefits of available practical options for change and embedding preferred options in a concerted ethical challenge to capitalism's imagination of the future as an endless, but unsustainable, spiral of accumulation.

In the third volume of *Capital*, based on unfinished notes collated after his death, Marx endorses a powerful moral economy of our social responsibility toward the natural world, arguing that:

> a nation, or all simultaneously existing societies taken together, are not the owners of the earth. They are simply... its beneficiaries, and have to bequeath it in an improved state to succeeding generations.
>
> (Marx, 1981, p. 911)

This ethos of custodianship has always informed the economic organization of commoning that supported the social organization of indigenous and peasant communities. As Marx knew all too well, having witnessed the enclosure of the historic forests around Trier where he grew up, capitalism's dynamic of accumulation requires this ethos to be silenced and consigned to history, so that shared resources can be continually converted into private property and exploited in the pursuit of profit under the twin banners of "modernation" and "progress."

Retrieving the ethos of custodianship and devising ways of reorganizing communications systems and practices to embed it as a central value in contemporary economic and social organization presents critical political economy with an urgent and unprecedented challenge. The clock is ticking.

References

Baliga, Jayant et al. (2011). 'Green Cloud computing: Balancing energy in processing, storage and transport', *Proceedings of the IEEE*, 99(1), 149–167.

Berendt, J. (2018). 'Playing host to climate conference, Poland Promotes coal', *The New York Times*, December 4. www.nytimes.com/2018/12/04/world/europe/poland-coal-un.html

Bump, P. (2018). 'Trump's abdication on climate change is very on-brand', *The Washington Post*, October 10. www.washingtonpost.com/politics/2018/10/10/trumps-abdication-new-climate-change-report-is-very-on-brand/?noredirect=on&utm_term=.d7f332716dc3

Chan, G. (2014). 'Tony Abbot says "coal is good for humanity, while opening mine"', *The Guardian*, October 13. www.theguardian.com/world/2014/oct/13/tony-abbott-says-coal-is-good-for-humanity-while-opening-mine

Cisco (2017). Cisco visual networking index: Global mobile data traffic forecast update 2016–2021 White Paper. www.cisco.com/c/en/us/solutions/collateral/service-provider/visual-networking-index-vni/mobile-white-paper-c11-520862.html

Cole, B. (2018). 'Trump says his "Very high level of intelligence" means he can't belie in climate change, scientists despair', *Newsweek*, November 28. www.newsweek.com/trump-says-his-very-high-levels-intelligence-means-he-cant-believe-climate-1234608

DCMSC (Digital, Culture, Media and Sport Committee) (2019). *Disinformation and 'fake news': Final Report*. London. House of Commons HC1791.

Echols, E. (1961). *Herodian of Antioch's History of the Roman Empire*. Berkeley. University of California Press.

European Commission (2018). 'CO2 Time Series 1990–2015 per region/country', *Emissions Database for Global Atmospheric Research (EDGAR)*. http://edgar.jrc.ec.europa.eu/overview.php?v=CO2ts1990-2015

Gaffney, O. and Steffen, W. (2017). 'The Anthropocene equation', *The Anthropocene Review*. http://journals.sagepub.com/doi/full/10.1177/2053019616688022

Gibbard, S. et al. (2005). 'Climate effects of global land cover change', *Geophysical Research Letters*, 32(23), L23705.

Hausfather, Z. (2010). 'Common climate misconceptions: Atmospheric carbon dioxide', *Yale Climate Connections*, December 16. www.yaleclimateconnections.org/2010/12/common-climate-misconceptions-atmospheric-carbon-dioxide/

Holthaus, E. (2017). 'Bitcoin mining guzzles energy—and its carbon footprint just keeps growing', *Wired*, June 6. www.wired.com/story/bitcoin-mining-guzzles-energyand-its-carbon-footprint-just-keeps-growing/

IPCC-Intergovernmental Panel on Climate Change (2018). *Global Warming of 1.5 degrees C* October. www.ipcc.ch/sr15/

Kroll, Luisa, and Dolan, Kerry (2018). 'Meet the Members of the Three-Comma Club', *Forbes*, March 6. www.forbes.com/billionaires/#39b5d33f251c

Leiserowitz, A. et al. (2019). *Climate Change in the American Mind: December 2018*. Yale Program on Climate Change Communication, December. http://climatecommunication.yale.edu/publications/climate-change-in-the-american-mind-december-2018/2/

Lewis, P. (2016). 'Donald Trump on climate change: "I Believe it Goes Up and it Goes Down"', *The Huffington Post*, December 24. www.huffingtonpost.com/entry/trump-global-warming_us_5601d04fe4b08820d91aa753

Mann, M., Bradley Raymond, S. B., & Hughes, M. (1998). 'Global scale temperature patterns and climate forcing over the past six centuries', *Nature*, 392, 779–787.

Marcin, T. (2017). 'What has Trump said about global warming? Eight quotes in climate change as he announces Paris Agreement decision', *Newsweek*, June 1. www.newsweek.com/what-has-trump-said-about-global-warming-quotes-climate-change-paris-agreement-618898

Marx, K. (1973). *Surveys from Exile: Political Writings Volume 2*. London. Penguin Books.

Marx, K. (1981). *Capital: Volume Three*. London. Penguin Books.

Mazzucato, M. (2013). *The Entrepreneurial State: Debunking Public v Private Sector Myths*. London. Anthem Press.

Monbiott, G. (2018). 'Our natural world is disappearing before our eyes. We must save it', *The Guardian*, July 1 2018. www.theguardian.com/commentisfree/2018/jun/29/natural-world-disappearing-save-it

Morley, D. (2017). *Communications and Mobility: The Migrant, the Mobile Phone and the Container Box*. John Wiley and Son.

Murdock, G. (2018a). 'Reclaiming digital space: From commercial enclosure to the broadcast commons', in Gregory Ferrell Lowe, Hilde Van den Bulck, and Karen Donders (eds.), *Public Service Media in the The Networked Society*. Nordicom. University of Gothenberg, pp. 43–58.

Murdock, G. (2018b). 'Media materialities: For a moral economy of machines', *Journal of Communication*, 68 (2, April), 359–368.

OPEC (2019). *2018 World Oil Outlook*. Vienna. Organisation of Petroleum Producing Countries.

Rhodium Group (2019). *Preliminary US Emissions Estimates for 2018*. January 8. https://rhg.com/research/preliminary-us-emissions-estimates-for-2018/

Steffen, W., Grinevald, J., Crutzen, P., & McNeil, J. (2011). 'The Anthropocene: Conceptual and historical perspectives', *Philosophical Proceedings of the Royal Society*, 369, 842–867.

Tobias, J. (2018). 'The Zinke effect: How the US Interior Department became a tool of big business', *The Guardian*, November 12. www.theguardian.com/us-news/2018/nov/12/the-zinke-effect-how-the-us-interior-department-became-a-tool-of-industry

US Energy Information Administration (2017). *International Energy Outlook 2017*. www.eia.gov/outlooks/archive/ieo17/exec_summ.php

US Global Change Research Program (2018). *Climate Assessment Volume II: Impacts, Risks, and Adaptations in the United States: Report in Brief*. Washington, DC. US Government Publishing Office.

We Are Still In (2018). Who's In. www.wearestillin.com/signatories

White House (2017a). *Presidential Executive Order on Promoting Energy Independence and Economic Growth*. March 28. www.whitehouse.gov/presidential-actions/presidential-executive-order-promoting-energy-independence-economic-growth/

White House (2017b). *Statement by President Trump on the Paris Climate Accord*. June 1. www.whitehouse.gov/briefings-statements/statement-president-trump-paris-climate-accord/

15 Time, Globality and Commodity Fetishism

Wayne Hope

Commodities are objects, goods, or entities which are exchangeable, usually via the medium of money. Commodity status is not intrinsic, but assigned. In given circumstances, the process of assignation – commodification – has been studied by historians, anthropologists, sociologists, geographers, and other scholars. Marx argued that under capitalism, the very exchangeability of commodities obfuscated the social relations of labor exploitation which brought them into existence. The taken-for-granted appearance of market exchange attests to the power of commodity fetishism. In this regard, political economists of communication have historically explored the various processes of commodification associated with mass media and social media technologies. Thus, commercial ratings enable media organizations and advertisers to determine the exchange value of given media audiences. This negotiation process obscures the role played by media workers who produce the rateable media content. At the same time, the mass-mediated promotion of individual consumption amidst program content obscures the capitalist imperatives of commercial media, advertisers, and private corporations. More recently, the business models of Google, Facebook, and other social media platforms have allowed users' search histories and personal interactions to be monetized and sold to third parties. Further, the social ubiquity of iPhones, iPads, and other communication devices obscures the mass exploitation of digital assembly workers. Clearly, the materiality and obfuscation of these labor practices plus the logics of profit which drive them are central concerns for critical communication scholarship. In my view, however, the demystification of commodity fetishism needs to be retheorized and given a broader analytical framework. This would reenergize established critical perspectives within the political economy of communication and open up new research vistas. To this end, I will advance the following lines of argument and explore the interrelationships among them. First, certain epistemes of time, temporality, time reckoning, coevalness, and epochality open up new understandings of commodity fetishism. Second, from a time-related perspective, various manifestations of commodity fetishism obscure not just labor relations but the materialities of unequal socio-ecological exchange and the slow violence of socio-ecological destruction. Third, the preceding critical insights have a contemporary global resonance which requires urgent scrutiny.

Epistemes of Time and Commodity Fetishism

The fetishism of commodity exchange as an ideological process can be understood in psychological terms. For consumers in a capitalist society, purchasing, owning, and gaining pleasure from a commodity represses the realization that workers made such activities possible. This entails a shared sense of forgetting or social amnesia about the causal linkages between labor and the commodity (Billig, 1999). A geospatial dimension operates here; the awareness of labor exploitation within networks of production, transportation, and distribution is unrecognized. Labor-commodity linkages are also chronological; goods are produced and assembled before they are purchased and consumed. It is this beforeness which is elided, psychologically and socially, by the omnipresence of commodity exchange. The twin problematic of remembering-forgetting and before-after brings us to *temporality*, an epistemic ground for understanding the relationalities between past, present, and future. A digressive consideration of such relationalities will extend our critique of commodity fetishism.

Temporality is inherent to memory, expectation, and attention to the present. These are manifestations of lived time that have no necessary connection to any supervening conception of time deriving from religion or science. Temporality can be observed or experienced in the intersecting domains of self, intersubjectivity, social identity, bureaucratic institutions, and society at large. Various temporal orientations are also built into the operations of nation states, economies, polities, legal systems, international institutions, and transnational organizations. In these contexts, the study of memory draws together insights from psychology, sociology, anthropology, history, literary studies, and media-communication studies. In general, one can make a central distinction between personal recall and constitutions of collective memory that may be institutionalized, oppositionally expressed, and/or fundamentally contested on the grounds of religion, culture, or political ideology (Zelizer, 1995). Of course, orientations toward the past and memories of the past could not occur if they did not coexist with the present. Without examining the intricacies of this coexistence, one can acknowledge an equally problematic relationship between present and future. Here, Barbara Adam and Chris Groves' sub-definitions of futurity and its lack are illustrative (Adam & Groves, 2007). For example, habits of mind that are subsumed by present interests and imperatives regard the future as a void to be filled by unfolding events as chronological time passes. Such events, as they arise, will simply reflect the modus operandi which prevails in the present. By contrast, scenario planning describes possible futures, according to internally consistent assumptions about key development potentials within institutions and social totalities. Obvious examples include macroeconomic and intra-sectoral planning along with technological research and development. A related concept, futures-in-the-making, refers to future-orientated actions that are progressing within an unfolding present. There are general parameters of future-oriented change, but the content of this change cannot be fully established in advance. The full temporal context of futurity is exemplified by memories of the future. In this formulation, the past contains plans, visions, and ambitions concerning the future which were (in retrospect) either realized or unrealized (Adams & Groves, 2007). In the latter case, the recovery of potential futures from the past may facilitate or inspire contemporary orientations toward the future.

Consumer culture induces myopia as well as amnesia. Commodity exchange in the purchase of commodity objects or services elides critical appreciations of futurity at two levels. Specifically, when an owned commodity is resold, given away, or discarded, its future is of no consequence for the (former) consumer. Such a commodity may be refined, repurposed, reassembled, and/or redistributed in ways that involve further labor exploitation. A discarded commodity may deplete ecological and biospheric surroundings. In the case of electronic equipment, devices, wirings, and screens, toxic dumps attract waste pickers; these are informal laborers who work to construct further nodes of commodity exchange. At a general level, myopia concerning the future life of commodities precludes any prospective understanding of how labor-commodity relationships might develop over time. The possible futures of given capitalist economies are, therefore, likely to elude public depiction. Because commodity fetishism entails the repression of memory and futurity, it foregrounds an atemporal present. Mass-mediated advertising has long served to reify the immediacy of consumer desire. From the mid-1990s, MP3 players, digital cameras, internet search engines, handheld remotes, and multifunctional phones opened up new time-saving opportunities for consumers. Personal media technologies were easy to operate, ready-to-hand, and offered instant access to purchasable commodities. The culture of consumption shifted from an emphasis on the enjoyment of continued possession to that of "the immediate and repeated appropriation of new goods" (Tomlinson, 2007, p. 137). Quickening rhythms of consumption became intimately associated with technological mediations of presentness.

Let us now examine commodity fetishism as an extension of the labor process itself. Here, the operational imperatives of worker exploitation and the material linkages between production and consumption can be analyzed in terms of *time reckoning*. This episteme refers to the numbering, measurement, and standardization of time independently of socially lived time and inbuilt natural processes within geology, biology, the biosphere, and the solar system. Historically, advancing precision in the devices and measures of time reckoning increases the degree of abstraction from natural processes. Mechanical clocks and time pieces, for example, can be distinguished from water clocks, sundials, and sandglasses. In early modern Europe, the precise time reckonings enabled by the mechanical clock in tandem with the calendric system became standardized within commercial enterprises, trading networks, oceanic navigation, and the early modern state. Subsequent standardizations of clock time coincided with the emergence of the telegraph, telephony, and wireless telegraphy. These innovations presaged radio transmission, terrestrial television, satellite television, networked computers, the Internet, and social media. Barbara Adam has remarked that the sum of these developments represented an historically new kind of time reckoning: "time has been reconstituted; instantaneity and simultaneity have replaced sequence and duration" (Adam, 2004, p. 120). Within social lifeworlds, this transition is not clear-cut. Different kinds of time reckoning are, to some extent, integrated with everyday routines. At a macro level, though, advances in real-time communication technology challenged the ascendancy of clock time.

For capitalist enterprises, calculations of profit and labor productivity have long depended upon the standard reckonings of clock time. The process is delineated in E.P. Thompson's seminal 1967 article "Time, Work Discipline and Industrial Capitalism". In 18th-century England, small domestically based workshops developed simple divisions of labor. The eventual arrival of machine-powered industry in the mid-19th century required greater exactitude in time regimes and a more substantial synchronization of labor processes. In Western economies, from about 1890, Frederick Taylor and his followers broke down labor processes into simple, complementary tasks so that managers could eliminate periods of inactivity and rest time from the working day. Henry Ford built upon Taylor's work by introducing a moving assembly line with labor-saving machinery, interchangeable automobile parts, and standardized job tasks. In American, Western European, and Japanese factories of the 1980s, microchip computers and robotics began to drive assembly lines. These and other technologies enabled the development of "lean production," a system of task integration, worker flexibility, and teamwork psychology. The general purpose was to "accelerate the entire factory"; to this end, special time studies software allowed "management to simulate the production process and test different compositions of tasks" (Hermann, 2014, p. 71). Lean production became integrated within just-in-time (JIT) delivery systems, whereby parts were delivered to the assembly line as they were needed. And, levels of output across different product types were matched with variations in consumer demand. On the basis of such calculations, corporations could ratchet up clock-based rates of labor exploitation worldwide. How this strategy was developed can be briefly outlined as follows. From the 1980s, information and communication technologies intermeshed with the established labor-based logistics sector to integrate transnational supply chains and transport products to their point of consumption. To this end, the very nature of logistics was transformed. It was possible to utilize "electronic communication to integrate all forms of transportation with systems of wholesale trade or distribution in order to deliver products immediately if not instantaneously in response to market demand" (Sealey, 2010, p. 27). This, in turn, required subcontracted workforces flexible enough to absorb redundancies, increases or decreases in work hours, and shorter spans of "downtime." From a labor-commodity standpoint, then the severity of clock-based worker exploitation is ultimately driven by unfolding real-time variations of consumer demand. Yet this business model, which shapes the operations of transnational retailers, ICT corporations, and other transnationals, is obscured by the hyper-mediated present of consumer culture and commodity fetishism.

The time reckoning of labor exploitation excommunicates unwaged and precariously waged populations. Within contemporary capitalism, the entire process constitutes a denial of *coevalness*. This episteme concerns intersubjective and reciprocal communication with regard to different awarenesses of time. Conversely, narrow univocal assumptions about time may predominate and thus damage communication among individuals, groups, institutions, and cultures with disparate, historico-temporal experiences. Johannes Fabian's (1983) critique of Western anthropology, *Time and the Other*, maintains that such research constructed its object in a way that erased the historical and temporal perspective of the cultures under investigation. They were externally characterized through the anthropological lens as backward, traditional, savage, tribal, and/or peasant. This positioning obscured the cultural impact of a Western time consciousness shaped by the myth of progress and the sequential precision of calendar and clock time. With the decolonization of European empires and the spread of postcolonial sensibilities, one can argue that the Eurocentrist preconditions for the denial of coevalness no longer hold (Fabian, 2007). In my view, however, the denial of coevalness has become reexpressed within global configurations of capitalism.

Workforces and the precariously employed are treated as a collateral or disposable component rather than as a fixture internal to capital-labor relations. In this context, Ankie Hoogvelt observed in 2006 a configuration whereby 20% of the world's population were able to borrow funds (wealthy elites, securely employed professionals, and waged workers), while other waged workers, informal workers, service providers, and their families lived precariously. The outer layers of the world's poor were individually expendable as a structural depressant on global wage levels (Hoogvelt, 2006). Their temporal experiences, within burgeoning slums, became the unrecognized other to the capitalist imperatives of profit maximization and wealth defense (Davis, 2007). The material denials of coevalness involved here were, and are, naturalized by global disseminations of consumerist cosmopolitanism. This is a contemporary form of commodity fetishism, whereby openness toward peoples, places, and experiences from different cultures and nations is superficially celebrated through branded products and advertising via images of food, fashion, film, real estate, tourist destinations, and sport and celebrity figures. From the early 1990s, this consumerist cosmopolitanism was continuously reproduced through the Internet, mobile phones, airline travel, billboards, neon signs, and television.

Reflecting upon the episteme of *epochality* allows us to historicize the contemporary time-related features of commodity fetishism. The commonsense idea that there are marked periods or epochs in history raises several vexed questions. When do epochs begin and end? Is the unfolding of history expressive of continuity or discontinuity? Does the naming and demarcation of epochs illuminate or obscure historical reality? Amidst these and other related questions, I advance the following proposition. In the late 19th century, the development of telegraph networks, modern sea and transport systems, and world time zones gave capitalism a rudimentary global shape. From about 1980, a confluence of epochal events and processes brought a fully fledged global capitalism into being. These included the collapse of Fordist Keynesianism; national Keynesianism, Bretton Woods, and Soviet Communism along with First, Second, and Third World demarcations; the international proliferation of neoliberal policy regimes; and the growth of transnational corporations with far-reaching supply chains and dispersed subcontracted workforces. Just as importantly, the globalization of financial institutions and financial flows weakened national-economic boundaries (Dicken, 2003; Hope, 2016; Robinson, 2004; Sklair, 2002). Critical representations of these developments are precluded by consumerist cosmopolitanism and a transnational corporate imaginary, in which disparate communities form around branded products and services to celebrate global connectedness and universal humanism. A longitudinal analysis of 2,400 transnational corporation television advertisements in telecommunications, ICTs, finance, biotechnology, energy, automobile manufacture, aerospace, defense, and pharmaceuticals by advertising researchers Robert Goldman and Steven Papson discerned a narrative whereby "free, open and vast communication eliminates all discriminations associated with race, gender, ethnicity and social positioning." They concluded that such advertising tells a "dehistoricised story about capital." It has no apparent source and exists in "the form of grand signifiers that appear to be autonomous in every sense except for their relationship to the individual subject" (Goldman & Papson, 2011, p. 202). Goldman and Papson's summation expresses perfectly the global-epochal dimension of commodity fetishism.

Time, Global Capitalism, and Unequal Socio-Ecological Exchange

Within global capitalism, the exploitation of subcontracted workforces and the marginalization of unwaged populations also depletes environmental surroundings. In such circumstances, commodity fetishism works to efface unequal structures of socio-ecological exchange. Over 25 years ago, James O'Connor identified two contradictions of capitalism. The first, well understood in Marxian literature, is expressed through "capital's social and political power over labor and also capitalism's inherent tendency toward a realisation crisis or crisis of overproduction." Increasing rates of labor exploitation would drive the need "for a vast credit structure, aggressive marketing, constant product innovation and intensified competition" to maintain aggregate demand (O'Connor, 1991, p. 107). O'Connor also sought to link the size and value of mass consumption, natural elements entering into production, and the socioeconomic costs of environmental depletion (O'Connor, 1988). This brings us to the second contradiction: "capitalism's economically self-destructive appropriation and use of labor power, urban infrastructure, space and external nature or the environment" (O'Connor, 1991, p. 108). One must acknowledge here that capitalism's appropriation of "external nature or the environment" is a long-standing historical process. The environmental historian Jason Moore has detailed the intercontinental expansion of mercantile capitalism and the instrumentalization of ecological nature from 1450 to 1750. This period saw the deforestation of European landscapes, the plunder of gold, silver, copper, iron, forest products, and wildlife from the Americas and the enslavement of indigenous and African populations. Plantation agriculture, trade, and commodity exchange based upon spices, cereals, tobacco, sugar, and cotton depended upon cheap appropriations of labor, food, energy, and raw materials (Moore, 2016). In this context, the instrumentalization of ecological nature, including its inhabitants, was premised upon new imaginations of reality. Moore remarks that "early forms of external nature, abstract space and abstract time enabled capitalists and empires to construct global webs of exploitation and appropriation, calculation and credit, property and profit on an unprecedented scale" (Moore, 2017a, p. 620). Thus, geographic space was apprehended by cartography and historical time was fused with chronological measurement and the teleology of civilizational progress. Indigenous comprehensions of time and ecological nature, in the face of imperial encroachment, were thereby marginalized. In sum, the relations of power and wealth that emerged after 1450 became encompassed by the time-space dynamics of unequal socio-ecological exchange. Such a realization was unimaginable within the incipient commercial cultures of European metropoles.

Within a modernizing 19th-century world economy integrated by trade, transport, communication, and time zones, the British industrial revolution accelerated coal extraction and CO_2 emissions. This was the underpinning of fossil fuel capitalism, a form of unequal socio-ecological exchange which would have enormous long-term repercussions (Malm, 2016a). The extraction, combustion, and consumption of fossil fuels drove subsequent capitalist development in Western Europe, North America, and beyond. Eventually, the entirety of industrial capitalism became locked into carbon energy extraction, CO_2 emissions, and the multiple feedback loops of anthropogenic climate change. This contemporary plight leads us to consider the epochality of global capitalism from a socio-ecological perspective. Before doing so, a brief critical discussion of anthropocenic narratives will be required.

In 2000, the earth scientist Paul Crutzen declared that the Anthropocene should follow the Holocene on the geological timescale (Crutzen, 2002; Hamilton, Bonneuil, & Gemenne, 2015). He and fellow researchers argued from stratigraphic evidence that human activities involving large-scale carbon emissions had measurably changed the global climate such that a new geological turning point could be identified. Subsequently, a range of other scientists from climatology, oceanography, geochemistry, atmospheric geochemistry, and orbital satellite programs maintained that the earth system was shifting into an Anthropocene epoch characterized by anthropogenic global warming, ocean acidification, melting ice sheets, sea level rise, and species extinction. These outcomes, in the absence of adequate countermeasures, point to a hotter world, unruly climate, extreme weather events, submerged coastal settlement, mass migrations, destroyed agricultural systems, and violent geopolitics. Metanarratives of progress, which assume nature's externality, are therefore redundant. Natural history and human history have converged. However, popularizations of this insight within conventional anthropocenic narratives overlook historical and contemporary understandings of unequal socio-ecological exchange. The argument is succinctly put by Christophe Bonneuil and Jean Baptiste Fressoz in the *Shock of the Anthropocene*. They did not criticize the scientific value of anthropocenic research, only its insufficiency:

> It is rather a matter of opening up the official narrative of the Anthropocene to discussion so as to enable closer reflection on the particularities of our representations of the world. So that other voices from and for the earth can be heard coming from other cultures and other social groups, so that other explanations of 'how we got to this

point' and other proposals for 'what is to be done' may also have their say. Otherwise the seductive Anthropocene concept may well become the official philosophy of a new technocratic and market oriented geo-power.

(Bonneuil & Fressoz, 2016, p. 49)

Conventionally, the Anthropocene concept points to the conscious realization of a worsening human predicament. The multiple feedback loops associated with CO_2 emissions, global warming, and climate change must be understood and mitigated by humanity before it is too late. However, this unfolding narrative elides from view the historical significance and vested interests of fossil fuel capitalism (Malm, 2016a). And, the temporal assumption that anthropocenic impacts could become catastrophic at some future time obscures the fact that some are experiencing life-changing disruption now. Hotter temperatures for sub-Saharan tribal communities and sea level rises for Bangladeshis and South Pacific Islanders are existential threats. Massive tar sand extractions in Alberta, Canada, are displacing First Nation inhabitants. The affected populations in all these cases have been denied the right of coeval communication, an injustice which is obscured and reinforced by the undifferentiated "we" of standard Anthropocene discourse.

From a left-ecological perspective, the Anthropocene is difficult to periodise because of the time delay between causes and consequences. One view is that contemporary global warming stems from the development of steam power in the mid-19th century. The biospheric effects of rapidly increasing CO_2 emissions were cumulative and exponential (Malm, 2016a). The same can be said of the upsurge in oil-based CO_2 emissions after 1945 (McNeill & Engelke, 2014). However, it is also true that the carbon footprint of global capitalism is epochally distinctive. Andreas Malm notes that between 1751 and 2010, half of all CO_2 emissions from fossil fuel combustion occurred after 1986. Between 2000 and 2006, 55% of such growth derived from China. There, a massive economic transition from agriculture to industry depended upon cheap labor, domestic coal and imported oil. The building of power plants and electricity grids delivered coal-based energy to factories and work dormitories. Finished goods were sent to domestic and overseas markets via oil-consuming road, rail, air, and sea transport. The net result was, and is, a huge unprecedented separation between energy production and consumption across national boundaries. Major corporations profit from the extraction, combustion, and consumption of fossil fuels and their embodiment in commodity exchange. Meanwhile, global consumer culture obfuscates the capitalist origins and temporal dynamics of carbon-driven climate change.

The unprecedented spread of transnational carbon footprints and anthropocenic feedback loops coincides with the "end of cheap nature" (Moore, 2014, p. 285). The costs of monetizing labor, raw materials, energy, and food are growing irreversibly because the very globality of capitalism has erased the inside-outside frontier, whereby appropriations of external nature were always in prospect. Thus, labor productivity growth in China's industrial heartlands is likely to slow as workers mobilize for higher wages. The cheap supply of migrant rural labor from the central and western provinces is not inexhaustible. Beyond China, available reservoirs of soon-to-be-exploited workers are diminishing. From 2003, rising and volatile world prices for metals, energy, and food staples suggested that these resources could no longer be cheaply appropriated from outside the immediate circuits of capital (Moore, 2014). In this regard, food production is especially vulnerable to the effects of global warming. One cited study predicts an inevitable output decline for tropical and semi-tropical agricultural systems in Pakistan, North Western India, the Sahel, the Maghreb, the Caribbean, Mexico, parts of southern Africa, and the Middle East (Cline, 2007; Davis, 2018). The epochal significance of global capitalism's impact upon social ecologies and the earth system is not readily apparent. To explain why, one must consider the mutually reinforcing opacities of ecological destruction and mediated commodity fetishism. It is to this task that I now turn.

Socio-Ecological Destruction, Slow Violence, and Commodity Fetishism

Vivid depictions of labor exploitation can potentially de-reify commodity fetishism. Video footage of factory compounds, surrounded by wire mesh and policed by security guards, reveal the physical environments of subcontracted workforces. This is where clothing and apparel is produced for major transnational brands such as Gap, Nike, and Reebok. The websites of labor rights NGOs show Chinese Foxconn workers on huge production lines, assembling the screens and circuitry of Apple devices. In these and other cases, one can potentially associate branded products with the human toil needed to produce them. It is more difficult, though, to draw causal connections between the accretions of socio-ecological destruction and mediated consumer culture. The linkages which conjoin fossil fuel extraction, CO_2 emissions, temperature rise, ocean acidification, other greenhouse effects, disintegration of pan-regional ecologies, and the proliferation of carbon-based consumer lifestyles are difficult to represent. The same holds for an agribusiness system which displaces local farming practices, creates landless rural laborers, damages the environment, and sustains retail cultures of food consumption. Literary scholar and environmental activist, Rob Nixon, attributes this representational difficulty to "slow violence":

> By 'slow' violence' I mean a violence that occurs gradually and out-of-sight, a violence of delayed destruction that is dispersed across time and space, an attritional violence that is typically not viewed as

violence at all. Violence is customarily conceived as an event or action that is immediate in time, explosive and particular in space and as erupting into sensational visibility. We need, I believe, to engage in a different kind of violence, a violence that is neither spectacular nor instantaneous but rather incremental and accretive, its calamitous repercussions playing out across a range of temporal scales.

(Nixon, 2011, p. 2)

From these insights, different levels of analysis can be presented. First, it should be acknowledged that the actual materialities of slow violence are not fully visible. Ocean acidification, species extinction, water supply salination, and depletion of soil nutrients and fish stocks are complex ecological processes which are difficult to encapsulate. By contrast, fractured icecaps, deforestation, forest fires, and extreme weather events can be readily observed. Consequently, sensational images referring to certain kinds of environmental and social destruction circulate instantaneously throughout mass media and social media networks. In these circumstances of uneven visibility, it is difficult to depict the global totalities of socio-ecological destruction and the culpability of powerful corporate interests. Second, one can argue that the opacity of slow violence intensifies the global and technological opacities of commodity fetishism. The processes at work here are time-related. Global telecommunications and television networks generate a 24/7 real-time world of rolling news, cosmopolitan consumerism, and corporate image advertising. Simultaneously, information communication technologies, social media search engines, big data, and virtual environments routinely intervene between reality and its appearance. Such developments normalize quickening consumption, presentist consumer gratification, and continuous promotions of the digital self. These conditions of social life reify the material invisibilities of slow violence and bracket out temporal understandings of socio-ecological destruction. Here, Barbara Adam and Chris Groves' conception of "timeprint" points to an underlying global-ecological dimension of futurity. Certain economic, political, and environmental practices in the present may undermine the future prospects of successor generations. The growing intensification and extension of this timeprint suggests a recurring inability to learn from past courses of action and anticipate their consequences. Saulo Cwerners' "chronopolitan ideal" furthers our understanding of this predicament. He argues that constructions of citizenship, sovereignty, and democracy at the global level should entail "the extension of rights and responsibilities in the polis across time as well as space" (p. 335). Cwerners' chronopolitanism insists that the rights of future generations should be "inscribed in the actions and thoughts of the living" (p. 337). Thus, future socio-ecological depredations must be anticipated just as earlier depredations are publicly recovered and acted upon. Future projections of the relationship between slow violence and commodity fetishism should explore the growing plutonomy of super wealthy elites committed to production growth and the unsustainable practices of luxury consumption. Tom Di Muzio argues that these "pursuits are actively destroying the ecosystems upon which future generations of humans and other species depend" (2015, p. 510).

Global Commodity Fetishism, Collective Action, and the Political Economy of Communication

Within global capitalism, commodity fetishism obfuscates labor relations and unequal structures of socio-ecological exchange. Yet this is not a total, irreversible accomplishment. By drawing upon certain epistemes of time – temporality, time reckoning, coevalness, and epochality – the key practices of obfuscation can be identified and challenged. Enveloping commodity fetishism induces amnesia, myopia, real-time presentism, and denials of coevalness, yet militant opposition against global capitalism has occurred. Without detailing actual events, the minimal coalitional threshold for effective collective action can be defined. Organized labor worldwide must expand its capacity to disrupt synchronically the JIT supply chains of transnational corporations; successful strategic outcomes will require multilevel alliances of the precariously employed and wageless poor. From an eco-socialist perspective, resolute defenses of the ecological commons should be headed by the transnational climate justice movement. To this end, Andreas Malm has proposed a complete moratorium on all new facilities for extracting coal, oil, or natural gas, the nonfossil fuel generation of electricity, especially wind and solar, major public investment in renewable energy projects, the cessation of forest burning, and the advancement of massive reforestation programs (Malm, 2016b). Ecological and socialist activists must challenge the capacity of global commodity fetishism to efface the material realities of global capitalism. Beyond the standard rhetoric of ethical consumption, ethical investment, and personal carbon footprint reduction, underlying totalities of structural power can be depicted and explained. I refer here to the following overlapping configurations: transnational corporations, workforces, and the wageless poor; fossil capitalism, growing CO_2 emissions, and temperature rises; along with a world ecology map indicating the exhaustion of "the four cheaps" – labor, food, raw materials, energy. Oppositional movements against global capitalism should also invoke a radical conception of global humanity which recognizes coeval communication, differential suffering, and contemporary responsibility for the prospects of future generations.

Finally, the arguments of this article open up new interrelated research questions for the political economy of communication. The list of these below is indicative rather than exhaustive:

- How do the epistemes of temporality, time reckoning, coevalness, and epochality clarify global understandings of capitalism, political economy, and communication?
- How should the time-related aspects of commodity fetishism be situated within the political economy of communication oeuvre?
- On what theoretical grounds can one reconcile class and ecological critiques of global commodity fetishism?
- From a time-related perspective, how should other related opacities of fetishism be analyzed, i.e., spectacularity, algorithms, abstract money, financial technologies.
- How can research on the preceding questions advance an eco-socialist praxis of communication?

References

Adam, B. (2004). *Time*. Cambridge, UK: Polity.

Adam, B. & Groves, C. (2007). *Future matters: Action, knowledge, ethics.* Leiden, Netherlands: Brill.

Billig, M. (1999). Commodity fetishism and repression: Reflections on Marx, Freud and the psychology of consumer capitalism. *Theory & Psychology* 9(3), 313–329.

Bonneuil, C. & Fressoz, J.B. (2016). *The shock of the Anthropocene*. London: Verso.

Cline, W. (2007). *Global warming and agriculture: Impact estimates by country.* Washington, DC: Centre for Global Development.

Cwerner, S.B. (2000). The chronopolitan ideal: Time, belonging and globalisation. *Time & Society* 9(2–3): 331–345.

Davis, M. (2007). *Planet of slums*. London: Verso.

Davis, M. (2018). *Old gods, new enigmas*. London: Verso.

Di Muzio, T. (2015). The plutonomy of the 1%: Dominant ownership and conspicuous consumption in the new gilded age. *Millennium: Journal of International Studies* 33(2): 492–510.

Dicken, P. (2003). *Global Shift* (4th ed.). London, UK: Sage.

Fabian, J. (1983). *Time and the other: How anthropology makes its subject.* New York, NY: Columbia University Press.

Fabian, J. (2007). *Memory against culture: Arguments and reminders*. Durham, NC: Duke University Press.

Goldman, R. & Papson, S. (2011). *Landscapes of capital: Representing time, space and globalisation in corporate advertising*. Cambridge, UK: Polity.

Hamilton, C., Bonneuil, C. & Gemenne, S. (2015). *The Anthropocene and the global environmental crisis*. New York, NY: Routledge.

Hermann, C. (2014). *Capitalism of work time and the political economy*. New York, NY: Routledge.

Hoogvelt, A. (2006). Globalisation and postmodern imperialism. *Globalisations* 3(2), 159–174.

Hope, W. (2016). *Time, communication and global capitalism.* London, UK: Palgrave.

Malm, A. (2016a). *Fossil capital: The rise of steam power and the roots of global warming.* London, UK: Verso.

Malm, A. (2016b). Revolution in a warming world: lessons from the Russian to Syrian Revolution. In L. Pantich & G. Albo (Eds.), *Socialist Register*, 2017 (pp. 121–142). London: Merlin Press.

McNeill, J., & Engelke, P. (2014). *The great acceleration: An environmental history of the anthropocene since 1945.* Cambridge, MA: The Belknap Press of Harvard University Press.

Moore, J. (2014). The end of cheap nature. Or how I learnt to stop worrying about 'the' environment and 'love' the crisis of capitalism. In S. Suter and C. Chase-Dunn (Ed.), *Structures of the world political economy and the future of global conflict and cooperation* (pp. 285–314). Berlin: LIT Verlag.

Moore, J. (2016). The rise of cheap nature. In J. Moore (Ed.), *Anthropocene or capitalocene? Nature, history and the crisis of capitalism* (pp. 78–115). Oakland, CA: PM Press.

Moore, J. (2017a). The capitalocene Part I: On the nature and origins of our ecological crisis. *The Journal of Peasant Studies* 44(3), 594–630.

Moore, J. (2017b). The capitalocene part II: Accumulation by appropriation and the centrality of unpaid work/energy. *The Journal of Peasant Studies* 45(2), 237–279.

Nixon, R. (2011). *Slow violence and the environmentalism of the poor.* Cambridge, MA: Harvard University Press.

O'Connor, J. (1988). Capitalism, nature, socialism: A theoretical introduction. *Capitalism, Nature and Socialism* 1(1), 11–38.

O'Connor, J. (1991). On the two contradictions of capitalism. *Capitalism, Nature and Socialism* 2(3), 107–109.

Robinson, W. (2004). *A theory of global capitalism: Production, class and state in a transnational world.* Baltimore, MD: John Hopkins.

Sealey, R. (2010). Logistics workers and global logistics: The heavy lifters of globalisation. *Work, Organisation, Labor & Globalisation* 4(2), 25–38.

Sklair, L. (2002). *Globalisation: Capitalism and its alternatives* (3rd ed.). Oxford, UK: Oxford University Press.

Thompson, E.P. (1967). Time, work discipline and industrial capitalism. *Past and Present* 38, 56–97.

Tomlinson, J. (2007). *The culture of speed.* London: Sage.

Zelizer, B. (1995). Reading the past against the grain: The shape of memory studies. *Critical Studies in Mass Communication* 12(2), 214–239.

Index

Printed in Great Britain
by Amazon

18655163R10181